the BACKYARD
Bird Feeder's
B·I·B·L·E

A RODALE ORGANIC GARDENING BOOK

the BACKYARD Bird Feeder's B·I·B·L·E

THE A-TO-Z GUIDE TO FEEDERS, SEED MIXES, PROJECTS, AND TREATS

Sally Roth

RODALE

© 2000 by Sally Roth
Illustrations © 2000 by John Burgoyne

First published 2000
First published in paperback 2003

We're always happy to hear from you. For questions or comments concerning the editorial content of this book, please write to:

Rodale Book Readers' Service
33 East Minor Street
Emmaus, PA 18098

Look for other Rodale books wherever books are sold. Or call us at (800) 848-4735.

For more information about Rodale Organic Living magazines and books, visit our Web site at:

www.organicgardening.com

Editor: Deborah L. Martin
Contributing Editors: Susan B. Burton and Sarah S. Dunn
Cover and Interior Book Designer: Nancy Smola Biltcliff
Interior Illustrator: John Burgoyne
Cover Photographers: Mitch Mandel (hardcover and paperback), Robert P. Carr/Bruce Coleman Inc. (hardcover), and John Sorensen (paperback)
Photography Editor and Cover Photo Stylist: Lyn Horst
Layout Designer: Keith Biery
Researchers: Diana Erney, Sarah Wolfgang Heffner, Pamela R. Ruch
Copy Editor: Nancy N. Bailey
Manufacturing Coordinator: Mark Krahforst
Indexer: Lina Burton
Editorial Assistance: Kerrie Cadden

RODALE ORGANIC LIVING BOOKS

Executive Editor: Margot Schupf
Art Director: Patricia Field
Content Assembly Manager: Robert V. Anderson Jr.
Copy Manager: Nancy N. Bailey
Editorial Assistant: Sara Sellar

Library of Congress Cataloging-in-Publication Data

Roth, Sally.
  The backyard bird feeder's bible : the A-to-Z guide to feeders, seed mixes, projects, and treats / Sally Roth.
        p.   cm.
  Includes bibliographical references (p.   ) and index.
  ISBN 0–87596–834–1   hardcover
  ISBN 0–87596–918–6   paperback
  1. Bird feeders.   2. Birds—Feeding and feeds.   I. Title.
QL676.5 R6683   2000
639.9'78—dc21   00–009063

Distributed to the book trade by St. Martin's Press

            6 8 10 9 7 5   hardcover
    2 4 6 8 10 9 7 5 3 1   paperback

In memory of Rachel Carson,
in hope of never a silent spring

Rodale
Organic Gardening Starts Here!

Here at Rodale, we've been creating organic gardens for more than 50 years—ever since my grandfather J. I. Rodale learned about composting and decided that healthy living starts with healthy soil. In 1940 J. I. started the Rodale Organic Farm to test his theories, and today the nonprofit Rodale Institute Experimental Farm is still at the forefront of organic gardening and farming research. In 1942 J. I. founded *Organic Gardening* magazine to share his discoveries with gardeners everywhere. His son, my father, Robert Rodale, headed *Organic Gardening* until 1990, and today a fourth generation of Rodales is growing up with the magazine. Over the years we've shown millions of readers how to grow bountiful crops and beautiful flowers using nature's own techniques.

In this book, you'll find the latest organic methods and the best gardening advice. We know—because all our authors and editors are passionate about gardening! We feel strongly that our gardens should be safe for our children, pets, and the birds and butterflies that add beauty and delight to our lives and landscapes. Our gardens should provide us with fresh, flavorful vegetables, delightful herbs, and gorgeous flowers. And they should be a pleasure to work in as well as to view.

Sharing the secrets of safe, successful gardening is why we publish books. So come visit us at the Rodale Institute Experimental Farm, where you can tour the gardens every day—we're open year-round. And use this book to create your best garden ever.

Happy gardening!

Maria Rodale

Maria Rodale
Rodale Organic Gardening Books

Contents

Acknowledgments

Thank you first of all to my tolerant son, David—I'm so glad you're a nature lover, too, even if it isn't cool for a teenager to admit it. And thank you to my daughter, Gretel, and granddaughter, Erica, who find joy in the world every day.

Thanks to my understanding friends, who remind me there's more to life than birds but who never argue with "I'm working."

Dear Deb, what would I have done without the endless Diet Coke breaks and discussions of human nature? Dear Pauline, thanks for sharing the joy of God and love. Dear Jim, thanks for the always-entertaining political conversations. Dear Heidi, thanks for your painstaking work in matters of science, but even greater thanks for your kindred spirit that makes nature walks—a very private time—so much fun to share. I'll never forget stumbling through the dark to find the *Xanthopastis* caterpillars! Dear Paul, thanks for always being yourself—but Indian bikes still rule. Dear Lynn, thanks for ever-patient listening, high-energy dancing, and that wild-woman insight. Dear Randy, thanks for sharing yourself through your songs—the Taylor sounds beautiful in your hands. Dear Paul, thanks for pondering the big questions and offering shelter from the storm. Dear Ben, thanks for Vangelis and for coming to the rescue of the cecropia moth at 4:00 A.M. Dear Beth, Jill, Barbara, Tracey, Jane, and Peggy, thanks for the shared voices and shared strength of good women. Dear Larry, thanks for loving music as much as I do and for taking me back to my roots. Dear Pati, thanks for being part of this wonder-filled world. I am truly blessed.

Thanks to Nancy Bailey and Sue Burton for polishing my language and organizing my thoughts with incredible patience and inexhaustible goodwill.

Finally but foremost, a big bear hug to Deb Martin, my editor, whose sense of humor let us both survive the creation of this book—you made working fun! You and GI Joe will always be my heroes.

The Best Part of Bird Watching

I was exploring a local birding hot spot with my friend Heidi last year when both of us were taken completely by surprise by a couple of bald eagles that came flapping out of a little woods to soar over our heads. We stood spellbound in the open field where we'd been hunting for rocks.

"That's the way it is with birds," I remarked. "Go look for an eagle and you won't find one. Look for rocks, and you get an eagle."

We laughed about what terrible birders we were, having spent the beautiful sunny day looking at everything around us and totally forgetting to watch for the birds that draw "real" bird watchers to this area. We'd admired prairie grasses bent from the November winds, common-as-dirt song sparrows singing in the weeds, delicate pearly shells glinting in a drought-stricken lake bed, red hawthorn berries glowing in the sun, clouds forming and re-forming in the impossibly blue sky.

"I figure I just skipped a few steps in that old joke," said Heidi. "The one about the stages of a birder, you know, like the stages of man?"

I hadn't heard it, so she filled me in. Bird watchers begin by watching birds, goes the story: They watch them singing from a bush, pecking at seeds on the ground, pulling a worm from the lawn.

Then they take the next step and start learning their names; soon they are making lists and searching for species to fill the gaps. Once they reach the next stage, they are obsessed, traveling far distances to focus binoculars on their quarry, thinking "Ah, number 527! Number 528!" Lost in the thrill of the hunt, they no longer see the birds as birds but as quests—they forget to watch them. Eventually, though, bird watchers return to their beginnings, enjoying the birds without caring whether they're the rarest of the rare or the most common of backyard residents.

The joke is an exaggeration, of course, because many life-listers still watch the birds, but I like it because it emphasizes what to me is the best part of being a bird watcher. It's not how many you've seen, or what rarities you have notched in your belt— it's the wonder of watching a bird, any bird, as it lives its perfect natural life.

Although I love a beautiful bird as much as anybody—seeing a bluebird can make my whole day!—I still enjoy watching the antics of the ill-mannered house sparrows that congregate at my feeders. (Of course, I did travel 2 hours to see a big rare gyrfalcon that had strayed from the Arctic to a Pennsylvania quarry, but only because I love hawks and Audubon's print of gyrfalcons has hung over my bed for half my life.)

I can't imagine a yard without birds, and that's why I do everything I can to make my place tempting to them. It's a win-win proposition for both of us: I get the pleasure of watching them at their daily lives, and they get a reliable and constant source of food as well as the added attractions of fresh water and a safe and sheltered place to rest or nest.

I've been lucky to have been a country girl for most of my life, but I live in town now, and I've learned that the same tricks that brought birds to my feeders when I was surrounded by wild space are just as effective in a small yard amid neighbors. It's not all house sparrows and starlings, either: More than 40 different kinds of birds have visited here in just 2 short years (but who's counting?).

Food Brings in the Birds

Food is the number one attraction for birds because most of their everyday life is given over to finding the food to stoke their high-metabolism bodies. "She eats like a bird" means something very different to birds than it does to us: If we ate like they do, we'd be at the table all day long.

I learned about feeding birds at my mother's knee. I helped her toss bread crumbs and leftovers out the door to hungry cardinals and blue jays. We had no feeder, but the birds didn't care; they'd descend in minutes to vacuum up the offerings. Only potato peelings went untouched, and I remember asking my mother why. "Birds don't eat potatoes," she told me, "but the bunnies will."

Those were my first lessons in what birds like to eat—and don't. Watching birds in the natural world as I explored the woods and fields and setting up my own feeding station taught me a lot more about bird diets. I laughed the first time I read about scientists' inventories of the contents of bird stomachs—what a job!—but I've realized that other than firsthand observation, that is the only way to get a handle on who's eating what. Now I'm in awe of the botanic skills of those scientists, who had to be able to recognize the seeds of hundreds of plants. But I also recognize the limitations of the method: What was in the stomach depended upon where the bird was

American goldfinches sparkle in the spring when the males trade their drab winter feathers for bright yellow plumage trimmed tidily in black. These birds go for a tube feeder filled with sunflower or niger seed.

collected and what the wild crops were like that year. While stomach inventories are a good starting place to tailor-make a menu, they're not the final word.

My science has always depended on my own observations. With so much variation in the plants of this wonderfully diverse country of ours, what my birds are eating may not be the same as what yours are dining on. Luckily, a few seeds are so welcomed by so many birds that they function as "one seed fits all." It's no secret why millet and sunflower are top sellers everywhere: Birds eat them with relish. Fill your feeders with these seeds, and you're guaranteed a steady stream of customers.

That's the great thing about bird feeding. You can keep it that simple: Go out and buy just two kinds of seed, never read a "how to attract birds" book, and enjoy a lifetime of birds at your feeder.

Or you can go the route I've chosen, and learn what foods are preferred by birds and what foods will lure birds that aren't interested in the standard fare. You can fill your yard with practically every kind of bird that lives nearby or passes through your area. You can thrill to a brilliant tanager at your window feeder or a shy thrush in your garden. You can call the kids to see their first bluebird, and you can invite your neighbor for tea and chickadees. It's a wonderful life!

What You'll Find in Here

This book includes just about everything I've learned in four decades of watching birds every day, in every season, in every kind

Key to the Symbols

Plants for Food

Fruits and flowers, tall shade trees, twining vines, and blooming bushes—they all say "Stop here!" to birds seeking a spot to dine or a place to nest. Grow your own bird-welcoming and beautiful landscape!

Bird Foods

Out of bird seed? What's in your cupboard to offer the birds instead? Create custom seed mixes and whip up tasty treats from your kitchen to entice your favorite birds to your yard. These entries make it easy.

Birds

Learn more about the common—and uncommon—birds that show up at feeders across North America. Each of these bird-focused entries features a quick-reference list of "Feeder Foods" that are most likely to attract that bird.

Bird Behaviors

The more you watch the birds in your yard the more bird activities you'll see: communication, competition, mating, mimicry, and more. These entries explain what it means when birds behave the way they do.

of weather. The eastern birds of my childhood are in here as are the northwestern friends that visited my feeders in Oregon and the Midwest birds that keep me company here in Indiana. So are all the northern, southern, and western birds I've met on travels and at friends' feeders.

You'll learn about the birds themselves and what their behaviors mean. You'll find the tricks to supplying their favorite feeder foods. You'll discover plants that they prefer. You'll find out how to make your yard a safe haven. As you browse through this book, look for the little symbols at the beginning of each entry. There are eight different ones, and they serve as a key to the general subject of an entry (the symbols are defined below).

Sample the entries in any order you like, according to what you're most curious about. I guarantee that your feeders will entertain more birds than ever once you start putting the suggestions in this book into practice.

One caution before you dig in: Bird watching and bird feeding are lifelong passions. You'll spend more time outside or looking out the window than ever before. You'll start watching birds while you're stuck in traffic jams or in the parking lot at school, waiting for your kids. You'll become an evangelist even without trying, as friends and family get hooked on the lively action at your feeders. Before you know it, you'll be thinking like a bird as you work in the yard and choosing plants and designs because the birds will like them. And, of course, the chair by the bird-feeder window will become the most popular seat in the house.

Bird Watching	**Animal Visitors**	**Feeders and More**	**Seasonal Subjects**
Take your backyard-bird viewing to a new level with techniques from these entries. Choose the most useful binoculars and field guides, find out more about bird photography, or participate in your first bird count.	Who else visits bird feeders? Discover the other critters that dine on seeds, suet, fruit, nectar, and other bird foods. Find out how to enjoy the extra wildlife in your yard—and how to thwart unwelcome feeder raiders.	From making your own tube feeder to cleaning the bird bath, these entries describe all the best equipment—homemade and store-bought—to put the food and feeders right where birds are most likely to find them.	What do birds do when it rains? What kind of foods should you offer in the middle of summer? Find out how you can get the most out of your bird-feeding efforts every season of the year.

Accessories

MANUFACTURERS OF BIRD FEEDERS are making it easy for consumers to jump on the bird-feeding bandwagon. Of course, all you need to make the birds happy is a supply of seed and a tray to put it in. But if you feed birds on a regular basis and have a feeding station that includes several types and sizes of feeders, you'll appreciate the new labor-saving devices. You can buy gizmos that clean or hang your feeders, contraptions to keep out squirrels, and technological marvels to bring the bird world closer to you inside. Here are some of the accessories I've found most useful. Look for them in well-stocked bird-supply stores, home improvement stores, or discount stores, or order from catalogs such as those listed in "Resources" on page 348.

Scrub-brush hose attachment. This short-handled brush attaches directly to your garden hose. A stream of water travels through a narrow tube in the handle and loosens grime and stuck-on seed from your birdbath or feeder.

Brush for plastic tube feeders. Slide this long brush into your tube feeder and rotate to clean out old seed in a jiffy. Soft bristles won't scratch plastic.

Niger seed bags. Add extra feeding places for finches in a snap by hanging seed-stuffed pouches brimming with niger. Birds cling to the mesh and extract the seeds through the small openings.

Add-on trays for tube feeders. Cut down on spilled seed by attaching a plastic tray to the bottom of your tube feeder to catch niger or other seeds that fall from openings. *Bonus:* The tray adds perching room for cardinals and other customers.

Bell-shaped ant guard. Hook this plastic bell above your nectar feeder, coat the inside with petroleum jelly, and prevent ants from raiding your sugar water supplies. Longer lasting, more effective, and much less messy than smearing petroleum jelly on the feeder hanger itself.

Shepherd's crooks. Easy to push into any soil, these low-cost metal posts let you install feeders quickly and easily by stepping onto the anchoring

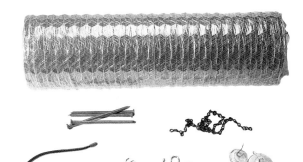

Accessories make your feeders more versatile: Suction cups with screws or hooks let you put a feeder right on your window. Use large nails to skewer citrus fruit or apples; chicken wire is handy for shaping a temporary cover or squirrel guard around a feeder.

support. Some feature more than one curved hook, for multiple-feeder capacity.

Extra arms for feeder poles. A simple clamp lets you add extra hooked arms—and that means extra feeders—to poles up to 1¼ inches in diameter.

Steel feeder stand. Heavy, tip-proof, flat base accepts a metal post, such as a shepherd's crook, so you can enjoy feeders on your deck or patio.

Tree-mount feeder bracket. Never have to pound a nail into living wood again. This stretchy cord wraps snugly around a tree to hold the included feeder-supporting hook. To avoid inadvertently girdling your tree, use this type of support for a winter-time feeder that you remove—along with the stretchy cord—when spring arrives.

Bird monitor system. Bring the sounds of the feeder area indoors with this wireless monitor system. It works like a waterproof baby monitor. The sensitive microphone picks up chirps, songs, and even the sounds of cracking seeds and rustling wings.

Accidents

BIRDS REPRODUCE IN BROODS to compensate for the many individuals lost to predators, disease, and accidents. Sad to say, human activity causes most bird accidents. The leading causes of bird fatalities include collisions with vehicles, fatal encounters with glass windows, knockouts at tall radio, television, or cell phone towers during migration flights, and bashes with big city buildings. Lighthouses, ocean oil slicks, and chemicals also take their toll on birds. Add the predations of our feline friends to the list, and you can see what a danger our human habits are to wild birds.

Apart from the widespread dangers birds face, there is a long list of other accidents that may befall them. Songbirds may become trapped in garages and other outbuildings. Quail, pheasants, and other game birds have had unfortunate entanglements with barbed wire. Lawn mowers and farm equipment endanger ground-nesting field birds.

Even water can pose a problem to swallows, which skim low across the surface to collect insects. One wing beat too low, and the bird may be unable to regain the air. In the feeder area, most accidents happen when birds fly into windows. Use fruit-tree netting, stretched tightly so it's barely visible to human eyes, to break up reflections and keep the birds in your yard safe.

Tribulations of Being Tiny

Hummingbirds are particularly prone to accidents due to their small size. They may become fish food or frog dinner at ponds. A friend of mine found a hummer hanging by its beak from her screen door. Bird watchers have found the little birds trapped in the sticky threads of orb weaver spiders.

> Even spider webs may prove to be hazardous for hummingbirds and other tiny birds.

Acorns

Attract chickadees, jays, nuthatches, quail, titmice, wild turkeys, woodpeckers

PACKED WITH PROTEIN, acorns are a huge hit with all nut-eating birds, including chickadees, jays, nuthatches, titmice, and woodpeckers. They're also tops with game birds like wild turkeys and quail. Lacking the necessary whacking power to get at acorn nutmeats themselves, smaller birds such as buntings, finches, juncos, and sparrows will clean up crumbs dropped by larger birds or acorns smashed by the bird-feeder filler (that's you).

Oak (*Quercus* spp.) trees of any kind are magnets for birds when the acorns are ripe for picking, which may be late summer to fall, depending on the oak species. Beating the birds to the harvest may sound a little mean, but you're really just stockpiling acorns for winter feeding when acorns can be hard to find.

Meaty acorns taste bitter to us, but they are beloved by birds, from chickadees to wild turkeys. Stockpile a few in the fall to offer as winter feeder treats.

Plant for the Future

MATURE OAKS add majesty to a landscape, but even young oak trees are of great value to birds. Many oaks begin producing acorns when they're 5 to 7 years old, and the crop only gets better as the trees mature. Even before they start to bear acorns, young oaks provide homes for tasty caterpillars and other bird-nourishing insects.

Before you plant, make sure you have room for an oak. Squint your eyes and picture a 100-foot-tall giant in your site, not that 4-foot nursery specimen you've been looking at. To keep maintenance to a minimum, choose an oak species that's native to your region rather than a nonnative species that may struggle in your local soil and climate.

Check your local nursery or refer to "Resources" on page 348 for nurseries that specialize in native plants. Or you can go the freebie route and simply plant a few of the acorns you've collected. Wrap the acorns loosely in a little cage of ½-inch-mesh hardware cloth to protect them from squirrels, then set them in the ground about 3 inches deep. Cover with a thin layer of fall leaves, and mark the spot with a plant label stake as a reminder to watch for sprouts in the spring.

Harvesting, Storing, and Serving Acorns

It doesn't take a lot of effort to gather a supply of acorns for winter bird feeding. Just fill your pockets whenever you notice the fallen nuts on your nature hikes or while strolling your yard. Although some acorns taste sweet to human palates and others are extremely bitter, birds seem to appreciate all of them.

Some acorns begin to germinate soon after hitting the ground, while others need a rest period over winter before they sprout. To keep your acorns fresh, store them outdoors or in an unheated garage in a moisture-proof metal container with a secure lid, so that squirrels don't help themselves to your hoard. When you want to give your feeder birds a treat, put a handful of acorns in an old sock, fold over the top, and use a hammer to split open the acorns. Pour the broken nuts into a tray feeder and sit back to watch the show.

Age

OUR STUDIES OF CAPTIVE BIRDS indicate that if a bird manages to avoid predators, disease, accidents, and starvation, it can achieve a ripe old age of 10 years or more. Sheltered from natural disaster, robins have been reported to live as long as 15 years, and a captive cardinal reached the rather incredible age of 28 years!

Unfortunately, in the wild, birds rarely achieve their potential life span. Many of them live a very short life: from 6 months to a year or two, with an estimated two-thirds of birds that reach flying stage never making it to their first birthday. Records retrieved from banded birds show that representatives of many species, from chickadees and goldfinches to grosbeaks and jays, manage to notch 5 years or more, with some lasting into their teens. In general, very small birds such as warblers have shorter lives than larger birds. Hawks, owls, geese, and gulls and other seabirds hold the old-age records for birds: Some individuals have thrived for more than 40 years.

If you can distinguish an individual bird in your backyard, perhaps because of albinism or unusual behavior or song, you can keep track of its age yourself. A tufted titmouse with a white tail feather visited my feeder for 6 years, then disappeared in year 7. A blue jay that produced a distinctive imitation of a red-tailed hawk scream was a feeder patron and a nesting resident for 4 years.

> About two-thirds of the birds that reach flying stage never make it to their first birthday.

Albinism

BIRDS OF A FEATHER FLOCK TOGETHER, and those birds that display the white feathers characteristic of albinism may not be accepted among their species. A flock of birds may harass or shun a mostly white bird, perhaps because its high visibility draws the attention of predators.

Partially albinistic birds are an oddity but not a real rarity. Once you begin watching the birds around you, you're likely to spot a robin or house sparrow or other bird with white feathers where there should be color. Stress or shock, injury, environmental factors, or genetics may cause the lack of pigment in the colorless plumage. Complete albinos, which lack pigment even in their bill, legs, and eyes so that these features show up as pink, are much rarer than partial albinos.

Identifying a bird with mostly or totally white feathers is tricky. Bird watchers must rely on body shape, song, or behavior clues to provide enough information to pinpoint the species.

Birds that normally are brown or black like this robin are more likely to display albinistic feathers than brightly colored birds such as goldfinches and tanagers.

Aloes and Agaves

Attract hummingbirds, orioles

SPIKY, STIFF-LEAVED ALOES (*Aloe* spp.) and agaves (*Agave* spp.) hail from desert country, and so they make great garden plants in warm, dry climates. Agaves are American plants and are a familiar sight in the Southwest, where their tall flowering stalks attract thirsty hummingbirds. Aloes, including the well-known *Aloe vera*, come from Africa.

Separating aloes from agaves can be a challenge because the plants look similar. Some agaves even go by the common name "aloe," like the American aloe (*Agave americana*), better known as century plant.

These plants are a prickly bunch overall. They grow in a cluster of spearlike, succulent leaves armed with sharp spines to deter thirsty desert animals from munching on the juicy leaves. At bloom time, a flowering stalk arises, bearing clusters of tubular flowers. In some species, the main plant dies after flowering, and new plants form around the "parent."

Agaves and aloes are at home in desert gardens, where their nectar-rich blooms draw crowds of hummingbirds and orioles. Outside of USDA Zone 8 or 9, treat them as indoor-outdoor plants: Keep them on a sunny windowsill in winter, then move them outside in summer. To encourage flowering, withhold water for 6 to 8 weeks in winter and early spring, then water well to mimic desert rains.

Some large agaves such as the century plant may take 20 years or more to bloom.

Altruism

BIRDS LOOK OUT FOR EACH OTHER in fascinating ways. A covey of quail usually posts a lookout bird, who alerts the others if danger threatens. The sentry may choose an elevated perch, the better to see its surroundings. Although this conspicuous watch post increases the danger for the individual bird (from hawks, particularly), it provides safety for the flock. Doves and pigeons, too, may keep watch for others of their kind when feeding.

Jays and crows act like the police officers of the bird world, alerting all within hearing when a predator threatens. Of course, jays aren't above using their raucous alarm call to clear a feeder area so that they can have it all to themselves.

During nesting season you may see one of the most amazing acts of bird altruism in action. Tree-climbing snakes and squirrels, which have a hearty appetite for bird eggs and nestlings, often run into a full-bird defense when approaching a nest. Usually the nest owner raises the initial alarm, and every nesting bird in the area quickly joins in the attack. With loudly flapping wings and dive-bombing threats, the birds try to deter the snake, and they are often successful. This is an example of reciprocal altruism: The adult birds, no matter what species, vigorously defend the endangered young, and should the need arise, their young will also be guarded by this band of protective parents.

Learn to recognize the alarm calls of your local birds, and hurry to the scene when you hear them. You may witness a fascinating life or death struggle or even help deter a predator in search of avian prey.

> Adult birds will band together to protect nestlings—even of other species—that are in danger.

Amaranth

Attracts juncos, tree sparrows, and many other seed eaters

BIRD BRAINS NEVER HAVE TO WORRY about making grain into flour, which is why amaranth remains a favorite food crop with our avian pals. When a beak is your main utensil, tiny amaranth seeds will do just as well as fat kernels of wheat. (Humans have a different perspective, which is why ancient amaranth, once a widespread grain crop in hot, dry places of the world, lost favor to easier-to-handle grains.)

Pigweed (*Amaranthus retroflexus*) is perhaps the most well-known amaranth. Tough and hardy, it pops up everywhere—much to the delight of small birds that feast upon its prolific seeds all winter long.

You're likely to spot pigweed sprouting near your bird feeder, thanks to deposits from your feeder guests. If you let a few plants grow, you'll find they're as popular with birds as your feeder. And the tough, densely branched plants make great shelter for small birds, all the way through winter. Let frost-killed pigweed stems stand and you'll see juncos, tree sparrows, and other seed eaters amid the plants.

If you prefer a more refined amaranth for you and the birds, try the dramatic love-lies-bleeding (*A. caudatus*), with hot pink drooping tassels that look like fat, fuzzy yarn. Or go for bold with the multicolored foliage of 'Joseph's Coat', 'Molten Fire', and other showy cultivars of *A. tricolor*. All amaranths are easy to grow as annuals in any zone, but they take their time coming into flower. Start them indoors early if your growing season is short.

> If your growing season is short, start amaranth indoors to give it time to produce flowers.

Amelanchier

Attracts bluebirds, catbirds, great crested flycatchers, jays, mockingbirds, orioles, tanagers, thrashers, thrushes, waxwings

BIRDS SHOW GOOD TASTE when it comes to their favorite shrubs and trees—many of the most popular plants with birds are also beautiful in a garden. Among the best for birds and gardens is amelanchier, also known as Juneberry, shadblow, shadbush, or serviceberry. This group of shrubs and small trees bursts forth in a flurry of snowy white flowers in early spring. Deep blue-purple berries follow the flowers and are so tasty that you may find yourself enjoying them right along with the birds. The good looks and the (literal) good taste of amelanchiers make them a great foundation for a bird-feeding station *and* a handsome addition to your landscape.

Versatile and Attractive

Various amelanchier species are native to just about every part of North America, from the cold North to the mild Northwest to the hot desert regions. Depending on your garden style, you can choose plants that grow by suckering roots to form a tall hedge (*Amelanchier alnifolia, A. canadensis,* or *A. ovalis*), or low ground-covering shrubby species (*A. stolonifera*) that look wonderful on hillsides. The single-stemmed, small-tree types (*A. arborea, A. asiatica, A. × grandiflora, A. laevis,* or *A. lamarckii*) are as pretty as a dogwood in the landscape. In addition to their spring floral display and bird-pleasing berries, most amelanchiers develop colorful fall foliage. Most amelanchiers are hardy through Zone 4.

Plant amelanchiers in full sun to shade, in average, well-drained garden soil. When the berries ripen from red to blue-purple, watch for bluebirds, catbirds, great crested flycatchers, jays, mockingbirds, orioles, tanagers, thrashers, thrushes, and waxwings to visit in search of the mild-flavored, blueberry-like fruit. You may like fruit so much that you want to plant an extra bush or two for yourself. A bit seedier than blueberries, amalanchier berries taste great atop a bowl of cereal and make a delicious filling for pies or crisps.

Shadblow gets its name from its habit of blooming when fish called shad move from the ocean into rivers to spawn. "Blow" is an old word that means bloom.

Beautiful berries that ripen from red to purple don't stay on the tree for long. Birds can strip a tree of its fruit before you get a taste of the blueberry-like flavor.

Best Small-Tree Amelanchiers

DO YOUR part to lift ame-lanchiers out of undeserved anonymity and enjoy the benefits these plants have to offer: pretty spring flowers, bird-pleasing (and people-pleasing) fruits, and attractive fall foliage color. Here are several selections that form excellent small trees, worthy of any landscape. Except where noted, most will reach a mature height of 12 to 15 feet.

'Alta Glow' (*A. alnifolia* cv.): Columnar form, to 18 feet tall; unusual cream-colored fruit; yellow, cream, and maroon fall foliage colors

'Autumn Brilliance' (*A. × grandiflora* hybrid): More upright form than others; larger-than-usual white flowers; gorgeous red fall color

'Ballerina' (*A. × grandiflora* hybrid): Strong grower; lots of flowers and thus lots of good-size, sweet fruit; purple-bronze to red fall foliage

'Cumulus' (*A. laevis* cv.): Upright and oval-shaped with clouds of flowers; good for fruit, too; orange-red fall color

'Prince Charles' (*A. laevis* cv.): Vigorous grower, to 25 feet tall; abundant flowers bloom before the leaves open in spring; flavorful fruits; orange-red fall foliage

'Princess Diana' (*A. × grandiflora* hybrid): Very graceful form; loads of white flowers; good red fall foliage color

'Robin Hill' (*A. × grandiflora* hybrid): Upright rather than spreading; pink buds open to white flowers that yield small red fruit; yellow-red fall foliage

'Strata' (*A. × grandiflora* hybrid): Elegant horizontal branching habit with a substantial floral display; looks beautiful growing in perennial beds

'Tradition' (*A. canadensis* cv.): Oval form to 20 feet tall with graceful branching; early blooming; produces abundant fruit; brilliant orange-red fall color

Ants

Attract jays, robins, woodpeckers

WHEN YOU SPOT AN ANTHILL in your yard, count yourself lucky to host insects that birds love. Jays, robins, and woodpeckers are especially fond of ants, but lots of other birds eat ants, too. The critters are plentiful, apparently delectable, and easy for birds to find and eat.

Ants also figure in one of the more bizarre bird behaviors: anting, in which a bird uses an ant like a bath sponge to wipe down its feathers, especially under the wings. Ant bodies contain formic acid, which ornithologists think acts like a natural pesticide to keep feather lice and mites in check. Watch for jays and other birds lolling directly on top of anthills and contorting their bodies as they rub the ants among their feathers.

There's no need to attract ants to your garden—they're already there, going about their busy subterranean lives and venturing out to collect morsels of food for the storehouse.

You may also find ants herding aphids in your garden. The ants feed on the sticky sweet "honeydew" that the aphids secrete; in exchange, they protect aphids from predators and may actually carry the aphids to your plants. This fondness for sweets means that ants may seek out nectar feeders. If they do, deter ants by smearing petroleum jelly on the hanger or by using a commercial bell-shaped ant guard or a plastic water-filled moat to prevent access. Such solutions are easy, quick, and cheap—less than $5 for permanent nectar protection.

> Many feeder and backyard birds enjoy a meal of ants. Some birds freshen their feathers with them, too.

Apples

Attract bluebirds, chickadees, jays, mockingbirds, robins, starlings, thrashers, titmice, towhees, Carolina wrens

AN APPLE A DAY may deter the doctor, but it will bring birds flocking to your feeder in fall and winter. Roughly chop an apple into chunks, spread them in your feeder, and you'll soon have jays, mockingbirds, and Carolina wrens nibbling away at the treasure. Scatter some chopped apple on the ground and robins, brown thrashers, and towhees may also partake of the feast. If bluebirds are in the area, they too may fly in to enjoy a regular offering of apple.

Apples for birds needn't be perfect—they'll eagerly gobble up mushy or wormy fruit. Chopping an apple makes it easier for smaller beaks to eat, but slicing the fruit in half will attract customers, too, who will carefully eat every bit of flesh and leave just the hollowed-out skin behind.

Apples are also tops with starlings. Slice a couple of apples in half, place them on the ground, and you'll get a starling circus outside your window, as the birds joust and squabble over the sweet flesh. Kids love to watch the activity!

If you're trying to deter starlings from your feeding area, save your apples for feeders they can't frequent. A coffee can hung horizontally, with a small entrance hole that allows titmice and chickadees to enter but bars starlings, is a good place to put a small amount of chopped apple. Weighted feeders that deter larger birds will also prevent starlings from getting your apple offerings. But since apples, especially those past their prime, are usually easy to come by (just ask your grocer), you can also include starlings in this feast. Slice whole fruits in half and place them in a decoy feeder, away from those that your more desirable birds frequent.

If you find yourself with an abundance of apples and no room in the fridge for storage, take time to

A vertical feeder keeps apples in easy reach of agile wrens and other desirable fruit eaters but helps keep crowds of starlings from gobbling your offerings in one sitting.

slice and dry them for later use. There's no need to remove the cores—birds like the seeds, too. Just slice the apples thinly with a sharp knife, and loosely string the slices with a heavy-duty carpet needle and thread. Hang to air-dry. Or spread the slices on cookie sheets, and bake at 200°F. How long they take to dry in the oven depends on the moisture content and thickness of the apple slices. Check the slices after 15 minutes, then increase the time as needed by 10-minute intervals. Store dried apples in resealable plastic bags. Chop or serve whole in feeders, or use strings of dried apple slices to decorate outdoor evergreens or a discarded Christmas tree.

Baby Birds

MANY BIRDS WILL TAKE UP RESIDENCE near a reliable food source such as your well-stocked feeder, as long as your yard holds the plants or nest boxes they need to raise a family. That means you may get to see fledglings at your feeder, a sight that will bring a smile to even the grouchiest curmudgeon. With their fuzzy heads and stubby bodies, baby birds are delightful.

Should you come upon a baby bird in your yard, the best advice is to leave it alone. Nearly all songbirds leave the nest a few days before they can fly. The parents bring them food as they hop about and flap from one place to another, trying out their wings. The best thing you can do for these not-yet-airborne babies is to keep your cat inside. If a baby bird moves so fast that you have trouble catching it, it does not need your help. If, however, you find an obviously helpless nestling on the ground, you may be able to save it. Fill a berry box or shoe box with facial tissues, and add a 20-ounce soda-pop bottle filled with very warm water to provide vital heat. Nestle the baby in the makeshift nest, cover with a hand towel to preserve the heat, and get the baby to a bird rehabilitator as fast as possible. Your veterinarian or local nature center should be able to supply the name and phone number of one of these dedicated, experienced, and legally licensed people. In spite of your good intentions, it is very difficult—and illegal—to raise a baby songbird.

> If you discover a baby bird in your yard, leave it alone—and keep the cat indoors.

Bacon

Attracts bluebirds, crows, jays, ravens, starlings, woodpeckers, Carolina wrens

IN THE OLD DAYS when bacon was a regular part of breakfast, cooks were happy to share the leftover grease with their feathered friends. In today's fat-conscious society, many people have sworn off bacon, but birds don't need to fight fat! Bacon grease is still a great food for backyard birds.

The simplest way to package bacon grease for bird feeding is in metal tuna or cat-food cans. Punch a hole in the side wall of the can with a nail. Use pliers to bend the tip of a wire into a knot that won't slip through the hole, and thread the wire through the can for hanging. Fill the can to the brim with cooled, but still-liquid bacon grease, then stick it in the refrigerator to solidify. Once the grease is no longer runny, hang the can from a branch.

Bluebirds, jays, woodpeckers, and Carolina wrens readily accept this source of fat, whether you offer it straight or use it in bird-treat recipes. Bacon grease also draws crows, starlings, and even ravens.

Pour cooled but still-liquid bacon fat into empty tuna or cat food cans. After it solidifies, punch a hole in the side, and run a wire through it for easy hanging.

Baffles

Squirrels, raccoons, and similar animals may be welcome guests in your yard, but most birders prefer that these critters stick to their own feeders and leave the bird feeders alone. Not only do they tend to clean out a bird feeder in a hurry, but a resident squirrel will also deter most birds from visiting the feeder while it dines. For reasons unclear to us humans, squirrels will almost always go for the bird feeders first. To prevent them from hogging feeders intended for birds, it's time for that ounce of prevention.

Baffles are metal or plastic guards that stand between the feeder and the tree or post, so that climbing animals can't mount a sneak attack on the food. Keep in mind that squirrels are determined creatures, and they may eventually overcome a baffle. They may figure out an alternate approach route and leap directly to the feeder. Or they may learn the acrobatics necessary to keep from sliding off the baffle. At best, a baffle will keep squirrels thwarted all season long; at least, it will slow them down a bit.

If your feeder is mounted on a post, first be sure that squirrels can't reach it by leaping onto it from a tree or roof. Then install a metal cone-shaped or tubular baffle below the feeder. Tubular baffles must be about 14 inches long to deter squirrels and 24 inches long to keep out raccoons. You can make your own baffle from a section of pipe, chosen to fit the diameter of your post, or you can purchase a commercial baffle for easy installation. A section of plastic PVC pipe slipped over the post will deter squirrels for a little while, although they may eventually gnaw through it. Spray-paint the pipe dark green or black to make it less obtrusive in the landscape. Commercial baffles are widely available for both tubular metal posts and thicker wood posts; for a well-made design that will last for years, expect to pay between $15 and $30.

To protect hanging feeders, slip a metal or plastic baffle between the feeder and its hanging hook. These baffles prevent access by tipping as the squirrel climbs

Baffles put a barrier between seed and squirrel, but they may not baffle a determined and agile squirrel forever. A door that slams shut does the trick on this weighted feeder.

onto it, sending the animal sliding off the side or scurrying back where it came from. The slick plastic or metal also prevents the squirrel's feet from getting a secure grip. If you have a choice, go for a metal baffle. Remember that a determined squirrel will gnaw its way through a plastic device. No matter what type of feeder guard you install, keep an eye out—the most persistent of squirrels may eventually figure out a way around even the most well-designed feeder guard.

Some newer models of feeders now come equipped with weight-activated baffles. When a squirrel—or even a large, feeder-hogging pigeon—puts its weight on the perch bar, the pressure pulls down a solid metal wall between the unwanted guest and the food within the feeder. You can even adjust the balance to give only lightweight songbirds access to the seeds. Sturdy steel construction adds heft and cost to these bird-food fortresses, but you can recover the price rather quickly in savings on seeds.

Banding

A TINY ALUMINUM BAND on a bird's leg is an important link to the body of scientific knowledge about birds. The band identifies where the bird was banded and includes instructions on where to send the band if the bird is later found dead. Retrieved bands help researchers fill in the missing pieces of bird ranges and migration routes and dates.

If you're interested in banding, get involved in an existing program. There you will learn techniques and record keeping, and you'll make contacts who will vouch for your abilities should you later decide to apply for your own federal permit. Call your local chapter of the National Audubon Society, or check with nearby nature centers to track down a banding program to join. Or call 1-800-327-BAND (2263) to find out more.

Lightweight leg bands supply scientists with serious information about where birds have been. Find out how you can help through local nature centers.

Beneath the Feeder

BIRDS AT THE FEEDER mean debris beneath it, especially if you're serving up sunflower seed. If you are feeding a large contingent of hungry birds, the fallen seeds and hulls can quickly pile up into a layer several inches deep. You can rake up the hulls, but I prefer to disguise them instead.

Spread a 3-inch layer of wood chips underneath your feeder. Not only will it cover any unsightly accumulation of hulls, it will give a tidy look to your feeder area. The chips also allow ground-feeding birds, such as doves and juncos, to pick through the pile and find edible seeds. Every so often, I drag a garden hoe over the area to turn over a layer of chips on top of newly fallen hulls. The wood chips disguise bird droppings, too.

If you prefer to eliminate debris altogether, offer hulled sunflower seeds, peanut pieces, nutmeats, suet, and other no-mess foods. Niger seed hulls are so small that they rarely become unsightly, so include some niger in your mix to keep the finches happy.

Keep the area around feeders looking neat with a layer of inexpensive wood chips or bark mulch. Refresh the layer by burying seed hulls with a hoe.

Berries

Attract many kinds of birds at various times of the year

BERRIES ARE ONE OF THE BIG REASONS for dramatic declines in bird traffic at feeders in the summertime. Even premium birdseed can't compare to the temptation of ripening blackberries (*Rubus* spp.), blueberries (*Vaccinium* spp.), huckleberries (*Gaylussacia* spp.), mulberries (*Morus* spp.), salmonberries (*Rubus spectabilis*), and dozens of other kinds of wild and cultivated berries.

You'd think that since birds are this attracted to berries, they'd come like magic to a feeder full of these favorites. That's true—sort of. Berries are a big attraction at a feeder, with one big caveat: *if* you offer them at times when they aren't available from natural sources.

Scarlet tanagers stay in the treetops unless there are tasty berries to draw them closer. The purple fruit of a pokeweed plant has strong bird appeal.

Berries at the Feeder

If you find yourself with extra berries of any kind in summer—the last few strawberries in the box, a handful of slightly shriveled blueberries—don't bother putting them in the feeder. You'll probably get no takers when nature's bounty is all around. Instead, pop your leftover spring, summer, and fall berries into a plastic bag or container, and freeze them. In wintertime, the birds will gobble up bruised or battered berry bits as if they were rare treasures (at that time of year, they are!).

Gather berry-laden branches of dogwoods (*Cornus* spp.), hawthorns (*Crataegus* spp.), hollies (*Ilex* spp.), cedars (*Juniperus* spp.), or other bird favorites, and offer them in a tray feeder or on the Berry Branch Feeder on the opposite page. The perch gives robins, thrushes, and other birds easy access to the berries.

Like other thrushes, eastern bluebirds are quick to arrive on the scene when berries ripen. Tempt them to your yard by planting a berry patch for the birds.

Berry Branch Feeder

Here's a simple way to bring berry-loving birds to a spot where you can watch them while they dine.

MATERIALS

Screw eye

Board, approximately 8 × 20 inches

Screws

Sturdy branch

Berried branches of cedar, dogwood, or holly

Flexible wire, such as floral wire

Nails (optional)

Step 1. Screw the screw eye into the middle of the upper third of the board.

Step 2. Using screws, fasten the branch to the lower end of the board, where it will serve as a perch for your visitors.

Step 3. Gather berry-laden branches into a bundle, and wrap wire around the stems to hold them together. Leave enough wire at the end to wrap around the screw eye a few times to hang the bunch securely on the board at bird's-eye level.

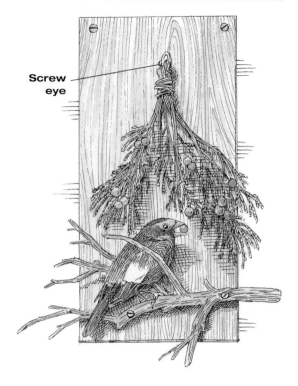

Screw eye

Step 4. Nail or screw the board to a tree, post, or fence, and wait for birds to arrive. Stockpile branches with berries for refilling the feeder.

Berries Bring Them In

If you really want to see the berry-eating birds of summer, growing your own fruit is the way to go. Seasonal fruit on the bush holds much more appeal for a greater variety of birds than the most attractively filled feeder. And you'll see birds that would never venture near your feeders, no matter what you put in them. You may play host to brilliant red tanagers; vivid orange or yellow orioles; soft olive-green vireos, thrashers, and catbirds; and golden-voiced thrushes. Everybody's favorite, bluebirds, are also big fans of berries. When berries ripen, also look for the big and brash great crested flycatcher and flocks of elegantly understated cedar waxwings.

If you never guessed you could enjoy watching such wonderful birds in your own backyard, guess again. If it's loaded with berries, even the smallest yard can attract these birds. Birds are opportunists. When they spot a bush brimming with tasty fruit, they'll move in for the feast, whether that berry bush is in a landscaping strip at the mall, a postage-stamp–size backyard, or a 100-acre estate.

Keep in mind, though, that berry season is sweet but short. From ripening to going, going, gone takes only about 2 weeks, no matter what kind of berry you're growing. You can extend the season by planting different kinds of berries and different cultivars of each berry.

(continued on page 16)

Berries for Birds

INSTEAD OF offering berries at your feeder in the summer, plant berry bushes. It's a guaranteed way to get more birds into your yard when the crop ripens. And what birds they might be! Glorious songbirds that normally will have nothing to do with a feeder will gladly come for berries-on-the-bush. Check out this listing to see what you can plant—and what you may already have—to tempt an array of beautiful birds into your yard.

Berry	Description	Birds Attracted
Strawberries (*Fragaria* spp.)	Clump-forming plants with familiar tasty red fruits; spread into colonies by runners	Catbirds, prairie chickens, crows, grosbeaks, grouse, mockingbirds, pheasants, quails, robins, sparrows, thrashers, thrushes, towhees, wild turkeys
Hollies (*Ilex* spp.)	Evergreen and deciduous shrubs and trees with attractive foliage and red berries	Bluebirds, bobwhites, catbirds, doves, flickers, grouse, jays, mockingbirds, quails, robins, sapsuckers, sparrows, thrashers, thrushes, towhees, wild turkeys, vireos, waxwings, woodpeckers
Cedars, junipers (*Juniperus* spp.)	Evergreen conifers with short gray-green needles, of various habit, from ground-hugging creepers to upright or gnarled trees	Bluebirds, catbirds, Clark's nutcrackers, crossbills, finches, flickers, grosbeaks, jays, mockingbirds, robins, sapsuckers, tree swallows, thrashers, hermit thrushes, yellow-rumped warblers, waxwings
Spicebush (*Lindera benzoin*)	Shrub or small tree, often suckering into small group, with yellow flowers on bare branches in early spring; has glossy red berries; all parts have delightful spicy scent	Bluebirds, bobwhites, catbirds, great crested flycatchers, pheasants, robins, thrushes, vireos
Mulberries (*Morus* spp.)	Deciduous trees with white, red, purple, or black-purple fruits; messy and invasive by seed but tops with birds	Bluebirds, cardinals, catbirds, doves, flickers, flycatchers, grackles, grosbeaks, jays, mockingbirds, orioles, phainopeplas, band-tailed pigeons, robins, house sparrows, tanagers, thrashers, thrushes, titmice, vireos, waxwings, woodpeckers
Virginia creeper (*Parthenocissus quinquefolia*)	Climbing or ground-covering perennial vine with five-part leaves that turn beautiful crimson in fall; has grapelike clusters of deep blue berries	Bluebirds, catbirds, chickadees, flickers, great crested flycatchers, mockingbirds, nuthatches, robins, sapsuckers, tree swallows, thrashers, thrushes, titmice, woodpeckers
Buckthorns (*Rhamnus* spp.)	Many species of shrubs or small trees, both native and introduced, frequently thorny, with small fleshy berries that ripen from red to black; deciduous or evergreen depending on species	Topnotch for pileated woodpeckers; also catbirds, mockingbirds, phainopeplas, band-tailed pigeons, robins, sapsuckers, thrashers, thrushes

SEASON WHEN BERRIES ARE PRESENT ▮ SPRING ☐ SUMMER ☐ FALL ▮ WINTER

Berries for Birds—*Continued*

Berry	Description	Birds Attracted
Sumacs (*Rhus* spp.)	Shrubs or small trees, often spreading into thickets; often brilliant scarlet fall foliage; fuzzy upright clusters of tiny red berries	Bluebirds, bobwhites, cardinals, catbirds, prairie chickens, crows, finches, flickers, evening grosbeaks, grouse, jays, juncos, magpies, mockingbirds, pheasants, band-tailed pigeons, quails, robins, starlings, tanagers, thrashers, thrushes, wild turkey, vireos, pine warblers, woodpeckers, wrens
Blackberries, raspberries, salmonberries, thimbleberries, wineberries (*Rubus* spp.)	Bramble fruits of various sizes and colors, including red, orange-yellow, purple, and purple-black; most species produce shrubby clusters of arching canes that may be prickly to thorny. Some brambles spread readily from suckers and by rooting where cane tips bend over to the ground to form protective thickets where birds may nest and dine.	Blackbirds, bluebirds, bobwhites, buntings, cardinals, catbirds, chickadees, prairie chickens, crows, grackles, grosbeaks, grouse, jays, mockingbirds, orioles, pheasants, band-tailed pigeons, quails, robins, sparrows, tanagers, thrashers, thrushes, titmice, towhees, wild turkeys, vireos, waxwings, woodpeckers, wrens
Elderberries (*Sambucus* spp.)	Deciduous multistemmed shrub with attractive white flowers in early summer that develop into clusters of small blue-black fruit	Rusty blackbirds, bluebirds, buntings, cardinals, catbirds, flickers, grosbeaks, grouse, jays, kinglets, magpies, mockingbirds, nuthatches, orioles, phainopeplas, pheasants, band-tailed pigeons, robins, sapsuckers, sparrows, starlings, tanagers, thrushes, titmice, towhees, wild turkeys, vireos, waxwings, woodpeckers, wrens
Snowberries (*Symphoricarpos* spp.)	Shrub with nondescript deciduous foliage and pretty round white berries that are held into winter, when branches are bare	Bobwhites, prairie chickens, purple finches, evening grosbeaks, pine grosbeaks, grouse, magpies, pheasants, robins, thrushes, towhees, vireos, wrentits
Poison ivy and poison oak (*Toxicodendron radicans; T. toxicarium*)	Deciduous perennial vine or groundcover with shiny three-part leaves and white berries; causes dermatitis in humans but is a favorite of birds	Bluebirds, bobwhites, catbirds, chickadees, finches, flickers, grouse, juncos, mockingbirds, pheasants, quails, sapsuckers, sparrows, starlings, thrashers, thrushes, titmice, towhees, wild turkeys, vireos, waxwings, woodpeckers, wrens
Mapleleaf viburnum (*Viburnum acerifolium*)	Deciduous shrub with maplelike leaves that go pink-red in fall and berries that turn from red to black	Cardinals, great crested flycatchers, grouse, pheasants, robins, starlings, thrashers, thrushes, wild turkeys, waxwings, woodpeckers
Arrowwood (*Viburnum dentatum*)	Large deciduous shrub with showy white flowers and clusters of blue-black berries	Cardinals, great crested flycatchers, grouse, pheasants, robins, starlings, thrashers, thrushes, wild turkeys, waxwings, woodpeckers
Possumhaw (*Viburnum nudum*)	Large deciduous shrub with shiny, dark green leaves and bright red berries	Cardinals, great crested flycatchers, grouse, pheasants, robins, starlings, thrashers, thrushes, wild turkeys, waxwings, woodpeckers

SEASON WHEN BERRIES ARE PRESENT   ▮ SPRING   ▯ SUMMER   ▮ FALL   ▮ WINTER

Who Are Those Berries for, Anyhow?

When you've planted and nurtured young berry plants for a year or two, you may have a reaction you don't expect when birds arrive to sample the crop. "Hey you! Shoo!" is pretty much normal when you see the first brown thrasher come sailing in to steal your precious few blueberries.

Even lovely bluebirds and waxwings can evoke some strong responses, thanks to their ravenous appetites. It's hard to watch the berry-laden branches of your 'Winter Red' deciduous holly (*Ilex verticillata* 'Winter Red'), for instance, being stripped bare in just minutes. As you watch those pretty red branches being transformed to boring brown sticks, it can be difficult to remember that attracting birds was the reason you planted the holly in the first place.

Growing berries for the birds doesn't mean you have to let them have all the fruit. But keeping some for yourself means taking steps to keep some from the birds. If you have room, separate "your" berries from those intended for birds. As soon as fruits start forming, cover any plants you hope to harvest from with black plastic netting and remove it only when you need to get to the plants to pick.

Birds are gluttons when it comes to berries: They really can't eat just one. When they descend on a berry bush, you can bet it'll be empty of fruit by the time they leave. That flock of robins or tanagers will return day after day until every berry on your dogwood is history. And once the berries are gone, so are the birds.

It may seem a little ungrateful for the birds not to stick around after eating your landscape decorations, but don't take it personally. Just go plant some more berry bushes so that next year your company will stay longer. And remember—your neighbors may still have berries on their hollies. But you're the one who had the pleasure of watching the bluebirds.

> Birds will visit berry-laden bushes and trees until every piece of fruit has been devoured.

Billing and Cooing

"BILLING AND COOING," an old-fashioned expression—popular a half century ago or more—for romantic human behavior, was snitched from the birds. Some species, particularly ground doves, mourning doves, rock doves, and other members of the pigeon family, engage in a seemingly tender display of affection during courtship, which for these "hot-blooded" species can be almost any month of the year. They coo to each other and take turns "billing," a clasping of beaks or reaching into each other's open mouths in an avian "kiss." Some birds, including cedar waxwings, herons, and some water birds, bill but don't coo.

Scientists call this kind of billing by the humanized term "kissing." The male is usually the initiator, although both members of the couple have to cooperate to make it work. When a pair of waxwings are in the mood, for instance, the male bird sidles up close to the female, then tenderly inserts his closed bill into the female's opened beak briefly. Ravens kiss for a longer time, holding each other's bills and sometimes even closing their eyes. Among herons, kissing can be a frightening sight, thanks to those gigantic swordlike beaks. Still, the birds know how to handle the exchange with delicacy so that no harm is inflicted.

Watch for billing and/or cooing in the feeder vicinity. When you spot such behavior, you may notice that other rituals of courtship are also being performed, such as the male pursuing a reluctant female, or the male offering the female a tidbit of food. It's fun to see how various species of birds play the mating game.

> Even ornithologists use the word "kissing" to describe the odd bird behavior of billing.

Binoculars

IMAGINE HAVING A HAWK'S KEEN EYESIGHT: able to see a tiny mouse scurrying through the grass far below as you slowly circle in the sky. People ages ago tried (unsuccessfully, as you can imagine) to improve their eyesight by ingesting the juice of hawkweeds (*Hieracium* spp.). Today, all you have to do is sling a pair of binoculars around your neck to come as close as human eyes can to a hawk's visual acuity.

All binoculars are not created equal. To find the pair that's right for you, consider four factors:

Magnification power. The first number ("7" in a pair of 7 × 35 binoculars, for example) tells you how many times the image is magnified. In a pair of 7 × 35 binoculars, what you see is seven times larger than with normal unaided vision.

It would be great to be able to see 20 times better, but binoculars of high magnification power have a limitation: They also magnify the slightest movements of the hands that are holding them. Binoculars with 7 or 8 magnification power will give you a clear larger picture, but binoculars of 9 or 10 power are best used only if you have a remarkably steady grip or can brace your elbows on a flat surface. Although you can buy binoculars with lenses of even higher magnification, they will be very difficult to hold still and are best used only when attached to a tripod.

Light-gathering ability. The width of the bottom lens, indicated by the second number in binocular designations (the "35" in 7 × 35), determines how much light can enter the lens during viewing. Common lens sizes are 35—the most popular for all-around use—40, and 50. Ultra-lightweight mini-binoculars sacrifice lens width for portability, using sizes such as 20 for the larger lens. These smaller lenses are fine for bright-light viewing but tricky in dim situations, where you may have difficulty distinguishing a bird from its leafy background. In general, a lens size of 35 or higher designation is well suited to most bird-watching needs, although larger lenses mean larger, heavier binoculars.

Practice is essential for focusing on fast-moving birds like this warbler. When you spot movement in the trees, pinpoint the location, then swing the binoculars to focus on the spot.

Economical 7 x 35 binoculars are powerful enough to give you a good view from a distance, but for magnified detail of head markings or other fine points, try higher power 9x or 10x lenses.

Field of view. How big a picture you see is important because it allows you to find a bird faster by pinpointing it against nearby surroundings—that tree to its left, the branch above its head. The second number is also a clue to the size of field of view: The larger the number, the more you'll see.

Special features. If you tend to be a klutz, look for "armored" binoculars that are covered with a protective rubberized shield to prevent them from getting jarred by knocks and falls. If you'll be spotting birds in places with very bright light, such as on or near water, you'll want coated lenses to reduce glare. A padded strap relieves the tension on your neck from carting around binoculars on long expeditions.

Best All-Around Binoculars

Most birders use 7 × 35 or 8 × 42 binoculars, which offer plenty of magnification, a decent field of view, as well as adequate light for telling one warbler from another. Prices range from $20 at discount stores to more than $1,000 for super high-quality binoculars of this size. A cheap pair is fine for beginners; if you notch the price up to the $100 range, you'll get a fine pair of glasses that will give you years of use. To choose a brand, ask bird-watching friends for their recommendations, look for manufacturers endorsed by national bird-watching societies, and try the binoculars out yourself to make sure they are comfortable for your eyes and are easy to handle.

Practice Makes Perfect

Using binoculars is easy—finding a bird through them and focusing on it before it flies away takes practice. Start by using your binocs on any bird that crosses your path. Track it through your binoculars, following it with the glasses as you would with your eyes. If you lose the bird, drop the binoculars, pinpoint it with your eyes, then raise the glasses for another look. Soon, your binoculars will feel like a part of you, and you'll be following birds with the binocs as naturally as you do with your eyes. Once you are adept at zeroing in on a moving target, practice using the glasses to note smaller features and details such

as the shape of the bill, notable markings, and activity that may give you a clue to the bird's identity.

But binoculars are not just an indispensable aid to identification. They also give you a window into bird life, letting you get fascinating, close-up look at nest building, group dynamics, and individual behavior that you would otherwise miss. Focus on a starling stalking your yard, for instance, and you may be gratified to see the bird suddenly stab the ground and yank out a grub. Zero in on a noisy, squabbling bunch of house sparrows in the street, and see if you can pick out what they are quarreling over—a discarded sandwich crust or a strip of plastic, perhaps. Watch a robin on the lawn for a little while, and see if you can begin to guess where its next worm will come from according to how the bird cocks its head.

Spotting Scopes

For watching feeder birds or songbirds in your yard at moderate distances, a magnification power of 7 or 8 is fine. But if you're planning on doing long-distance viewing, such as spotting shorebirds or ducks, you'll want the highest power of magnification you can find, which may mean stepping up from binoculars to a spotting scope mounted on a tripod. The tripod gives the scope stability that your hands just can't provide. Especially with high-magnification binoculars trained on a distant target, even the slightest tremor of your hands affects the view.

Spotting scopes offer incredible powers of magnification—you'll be able to see the scales on a fish being carried off by a flying heron, as well as many other close-up marvels your unaided eyes can't discern. A scope is also a pleasure for viewing backyard birds at the bath or squirrels visiting their feeder. It's a little trickier to locate and focus on a moving target with a scope, but if you set it up in your house, aimed at a water feature or a feeder, you're bound to get a ringside seat at the activity.

> Bigger binoculars may not be better if they're too heavy to carry and use comfortably.

Birdbaths

THE OLD-FASHIONED CONCRETE birdbath, a simple basin balanced atop a sturdy pedestal, has been popular for almost 100 years. That kind of longevity can mean only one thing—it works.

Many birds have become accustomed to seeking birdbaths to get a drink of water and have a refreshing splash. Common backyard birds like chickadees, house finches, goldfinches, grackles, robins, and house sparrows will readily use this style of birdbath.

Other birds, generally the shyer types that live in woodlands or large open natural areas, are difficult to tempt to the unfamiliar height and structure of a birdbath. You can increase your bath's appeal by lowering it. Place the basin at ground level to entice the birds that usually drink from puddles and steams.

You can try another tactic and make the landscape around the bath more inviting to shy birds than the typical wide-open expanse of lawn that usually surrounds the birdbath. Groups of shrubs or other corridors of safety will encourage birds to approach without feeling unsafe from exposure.

Advantages of Birdbaths

Over the years, I have added more naturalistic water features in several of my gardens. These features expand the guest list of bathers and attract unusual visitors such as warblers and vireos, but I still keep a pedestal birdbath. It puts birds where I can see them easily—and you will definitely want a view of the antics. Bathing birds are downright comical as they splash and ruffle their feathers. Some are as wary as a toddler about dipping a toe in the water, while others enter the bath with abandon.

My birdbath also functions as a garden accent. It draws the eye, so that I can lengthen a view or focus attention on nearby shrubs or flowers.

Budget Birdbaths

Concrete birdbaths are a real value for the money. Expect to pay about $20 for a fine, classic model that will last for many years. Because the basins may

Water is as big a draw for birds as food, especially in summer when natural H_2O is hard to find. A drip tube lures them with the inviting sound of trickling water.

break, you can also buy the top and bottom sections separately. This gives you another good option for providing bathing space for birds. I dot my gardens with just the basins from birdbaths, set directly on the ground or on a low stack of bricks. These low-level birdbaths are just as attractive to my clientele as the one that's parked on a pedestal.

Large, shallow clay saucers, sold for catching drips beneath potted plants, also are ideal for birdbaths. Comparison shop before you buy—a standard birdbath basin may cost less than a clay saucer, and it will hold up to the ravages of weather much longer.

Plastic plant saucers are another option, although they may be too slippery for the birds' comfort. I buy them anyway and rough them up with very coarse sandpaper to give birds something to grip. At a cost of just a couple of dollars each, they're a great way to provide water, and they can withstand freezing and thawing. Keep a few on hand to rotate in the winter—when one freezes up, bring it in to thaw and replace it with a freshly filled saucer.

Seasonal Use

Birdbaths are popular all year because resident birds soon learn to depend on an always-available supply of fresh water. The very presence of birds at the bath may lure stopover migrants, even without the addition of a pump or mister to create water music.

The dry season is prime time for birdbaths. That's when the water source will mostly likely entice unexpected visitors, as natural supplies of the precious liquid dry up and the lack of rain means no roadside puddles.

Winter in cold areas is also a popular time for birdbaths. As freezing temperatures turn natural water sources to solid ice, birds will become loyal visitors at a birdbath with open water. Some birds, including starlings, splash wholeheartedly in water even in winter, but most will content themselves with just a drink. If you live in a cold-winter area, it's well

---

PROJECT

Make an Insulated Birdbath

Boost the power of an immersion heater—and cut your electricity costs—by insulating your heated birdbath for the winter. Even if you don't use an immersion heater, this design will keep a pan of water from freezing as quickly as it would if unprotected from the cold.

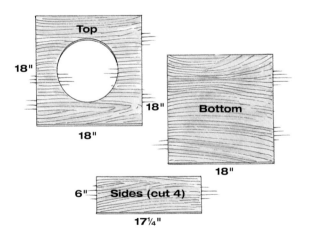

MATERIALS

Four 6 × 17¼-inch pieces of 1 × 6 lumber

Nails

Two 18 × 18-inch squares of plywood

Shallow bowl or pan for birdbath

Insulation (Styrofoam peanuts, fiberglass, or foam)

Submersible heater (optional)

Step 1. Nail the four pieces of 1 × 6 into a box frame.

Step 2. Nail one square of plywood to the frame to form the bottom of the box.

Step 3. Fill the box with insulation.

Step 4. Cut a hole in the remaining plywood square to hold the water pan while allowing the edges of the pan to rest atop the plywood.

Step 5. Attach the top to the box. Insert the pan, adjusting the insulation as necessary.

Step 6. Fill the pan with water. Add a submersible heater, if desired.

worth investing a few dollars in additional aids to keep your birdbath ice-free.

A submersible electric heater, which retails at about $20 and up, is the top de-icer choice of most backyard birders. In severe cold, don't expect the heater to keep the entire container unfrozen. It may allow only the part of the water very near the heater to stay in a liquid state in frigid weather. Birds will quickly find the open water.

Solar-heated birdbaths are also available. They depend on the warmth of the sun to keep the dark plastic dish ice-free. If your winter weather is mostly overcast as well as icy cold, a solar-heated bath won't be very effective.

Cleaning Birdbaths

Like any pool of stagnant water, a birdbath can harbor a fine crop of algae if you let it go without cleaning for several days. Even worse than the slimy stuff is the fact that a birdbath is the perfect breeding place for mosquito larvae. Those two considerations are more than enough reason to clean the bath frequently.

Any abrasive will get rid of algae. You can use a plastic scouring pad, a scrap of sandpaper, a handful of sand, or a scrub brush. A few stems of horsetail (*Equisetum* spp.), a plant with high silica content, will also work very well. To save steps on cleaning chores, you can keep your scrubbies inside the hollow pedestal of the birdbath. Loop a wire around the top of the pedestal and through the handle of the brush or corner of the scouring pad. When you're ready to clean, tilt the basin to empty it, lift it from the pedestal, and fish out your scrubbing tool. Before refilling the basin with fresh water, drop the tool back into the pedestal.

Landscaping the Bath

Planting around a birdbath to make it safe and enticing requires a careful balance. You need to supply shelter for wet birds but also make sure there is a clear view of approaching danger.

Cats are a real menace around a birdbath. If a stalking kitty is plaguing your birds and you can't exclude the animal from your yard, it's best to keep an open area of at least 10 feet around the bath. That should give birds enough time to become airborne once they spot the stalker. Beyond the bare zone, plant shrubs for birds to dive into for safety.

If cats are infrequent or absent in your yard, plant a shrub close to the bath (or place the bath close to a shrub). Birds like to move from branch to water, then hop back into the shrub to shake and preen their feathers. I plant pussy willows (*Salix discolor*) beside my birdbaths. They appreciate the extra water I dump on their roots every time I fill the bath, and the large bush supplies plenty of room for after-bath primping. Its branches also shelter the bath from overhead attacks by passing hawks.

Added Attractions

Birds won't be your only customers at a birdbath. My fat, lazy fox squirrels are surprisingly adept at leaping onto the rim of my pedestal bath to lap up fresh water. At my low-level basin-only baths, I've also spotted chipmunks, toads, butterflies, and once even a beautiful black snake. Visitors may also show up at night. I suspected my dogs of knocking the basin off my birdbath night after night, until I happened to spy a very large raccoon hanging on to the edge and trying to haul itself up for a drink.

Save steps by hanging a scrub brush from your birdbath's pedestal. Drop the brush into the pedestal if it's hollow, or let the brush hang down the back.

Bird Blinds

THE CLOSER YOU GET to a bird, the more fun it is to watch. You will see details of plumage and anatomy you might have missed from a distance—the position of the toes of a woodpecker compared to those of a sparrow, for instance. You'll spot nuances of body language that give you clues to upcoming bird behavior, such as quick movements of the head that show deference or aggression and that precede the more noticeable behaviors of lowered wings and puffed body feathers.

Watching birds from close quarters also gives you a peep at their private lives. You may hear quiet love songs or lullabies. You can watch the fascinating and intricate process of nest building. You may spot young birds being fed, and with the aid of binoculars, find out what's for dinner. And you may see fledglings practicing their skills before that big first takeoff.

But because birds are naturally wary creatures, you are not likely to get a glimpse of these behaviors as long as the birds are aware of your presence. A portable or semipermanent bird blind that keeps you hidden while you watch is easier to make than you might think, depending on what kind of habitat you want to watch birds in and what kind of materials you have handy. Use your ingenuity.

For watching feeder birds, the windows of your house make the perfect vantage point as long as you avoid drawing attention to your presence with vigorous or sudden movements.

- For the best view, position your feeders as close to the window as you can. Windowsill feeders are a wonderful choice because they bring the birds near enough to let you see every detail.

- Install inexpensive stick-on film that turns the window into a one-way mirror, from which you can see out clearly but the birds outside see only a reflection of themselves.

- A terrific but costlier alternative is to bring the birds "inside" by installing a feeder that replaces the lower part of your window and extends inside the room. (Expect to pay $100 or more for an in-the-window feeder, not including installation.)

For watching water birds, such as ducks, egrets, geese, herons, and roseate spoonbills at refuges or wild places along roadways, your car makes the ideal blind. Stay inside your car and observe through the open window to avoid frightening away the birds.

Your car is also perfect cover for watching hawks as they perch along roadsides watching for prey.

- When you spot a bird of prey on a utility pole or other perch, turn around when you can do so safely and return to a parking place within view of the bird.

- Watch the bird closely as you approach slowly; if it shows signs of nervousness, such as shifting its position or watching your vehicle intently, you will know you have reached the limits of approach. Park safely and sit quietly to observe through the windshield or side window. Remember that hawks have famously sharp eyesight; avoid sudden attention-getting movements.

In your own backyard, try one of these tricks to blend in to the scenery.

- Birds that live or move about in the trees will quickly become accustomed to your presence in a hammock or chaise longue, the most comfortable devices for overhead viewing.

- To cover up a backyard observation post for lower-level bird watching, surround your chair or bench with camouflage netting, sold at hunting-supply stores, draped over the metal poles used to prop up clotheslines.

- Ask at an appliance store for a box from a refrigerator or other large item. Flatten and fold the box for transport. Although the presence of the box blind may alarm birds at first, they will soon become used to its presence. Staple branches, grass, vegetation, or a piece of camouflage netting to the box to make the birds accept it more quickly as just part of the scenery.

Bird Counts

COUNTING BIRDS has been an annual bird-watching ritual for more than a century. Bird counts supply lots of important information, starting with population figures. By counting birds in the same area over a period of years, it's immediately obvious when, for example, numbers of wood thrushes drop to precipitous lows, or that catbirds begin regularly wintering far north of their usual haunts. This alerts scientists who can then look at factors that may have contributed to the change in population or range. Although banding birds offers solid data, too, counting birds supplies more information. Participating in an official or just-for-fun bird count also increases your awareness of just what kinds of birds, and how many of them, are visiting your feeder, backyard, or nearby wild places.

Contribute to science by keeping track of your feeder birds on a designated day. Regional and national counts let you see how your bird traffic compares.

Counting at Home

One of the simplest ways to participate in a bird count is Project Feederwatch, a joint project of several institutions, including Cornell University and the National Audubon Society. From the comfort of home, you can join tens of thousands of participants reporting regularly on their feeder guests. You'll be adding to the bank of important data gleaned from this project, including information on the spread and decline of diseases, population swings of species, and expanding ranges of songbirds. For information on Project Feederwatch, see "Resources" on page 348.

Join a Counting Crew

You don't need to be an expert to join an organized count. Every pair of eyes and ears are important, and even if you are shaky in your identification skills, you'll still be a help to more experienced birders. If you're shy about joining a count for the first time, as I was, never fear. The folks are invariably friendly and helpful to beginners, and it's just plain fun for adults and kids alike. As you're counting, you'll also enjoy traipsing around, looking at birds, wildflowers, and other great surprises, whether it's a praying mantis or a rare tanager. But beware to the very beginner bird watcher: Although spotting birds is usually done at a snail's pace, without strenuous physical exertion, the intensity of being alert for hours at a stretch can wear you out, and you'll be surprised how tired you are at the end of the day.

To get involved in a count of wild birds in your area, contact the National Audubon Society or a local nature center. Ask about one of my favorite counts, the National Audubon Society/U.S. Fish and Wildlife annual Christmas count, held in the 2 weeks surrounding Christmas. You'll find Web sites, phone numbers, and mailing addresses in "Resources" on page 348.

Bird Feeding on a Budget

BIRDS WON'T EAT YOU OUT OF HOUSE and home, but they can put a crimp in your wallet if you're feeding lots of customers. In winter, when feeder traffic is at its peak, it's not unusual for me (actually, my bird visitors) to go through 50 pounds of sunflower seed and about 20 pounds of millet in a week. Add suet and all those high-priced nuts, fruits, and other treats, and it's easy to rack up a $30 bird-food bill every week.

Limit the Menu

To keep costs reasonable, I limit my seed choices to three main foods. I still get plenty of feeder visitors, including all my favorite birds. Here are my recommendations to limit food costs but not avian visitors at your feeders.

- Serve **black oil sunflower** for cardinals, chickadees, jays, titmice, woodpeckers, and other strong-billed seed crackers.

- Offer **millet** for smaller seed eaters, such as finches, juncos, and sparrows.

- Supplement the menu with **cracked corn,** which takes care of visiting blackbirds and starlings.

I also keep one tube feeder filled with niger, and I ration out treats like fruit and nuts in small quantities. And instead of buying those all-too-convenient suet blocks, I stuff my wire suet cages with free (or practically free) fat trimmings from the butcher.

Feeding a multitude? Trim the budget by sticking to millet and sunflower seed, eagerly sought by feeder favorites like this cardinal.

Buy in Bulk

Picking up a plastic bag of birdseed at the supermarket can bring the cost of seed to almost $1 a pound. For bargain prices, buy in bulk. A 50-pound sack of sunflower seeds often costs less than 20 cents per pound. If that seems excessive, arrange to split the cost with a neighbor and fellow bird lover. Once you get the seed home, perhaps your neighbor can also help you unload it.

Peanut butter is one of the best foods for bringing bluebirds to your feeder, but a small jar can come with a hefty price tag. Stock up on economy-size jars of your

---

Skewered Suet

HERE'S AN easy way to provide suet to your bird guests without any cost to you. Save your empty plastic yogurt cups, and fill them halfway with bacon grease or meat drippings. Cover them and put them in the freezer until you're ready to use them. When it's time to feed, remove the lid and trim off the extra part of the cup, leaving only about 1 inch above the level of the frozen suet. Bend a piece of wire into a hanger on one end, and poke it through one side of the cup, twisting it to hold it in place. To provide a stable perch, push the pointed end of a wooden skewer all the way through the fat and the bottom of the cup. These may not be the most beautiful feeders, but when it's 10°F outside, I don't get any complaints from the bluebirds, chickadees, and other customers who come for a bit of high-energy fat.

10 Tricks to Trim the Birdseed Budget

1. Stick to cracked corn. A 50-pound sack costs only about $6 at feed stores. Most birds will readily eat corn if their favorite other seeds aren't available.

2. Offer chick scratch, available at very low cost at rural feed stores. It's welcomed by cardinals, doves, quail, and other birds.

3. Buy birdseed whenever it's on sale and store it in airtight containers for later use.

4. Make your own seed mixes instead of buying packaged products. If you do buy commercial mixes, read the ingredients so you know what you're getting. Fillers like wheat and milo are no bargain.

5. Use small, squirrel-proof feeders to serve more expensive seeds and nuts to favorite songbirds.

6. Install a feeder with a wire cage that prevents larger birds like starlings from entering and gobbling up your seed (see page 100).

7. Ask the produce manager at your supermarket for free, discarded fruit.

8. Grow your own sunflowers, buckwheat, and corn to supplement the feeders. I prefer to let the seedheads stay on the plants, so I can have the fun of watching birds extract the seeds.

9. Collect sprays of seedheads (snip the mature plant at the base) from dock, foxtail grasses, lamb's-quarters, mustards, and other likely weeds. It's interesting to see which birds they appeal to.

10. Plant a patch of amaranths (*Amaranthus* spp.), bachelor's-button (*Centaurea cyanus*), cosmos (*Cosmos* spp.), tickseed sunflower (*Bidens aristosa*), or zinnias (*Zinnia elegans*)—all bird favorites for seeds. You can find seeds for most of these at low prices in spring or at closeout time in fall; the seeds are often sold at 10 packs for $1. Plant the seeds within view of a window, so you can watch the plants sway with birds from fall through winter.

---

local store brand instead. The birds won't be offended that you're not serving them the high-priced gourmet blend: They will eagerly gobble any old brand.

Avoid Impulse Buys

Just as you'll pay more for those last-minute checkout-counter purchases, your birdseed budget can be blown if you forget to plan ahead. Filling in gaps with costly small bags of seed or buying from stores where seed is more expensive than your usual supplier is convenient but pricey. I like to keep an unopened sack of sunflower seed (at least 25 pounds' worth) in reserve, so that I can still satisfy the birds even when I have unforeseen problems with transportation, daily schedules, or bad weather.

A big metal trash can is the perfect storage container for your emergency seed supply. It will hold many pounds of sunflower, millet, or mixed seed and keep out unwanted nibblers, like small rodents or insects. Store a large scoop on top of the seeds, and you'll be all set for those times when your supply runs short. Be sure to replenish your reserve supply whenever you find yourself dipping into it.

Common redpolls, house finches, chickadees, and other small birds quickly adopt a tube feeder. Tube feeders prevent spills and limit the number of guests.

Bird-Friendly Backyard

STAYING ALIVE is the number one concern of all birds. Keep that in mind as you plan your bird-friendly backyard, and your landscape will soon be brimming with birds. Feeders are only the start—birds need more than just food to be safe, healthy, and happy in your yard. You'll also want to include as many plants as possible—to most birds, a big sweep of lawn grass is about as appealing as the Sahara—for food, cover for a quick getaway from predators, nesting sites, and cozy roosting areas. And don't forget water, another important incentive for

Food, water, and sheltering plants make a yard inviting to birds. Shrubs and other plantings allow them to safely navigate across open space under cover.

birds to visit and return to your yard. Safe nesting places, either natural homes in trees and shrubs or bird boxes supplied by you, will boost the population. Supplying nesting materials, grit, and salt are also welcome mats for birds looking for a place to settle down. Provide all this—and discourage predators, too—and your efforts toward encouraging a bird population in your yard will pay off.

Food

A feeding station is guaranteed to bring birds to your yard because those active little bodies need almost constant fueling to keep going. You can't go wrong with a general menu of sunflower seed, millet, and suet; adding occasional treats like nuts and fruits makes bird feeding more fun and attracts a wider variety of birds.

Fruit feeders may bring you catbirds, orioles, thrushes, wrens, and other unusual birds. Nectar feeders, for hummingbirds, of course, also appeal to orioles, finches, warblers, and woodpeckers. Mealworms are a treat for bluebirds and even purple martins. Peanut butter, combined with cornmeal to make it stretch a little further, is a big draw for many birds.

Bread and other soft foods may tempt robins and other birds that usually rely on insects.

Speaking of insects, the plants in your yard provide a steady diet of these delectable delicacies to birds. Trees, shrubs, perennials, grasses, and other plants hold a bounty, from bite-sized beetles to juicy caterpillars. Even in winter, birds will scour the plants to find eggs, cocoons, and overwintering insects. In summer, a yard with plenty of plantings is particularly welcome to birds because they need mass quantities of insect food for their young.

Naturally you will want to avoid using any toxic chemicals on your plants, which will kill off the insects and make your yard less appealing to birds, not to mention the possibility of making the birds sick as well. When you notice an outbreak of pests in the garden, you can either wait for birds to clean it up themselves, or, for vegetable plants, you can step in and handpick the offenders. Be careful with applications of "safe" organic pesticides, too. Even though

Fill Your Yard with Bird-Friendly Plant Choices

WHEN YOU'RE adding plants to your yard, make selections that will satisfy you and your bird visitors. Choose from among those plants that produce berries, fruits, and/or seeds that birds favor.

Look for plants that do double-duty, providing food and shelter for birds as well as "eye appeal" for you, and the birds will enjoy your landscape while you enjoy watching and listening to the birds.

■ Instead of planting a hedge of forsythia, which has little bird value, try a food-providing hedge of bayberry, blueberries, elderberries, or sumac.

■ Add cosmos (*Cosmos* spp.), bachelor's-button (*Centaurea cyanus*), sunflowers, and zinnias to your beds of annuals to satisfy seed-seeking goldfinches and sparrows.

■ Brighten your landscape with the showy spring flowers of handsome small trees such as dogwood, amelanchier, and callery pear, and you'll enjoy the birds that arrive to dine on fruits later in the season.

it doesn't harm birds, the commonly used product BTK (*Bacillus thuringiensis* var. *kurstaki*) will kill a wide variety of leaf-eating caterpillars. That's bad news for birds that might make a meal of those caterpillars (and it can cut down on the number of butterflies you enjoy in your yard, too). When you can, let birds handle caterpillar problems in your yard and garden. If caterpillars descend en masse on your plants, be patient: Chances are that catbirds, orioles, and other aficionados of these crawly creatures will soon arrive to snap them up.

Cover

Keeping out of sight is the modus operandi for most birds. Sheltering shrubs and other plants protect them from the gaze and the grasp of cats, hawks, and other hungry bird eaters. Design your yard so that there are only small stretches of open space between plantings, so that birds can move throughout your property safely.

Be sure to consider winter cover, too, when you're selecting plants. You'll want to include evergreens for the valuable shelter their branches offer in the off-season, when deciduous species are bare. Remember to choose first those plants that offer food sources in addition to cover: Hemlocks, pines, and other evergreen conifers will eventually produce a bounty of seed-filled cones as well as insects among their needles. Broad-leaved evergreens, such as bayberries (*Myrica* spp.) and Oregon grape hollies (*Mahonia* spp.), are other good choices.

Nest Sites

When birds feel comfortable and protected in your yard, they are more likely to move in to raise a family. The plants you provide for protective cover will also supply birds with many good sites for nesting. Shrubs with dense branches, especially those with thorns or prickles, are eagerly sought as nest sites because their branches deter predators. An overgrown patch of raspberries or other brambles is ideal. Hawthorns (*Crataegus* spp.), with their spiny branches, and hollies (*Ilex* spp.), with their prickly leaves, are other plants with good nesting potential. A dense tangle of vines, such as autumn clematis (*Clematis terniflora*), may also be used as a nest site.

Robins and phoebes may quickly adopt a horizontal, covered shelf—a simplified, open-walled structure that appeals to these birds—as a nest. Birdhouses themselves are eagerly sought by cavity nesters such as chickadees, woodpeckers, wrens, and even owls, as well as the popular bluebird.

Roosting Places

A densely planted yard also offers birds safe areas to roost at night or in bad weather. Evergreens are especially welcomed for roosting places. If you are lucky enough to already have a large spruce or other evergreen, watch in late afternoon to see what birds fly into its branches. A single 15-foot-tall eastern red cedar (*Juniperus virginiana*) at the corner of my former Pennsylvania home held catbirds, mockingbirds, robins, brown thrashers, and a horde of house sparrows within its dense, prickly branches at night. At my Indiana home, the same kind of tree shelters more than 50 birds every evening in winter: more than a dozen cardinals, plus robins, fox sparrows, white-crowned sparrows, white-throated sparrows, and the ubiquitous house sparrows.

Not all birds seek plants for roosting places. Carolina wrens are apt to wiggle their way into garages, sheds, and other outbuildings. My garage at a former home had a circular opening in one wall where a stovepipe had been removed. In the evening, I watched cardinals, Carolina wrens, chickadees, robins, and titmice enter the hole to roost overnight.

Nest boxes, roosting boxes, and natural cavities in trees are also sought for roosts. On cold winter nights, several birds-of-a-feather may pile into one communal box for warmth.

Water

Adding a water feature to your garden, whether it's a simple birdbath or an elaborate running waterfall, will make your property more inviting to birds, including those that don't visit a feeder. Incorporate the sound of water by adding a recirculating pump, and you will quickly attract migrants and other birds.

Water is a hot item during summer heat and drought, when natural puddles are scarce and birds need a cooling drink and splash. It's also a big draw in winter in cold regions, when creeks and ponds are locked in ice. An electric or solar de-icer is a great investment if you live in a cold-winter area because fresh water in winter is very attractive.

Grit and Salt

A few handfuls of crushed eggshells, fine gravel, and a brick of salt will supply the mineral needs of your birds. Finches, crossbills, and doves welcome a regular source of salt. All birds need grit to provide the necessary abrasion for their grinding digestive processes. While these substances alone won't bring birds flocking to your yard, their presence will make it easy for your feathered friends to fill these supplementary needs while they visit your yard. And that means they will stay longer and return more often.

Predator Control

You can't keep every bird safe from every predator, but you can help to eliminate one major threat—cats. Keep your own feline pets indoors, especially during nesting season, and do your best to discourage strays.

To protect birds from the depredations of hawks, provide them convenient close shelter at feeding areas and water features, so they can dive into dense bushes for a getaway if needed.

Snakes, raccoons, opossums, and owls may also prey on birds, but there's not much you can do to keep these animals out of your yard. Do, however, protect any bird boxes you put up with antipredator baffles on the posts below them. Those sold to keep squirrels or raccoons out of feeders will do the trick for birdhouses as well. Antipredator door guards on nest boxes are also a plus. These plastic or metal tubes extend outward from the entrance hole, making it impossible for a raccoon's paw to reach the eggs inside.

Bird-Friendly Neighborhood

MAKING YOUR YARD ATTRACTIVE to birds is a great start, but if you really want to bring more—and different types of—birds to your yard, inspire your neighbors to join you. If the yards surrounding yours include the same kind of welcoming features as yours does, you'll end up with a bigger bird-friendly space.

Property lines are meaningless to birds—an appealing space is just that. If your appealing bird-safe space flows into a neighbor's, birds will move freely from one place to another. Bigger bird-friendly spaces mean more birds, so both you and your neighbors will benefit. If neighboring yards border a wild area, the extension of plantings may eventually create corridors that birds will use to move back and forth from your backyards to the natural areas. That can result in species that you wouldn't otherwise see visiting your feeder or watering hole, such as bobwhites or bluebirds.

Often, just the appealing sight of a well-planted yard alive with birds is all it takes to make your neighbors want to create their own little sanctuary. A couple of chats over the backyard hedge can also encourage a boomlet of bird-friendly planting in a neighborhood. Talk to your neighbors about the pleasures of watching birds: the fun of seeing a robin splash in its bath, the thrill of your first junco of the season. Invite neighbors for coffee, and let them watch the birds out your kitchen window

Robins often nest close to our homes. Talk to your neighbors about the delights of bird life and your neighborhood may become an impromptu bird sanctuary for other species, too.

or from the patio. Show them the zippy little visitors at your hummingbird feeder or the oriole at the oranges. Tell them about the day last winter when you counted 20 different species of birds visiting the feeders in your yard. Chances are, once your neighbors see how much pleasure you're getting from feeding the birds, they'll want to take part in the fun.

Share the Wealth

DO YOU have neighbors who you suspect are leaning toward bird watching, but you think might need a small push? Help them out with "donations" of bird-friendly plants and other supplies. Purchase larger quantities of plants that attract birds than you need for your yard. (Often, you can save money this way as well.) Then, give the "extras" to the neighbors to plant. Buy feeders at a 2-for-1 sale, then ask your neighbors if they would like one for their yard. Before they realize what's happening, their yard will be full of the overflow birds from yours, and they'll be hooked!

If your neighborhood tends toward lawn competition rather than dense plantings, be sure to tell your neighbors what you're working on as you go about changing the look of your land. Wide, welcoming paths through your garden will do a lot to allay their fears that you may be creating a weedy jungle. Straight paths and fences add a touch of formality to even the wildest garden, showing neighbors that a guiding hand is still in control.

Birding Hot Line

BEING PART OF A CIRCLE OF BIRDERS helps you get reports of unusual sightings quickly, but you can't depend on word of mouth to pass the news when a rare bird rolls into town. By the time a friend remembers to call you, the bird may be already winging its way out of town. And if you're a birder who keeps a life list, you may be willing to travel 100 miles or more to lay eyes on an unusual bird. Once, when a gyrfalcon showed up at a quarry about 50 miles from me, I met birders from 500 miles away who had come to get a look at the highly unusual and beautiful visitor from the Far North. European, Siberian, and far-wandering bird species that turn up in the United States get star treatment, with birders trekking hundreds of miles to lay eyes on them.

Modern technology makes it even easier to track the occasional rare bird and to follow the movements of familiar species. There are numerous birding hot lines (and now Web sites) with recorded telephone messages that birders use to keep up-to-date on visiting birds. You can call in or log on to find out what unusual visitors are nearby. On many, you can also pass along your own observations. Some hot lines and Web sites also include information on migrants: when the first junco was spotted in fall, or the first hummingbird in spring. Hot lines include all bird species, not only songbirds, so you'll also find notices about gulls, shorebirds, herons, birds of prey, and others.

Visit www.americanbirding.org/wgrbaadd.htm, the American Birding Association Web site, to find a state-by-state listing of birding hot lines and Web sites. You can also visit www.birdcast.org, a site sponsored by numerous organizations, including the National Audubon Society and Clemson University.

> To locate a birding hot line in your area, search the Internet or call the National Audubon Society.

Bird Names

A BIRD'S "COMMON" NAME refers to the name we call a bird in conversation. We know spring has arrived when we see a *Turdus migratorius*, but we point and exclaim, "Oh, look! The first robin of spring!" A bird's common name is usually a sensible, descriptive moniker that tells you the type of bird—finch, grosbeak, hummingbird—and supplies a clue to its looks or likes (such as "robin redbreast"). Sometimes the adjectives are uncommon, but don't be discouraged: If you look "pileated" up in a dictionary, you'll discover that a pileated woodpecker is a woodpecker with a crest.

A Bird by Any Other Name

Most birds have more than just one common name, having been tagged simultaneously by locals in various regions. The field sparrow, for instance, was also known at one time and in various places as the bush sparrow, huckleberry sparrow, rush sparrow, wood sparrow, ground bird, and field bunting. Common names in this sense of the word—those invented by common people—are becoming a thing of the past. Most modern birders know birds only by the common name that's listed in their field guide. Whenever I find someone who calls the cedar waxwing "cherry bird," I smile with memories of my mother, who passed to me the names she'd learned from her father. The "official" (guidebook) common names of birds are occasionally changed, which can lead to cries of protest from birders, who rarely bother to memorize the Latin names of even the most familiar feeder birds.

Sometimes, a bird is named in honor of a person, not for attributes of the bird itself. Bachman's sparrow and Bachman's warbler, for instance, are fine tributes to Reverend John Bachman, a John James Audubon crony who supplied his friend with many specimens. But the common names of Bachman's birds don't tell us anything additional about the sparrow or the warbler. If you're interested in the history as well as the attributes of these birds, take your field guide along to the public library, and check the biography section for the scoop on big names in birds.

Old common names are often highly colorful and may reflect old regional dialects or language derivations. In New England, the name "Peabody bird" makes perfect sense for the white-throated sparrow; reflecting their British heritage, they pronounce the word "PEA-biddy." To non-Yankees who say "pea-body" instead and have read a description of the sparrow's song as "old Sam Peabody," there's a language barrier that keeps them from recognizing the true rhythm of the song.

"Pileated" simply means "crested," and the pileated woodpecker definitely has an eye-catching one atop its hammering head.

Deciphering Names

Many species of birds have common names that can give you clues about their lives. These include where a bird lives or feeds, what it looks like, how it sounds, and what its habits (usually feeding habits) are. Here are some birds who fit into that category.

Habitat: field sparrow, swamp sparrow, barn swallow, cliff swallow, house wren, marsh wren

Physical attributes: blue jay, red-tailed hawk, horned lark, fox sparrow, golden-crowned sparrow, white-crowned sparrow, white-throated sparrow, waxwings, and many wood warblers (orange-crowned, black-throated green, etc.)

Voice: catbird, mockingbird, pewee, phoebe, towhee, veery, vireo

Habits: gnatcatchers, nuthatch, grasshopper sparrow, hermit thrush, worm-eating warbler ("worms" meaning caterpillars, not earthworms), house wren

---

A Bit of Bird Lingo

THERE ARE many terms, some derived from Latin names, that have a specific meaning when they're part of a bird's common name, no matter what type of bird they describe.

Boreal: of the north

Cerulean: blue

Ferruginous: reddish (like rusted iron)

Grosbeak: large beak

Hatch (as in nuthatch): hack, hacker (as in hacking nuts, not computer hacker)

Hepatic: red (liver-colored)

Hoary: whitish

Lazuli: rich blue

Pileated: crested

Rufous: reddish brown

Tit (as in titmouse, bushtit): a small, active bird

Vermilion: vivid red to red-orange

Bird Recordings

WHETHER BIRDS use them to greet the dawn, to warn others of danger, or to announce ownership of a tasty treat, birdsongs and calls are hot topics among bird lovers. As evidence, one of the hottest gift items in recent memory is the bird clock, with bird pictures at the numbers on the face and the birdcalls of the 12 species sounding the hours. (A dedicated bird-watcher friend of mine received one as a gift and expected to be irritated by it, but he found he enjoyed it very much—especially when the thing got off-kilter and at the blue jay hour, it honked like a goose.)

Wood warblers are hard to get a good look at as they flit among foliage. Sort them out by song. The ascending trill of the northern parula warbler ends on a loud final note.

Sparrow Sing-Along

While the quality of the calls on bird clocks is nowhere near reality, serious birders can buy recordings of actual bird calls, with a commentator quietly introducing each bird by name before the vocalization. (See "Resources" on page 348.) High-quality tapes and CDs are a great education, and you'll be astounded at the diversity of bird music. Many people find these recordings useful for learning to identify birds by ear. Some bird watchers use specific calls to "lure" birds, not to capture them but to let them know of a food source so that they can enjoy watching them dine and hearing their songs live.

Flushing Out the Finches

Some bird watchers purchase taped alarm calls and owl calls to bring songbirds out of bushes. This is a controversial use for taped songs because the realistic sounds are distressing to birds, who hear "bird in danger," and fly out in fright. I prefer to use these tapes outside sparingly, if at all. Birds have enough panic in their lives without us adding to it.

The western meadowlark is a true songster, while eastern species sing just a few slow notes.

B

Birdseed

Attracts many kinds of birds at various times of the year

FEEDING THE BIRDS isn't just for the birds. Producing and selling birdseed is a huge industry. The roughly 63 million of us who feed birds spend a whopping *$2 billion* on birdseed every year. That cash outlay has far-reaching effects. It helps support more than just the farmers that raise the sunflowers, millets, sorghum, and other seeds that we pour into our feeders. It helps keep in business the makers of birdseed sacks, the shippers, the distributors, and all the other folks who play a part in getting birdseed from flowering plant to feeding station.

"Birdseed" doesn't describe a single seed. It includes a sampling of many grains and other seeds—from feeder staples like sunflower seed and millet to the wheat, corn, and milo fillers used in inexpensive seed mixes. Safflower and other specialty seeds that we pay dearly for to tempt special birds are also birdseed.

Thanks to the large market for the seed and the increasing savvy of those of us who stock the feeders, birdseed suppliers are adding an ever-growing lineup of seed mixes to the shelves. You can find bags of seed just for finches or bags of heftier seeds designed to bring cardinals and grosbeaks. Armed with some knowledge of which birds prefer what seeds and some information about the seeds themselves, you can become a smarter shopper and spend those big birdseed bucks more wisely.

The Staples

If you stocked your feeder with nothing but **sunflower seeds,** you would be able to satisfy more than 20 different species of feeder birds. All large-beaked seed eaters, including cardinals, grosbeaks, and jays, readily eat sunflower seeds. These birds, who use their big bills to easily crack the shells to free the meaty morsels inside, relish both black oil and gray-striped sunflowers. Chickadees, finches, nuthatches, titmice, and many other smaller-beaked feeder regulars also head for sunflowers as their staple seed of choice.

Birds will eat more—and waste less—of the mix on the lower left, which contains a greater percentage of appealing black oil sunflower and tiny tan millet.

Black oil sunflower seed is the more economical option because the smaller seeds go further than the big, plump gray-striped variety, which has fewer seeds per pound. It also has a higher oil content, so it gives the birds more calories when they eat it. The other advantage to black oil sunflower seed is that smaller birds can crack it readily. That may or may not be a plus, depending on how many house finches you're hosting! When hordes of these smaller-beaked birds descend, you might want them to spend a little longer working for their supper.

Sunflower seeds take care of most fall and winter feeder birds, with some notable exceptions: mainly, the sparrows. Native sparrows will crack sunflowers when they're desperate, but they prefer smaller seeds that they can pick up quickly. They prefer white or proso **millet,** a small, round, tan-colored seed that you probably have noticed in birdseed mixes. Though they will eat red millet, white seems to be more popular.

Not only sparrows siphon up millet. It's favored by bobwhites, buntings, doves, juncos, quail, house sparrows, towhees, and Carolina wrens—the regular cast of characters at most feeding stations. Tanagers also devour millet. Should sunflower seeds be lacking at your feeder, cardinals, purple finches, goldfinches, grosbeaks, jays, and pine siskins will turn to millet.

Millet is a bargain for bird feeding. Because it is so small and lightweight, you will get zillions of seeds in a 50-pound sack, enough to take care of your small feeder birds for weeks.

Budget Alternatives

Cracked corn and **chick scratch,** a crushed feed of corn and other grains, are low-cost replacements for sunflower seeds and millet. If your budget is tight, you can augment the basics with one of these seeds, or you can switch to them entirely. Eliminating sunflowers and millet, however, may cause you to lose the loyalty of purple finches, goldfinches, and some other feeder birds, which may shift to your neighbor's feeder if their favorites are no longer on your menu.

Cracked corn and chick scratch can be a great distraction at the feeding station. Birds that tend to show up in multitudes like starlings, blackbirds, grackles, and house sparrows favor these inexpensive foods. By serving abundant helpings of corn and scratch away from your other feeders, you can segregate the feeding station so that sunflower and millet eaters can dine without feeling pressured by the mobs.

Like coffee, chick scratch varies in the fineness of its grind, as various grades are manufactured to feed baby chicks of different ages. Ask your supplier for a coarse blend. The finely ground, almost powdery type tends to clump up into unpalatable lumps when it absorbs moisture, causing waste and inviting vermin.

Cracked corn, too, may vary in the grind. Most suppliers don't mind if you ask to see a sample. A bag of cornmeal isn't much good for feeding birds for the same reasons that powdery chick scratch is inappropriate. Also, a fine-ground cornmeal doesn't attract larger seed eaters. Coarsely cracked corn will satisfy the most customers.

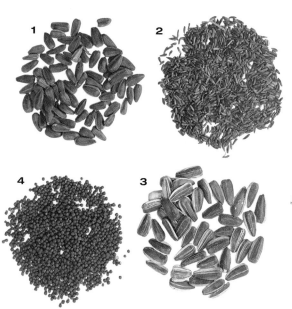

Finch heaven! Black oil sunflower (1), niger (2), striped sunflower (3), and rapeseed (4) will delight all small finches plus siskins, buntings, and larger cardinals and grosbeaks.

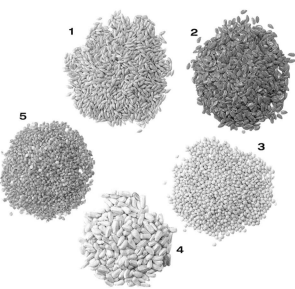

Canary seed (1) and flax seed (2) are special treats for finches; white (3) and red (5) millet are sought by all small seed-eating birds; cardinals enjoy safflower seed (4).

Special Seeds

The basic sunflower/millet/cracked corn menu will keep all but the fruit-eating and suet-eating birds at your feeder well fed and coming back for more. Adding special seed treats to the menu, however, will increase the desirability and appeal of your feeding station, and that, after all, is the object of the game. Besides, it's fun to keep an eye on the feeder and observe the visiting birds' individual tastes.

It can be difficult to generalize about the appeal of various specialty seeds because birds vary in their tastes. Midwestern sparrows may eagerly descend on an offering of rapeseed, while eastern sparrows spurn the stuff. Buy specialty seeds in small quantities at first to introduce them at the feeder. When you see which ones have become a hit, you can include them in your daily specials.

Do give birds at least 2 weeks to become accustomed to unfamiliar specialty seeds. It took more than a week for the purple finches at my feeder to sample the flax seeds I offered, but once they tasted them, the flax became their favorite.

Niger. One specialty seed—niger—has almost reached the class of staple, thanks to its guaranteed acceptability. Also called—albeit inaccurately—thistle seed, these tiny black seeds draw goldfinches without fail and also hold great appeal for house finches, purple finches, juncos, and siskins. Doves, house sparrows, native sparrows, and towhees may arrive to enjoy niger seeds, too. You can conduct your own informal inventory of customers by checking which birds are scratching for dropped niger below your tube feeders.

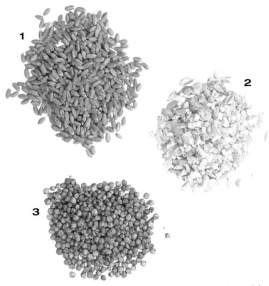

Buyer beware—make sure seed mixes aren't padded with low-cost yet undesirable fillers like wheat (1), cracked corn (2), and milo (3).

Safflower seed. After niger, safflower seed probably ranks next in popularity among the specialty seeds. This hard, white seed appeals to a limited number of species, but it can rapidly become a favorite of those birds. Cardinals are the number-one customer for safflower seed. Doves, purple finches, grosbeaks, jays, and titmice may also partake. As with other unusual seeds, it may take a while to build a client base for safflower. Offer the seed sparingly at first, and be patient.

Other specialty seeds. Other seeds that may convert birds into avid eaters at your feeder include

This Bird Favorite Is a No-No

IN THE more innocent days before the psychedelic '60s, one of the most highly recommended and most eagerly eaten seeds at the feeder was hemp. "Almost all seed-eating birds prefer hemp to any other seeds offered them," explains Thomas McElroy, Jr., in the 1950 *Handbook of Attracting Birds* (Knopf).

Unfortunately, birds aren't the only ones who will show up at your doorstep if you offer hemp seed today. The law would be close behind because the central Asian plant called hemp is also known as *Cannabis sativa*, or marijuana. With efforts now underway to reintroduce hemp as a legal farm crop in this country, perhaps someday our birds can go back to eating this old favorite. In the meantime, stick to millet, niger, and sunflower seed—your feeder will be full of customers, and you'll be home to enjoy watching them.

canary seed, flax, and rapeseed. The same birds that peck up millet at the feeder will eat all three. Mixtures that are advertised as "Just for Finches" often include a generous helping of canary seed and flax in the blend.

Seed Mixes

Not all seed mixes are created equal, and you can't judge a bag by its cover. Manufacturers decide what seeds to include, and in what percentages, and the recipe varies widely from one supplier to another. The names of the mixes can be misleading, too: "Seed Mix Deluxe Blend" may be nothing special at all.

To make sure you buy a good product, examine the mix if the bag is transparent or read the label. Laws require manufacturers to state the contents, listed in order of the most used to the least used. The lists usually include content percentages, too. Look for a high percentage of millet and sunflower, the top feeder favorites.

Additions of corn, wheat, and milo or sorghum often fill the balance of the bag. These inexpensive fillers cost much less per pound when you buy them as single-ingredient bags. As part of a mix, they add to the weight and jack up the price. Niger, flax, rapeseed, safflower, and canary grass, if they are included in small amounts, can be a bargain in a mix. But remember, with the exception of niger, your feeder birds may not readily accept these seeds.

Waste-Free Mixes

Bird feeding can be a messy business because hulls will rapidly accumulate beneath your feeders. Most people simply mulch over or scoop up the excess shells. But if you want things tidy, or if you're feeding birds on a balcony, windowsill, or patio, a waste-free mix will keep the feeder area neat and clean.

Naturally the price per pound of these mixes is more than seeds with hulls. But every bit of what you're paying for is edible and the convenience is worth a pretty penny itself.

Waste-free mixes usually include hull-less sunflower seeds (which you can also buy separately), plus bits of peanuts, finely cracked corn, and perhaps some canary seed, millet, or niger, which produce little waste. Compare the price per pound of this mix with

Ingredients are listed on the label beginning with the most plentiful. If fillers like milo top the list, keep shopping unless the bargain bag is your only choice.

the price of individual ingredients like sunflower chips, cracked corn, and chopped peanuts, and you may decide it's more cost-effective to make your own blend. Birds absolutely adore waste-free seed mixes, whether you buy them or stir them up yourself, because they don't have to work to eat the seeds. All large- and small-seed eaters relish the blend. Birds that don't usually eat seeds, such as bluebirds, catbirds, mockingbirds, robins, thrashers, and thrushes, also readily visit a feeder stocked with no-waste mix, where they can find an accessible, nutritious meal.

Treated Seed

To boost the birdseed's food value, manufacturers sometimes treat it with trace minerals or extra nutrients. This is usually unnecessary because birds don't eat only the seeds from your feeder. They also forage for wild foods, insects, and gravel that supply these needs naturally. But these treated seeds won't harm your birds.

Another treatment for birdseed is a great aid if squirrels and other animals are your nemesis. Capsaicin, the burning chemical of hot peppers, is effective at repelling animals from birdseed because it has the same effects on them as it does on us: burning mouth, watering eyes, and an afterburn that makes you yell "Water!" Birds, interestingly enough, are completely unaffected. Treatment methods vary. Some brands are dusted with capsaicin powder while others are soaked in a liquid extract that soaks into the seeds. Researchers at Cornell University tested the effectiveness of the presoaked seed in scientific trials. They found it to be very effective, except during severe winter weather, when squirrels apparently decided that spicy food would be better than no food at all.

Use care when filling feeders with capsaicin-treated seed. Avoid getting the dust into your eyes or breathing it in. Wear rubber gloves to prevent the burning substance from contacting your skin. If you have small children that play in the yard, it may be better to turn to squirrel-proof feeders or other remedies than fool with hot-pepper–treated birdseed. The stuff may hurt your pets, too.

Birdsong

MANY OF US TAKE THE GLORIES of birdsong for granted. When the birds grow quiet in late summer, we realize something is missing from the morning. If you have never spent the dawn hours sitting quietly in your yard, listening to the birds wake up, get up and give it a try. The breeding season, generally April through early July, is the best time to listen to the concert. That's when our migrant songbirds are passing through or have returned to their territories, full of hormones that make them burst into song to proclaim a match, attract a mate, or defend a territory.

You may hear snatches of song practically any time of year, especially if you live in a warm-winter area where nesting of some species continues into winter. Birds sing year-round in places where winter brings snow and cold, too, although there will be fewer performances in December than in June. Still, a melancholy phrase from a white-throated sparrow sounds heavenly in the afternoon dusk of a winter day.

If you pay attention to singing birds during breeding season, you will be able to tell who lives where. Male birds mark the boundaries of their nesting territories by voice, a charming way to tell other males to keep their distance. If you hear a cardinal singing its trademark "What cheer!" couplet, you know there is or soon will be a nest nearby. Late in the summer, listen for the haunting "whisper song" of mockingbirds, tanagers, and other singers, a very quiet, very private performance that takes place from a concealed perch.

Identifying singing birds can be a challenge, but all it takes is a bit of persistence. The best way to do

Common in backyards across America, the well-named song sparrow begins its concerts in late winter and continues serenading for months.

it is by tracking down the singer. Follow your ears and use your binoculars to identify the songster. Some people find recordings helpful, but I find it too difficult to remember the recording after turning off the stereo or remember the birdsong in question when I am back inside with the stereo.

Begin your voice lessons early in the season, when singers are still few and far between. Listen for chickadees and titmice in late winter, bluebirds in late winter to early spring, and then brace yourself for the rush of migrants in midspring. Thrushes are famed for their singing abilities, and one of the best of the family is our common robin. If you have never taken the time to appreciate a robin's song, make it a point to listen this season.

Bird Watching

If you're a bird watcher, keeping a bird feeder not only gives you a close look at birds but you also have the pleasure of knowing you're doing them a good turn by feeding them as you enjoy watching their behavior. Birds display many fascinating activities, from sparring to courtship, at or near feeders.

Bird watching is great fun at any age, from toddler on up. Get your kids involved by asking them to help fill or make feeders and by talking about the birds you see and what they're doing as you watch through the window.

You don't "need" any equipment to watch birds, but a field guide and a pair of binoculars will greatly increase your pleasure. Use the field guide to identify the birds you see at home and afield and to identify the type of foods they like best. The binoculars give you a close-up look at details and make it easier to tell who's who in your local bird world.

The feeder window (the window that looks out onto the feeder) will quickly become the most popular seat in the house. If you spend a lot of time inside—by choice or by necessity—you'll find that birds can be good company. The antics and activities of birds at feeders can be calming, cheering, and even therapeutic. Think about places you could put a bird feeder to educate or provide "therapy"—schools, daycare centers, or nursing homes.

The key to being a good bird watcher is to spend time really watching a bird. Observe the bird as long as you can keep it in view, with or without binoculars, and you'll quickly become familiar with typical postures and behavior. As you gain experience and a solid knowledge of the birds you encounter, you'll find it easier to notice birds in the first place and to identify them quickly. A large sparrow scratching vigorously with both feet beneath your shrubs in April could well be a fox sparrow; a large, long-tailed bird singing from your rooftop is likely to be a mockingbird. To attract these birds and keep them coming back, you'll want to plant or put out foods that they particularly enjoy.

Keeping your eye on the birds will also put you in the right place at the right time when more unusual events occur. You may get to see a starling stripping loose bark from your grapevine for nesting material or a house sparrow snapping up Japanese beetles at your roses. Or you could be privy to more intimate moments, such as mating scenes or whisper-song performances. Whenever you watch birds, ask yourself what is the bird doing, and why. You'll learn a lot about behavior as well as about the connections between plants, insects, and birds.

The terms "birding" and "bird watching" generally describe the same activity. In some circles, casual observers may call themselves bird watchers, while birders are considered to be professionals (or dedicated amateurs). To me, when someone says they're birding, the streamlined word may simply be time-saving, or it may be subtle snobbery. I vote for eliminating any distinction between the two. Call yourself a birder or a bird watcher—we're all watching birds.

Simple Feeders for Kids

CHILDREN DELIGHT in the colors, sounds, and lively activity of birds at the feeder. Letting kids watch bird activity from a window overlooking a feeding station is a great way to introduce them to what might become a lifelong passion—without the enforced stillness and quiet of "serious" bird watching. Kids will feel even more enthused if they're involved in filling, maintaining, and even building feeders.

This book contains several simple feeder projects that are great for making with kids inside on a rainy or wintry day. Check out these projects, as well as "Treasures from Trash" on page 299, for fun and easy bird-feeding activities for kids of all ages.

- Roofed feeder (see page 110)
- Soda bottle feeder (see page 257)
- Squirrel feeder (see page 273)
- Tube feeder (see page 306)

Blackbirds

AS A RULE OF THUMB, most medium-size, mostly black birds at your feeder are probably blackbirds. But there are exceptions to this rule, and most blackbirds aren't entirely black, so take care when classifying these birds.

Several common black birds may fool you. Adult starlings are black birds, but not blackbirds; they belong to an old-world family that includes myna birds. Big crows and ravens are not blackbirds. The lark bunting, a medium-size black bird found west of the Mississippi, is a large finch, not a blackbird.

Most blackbirds aren't entirely black. The **yellow-headed blackbird** of the West has a striking golden hood; the widespread **red-winged blackbird** has vivid shoulder patches of red and yellow; and the similar **tricolored blackbird** of far western marshes has red and white shoulder decorations. Those elegant, long-tailed strutters known as **grackles** (see Grackles on page 143) have glossy black feathers overlaid with a sheen of bronze, green, or purple. The name of the **brown-headed cowbird** speaks for itself; its relative, the **bronzed cowbird,** glistens with a metallic green-gold iridescence. The **rusty blackbird** and **Brewer's blackbird** come closest to the all-black coloration the name implies, especially at a distance. Upon closer inspection in certain seasons, you will see slight variations on the black dress code. The rusty has a weathered look, but only in fall, when the edges of its feathers show a brownish tinge. The Brewer's has slight purple or green iridescence.

A locally common member of the blackbird family, the black and white male **bobolink** and his brown-streaked mate flock in hay fields. In fall, the male exchanges his bright garb for an outfit similar to the female's, and the birds gather in enormous numbers like their other blackbird kin.

Female blackbirds of all species are much harder to identify than males. Most are brownish, with streaked breasts or bellies. Whenever a female redwing shows up at my feeder (usually in winter), it

Find a front-row seat in spring to watch the courting displays of the male red-winged blackbird. To impress his lady love, he droops his wings and shrugs his gorgeous red shoulders.

A piercing yellow eye stands out against the all-black plumage of the Brewer's blackbird. The shape of the bill is a sure way to identify members of this family.

Cowbirds Don't Linger for Long

WHEN COWBIRDS congregated at my feeders in spring, I used to worry that I was endangering my favorite songbirds by attracting these parasitic birds. Cowbirds lay their eggs in the nests of other species of birds. The unsuspecting foster parents then spend their energy raising the big, loudmouth cowbird nestling like one of their own—and sometimes in place of one of their own. Cowbird piracy increases as we carve our woodlands into pieces, allowing these birds easy access to nests of wood thrushes and other forest dwelling songbirds.

But I needn't have feared for my local songbirds—like other blackbirds, the cowbirds dispersed soon after their hormones began stirring. Once their mating instincts kicked in, the flock dwindled to one or two pairs of cowbirds, as the others returned to their traditional "nesting" territories, far away from my feeder area.

takes a minute before I recognize this unusual, large sparrowlike bird. Immature birds can be difficult to identify as their coloring is similar to a female's. To make things even trickier, the males of most species change their plumage after the breeding season for markings that also resemble the female's rather unremarkable garb.

All blackbirds have fairly long, pointed bills, perfect for their varied diet of seeds, grain, insects, fruit, bread, and just about anything else they encounter. Birds of fields, marshes, and open spaces, they usually walk about on the ground, so a low tray feeder serves them well. Blackbirds also easily adapt to higher feeders.

Blackbird populations at the feeder ebb and swell with the seasons. During nesting time, only a few resident birds generally visit. But during the times of fall and spring migration, and when wintering flocks are in the area, you may be hosting dozens of the birds. A generous handout of inexpensive cracked corn in a low feeder or directly on the ground will keep them busy and away from other feeders that hold pricier foods.

BLACKBIRD FEEDER FOODS
▓ Apples, blueberries, and other fruit
▓ Bread and other baked goods
▓ Chick scratch
▓ Corn in any form, especially cracked
▓ Millet
▓ Milo
▓ Mixed seeds
▓ Nuts
▓ Peanuts
▓ Raisins
▓ Suet
▓ Sunflower seeds

Blackbird Behavior

Listen for the interesting voices of blackbirds at or near your feeder. Many of them include phrases with a gurgling, liquid sound, like water bubbling over rocks, in their repertoire. They also emit ear-piercing screeches and squeals and hoarse squawks.

If you spend time watching the various blackbirds at your feeding station, you will see some interesting "body language." When blackbirds threaten each other, they droop their wings, fluff their feathers, and make harsh noises that make them appear more imposing. A similar behavior takes place during courtship season, with the bird's head generally raised with its beak pointing skyward. Often the male bird will stalk the female, pausing now and then to repeat the display, as if showing off his physique for her to admire.

It's hard to believe somber-colored blackbirds are in the same family as orioles, until you see the yellow-headed blackbird.

Black-Eyed Susans

Attract buntings, finches, sparrows, and other small-seed eaters

BLACK-EYED SUSAN (*Rudbeckia hirta*) is as all-American as a flower can get. One of the few wild-flowers that actually hails from this continent, these buttery daisies brighten summer roadsides and gardens from sea to shining sea. That's a good thing as far as birds are concerned because those black "eyes" hold a wealth of nutritious seeds. Related to the ever-popular sunflower, black-eyed Susan seedheads ripen in summer and hold their bounty of bird food into winter—a good reason to let those seedheads remain in your garden at the end of the growing season.

Another related dark-eyed yellow daisy, orange coneflower (*R. fulgida*), is sometimes also called black-eyed Susan. So is *R. triloba*, a more shade-tolerant species. Unfortunately, the highly popular 'Goldsturm' black-eyed Susan (*R. fulgida* 'Goldsturm') holds little attraction for birds. Its seeds lack the meaty centers of the unimproved species type, which is still available and still worth growing. Another cultivated variety, 'Gloriosa' black-eyed Susan (*R. hirta* 'Gloriosa'), offers hearty seeds like those of its wild parent, so it's a good choice for the bird garden. It's pretty, too, with big, beautiful flowers in shades of rust, gold, and bicolors.

Black-eyed Susans reach 2 to 3 feet tall. Their branching stems and dense leaves offer small birds safe shelter where they can forage for insects or seeds. Plant several near your feeding station to encourage buntings, finches, sparrows, and other small birds to linger within view. Black-eyed Susans will attract a flurry of butterflies (bird food on the wing!) to your yard, too, and they're pretty and long-lasting in bouquets. Even after black-eyed Susans lose their golden petals, their dark central "cones" will stand tall atop the stiff stems, holding up their cache of seeds for hungry birds. If you must clean up the faded flowers, gather them into bunches to hang from a feeder or weave them into a wreath of bird-seed treats. Easy to grow and drought-tolerant, these plants thrive in USDA Zones 3 through 10.

Stick to "unimproved" black-eyed Susans for attracting birds. Garden favorite 'Goldsturm' does not produce the nutritious seeds birds crave.

Standing stems of black-eyed Susans help shield birds from predators in the winter garden. Common redpolls and other seed lovers will work at the seedheads.

Blueberries

Attract bluebirds, mockingbirds, robins, brown thrashers, woodpeckers, Carolina wrens

BIRDS LOVE blueberries (*Vaccinium* spp.) as much as we do. When the fruits begin to ripen, birds descend on the berry patch and gobble up berry after berry until their bellies are so full they can barely fly. Spy on a catbird in a blueberry bush and you'll see some amazing feats as the bird swallows berries that look way too big to fit down that skinny beak.

Of course, if the berries that catbird is gobbling are the ones you intended for your breakfast bowl of cereal, you may feel a certain conflict of interests. Once a blueberry patch is established and growing for a few years, it produces enough berries for you and the birds to share. But when your bushes are new and small, you may want to throw a sheet of plastic bird netting over the patch to protect your precious crop.

If you've never tried growing blueberries, don't let the "finicky blueberry" reputation scare you off. If you can grow hollies (*Ilex* spp.), azaleas (*Rhododendron* spp.), or rhododendrons (*Rhododendron* spp.), you can grow blueberries. These American natives are well known for liking acid soil, a condition that's usually not hard to meet. Unless you live near a limestone outcrop or in one of the alkaline areas of the West, your soil should be reasonably close to blueberry range. A do-it-yourself soil test will give you the information you need. But if the azaleas in your yard are thriving, you can skip that step and go ahead and plant your berry bushes. An annual mulch of chopped oak leaves, cypress bark, beech leaves, or other acidic material will help keep your soil pH in the range that's just right for blueberries.

Sweet and juicy blueberries are so popular with birds, you'll have to act fast to get a handful for yourself. Plant in groups or as a hedge and put a bench nearby.

Blueberries at the Feeder

Save some blueberries to put in your feeder in fall and winter, times when natural fruit is hard to find. You can freeze or dry fresh berries for later use. To dry blueberries, spread them on a window screen in full summer sun, covered by a layer of gauze or cheesecloth to keep bugs away. Support the screen on blocks so that air can circulate on all sides of the berries.

Unless you're in the blueberry business, your stock will most likely be small. Dole them out a scant handful at a time so that they aren't wasted. Bluebirds, mockingbirds, robins, brown thrashers, woodpeckers, and Carolina wrens may be tempted by the handout. Many of these blueberry-eating birds prefer fruit, mealworms, peanut-butter dough, and other soft goodies to birdseed. To cut down on competition for feeder space, scatter the blueberries in an open tray feeder that you reserve for soft foods.

Bluebirds

BLUEBIRDS ARE THE CROWNING GLORY of any feeding station, and they are relatively easy to attract. Supply their favored foods of peanut butter, mealworms, berries, and other treats, and if they live nearby, they may become regular patrons. Of course, if bluebirds aren't in residence in your neighborhood, the only takers you'll get for your goodies are likely to be mockingbirds, starlings, and other soft-food fans.

Where do bluebirds live? Usually near wide open spaces, with areas of cover: in other words, in the country. Expect to see them in farming areas, in suburban developments bordered by wild space, on golf courses, in cemeteries, near school playing fields, in parks, at the edges of woods, in extensive hedgerows, and along rivers and streams. If you live in the city, where concrete covers most of the open space, don't hold your breath for a bluebird.

East of the Great Plains, the only bluebird you're apt to see is the appropriately named **eastern bluebird.** Like its closely related kin, the **western bluebird,** the male bird wears plumage of a breathtaking rich blue. Thoreau wrote that this exquisite creature "carries spring on its back." Although I think the color is closer to the hue of an October sky than that of

Build it and they will come—but only if your yard is near the wide open spaces where eastern bluebirds prefer to make their homes.

rain-washed April, I won't argue with the romance of Thoreau's feelings. Bluebirds evoke a sense of rhapsody in most of us.

Both eastern and western species sport similar coloration. Look for the blue throat and rusty shoulder patch of the western to distinguish it from the eastern bird. The **mountain bluebird** is blue all over and generally lighter in color—closer to what I think of as a spring sky. It lacks the rusty breast of the eastern and western bluebirds, being paler blue-gray beneath. Although mountain bluebirds live up to their name in nesting season, staying usually above 5,000 feet, in winter they wander to low elevations as food becomes scarce in the mountains. All female bluebirds are brownish blue, with a faded rusty breast in eastern and western species and a grayish brown breast in the mountain species.

Except for some regions in the mountains and plains, where winter cold is brutal, you may see a

BLUEBIRD FEEDER FOODS

- Bayberries (*Myrica* spp.)
- Blackberries (*Rubus allegheniensis*)
- Blueberries (*Vaccinium* spp.)
- Bread and other baked goods
- Dogwood berries (*Cornus* spp.)
- Juniper berries (*Juniperus* spp.)
- Mealworms
- Peanut butter
- Peanut butter/cornmeal dough
- Peanuts, chopped
- Pine nuts
- Raisins
- Raspberries (*Rubus occidentalis*)
- Suet, chopped or block
- Sumac berries (*Rhus* spp.)

bluebird at any time of the year. When insects become scarce, the birds supplement their diet with berries and other fruits.

Bluebird Behavior

You can spot an eastern or western bluebird from a distance once you become aware of their typical posture. These birds apparently never practiced walking with a book on their head—they typically sit hunched, with head drawn down into their shoulders. They frequently assume this position when perched atop a fence or other prominent lookout point, where you can identify them by their posture even without seeing their color.

Identify the mountain bluebird by its lack of red on breast or sides. These birds prefer high elevations during nesting season.

Bluebirds often come to a feeder for the first time during bad weather and the availability of appropriate food will keep them coming back. When I know snow, ice, or severe cold is on its way, I mix up a batch of bluebird-tempting food so it's ready for immediate serving at the crack of dawn. Often I'll find a bluebird has already come in and is waiting for its turn at the peanut butter or suet, while its cohorts linger nearby, calling to each other in gentle whistles.

Bluebirds are ideal company at the dinner table. They are reserved and well behaved, never picking a fight with other invited guests. Usually they are quick to depart or at least shift position should a more aggressive bird act threateningly. Provide their food in an open tray so it is easily visible. Once you have their attention, you can switch to a roofed feeder if necessary to protect food from snow or rain. Once they come to a feeder, bluebirds are unusually tame. Approach them slowly and quietly, and they may quickly accept eating from your hand.

Watch the bluebirds in your yard, and you will see that their hunting technique somewhat resembles that

As richly colored as its eastern counterpart, the western bluebird is also a cavity nester. Supplement the supply of holes in trees by mounting nest boxes.

12 Tricks to Tempt Bluebirds

IF YOUR yard is near the kind of open spaces that bluebirds like—farm fields, edges of woods, parks, golf courses, cemeteries—try these tricks to encourage the birds to visit your feeding station.

1. Put up bluebird houses, mounting them about 100 feet apart.

2. Keep a small amount of food to tempt bluebirds in plain view in winter in an unroofed tray feeder.

3. Mount a suet feeder with access for perching birds, such as a tray beneath a wire suet cage. Or mount a wire suet cage horizontally, so that bluebirds can perch on top while they eat.

4. Place a tray feeder stocked with a small supply of mealworms on the side of your property closest to good bluebird habitat.

5. Plant a hedge of sumac (*Rhus* spp.) or blueberries (*Vaccinium* spp.). Blueberries are a favored summer food; sumac will suffice in the dead of winter when other berries are scarce.

6. Learn bluebird calls so that you can tell when they are in your neighborhood.

7. Add a birdbath.

8. Keep a resealable plastic bag of chopped peanuts ready in the freezer in case bluebirds do come to visit your feeders.

9. Allow a plant of pokeweed (*Phytolacca americana*) to grow in your yard. The black-purple berries are a prime wild food for bluebirds.

10. Cover a trellis with Virginia creeper (*Parthenocissus quinquefolia*), another big temptation to bluebirds.

11. Indulge a poison ivy vine (*Taxicodendron radicans*) in a wild corner of your property; the white berries are manna to bluebirds.

12. Plant a group of bayberries (*Myrica* spp.), backed by columnar red cedar (*Juniperus virginiana*), to supply shelter and berries.

of a flycatcher. The birds will perch at a likely spot, then flutter out to nab a passing insect. Bluebirds aren't speedy fliers like flycatchers. They usually pursue the moth or other passing insect to near or at ground level before securing it in their beak. They may devour their catch there on the ground or fly to another perch to dine.

Water is a great draw for bluebirds, which will happily visit birdbaths or low-level water features. A pair that resided in my yard for several years often came to my dogs' outside water dish to drink deeply every morning. More than once when I have been slow about refilling their favorite pedestal birdbath, they turned for water to a bucket holding perennials for transplanting.

Bluebirds are cavity nesters, which means they seek a natural hole or a birdhouse for raising their families. One good way to find out if you have bluebirds living nearby is to put up a bluebird box. If you mount it, they will come: It's really that simple.

Bluebirds can certainly use a helping hand when it comes to real estate. They suffer from stiff competition for nest sites from house sparrows and starlings. Modern orchard management removes dead tree limbs as a matter of course, resulting in fewer natural cavities for these birds. Their natural habitat has declined with fewer woods' edges and hedgerows and with metal fence posts that have replaced wooden ones. Bluebird trails and individual efforts at providing nest boxes have helped bluebirds overcome the odds stacked against them. Populations that had become disturbingly low have rebounded to more comfortable levels, but bluebirds still need all the help they can get. If there's a chance you may have bluebirds in the area, put up a few boxes.

Bluebirds are early birds. They begin nesting as early as February. In northern regions, this is not always a wise move. Severe cold can have fatal effects on the brood and on the food available to parent birds. After deep freezes in the past, bluebird numbers took a nose dive. When not nesting, bluebirds roost together in cold weather in natural cavities or bird boxes—yet another good reason to mount a bluebird box in your yard.

B

Blueberry Bird Granola

Expect visits from bluebirds, mockingbirds, thrashers, woodpeckers, and wrens when you put out this nourishing granola.

INGREDIENTS

1 *cup granola flakes*

1 *cup dried blueberries, chopped*

½ *cup finely chopped peanuts*

½ *cup cornmeal*

½ *cup ground or chopped suet*

½ *cup corn oil or peanut oil*

Combine all ingredients in a large bowl, using your hands to squeeze oil throughout the mixture to bind. Serve in an open tray feeder.

Bluebird Tempter

A taste treat to lure bluebirds for a first-time visit. They'll keep coming back for more.

INGREDIENTS

1 *cup peanut butter, chunky or creamy*

1 *cup suet, chopped*

1 *cup raisins or dried currants, chopped*

1 *cup peanuts, chopped*

   Cornmeal

Combine first two ingredients. Add raisins, peanuts, and cornmeal, mixing by hand until the mixture reaches the consistency of medium-stiff cookie dough. Crumble into an open tray feeder.

Bluebird Winter Berry Mix

A welcome change of pace for eastern and western bluebirds that are already feeder regulars.

INGREDIENTS

1 *cup dried or frozen blueberries*

1 *cup frozen blackberries or raspberries*

1 *cup dried currants*

1 *cup dried cherries, chopped*

1 *cup bayberry, holly, sumac, or juniper berries*

½ *cup figs, chopped*

If the temperature outside is above freezing, thaw the frozen berries, and drain on paper towels to soak up the excess juice. If temperature outside is below freezing, use the frozen fruit as is. Combine all ingredients in a large bowl. Serve in an open tray feeder or scatter on packed-down, snow-covered ground where the mix will be easily visible.

Bread

Attracts blackbirds, grackles, jays, magpies, mockingbirds, robins, house sparrows, native sparrows, starlings, Carolina wrens, and many other species

OUNCE FOR OUNCE, even fortified bread can't compare to the food value of sunflower and other bird seeds, which offer the high-fat, high-protein diet that birds require. But bread is a fine addition to any feeding program—jays, magpies, mockingbirds, robins, native sparrows, Carolina wrens, and many other species will quickly gobble it up. Bread also brings in blackbirds, grackles, house sparrows, and starlings—so if you're trying to discourage these birds, think twice before adding it to the menu. Squirrels, ground squirrels, and chipmunks, as well as raccoons, opossums, and dogs, also eat bread.

I welcome all customers, no matter how unmannerly, at my feeders, but I use bread to keep my clients somewhat separated. Highly visible pieces of white bread seem to be irresistible to house sparrows, jays, and starlings, so I scatter them in trays and on the ground in a separate feeding area, away from the tube feeders and seed trays of sunflower and niger provided for the shyer birds. The ruse works well, and everybody leaves the bird café with a full stomach.

Scatter leftover bread or bread crumbs in feeders. It's best to use a roofed feeder (see page 110) because bread quickly turns moldy if it gets wet. I do feed bread directly on the ground in severe winter weather, when snow or ice makes it impossible for robins, towhees, and other ground-feeding birds to find natural foods. They appreciate a handout they can eat at ground level.

Birds will pretty much eat any kind of bread. As long as you're not feeding your bird guests a bread-only menu, you needn't worry whether it offers great nutrition. A stale slice of refined white bread is just as welcome to hungry birds as a fresh loaf of all-natural multigrain bread. Crumble the bread into small bits to make it easy for doves, sparrows, and other small-beaked birds to eat. Feeding bread as crumbs also keeps birds lingering at your feeder where you can watch them, instead of allowing them to fly off with a big chunk to eat out of your sight. Crumbs also cut down on the inevitable "It's mine!" "No, it's mine!" squabbles that result from offering larger pieces of bread.

Tidbits for Bird Breads

ADD BIRD-FAVORED treats to your favorite yeast bread or quick bread recipe, or try one of the recipes on pages 48 and 49. The following ingredients, in any combination, will help spice up a bread recipe for the birds:

- Acorn nutmeats
- Acorn or winter squash seeds
- Almonds, chopped
- Apples, chopped or coarsely grated

- Beechnut nutmeats
- Blueberries, fresh or dried
- Buckwheat kernels
- Canned whole-kernel corn
- Cantaloupe seeds
- Cherries, fresh or dried
- Currants
- Grapes, chopped
- Hickory nuts
- Hulled sunflower chips
- Millet, whole
- Oatmeal
- Oranges, chopped

- Pasta, leftover cooked, any kind, chopped if large
- Peaches, chopped
- Peanut butter, chunky
- Peanuts, raw or roasted
- Pears, chopped
- Pecans, chopped
- Pine nuts
- Plums, chopped
- Pumpkin seeds
- Raisins
- Strawberries
- Walnuts, chopped
- Watermelon seeds

Special Recipes

Baking bread for the birds is a fun weekend project that will fill your freezer with nutritious loaves. I load the dough with lots of extras to make the bread a real treat: dried and fresh fruits chopped into small pieces, nutmeats of any kind, oatmeal, raisins, grated apple, and even leftover pasta that may be lingering in the refrigerator. No matter how lumpy the loaves, the birds quickly flock to the results of my experiments.

Visit a health food store to find nutritious flours, such as millet, amaranth, or whole wheat, to bake into bread for birds. Experiment with bird breads: As long as your offerings are chock-full of nutty or fruity ingredients, birds will relish your efforts. Because the breads will be dense and moist, they may not be as dry in the middle of the loaf as your usual concoctions for human consumption, but the birds won't mind a bit.

RECIPE

Oatmeal-Raisin Bluebird Bread

Try this yeast batter bread for attracting bluebirds in winter. Catbirds, jays, mockingbirds, robins, thrushes, and Carolina wrens may also partake.

INGREDIENTS

1½ cups boiling water

¾ cup oatmeal, regular or instant

¾ cup raisins

¼ cup light corn syrup or molasses

3 tablespoons margarine

1 package active dry yeast

¼ cup warm water

4 cups whole wheat flour

Combine first five ingredients. Set aside to cool. Sprinkle yeast over warm water in a large bowl, and stir until dissolved. Stir oatmeal mixture into yeast. Stir in 2 cups flour. Add remaining flour, and blend with a mixer or with hands. Cover and let rise for 30 minutes in a warm place. Grease a 9 × 5 × 3-inch loaf pan. Beat dough 25 strokes with a sturdy spoon, then spread in the pan. Smooth the top with a greased spatula. Cover and let rise until about 1 inch from top of the pan. Bake at 425°F for 45 minutes. Cool; tear into small pieces to serve in an open tray feeder.

RECIPE

Delicious Date-Nut Bread for Birds

Finely chopped dates make this quick bread a magnet for fruit lovers like bluebirds, mockingbirds, robins, and thrushes, and the nuts are a bonus for jays and woodpeckers.

INGREDIENTS

2 cups sifted flour

3 teaspoons baking powder

1½ cups finely chopped dates (dip knife in hot water for easier chopping)

1 cup finely chopped walnuts, pecans, or almonds

1 cup milk

¼ cup vegetable oil

1 egg

Stir together flour and baking powder. Add dates and nuts. Mix milk, oil, and egg slightly to combine. Pour into dry ingredients, and stir with fork until moist. Spread in greased 9 × 5 × 3-inch loaf pan. Bake at 400°F for about 20 minutes.

B

Fruitful Feeder Bread

Bluebirds, jays, mockingbirds, robins, wrens, and even orioles may nibble this bread.

INGREDIENTS

2¼ cups sifted flour

½ cup sugar

2 teaspoons baking powder

1 cup blueberries, cranberries, raspberries, or other berries

1 cup finely chopped apple, peel left on

1 cup chopped orange pulp

2 eggs

1 cup milk

¼ cup melted margarine

Stir together flour, sugar, and baking powder. Add fruits. Whisk eggs with milk and melted margarine. Add egg mixture to fruit and flour mixture, stirring quickly with fork until moist. Scrape into greased 9 × 5 × 3-inch loaf pan, and bake about 55 minutes at 350°F. Cool, then slice into thin strips and offer at feeder.

Top-Banana Bread

Sweet, moist banana bread is a special treat for robins in winter. It's also welcomed by jays, mockingbirds, thrushes, and Carolina wrens. Add nuts to entice woodpeckers.

INGREDIENTS

2½ cups sifted flour

3 teaspoons baking powder

1 cup sugar

¼ cup margarine

1 egg, beaten

6 ripe, mashed bananas

¼ cup milk

1 cup chopped nuts

Combine flour and baking powder. In another bowl, beat together sugar, margarine, and egg. Mix in bananas and milk, then add flour mixture, and stir until smooth. Stir in nuts. Pour into a greased 9 × 5 × 3-inch loaf pan, and bake at 350°F for about 65 minutes.

Feeding Bread

To avoid waste, offer bread in small amounts at the feeder, until you can gauge how quickly the birds will eat it. Freeze leftovers for later use. Keep frozen bread, crumbled into resealable plastic bags, on hand for emergencies like snowstorms, when any bluebirds, robins, or other thrushes in the area will be grateful for a handout of this nutritious soft food.

Bread is soft and absorbent, which makes it ideal for soaking up bacon fat, melted suet, beef drippings from a roast or broiler pan, and other oils. Chickadees, jays, titmice, woodpeckers, and many other birds will accept such high-fat offerings eagerly, especially in cold weather. Cut the bread into cubes or crumble it into cool but still liquid fat, and serve in a large, shallow plastic tray to avoid grease stains on wood bird feeders. An old plastic plate or cafeteria tray nailed to the top of a flat post is an ideal feeder for these high-energy treats. Any leftovers will be enjoyed by raccoons, opossums, and cats at night.

Buckwheat

Attracts bobwhite, quail, pheasants, wild turkeys

NOT A WHEAT AT ALL but a relative of the pink-flowered smartweed you pull out of your garden beds, buckwheat (*Fagopyrum esculentum*) is a fast-growing annual with dark green, heart-shaped leaves and fragrant small white flowers. In bloom, it's abuzz with bees, who carry the nectar home to make superb honey. In seed, it's a great temptation to bobwhite, quail, pheasants, and wild turkeys, who relish its small, nutty seeds.

Gardeners and farmers use buckwheat as a summer soil-building crop because it grows quickly, producing lots of green material to till into the soil. Buckwheat is pretty when it flowers, and its small blossoms attract insects, including beneficials that will patrol your gardens for pests. Insect-eating birds will come, too, to dine on the insects visiting the buckwheat blossoms.

Plant buckwheat seeds after all danger of frost has passed in a sunny patch of prepared soil near your feeding area for game birds. It will sprout fast and grow like a weed, creating a solid swath of erect plants that bloom late in summer. In fall and winter, keep an eye on your buckwheat patch, which may attract a covey of foraging quail. These shy birds will appreciate the sheltering cover of the dense stems, where they can seek seeds while remaining hidden from predators.

Harvest some of your buckwheat seeds for winter feeding by shaking the seedheads into a large paper sack; you'll hear the seeds falling against the paper. Store the seeds in a tightly closed plastic container in a cool, dry place. During cold weather or snow and ice storms, buckwheat seeds make a good high-energy food that you can scatter directly on the ground for hungry birds.

Other members of the buckwheat family species also produce plenty of bird-attracting seeds, so you may want to think twice before you uproot every bit of smartweed or knotweed (*Polygonum* spp.) in your garden. But don't think about it too long—these weeds can grow quickly out of control! For more about buckwheat's weedy relatives, see Weeds on page 327.

> Game birds relish buckwheat's small, nutty seeds and prefer to feed in the shelter of the plants' dense growth.

Bullies

JAYS AND MOCKINGBIRDS are often tyrants at the feeder. It's not because of their gluttonous habits—they eat no more than any other songbird at the feeder. It's because of their bad manners and their aggressive "All mine!" attitudes.

These birds are bullies. They flaunt their large size and loud voices to scare other birds away from seed trays and suet feeders. And should these nonviolent approaches not clear the field, the bully birds will resort to a more physical approach, threatening with long, sharp beaks and flashing wings.

Jays are more talk than threat, and many smaller birds learn to retreat when the jay comes in, then quickly return once the bigger bird settles down. Mockingbirds, however, are real meanies. When they warn other birds that the feeder area belongs to them, they aren't kidding. They will mercilessly pursue any bird that crosses whatever invisible line the mockingbird defends.

The mockingbird doesn't take much time to eat because the big gray bird spends most of its energy dashing after invaders. If the weather is mild and I know the other birds can resort to foraging for themselves, I often let the mockingbird tire itself out. It usually takes no more than a couple of weeks before the bird wearies of its territorial game.

But if winter weather has settled in and food sources are scarce, I take defensive measures on behalf of my more timid customers. It's easy to add more feeders or move one of the existing ones to another side of the house—out of sight and out of mind for the mockingbird.

One year I discovered that even a flimsy trellis can make an effective barrier. Because I had limited space, I moved a feeder on an iron crook to the other side of a strip of lattice that supported a tangle of bean vines. Although the leaves had long since dropped, the thick, twining stems provided just enough camouflage to allow the birds to eat in peace. I sometimes wondered if the mockingbird could actually see them and was just saving face—not to mention energy.

Small but Mighty

Another notorious bully at feeders and in the garden is the tiny hummingbird. These itty-bitty birds will take on opponents of all sizes once they become obsessed with the notion that a nectar feeder or even a favored plant is their sole territory. Often they limit their attacks to other hummingbirds, but I have also seen feisty hummingbirds zip to the defense against other species. When the silver beech tree near one of my nectar feeders became a magnet for beechnut-eating flickers and blue jays, the male hummingbird who "owned" the feeder single-handedly chased away every last one of them. Its technique was simple: a high-speed approach with rapier bill held straight ahead, aimed at the other bird. No arguing

Just as pugnacious as the notorious bluejays, this red-headed woodpecker is well able to hold its own against their screamed insults.

with that! The other birds wisely retreated, at least for a little while, although the jays made sure everyone within earshot knew how unfair the situation was.

Should a hummingbird become the bully at your feeder, the best solution is to add another nectar feeder, as far away and as much out of the hummer's line of sight as possible. But when the hummingbird claims a plant—fuchsias are a favorite in my yard—there's not much you can do other than enjoy watching the territorial spats.

In recent years, nectar feeders have become battlegrounds for other birds, too. Woodpeckers, house finches, and dozens of other species have learned about this source of food, and the trend is spreading. Often, the very presence of a competitor at the nectar feeder is enough to deter hummingbirds. If a woodpecker or other feeder hog is draining your feeder dry, you may want to shoo the glutton away yourself. Simply approaching the feeder should do the trick.

Buntings

BUNTINGS ARE the size of chipping sparrows, have the same conical seed-eating bill, and belong to the same large finch family. But unlike their generally drab sparrow relatives, male buntings are real beauties. The **painted bunting**, found in Texas and the Southeast, is as vivid as a parrot, decked out in an incredible patchwork of red breast, blue head, and yellow-green back. The **indigo bunting** is common to the eastern half of the country with a range that extends sporadically westward. As brilliant as a sapphire, his color shifts from turquoise through cobalt blue, depending on how the light hits his iridescent feathers. In the western half of the country, the **lazuli bunting** maintains the colorful reputation of the group; the male wears plumage similar to the eastern bluebird's, with a rich blue head and back, a russet chest, and a snowy belly. The least common species, the **varied bunting**, has purple and blue feathers washed with red. Observers occasionally spot this beautiful bird just above the Mexican border. Female buntings are the complete opposite of their flashy mates—all species are dull brown, with perhaps a faint tinge of color. On the nest the females are practically invisible.

Because of their beauty, we cherish buntings at our feeders. Yet they can be as common as sparrows if your feeding station is close to their natural habitat of brush, hedgerows, or woods' edges. On migration, they can show up just about anywhere. Indigo buntings live in the farm fields outside my small town, but when they pass through in April on their way to breeding grounds, they stop off at my urban feeder for a handout of millet. Once they find a feeder to their liking, whether on migration or as

The intense blue of a male indigo bunting's feathers is a matter of light refraction, which is why this little jewel looks dull black on a cloudy day or in shade.

At first glance, the lazuli bunting looks like a bluebird, thanks to its red, white, and blue coloring. White wing bars are the distinguishing feature to look for.

residents, buntings return day after day, long enough for you to call your friends to come and see these beautiful little birds. Buntings winter south of the United States, so enjoy them during their spring, summer, and fall visits.

Bunting Behavior

Except for the painted bunting, who prefers to vocalize softly, the voice of a bunting seems too big for its body. These birds are tireless singers, persisting in their long, varied choruses even during the heat of a summer afternoon, when other avian singers are silent. They generally choose to sing from a high perch. Listen for a flight song, usually delivered just before dusk from a male bird that flutters high into the sky, then swoops down, singing exultantly.

BUNTING FEEDER FOODS

- Canary seed
- Millet
- Mixed seeds
- Nuts, chopped
- Peanuts, chopped
- Rapeseed
- Weed seeds

At the feeder, buntings are big fans of small seeds. They eagerly eat ragweed, lamb's-quarters, and other weed seeds, too, which is the excuse I use for letting my lawn and gardens look a little unmanicured. When dandelions go to seed in my yard (and along the roadsides), brilliant indigo buntings will soon arrive. I love to watch them compete with yellow goldfinches and fresh-plumaged white-crowned sparrows for possession of the seed-filled puff. They can be feisty little birds, squabbling with a thrust of an open beak and a harsh warning note, but when food is abundant, as at your well-stocked feeding station, they feed quietly.

Like sparrows, buntings prefer to eat close to the ground. I often find them picking spilled seed from beneath the feeders. Pour their seed into a low tray feeder to pique their interest. They will also eat at higher feeders but are quicker to fly in alarm when perched above the ground.

C

Cake and Cookies

Attract blackbirds, bluebirds, chickadees, crows, jays, mockingbirds, pigeons, robins, house sparrows, native sparrows, starlings, thrushes, titmice, Carolina wrens

IT'S NOT THE SWEETNESS OF CAKE that attracts birds, it's the energy they get from the flour-based food that makes them peck up cake crumbs in the feeder and on the ground. As with bread, white or light-colored cake pieces and crumbs are the easiest to see and attract birds fastest. Carrot, zucchini, and other moist homemade cakes are ideal for birds, especially if you add a heavy helping of nuts or fruit.

All soft-food eaters and many seed eaters dine on cake, including bluebirds, chickadees, jays, mockingbirds, robins, thrushes, titmice, house and native sparrows, and, sorry, blackbirds, crows, and starlings.

Cake absorbs moisture and turns moldy fast in wet weather or when spread on the ground or in a feeder where it's not protected from the elements. Feed sparingly, or stockpile leftover cake in resealable plastic freezer bags for winter feeding, when birds that eat soft foods, such as bluebirds, robins, and Carolina wrens, may visit feeding stations to seek sustenance.

Cookies

Like any grain-based product, cookies appeal to a variety of birds. Birds, such as bluebirds, mockingbirds, robins, thrushes, and Carolina wrens, that eat mostly soft foods may be tempted by an offering of oatmeal-raisin, chunky peanut butter, or other tasty bird-tailored cookies. Of course, keep in mind that blackbirds, crows, pigeons, house sparrows, and starlings also are fond of soft foods, including cookies.

Crush leftover cookies into coarse crumbs for serving to chickadees, titmice, and soft-food eaters at feeders. You can also toss a handful of stale cookies from your pantry shelf onto the ground, where house sparrows and other hardy sorts will quickly peck them into bite-size bits.

> Crumble up stale cookies and leftover cake into beak-size bites for birds that eat soft food.

Canary Seed

Attracts buntings, ducks, house and purple finches, geese, goldfinches, quail, redpolls, native sparrows

CANARY SEED WAS VERY POPULAR with caged-bird owners some 50 years ago, when singing canaries were resident pets in many kitchens and living rooms. As the popularity of these pets faded, the seed made a natural transition to wild birdseed mixes, where it remains popular with all the finch relatives of canaries. Goldfinches, purple finches, and house finches as well as buntings, redpolls, and native sparrows all eat canary seed.

Canary seed is a golden tan, smallish seed that you can buy by the pound or mixed with other choice seeds. The seed comes from a grass called canary grass (*Phalaris canariensis*), which has a notorious relative known as reed canary grass (*P. arundinacea*), a fast-spreading plant that has become a pest in many areas, especially along water. Ducks, geese, quail and other game birds, and songbirds eat canary seed.

Feeder birds can be finicky about canary seed. At feeders in some regions, they take to it readily, while at other feeders, it may join the milo (also known as sorghum) and wheat kicked onto the ground in favor of choicer seeds. Do your own tests to determine whether your birds will take to canary seed by offering a small amount by itself or by checking to see if birds eat the canary seed when it's part of a seed mix.

> Buntings, house finches, purple finches, game birds, goldfinches, and water fowl all eat canary seed.

Cardinal

THE MALE CARDINAL PROVES that a plain red dress is always an attention getter. Add the right accessories—a black face mask and a jaunty crest—and this bird is a welcome presence at any feeder. Yet cardinals are such routine feeder guests that many of us take these birds for granted. If you live in the Midwest, East, or parts of the Southwest where **northern cardinals** live year-round—count your blessings. Those who feed birds in the Northwest, Rockies, and parts of the Southwest never get even a glimpse of this glorious bird.

The female cardinal has paler, browner feathers than the male, but she is a beauty in her own right. Her big, bright orange bill, which you hardly notice in the male bird, stands out in vivid contrast to the subtle coloring of her feathers. It's not an optical illusion, by the way, that males seem to become brighter as spring approaches. Their breeding plumage almost glows with electric color.

Cardinals are beloved for brightening the landscapes of a northern winter. Against snow or the green of conifers, their color brings a welcome flash of life to the scene, like a reminder of summer flowers.

The **pyrrhuloxia**, a close relative of the cardinal, lives in the Southwest. A casual observer may confuse this bird with the cardinal. Both male and female pyrrhuloxia are gray above, with reddish wings and tail, and the male sports a speckled wash of red on the belly. The bill is smaller and more curved than the cardinal's.

Cardinal Behavior

The trademark love song of the cardinal, a loud, whistled "What cheer!" is a welcome antidote to winter doldrums. The birds begin singing in late winter and keep going strong through midsummer. The basic whistle is easy for our human lips to imitate. Try calling back to a singing cardinal and the male may investigate what sounds like a potential rival. A slurred trill is also frequently part of the song. The pyrrhuloxia sounds almost identical.

The male cardinal becomes even brighter as spring approaches and the dull-colored tips of his fall feathers wear away. By the time courtship time nears, the bird will be its most vivid red.

Beautiful in an understated way, the female cardinal wears colors that keep her concealed on the nest. Her strong, triangular bill is a finch-family hallmark.

At the feeder, cardinals may feed singly, in pairs, or as part of a large group. The birds frequently band together in winter, traveling thickets, roadsides, and backyards to search for food. Sunflower seeds are a guaranteed draw, but cardinals consume many other foods as well. Cardinals are one of the few birds that will stand up to a greedy jay at the feeder.

During courtship season, you may witness a tender ritual between the male and female birds. Imitating the posture of a baby bird, the female droops her wings and crouches low with open beak, begging for food. Her mate eagerly obliges her request, depositing a morsel of food into her waiting bill.

Cardinals may seem to be romantic suitors, but strong hormones rule the males during the breeding season. This leads to frequent attacks on other males—or against their own reflection. If a tapping on a window awakens you, you may find a cardinal viciously trying to drive away the phantom bird in the glass. A car mirror may also substitute for a rival. Because cardinals are so single-minded about attacking their adversary, do the bird a favor and cover the offending window or mirror before it batters itself silly. A piece of netting may break up the reflection adequately; if not, use an old sheer window curtain or other covering.

CARDINAL FEEDER FOODS
▪ Apples
▪ Bread and other baked goods
▪ Corn, any type
▪ Peanuts, chopped or shelled
▪ Safflower seed
▪ Suet, ground or chopped
▪ Sunflower seed, black oil or striped, hulled

Catbird

THAT KITTY MEWING in your bushes may not be a feline but an avian species. The gray catbird, a cousin of the mockingbird and thrasher, bears an appropriate name. Catcalls aren't the limit of this talented mimic's repertoire: The bird may also imitate squeaking gates, other birds, or your mail carrier's whistle.

A shy bird, the catbird ranges across most of the country except for the far West. It keeps to thickets and hedgerows and rarely comes out into the open. Because of its habits, a catbird can be difficult to tempt to the feeder. Your best course is to plant brambles and berried shrubs in a thick corridor, which will provide natural food for this insect- and fruit-eating species, as well as give the bird a route of safety through your yard. The abundant vegetation will also provide a ready supply of the beetles, crickets, grasshoppers, and other insects devoured by the bird.

Catbirds are a gardener's allies in the vegetable garden, which they may visit more readily than a feeder because the plants feel more like home. Dense

Often heard but not so easy to spot, the catbird skulks in shrubbery. Track it down by following the meowing or listen for its melodic song of repeated phrases.

flowerbeds and borders also attract the birds. The persistently pesty Japanese beetle is one of their favorite menu items.

Catbirds usually winter in the far South, coastal Southeast, and southward, though an occasional bird may stay in northern climes. Keep your feeding station stocked with fruit and soft foods year-round, and any catbirds in the area may eventually visit. As with other species, catbirds seem to be learning to associate feeders with a steady food supply. In my first 20 years of bird feeding, I never saw a catbird venture to the tray of food, although local residents did eat heartily of wild grapes and raspberries nearby. In the last decade, I have regularly hosted catbirds, summer and winter, at feeding stations in Indiana and Pennsylvania.

Catbird Behavior

This mimic thrush engages in a special kind of singing, especially in late summer. Listen for its very quiet whisper song, usually sung from dense undergrowth where the singer is well concealed. If you are "lucky" enough to have a tangle of Japanese honeysuckle (*Lonicera japonica*) on your property, you may find that vine an ideal location for both a catbird nest and a catbird song.

At the feeder, the catbird is quick to take flight at the first intimation of danger or signs of unrest from other birds. After winter storms, it is one of the first birds to arrive at the feeder and one of the last to leave. At my feeder, one of its favorite summer foods is the tiny champagne grape, a ¼-inch morsel that is similar to the bird's favorite wild grapes in size. Once a rarity in the fresh fruit market, these wine grapes are becoming more available in supermarkets.

CATBIRD FEEDER FOODS

- Blackberries (*Rubus* spp.)
- Blueberries (*Vaccinium* spp.)
- Bread and other baked goods
- Cereal
- Crackers
- Currants (*Ribes* spp.)
- Grapes (*Vitis* spp.), wild or cultivated
- Peanuts, shelled; chopped or whole
- Raisins
- Raspberries (*Rubus* spp.)

Cats

THAT DEAR PET SLEEPING PEACEFULLY on your lap is part of one of the biggest threats birds face. House cats, strays, and other wandering felines account for an unbelievable number of bird fatalities: One estimate suggests more than a million songbirds a year meet their fate at the claws of cats. I've done an informal survey of nesting birds for 2 years in my own small town, where cats claim their territories on every block. According to my records, only one in five nests goes unmolested by cats in the six blocks surrounding my house. And that doesn't include the adult birds that fall prey to predatory felines.

Whatever the actual figure of cat damage, keeping kitties out of your yard should be a prime consideration for any bird lover. Keeping your own pets indoors is a good place to start. They may protest for a while, but they will eventually become accustomed to house arrest. If you can't bear the thought of confining your pet year-round, at least keep it indoors during the peak breeding season, when birds are at their most vulnerable. A bell on the collar won't do the trick because cats can stalk without a single tinkle.

Because the cats that visited my yard were not my own, I couldn't control their comings and goings. But I did discourage them from making my yard their private lounge. The old chase-and-yell strategy is highly effective. If you're not the yelling type, drop a

> If you care about the well-being of your birds, keep your cat indoors and urge your neighbors to do the same.

handful of pennies into a soda can, tape the opening shut, and shake it as you chase out the intruders. A squirt gun or a blast from the garden hose will also do the trick. Of course, only use the water treatment in warm weather.

No matter how often you chase a cat, it probably will come back because all those birds in one place are just too much to resist. Two other options will give you more permanent results: a fence and/or a dog. After I erected a solid wood-board fence with little room to scramble under, the cat traffic dropped dramatically. The presence of a dog is just as discouraging, although it won't help your birds at night when Fido is asleep on the hearth inside. Combining fence and dog, I've found, works like a charm. After a few close calls when my dog thought he was actually going to catch a cat, the felines apparently passed the word. Now the cats avoid my yard for fear of getting cornered by the dog inside the fence.

Providing protective cover for your birds is a double-edged sword. Sheltering shrubs make it easier for a bird to dash for safety, but they also allow cats to sneak up on unwary birds. If cats are a problem at your feeding station, keep

That single-minded look strikes fear in any bird's heart, and for good reason. Pet and stray cats may kill as many as a million or more birds every year.

cat-hiding vegetation several yards away from feeders and water features. In the end, your observations will help you evaluate the cat-danger situation in your own yard.

Cereal

Attracts common feeder birds plus jays, pheasants, pigeons, quail, starlings

HUNGRY BIRDS IN YOUR BACKYARD will change your whole perspective on stale cereal—instead of seeing that last inch or two at the bottom of the box as a waste of good food, turn it into a popular treat for your feathered friends. You can scatter stale cereal directly on the ground or in a tray feeder, but birds will gobble it up faster if you make it more palatable by adding tasty peanut butter, peanut oil, or meat drippings to the dry flakes. It's easiest to mix peanut butter and other binders with cereal using your bare hands in a large, deep mixing bowl (kids love to help with this hands-on preparation). The result will be a crumbly mixture that the birds can easily pick up and enjoy.

Many of our favorite feeder birds appreciate leftover cereal, but so do pigeons, house sparrows, and starlings. If you're trying to discourage these birds from visiting your feeders, offer the cereal mixtures described on the opposite page in small quantities, scattering about a cup at a time among other seed in the feeders. You can also scatter the cereal mixes beneath a dense shrub or low-branching conifer to tempt jays, quail, pheasants, and native sparrows. Some of the traditionally troublesome birds are more reluctant to feed in those places than at open sites.

I like to collect a wealth of cereal-box leftovers in large resealable plastic bags, stored in the freezer, for winter feeding when blizzards bring crowds of hungry birds to the yard. I scatter the flakes and loops across the open areas of my backyard so that the flocks of birds can easily reach them, and I feel benevolent rather than annoyed as 100 or so starlings chow down.

Choose cereals for birds just as you would for your children or yourself (see "Serving Leftover Cereal" below): Those without sugar coating and marshmallows are healthier. Cereals with dried fruit bits or nuts are a special treat that birds will devour with gusto. They also make a great base for birdfood recipes.

Serving Leftover Cereal

SOME BIRDS will eat almost any kind of cereal, but I've found that some popular brands like Cheerios develop a particular following. Consult the chart below to find out how to prepare cereals or mix them with other foods, what type of feeder to put various cereals in, and what birds these grainy treats will please.

Cereal Type	How to Prepare	How to Serve	Desirable Birds Attracted
Bran flakes	Crush with a rolling pin.	Ground feeder	Doves, juncos, quail, pheasants, native sparrows
Cheerios	Offer whole.	Tray feeder	Blackbirds, chickadees, jays, mockingbirds, titmice
Corn flakes	Crush with a rolling pin.	Ground feeder	Blackbirds, buntings, doves, juncos, pheasants, quail, native sparrows, towhees
	Crush with a rolling pin; mix each cup cereal with ¼ cup peanut butter, peanut oil, bacon drippings, meat drippings, or melted suet to make a crumbly mix.	Tray feeder	Cardinals, chickadees, jays, nuthatches, titmice, woodpeckers, wrens
Crisped rice	Mix each cup cereal with ¼ cup peanut butter, peanut oil, bacon drippings, or meat drippings.	Tray feeder	Cardinals, chickadees, jays, nuthatches, titmice, woodpeckers, wrens
Fruit/nut cereals	Crush lightly with a rolling pin to break up cereal flakes.	Ground feeder	Buntings, robins, thrushes, towhees, native sparrows
		Tray feeder	Bluebirds, chickadees, grackles, grosbeaks, jays, mockingbirds, nuthatches, tanagers, titmice, yellow-rumped warblers, woodpeckers, wrens
Hot cereals (oatmeal, grits, Cream of Wheat)	Mix each cup dry cereal with ¼ cup peanut butter, bacon drippings, or meat drippings.	Tray feeder	Cardinals, chickadees, jays, nuthatches, titmice, woodpeckers, wrens
Puffed rice	—	—	Not appealing to birds
Shredded wheat	Crush with a rolling pin.	Ground feeder	Doves, juncos, pheasants, native sparrows
Sugar-coated cereals	—	—	Not appealing to desirable birds; serve in tray or ground feeder during winter storms only when food is scarce.

Chickadees

As CUTE AS A TIN wind-up toy, chickadees are endearing little creatures with jaunty attitudes and spiffy black caps. Their alert bright eyes seem to hold little fear of humans, and indeed these birds are among the easiest species to hand tame. The **black-capped chickadee** is the most widespread species, ranging across the northern half of America. Its "chick-a-dee-dee" call is one of the most widely recognized bird songs. Other chickadee species provide variations on the theme. The **Carolina chickadee** looks almost identical to the black-capped and inhabits

Black-capped chickadees are just downright cute. Active and unafraid, they are easy to befriend with a handout of their favorite foods. Plant a row of sunflowers for fall and winter snacks-on-the-stem.

the East and Southeast. Listen carefully and you may be able to distinguish its call, which is higher pitched and more rapidly delivered, often with a few extra "dees" tacked to the end of the phrase. In the mountainous West, it's the **mountain chickadee**, naturally enough, that entertains backyard bird feeders. It's distinguished by a black stripe through its eye, which splits the large white cheek patch. Along the Pacific coast, the beautiful **chestnut-backed chickadee** takes over. Its head markings look like the black-capped, but its belly is pure white and its back and sides are a rich russet brown. The **boreal chickadee** dwells in the extreme North, where, like other species, it devours a myriad of insects and frequents conifers to extract seeds from their cones. This species has a brown cap instead of the usual black attire, and a flush of chestnut tinges its sides and back.

Chickadees reside all year in nearly all of their ranges, but in nesting season they may temporarily disappear from your feeding station. Chances are, they will return when the duties of feeding a family are over—often with the young'uns in tow. There are not many things cuter than a row of fuzzy-headed

The chestnut-backed chickadee flits about in the dim light of moist Pacific Coast forests, from the moss-draped Northwest to the giant redwoods of California.

baby chickadees sitting shoulder to shoulder along a tree limb near the feeder.

Chickadee Behavior

You could spend all your feeder-watching hours observing the antics of chickadees. These birds are active little creatures, always in motion. They flit from tray feeder to tree branches, then to the suet feeder, then to sample a doughnut, then to examine a weed for insects. And that's just in the first 5 minutes of watching! Excellent acrobats, they are adept at hanging upside down or sideways and at contorting their bodies to reach a morsel that is just a bit out of beak range.

A white stripe above the eye, splitting the black cap, is the key to recognizing the mountain chickadee.

CHICKADEE FEEDER FOODS
■ Acorns
■ Bayberries
■ Bread and other baked goods
■ Cornmeal mixtures or baked goods
■ Doughnuts
■ Hamburger, raw
■ Mealworms
■ Nuts
■ Peanut butter
■ Peanut butter mixtures
■ Peanuts, any style
■ Pine nuts
■ Suet
■ Sunflower seeds, black or striped

Chickadees are talkative as well as dynamic. You will hear them calling at any time of year and any time of day. Listen for the whistled two- to four-note songs of chickadees in addition to their traditional calls. This vocalization varies from species to species. To my ears, it's as shrill as one of those supersonic dog whistles—I have an almost uncontrollable impulse to clap my hands over my ears whenever I hear it.

Chickadees readily visit any style of feeder. They are agile enough to handle a tube feeder or homemade coffee can feeder, and they can cling to suet feeders as well as woodpeckers can. Being birds of the trees, they prefer feeders at higher settings than food at ground level, although if you are slow to refill, they will glean seeds from the ground. They welcome nuts, seeds, suet, and soft foods.

In winter, watch for gregarious bands of chickadees mixed with kinglets, nuthatches, titmice, and downy woodpeckers roaming your yard or feeder area. These mixed-species groups can be heard before they are seen because the birds keep up a constant, reassuring call-and-response conversation.

RECIPE

Chickadee Delight

Mix this recipe for winter feeding, when high-activity chickadees need high-fat foods to keep their small bodies well fueled. Chop the suet finely so that it can be eaten in one bite.

INGREDIENTS

2 cups beef fat trimmings, ground or finely chopped

1 cup hulled sunflowers

1 cup pine nuts

1 cup peanuts, coarsely chopped

1 cup shelled almonds, hazelnuts, pecans, or walnuts, coarsely chopped

Spread the chopped fat on a tray in a single, shallow layer, and freeze until stiff. Break into individual small pieces with hands, and pour into a resealable plastic bag. Return to freezer, and freeze overnight. Dump suet pieces (loosen clumps if necessary) into a large bowl, and stir in other ingredients. Pour into an open tray feeder in a shallow layer.

Chipmunks and Ground Squirrels

CHIPMUNKS AND GROUND SQUIRRELS are hoarders that may spirit away food from your feeding station to store underground. These small, quick, ground-hugging rodents look like downsized, flatter-tailed versions of the larger, usually tree-dwelling squirrels. Most species sport long stripes down their backs.

If you live in the eastern half of the country, you are likely to enjoy the visits of the eastern chipmunk at your feeding station. Smallest of the ground squirrels, this fellow has a body about 9 inches long. In the central plains, Franklin's ground squirrel, an unstriped, solid grayish brown animal, is prevalent. In the West, the 13-lined ground squirrel, also known (albeit incorrectly) as a gopher, fills the same ecological niche. These little rascals can carry surprising quantities of food in their expandable cheeks. They hibernate in the winter and are active from spring through fall.

You can tame most ground squirrels with a bribe of bread or other baked goods. The chipmunk in my former Pennsylvania garden was particularly fond of buttered toast. It would take it daintily from my fingers, then maneuver into its burrow in a stone foundation wall. Chipmunks also munch on nuts and seeds.

These furry visitors can be troublesome, however. They eat young birds and bird eggs, along with tasty morsels from your garden, such as spring bulbs. Their burrows may destroy your favorite plants, too.

The presence of a cat or dog may discourage these rodents from making their home in your yard. You can also try tempting them into live traps for removal to a suitable wild area if they become a problem.

> Chipmunks love baked goods as well as seeds, but they also eat young birds and bird eggs.

Cicadas

Attract buntings, cardinals, chickadees, robins, warblers

THE INFERNAL BUZZING DRONE of cicadas in the summer may not be music to our human ears, but to birds it speaks a welcome message: Food here! Cardinals are adept at catching the buzzing insects in flight, while robins wrestle them to the ground, then stand on the vibrating body to dine. Even tiny buntings, chickadees, and warblers will capture and eat a cicada when they can.

With their loud droning and the large empty shells they leave about the landscape, cicadas tend to attract our attention more than most other insects. When cicada populations are high, you'll notice dead tips on tree branches damaged by egg-laying adults. Immature cicadas live in the soil. When they emerge at maturity and split their brown shells to reveal large, fearsome-looking winged adults, hungry birds will be waiting.

Large, buzzing cicadas may not look like the most delicious item on the menu, but to birds big and small, these summertime insects are a welcome feast.

City Birds

EVEN IN THE HEART of the city, a bird feeder can bustle with activity. You won't attract nearly as many species as you will in less urban areas, but the birds you feed will be just as appreciative of the handout. Birds of any kind are interesting to observe. When you have just a few species to watch, you will enjoy learning their habits even more than if you're trying to keep an eye on a dozen different kinds of birds. With city bird guests, you may even come to recognize individuals, which will give you a more personal pleasure in putting out seed for your "friends."

Love 'em or hate 'em, pigeons are a fact of life in the city. Give them a handout if you don't mind their messy habits.

In any city across America, you can attract house sparrows and starlings. Pigeons in a wonderful array of plumage colors and patterns may also visit. Mourning doves may turn up, too. Depending on just how much of a concrete jungle the neighborhood is, you may not attract any more species. If there are trees nearby, you may entice cardinals, chickadees, jays, and other birds. During migration time, your feeding station may draw passing birds if there are nearby trees or shrubs to shelter them while they rest.

Millet, seed mixes, and cracked corn are excellent choices for satisfying typical city birds—they're economical and eagerly eaten. Keep a small feeder of sunflower seeds for unexpected visitors; true city birds such as sparrows and starlings prefer smaller seeds and soft foods. Bread and cracker crumbs and baked goods are ideal for city birds, which have learned well how to scavenge edibles.

Feed your city birds in feeders that prevent seed from scattering on the ground, such as tube feeders with trays attached beneath them, or other enclosed feeders. Regularly clean up any spilled seed beneath feeders, and feed soft foods in small amounts so that none remains at the end of the day. You do not want to attract city mice and other urban rodents.

City birds greatly appreciate a birdbath as they may have no source of clean, fresh water. They will readily use the standard pedestal type.

Urban Pests

Should you be inundated by pigeons, house sparrows, and starlings and wish to discourage them, a couple of preventive actions will yank the welcome mat out from under their feet. First, switch to tube feeders. These birds have a hard time keeping their grip on the small perches, although they may still visit to vacuum up any seed that spills from the tubes. Weighted feeders that slam closed under the weight of larger birds will also prevent them from gobbling your goodies. You can also try serving only striped sunflower seed, which is difficult for house sparrows to crack. See Nuisance Birds on page 217 for more details on discouraging unwelcome birds.

C

Clark's Nutcracker

IN MOUNTAINOUS REGIONS of the West and Northwest, the Clark's nutcracker may visit your feeding station. This sturdy-looking, jay-size bird has soft gray body feathers and dashing black and white wings and tail. Look for this relative of crows, jays, and magpies near conifers, where it uses its stout bill to pry open the scales and retrieve the seeds of firs and pines.

CLARK'S NUTCRACKER FEEDER FOODS
■ Acorns
■ Bread and other baked goods
■ Chick scratch
■ Corn, cracked, whole kernel, or on the cob
■ Crackers
■ Juniper (*Juniperus* spp.) berries
■ Leftovers
■ Meat scraps
■ Pine nuts
■ Soup bones with marrow
■ Suet
■ Sunflower seeds

I made the acquaintance of this bird while camping near Yellowstone National Park. Like most birds that live near a campground, the nutcracker was unusually tame, snapping up crackers with alacrity from just a few feet away. Later, I saw the birds flying across the mountain valleys, their flashy feathers catching the eye from a distance.

Clark's nutcracker takes the first part of its name from one-half of the famed western exploring team, Lewis and Clark. The nutcracker classification comes from the bird's habit of whacking open cones to get at the "nuts" inside. Pine nuts, the plump kernels of pinyon pines, are a particular favorite.

Clark's Nutcracker Behavior

Like the rest of the crow family, nutcrackers are noisy, and they seem to like causing a commotion. Their voices are mostly unmusical. Squawking is what they do best, often enough to make you cover your ears, especially when the birds arrive in a flock.

Friend of the pine forest, the flashy, noisy Clark's nutcracker ensures a crop of young trees, thanks to its habit of burying seeds for winter use.

Watching a nutcracker at the feeder or in the yard, you might think it's related to the woodpeckers. The bird often clings to trees and hammers away with its strong beak to extract hapless grubs. But on the ground, the nutcracker gives away its heritage with its walk, strutting about like a crow, with an occasional hop. Watch for its flycatcher-like feeding behavior, too, when it dashes out to snatch a butterfly in midair.

If you live high in the mountains, you may host a Clark's nutcracker during nesting season, which takes place as early as late winter, when the high-elevation temperatures hover near zero or below. In fall and winter, the birds often shift to lower elevations, where they feast on berries, lupine seeds, carrion, and feeder offerings as well as conifer seeds.

Like jays and squirrels, these nutcrackers are friends of the forest because they "plant" new trees by burying cones and seeds for later use. A Clark's nutcracker can locate its cache even when it's buried under snow. Uneaten seeds start new pine trees.

Cleaning Feeders

THERE'S NO DENYING that keeping feeders clean can be a chore, but like any other maintenance job—think: weeding—it's a task that's much quicker and easier if you do it routinely rather than wait until the situation gets out of hand.

Clean feeders keep your feeder area looking good, but the benefits go much further than just appearance. Although disease problems seem to be thankfully infrequent at feeder sites, the high concentrations of large numbers of birds in a small feeding area is an unnatural situation that can lead to health problems for the birds. A clean feeder means clean, fresh seed, healthier feeder birds, and less risk of disease. Aspergillosis, for example, a common fungal disease of birds with pneumonia-like symptoms, may spread through moldy seed or infected droppings. Swabbing out feeders regularly with a germ-killing bleach solution helps eliminate potential problems.

Offer Fresh Foods

Given a choice, birds will not eat moldy seed. Like us, they prefer their food fresh. Because it is nearly impossible to keep all seed swept up off the ground, always be sure to have a supply of fresh seed readily available, so that birds are not reduced to picking up bad seed.

At my own feeders and in the wild, I have noticed that birds will peck at or sift through "spoiled" food to find any fresh morsels remaining. Take suet, for example. In summer, my suet feeders begin to look mighty unappetizing, with the fat taking on a covering of black and gray mold. Still, the woodpeckers and other birds work at the chunks of fat, ferreting out fresh white suet from within the blackened shell. I have seen birds do the same at roadkill carcasses. And birds will appreciate withered, bruised, or even fermented fruit that no longer appeals to you. The only danger that birds face from eating spoiled fruit is inebriation: The fermented juices may make them a bit tipsy.

A Clean Scrape

How often you need to clean your feeders depends on how much bird traffic you get and on the weather. I remove spoiled seed and empty hulls whenever they accumulate in the feeders, but I do full-scale disinfecting work only about four times a year.

A good rule of thumb is to swab down your feeders with a 10-percent bleach solution once each season, on approximately the following schedule:

- In late summer, just before migrating goldfinches herald the beginning of increased fall traffic

Stock Up on These Supplies

MAKE FEEDER cleaning easier by stocking up on a few useful tools. If you have the right equipment at the ready, you're much more likely to give your feeders an occasional cleaning when it's needed. Unless you have some particularly unusual or elaborate feeders in your collection, this assortment of basic tools will take care of nearly all of your feeder cleaning tasks. I keep my cleaning supplies stored in a single bucket so that they're within easy reach for my monthly cleanup sessions. Here's what I keep handy.

- A sturdy scraper tool, such as a rigid plastic or metal kitchen spatula, for lifting old seed out of tray feeders and scraping off dried droppings

- A brush with short, stiff bristles for removing caked-on seed from other feeders

- A long-handled, elongated brush—sort of like an oversized baby bottle brush—for swabbing out tube feeders

- A water supply, such as a garden hose in summer or a bucket in winter

- Chlorine bleach solution at a ratio of 9 parts water to 1 part bleach

- A scrub brush for applying the bleach solution

- In late fall, when the feeders are filled to capacity daily
- In late winter, when unusual visitors are apt to show up as natural food becomes scarce
- In late spring, when migrants have moved on and feeder traffic hits a lull.

But you'll also need to clean out your feeders much more frequently than this. Seed turns moldy quickly in damp weather and in rainy and snowy seasons, and even covered feeders can't completely protect seed from accumulating moisture. Every time I refill, especially if the weather has been wet, I scrape out any moldy, damp, or bad seed. Instead of pouring good seed in on top of bad, I stick a spatula in my back pocket when I go out in the morning to refill. A quick flip of the wrist and any damp seed is instantly removed from feeders before refilling.

Keeping Seed Dry

Keeping seed dry can be a problem when you have a high-traffic feeder or a particularly wet climate. Here are a few ideas to help you reduce waste and increase customer satisfaction.

- In wet weather, refill your feeders sparingly, so that the seed is consumed before it can absorb moisture. Refilling the feeders more frequently is better than wasting money on wet seed.
- To keep tiny niger seed fresh and dry in tube feeders, use an age-old kitchen trick: Add a few handfuls of uncooked rice to the seed when you fill the feeder. In the 3 years since I started this practice, I have not once needed to scrape out caked, spoiled niger seed from my tube feeders.
- Don't worry about the wet seed that drops and occasionally sprouts under your feeder area. In my experience, birds won't eat wet seed from the ground. But I have seen sparrows nibbling on the fresh green sprouts, especially during winter when tender greenery is scarce.

Cleaning Solutions

A garden hose with a high-pressure adjustable nozzle is my favorite labor-saving aid in the clean-

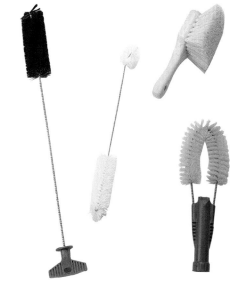

Inexpensive cleaning tools make feeder maintenance quick and easy. Choose scrub brushes that fit your feeders and that make it easy to reach into the corners of trays, hoppers, and tubes.

feeder campaign. I use the hose to spray feeders clean fast, without applying any elbow grease at all. A hose is great for washing out tube feeders, plastic suction-cup window feeders (take them down first), and other feeders with nooks and crannies that are hard to reach with a brush. Allow the feeders to dry thoroughly before you refill them.

When I do my once-a-season disinfecting, I use a bucket of bleach solution (9 parts water to 1 part bleach), a pair of rubber gloves, and a stiff brush. I scrub the surfaces, roofs, and sides of tray feeders and the feeding shelves and perches of other feeders, which are likely spots for germs to accumulate. Then I allow the feeders to dry in the sun, which my mother always told me kills germs, too. Whether that's true or not, I don't know, but it does make my feeders feel fresh and clean.

While the feeders are drying, I turn over the wood chip mulch below the feeder posts, or add a new layer to cover the accumulated droppings and seed hulls. A garden hoe makes this chore a simple operation.

Cleaning Gadgets

Specially designed brushes that have angled tips, long wire handles, or other improvements to make feeder cleaning easier may be worth investing in, especially since most of them cost just a few dollars. Examine each implement before you buy it to determine if you will actually use the tool enough to warrant adding it to your collection. Make sure it is the appropriate size, shape, or length for your particular feeder(s).

Once you begin cleaning your feeders, you'll develop an appreciation for the ones that are easy to clean. Those with decorative nooks and crannies in which seed can get stuck may turn out to be more trouble than they're worth. My favorite feeders are those that are easy for both me and the birds to use. Look for feeders that are sturdily built, simple to fill (don't require two hands to hold open), hold plenty of seed (at least a quart), and are easy to keep clean using basic cleaning tools.

Clematis

Attracts cardinals, catbirds, finches, juncos, sparrows

GIVEN A CHOICE between small-flowered clematis vines like sweet autumn clematis (*Clematis terniflora*) and big, bright-flowered clematis cultivars and hybrids, most gardeners will go for the color and splash of the fancified varieties.

From a bird's-eye view, though, the choice is exactly the opposite. Most large-flowered clematis put their energy into flowers, and the vines themselves are fairly puny things. Small-flowered types, on the other hand, are rampant growers that easily cover a trellis or fence with dense, twiggy growth in a single season. Who cares about flowers when you're seeking shelter on a cold, rainy night or when you need a hidden place to make your nest?

Autumn-flowering clematis (*Clematis terniflora*) makes a sweet bower for nesting birds. Clematis vines also supply nesting materials and attract insects for food.

Bird Benefits Galore

Plant a trellis or fence near your feeders with sweet autumn clematis (*C. terniflora*, also called *C. maximowicziana*) or other small-flowered types such as anemone clematis (*C. montana*), virginsbower (*C.*

virginiana), and your birds will have plenty of reasons to thank you. Here are some:

■ The vigorous, twiggy vines provide excellent shelter from rain or wind for any bird, and the vine is a great place to hide in a hurry should a hawk dive-bomb the feeders.

- The tangle of branches keeps nests of cardinals, catbirds, and sparrows hidden from predators.

- The multitude of tiny flowers are better at attracting insects than those large, colorful hybrid clematis blooms so dear to a gardener's heart. Birds will visit the flowering vines to snap up small flies, wasps, and other insects.

- In fall, when the fuzzy seedheads mature, cardinals, finches, juncos, and sparrows will work busily to tear away the fluff and get at the seeds.

- In spring, sparrows and other songbirds will tug off pieces of bare clematis vine to use in nest building.

Small-flowered clematis are speedy growers that thrive in sun to full shade and are perfect for quick coverage of a fence, wall, or trellis. You may plant these vines for the benefit of birds and find yourself enjoying them, too. What's not to like? These trouble-free vines never need fertilizer and require no additional watering after their first few weeks in the ground.

Just as they make great screens for feeders, they also provide quick and substantial privacy for your deck or patio. And the oodles of small flowers combine to deliver sweet fragrance that's often missing from the larger hybrid blossoms. Look to see what clematis options are available from your local growers, then turn to mail-order outlets, if need be, for an expanded selection. Most clematis grow well in Zones 3 through 8.

Communication

SOME ASPECTS OF BIRD communication are hard to miss. When a jay flies into the feeding station, hollering at the top of its lungs and sending all the other birds scattering for cover, you know that it means "Scram!" Other bird communications are less obvious, and you will need to watch closely to notice them. Learning the language of birds will give you a better understanding of the interactions between them, and that translates into making feeder watching more fun.

Here are some bird communiques to listen for:

- Listen for the shrill cheeping calls of fledglings demanding a meal. Even when they are old enough to get food on their own, the young call for parental assistance, and the parents generally oblige. When you hear a young bird squawking, it's probably perched some distance from the feeder. Locate it by watching to see where the parent carries the food.

- Birds communicate with others of their species using call notes—short, nonmusical chips and twitters. Listen for juncos keeping up a constant chittering as they hop about near the feeders.

During courtship, a female house finch may act like a hungry nestling, crouching with her wings lowered and her beak open for a gift of food from her partner.

During migration time, you may hear call notes filtering from the sky as birds pass overhead.

- Assembly calls gather the flock. Listen for these notes from quail and crows.

- Alarm notes are usually louder than normal bird "conversation," and birds deliver them in a harsh, scolding, attention-getting tone. Should you hear a sudden loud "Chip!" as you stroll about your yard, try to find the bird that's warning you away. A nest may be nearby.

- Danger signals are hard to miss because birds at the feeder will leave in a sudden panic. As you observe your feeding station, see if you can pinpoint the first bird to become alert, stop eating, and then deliver an alarm call. The note varies among species.

- Determining the pecking order makes for constant quarreling among feeder birds, especially if eating space is limited. Watch for birds to make shrill attack notes, usually accompanied by a thrust of the head or a flurry of wings.

Birds frequently use body language in place of verbal chit-chat. They communicate anger with threatening head motions or drooping wings and fluffed-out feathers. Courtship rituals may include the female assuming the posture of a begging nestling, dropping her wings, lowering her body, and begging with open bill.

One of the most fascinating everyday miracles of the natural world is the synchronized flight of flocking birds, such as starlings and blackbirds. As if guided by the same brain, they wheel and dive and change direction in one smooth motion, with no visible sign passed among the members of the group. If you are ever privileged to see a mass flight of dozens of American avocets, you will never forget the breathtaking display. These long-legged, long-beaked birds of coastal and western marshes and shallow lakes are decked out in bold zigzags of black against snowy white wings and backs. In a flock they look like a modern dance troupe in flight, flashing dramatic changes of costume as they shift their postures in midair in near-perfect synchronization.

Competition at the Feeder

IT'S HIGH STAKES FOR A SEAT at a bird feeder, thanks to the tempting spread of food you supply. No matter what you're offering—seed, suet, corn, fruit, nectar, soft foods—you will see birds squabbling over squatting rights. Naturally, the most desirable foods will attract the most competition. Birds will shoulder each other aside at the tube feeder, push and shove or threaten to peck one another at a tray feeder, and defend their perch vigorously at a nectar or suet feeder.

Less aggressive or smaller birds generally yield quickly to backyard bullies, which can leave you with a feeder full of starlings or jays and not much else. Luckily, the solution is simple, with a payoff for both you and the birds: Add more feeders. Increasing the accommodations will decrease the competition and result in more birds to watch.

Large tray feeders are your best choice for feeding a crowd because dozens of birds can pack the edges

Blue jays are not well mannered about sharing feeder space. If they monopolize tray feeders, add tube feeders so other visitors don't go hungry.

to reach the seed. A hopper or tube feeder, on the other hand, usually accommodates only a handful of guests because of limited eating space.

I follow an "All Birds Welcome" policy at my feeding station, but I do take steps to keep gluttons like starlings separated from dainty eaters like chickadees. A large, low tray feeder, homemade from plywood and wire mesh, serves as my all-purpose starling feeder. When the starling traffic increases, I dump my old bread, dog food, apple peelings, whole kernel corn, ground suet, meat scraps, and other starling delights directly on the ground. To birds that often eat out of dumpsters, such accommodations are a natural fit. Jays and the occasional brave crow also forage happily there.

Away from the downscale diner, I keep the usual assortment of trays and tubes, some tailor-made for small birds, some not. As long as I keep the starling arena chock full of goodies, they rarely infiltrate the songbird stations. If the smaller birds have a few feeders just for them, I don't worry about them going hungry should bullies shoulder them aside.

Blackbirds, grackles, or starlings can gather in flocks of thousands in fall and winter, vacuuming off feeders in nothing flat. If you consider these birds your nemesis, you'll want to replace traditional-style feeders with trays, hoppers, and tubes that have wire grids, cage bars, or weight-sensitive devices that deny larger birds access to the food within. Shop in a bird-supply store or catalog such as those listed in "Resources" on page 348 to find just the right model to eliminate most of your feeder competition problems.

Coneflowers

Attract goldfinches, tree and other native sparrows

IF YOU PLANT JUST ONE PERENNIAL to attract birds, make it purple coneflower (*Echinacea purpurea*). One of the longest blooming perennials, this sturdy plant starts putting forth flowers in early summer and keeps going strong right through the first light frosts. And, while it's putting out new flowers, the old ones are maturing into beautiful orange-tinged spiny seedheads, brimming with birdseeds. Snip off some of those seedheads with pruners and let them fall into a large paper sack to dry for fall and winter feeding.

Goldfinches are usually the first birds to take advantage of a ripening coneflower. They perch patiently for as much as half an hour at a time, extracting seeds and nibbling the meat free. During late fall and winter, tree sparrows and other native sparrows gather to take advantage of the bounty, either pulling seeds from the plant or searching out dropped seeds below.

The similar pale coneflower (*E. pallida*) and the coneflowers of the genus *Ratibida*, including

A male goldfinch gives purple coneflower the stamp of approval. The blooms attract insects, the plant itself offers cover, and the seeds are favorites of finches.

prairie coneflower (*R. columnifera*) and gray-headed coneflower (*R. pinnata*), also attract small seed-eating birds in fall and winter. Most of the coneflowers thrive in full sun to light or partial shade in average soil conditions. They're hardy across most of the United States, from Zone 3 in the North to Zones 8 and 9 in the South. Established plants tolerate drought conditions, although you and your bird guests will enjoy more flowers when your plants receive adequate moisture.

Use coneflower seedheads, collected after ripening and dried in shallow cardboard boxes, to decorate wreaths and swags for birds. You can also tie the seedheads into bundles and hook them on a nail in a spot where birds can perch and nibble on these tasty treats.

Butterflies and Other Bugs

All coneflowers attract butterflies and other insects, so when they're in flower they bring in live bird food, too. Small butterflies on their way to and from the plants are likely to be quickly snatched up by flycatchers or English sparrows, and smaller insects become a quick dinner for any wrens in the neighborhood. Because coneflowers attract so many insects, they also attract predatory spiders that often stretch their webs across the branches of the plants. The spiderwebs, in turn, may attract hummingbirds that will flit about, collecting the sticky webs for building their nests.

> Coneflowers mature into beautiful orange-tinged spiny seedheads, brimming with birdseed.

Coreopsis

Attracts doves, quail, white-crowned and white-throated sparrows, towhees

OUR AMERICAN PLAINS WERE ONCE ALIVE with great swaths of wildflowers and grasses and with the multitudes of birds that fed among them. It's fun to use native flowers to re-create even a small bit of that sweeping prairie heritage in a sunny spot near your bird-feeding station.

The prairie flowers of the genus *Coreopsis* include annual and perennial species, all of them loaded with tasty bird-attracting seeds. Other coreopsis hail from desert homes in North and Central America, so no matter where you live, you'll discover rewarding native coreopsis that are appropriate for your garden conditions. Members of the giant aster family, these bright daisies are usually yellow, with the exceptions of calliopsis (*C. tinctoria*), which also blooms in burgundy and bicolors, and pink tickseed (*C. rosea*), a pink-flowered species.

Native sparrows appear most often when coreopsis seeds are on the menu, although other birds also enjoy them. Look for white-crowned and white-throated sparrows among the plants in fall and winter. Towhees may scratch underneath to turn up overlooked bits of seeds, and doves and quail will also forage beneath the plants.

Calliopsis (*C. tinctoria*), a self-sowing annual once used as a dye plant, produces so much seed—thanks to its dozens of blooms—that you can easily harvest the seed for winter feeding. Snip sprays of the seedheads, and weave their thin, wiry stems into wreaths and swags for a decorative bird treat.

All coreopsis are easy to grow in a sunny site in average, well-drained soil. Hardiness varies by species. Two of the easiest and most widely adaptable perennial species are *C. lanceolata* and *C. grandiflora*, dependable performers with bouquets of sunny golden flowers. Start the seeds indoors in late winter for some bloom the same year. Expect to see butterflies at the flowers of any coreopsis you grow.

> Both annual and perennial coreopsis species are loaded with tasty bird-attracting seeds.

Corn

Attracts red-winged blackbirds, buntings, cardinals, grackles, jays, juncos, pheasants, quail, sparrows, towhees, wild turkeys, woodpeckers

IF YOU'RE A budget-minded bird feeder, or if you're playing host to hordes of birds, offering cracked corn is an inexpensive way keep your birds happy. A 50-pound sack can cost as little as $3, depending on the grain market. Corn is near the top of the list for cardinals, jays, and woodpeckers, which eagerly seek out whole ears, whole kernels, or cracked kernels. Red-winged blackbirds and other blackbirds also flock to corn, as do grackles, pheasants, quail, starlings, towhees, and wild turkeys. Smaller seed eaters such as buntings, juncos, and sparrows naturally prefer the cracked variety because of their smaller beaks. And of course, those bushy-tailed squirrels and quick little chipmunks also adore corn.

Dry corn on the cob is cheap entertainment at the feeding station. Here, a red-bellied woodpecker works a neat vertical row.

With all these fans, it makes sense and cents to include corn in your feeder program. Use the whole ears, on spike feeders or suspended from hangers, to keep squirrels and woodpeckers happy. Feed shelled corn—whole kernels separated from the cob—in tray or hopper feeders for cardinals, crows, and jays. Fill low tray feeders with shelled or cracked corn to satisfy blackbirds, doves, game birds, and other ground feeders. Pour cracked corn into feeders, low or high, for buntings, juncos, towhees, and native sparrows. Decoy flocks of blackbirds, house sparrows, and starlings away from other feeders by providing plenty of cracked corn in an area separated from the main feeding station by shrubs or other visual barriers.

Because the hard shell is left intact, cob corn and whole kernel corn keep much longer than cracked corn. Cracked corn may become infested by meal moths and other pests or grow rancid because of its high fat content. Keep only about a month's supply of cracked corn on hand to avoid problems. Store in a tightly lidded can in a cool area. I like to keep a 50-pound sack in the trunk of my car during the winter: The cold storage is ideal, and the extra weight improves traction on slippery roads.

Before you start pouring out cracked corn with abandon, gauge how much your birds can eat at one sitting. Cracked corn can become a real mess if you spread a thick layer and it goes uneaten. It becomes a solid, moldy mass when it absorbs moisture from dew or rain or the soil itself. Cracked corn, however, can be a real lifesaver during severe storms because you can feed great quantities of birds at little cost by simply spreading it over the snow- or ice-covered ground. Should snow cover the corn, rake it into nearby flowerbeds or add it to the compost pile when you find it after the spring cleanup.

Growing Corn

For a fast-growing and attractive hedge that has great bird appeal, you can't beat common corn. Plant a triple row of the kernels, and within weeks, you'll have a knee-high boundary of waving green leaves. By summer's end, ears will be fattening, ready to feed cardinals, jays, woodpeckers, and other birds throughout the fall and winter.

Growing corn is as simple as sticking kernels into the ground with your thumb, about 4 inches apart, in a sunny patch of fertile soil. Mulch around the young stalks to keep weeds away, or interplant with scarlet runner beans, which will twine their way up the stems and attract hummingbirds with their rich red blossoms.

For a dramatic effect, you can plant Indian corn, with foliage that is streaked or tinted in reds and greens. Highly ornamental varieties are now available, with wide leaves swirled in a fantasy of red, white, yellow, and green stripes. And why stick to yellow kernels? Birds like colorful ears, too. Try 'Painted Mountain', the mini-eared 'Wampum' and 'Little Jewels', blue-kerneled 'Shaman's Blue', or burgundy 'Ruby Red'. Birds devour popcorn, too—right from the ear, not fluffed in a popper. Experiment by growing little, plump strawberry popcorn or other varieties. For easy eating, your birds will appreciate

a cultivar called 'Shorty', which tops out at 12 to 18 inches tall, offering its bountiful ears in easy reach of ground-feeding doves, pheasants, wild turkeys, and smaller birds.

Unpopped Only, Please

Stringing chains of popcorn sounds like the perfect approach to decorating an outdoor Christmas tree for the birds. Yet if you try it, you'll quickly find out that your handmade garland goes uneaten. That's because the popping process has exploded the meaty part of the kernel into a fluffy mass that the birds apparently find unappealing.

Instead of decorating for the birds with popped popcorn, hang ears of unpopped mini-corn such as golden 'Tom Thumb', which are just a few inches long, or strawberry-type popcorn ears. You'll find chickadees, jays, titmice, woodpeckers, and, of course, squirrels taking you up on your offering.

> For a fast-growing and attractive hedge that has great bird appeal, you can't beat common corn.

Corn Feeders

SQUIRRELS ADORE IT, woodpeckers welcome it, cardinals crave it—and it's one of the cheapest foods around. All those reasons make corn an ideal menu item at your feeding station. As another plus, a cob of corn offers entertainment value, too. It's great fun to watch squirrels figure out a revolving wheel of corn, and I hate to admit it, but even I smile at the sight of a squirrel sitting at its own little table-and-chair corn feeder, a popular wooden contraption that only looks tacky until you try it.

You can make a corn feeder with nothing more than a scrap of wood, a big nail, a couple of smaller nails, and a hammer. Drive the big nail through the wood, attach the plank to a vertical or horizontal

post with the smaller nails, shove an ear of corn onto the protruding nail, and *voila!* In less than 5 minutes, you have yourself a new corn feeder for both birds and squirrels—and you—to enjoy. (Don't be surprised if it takes even less time for the squirrels to strip the ear of corn down to the cob.)

Whole-Kernel Feeders

A sack of whole kernel corn removed from the cob is excellent, high-fat food for cardinals and woodpeckers. A wire-grid feeder such as those sold for nutmeats and peanuts is also perfect for offering whole-kernel corn. If you want to make your squirrels and chipmunks smile, you can also offer the kernels in a tray feeder.

Squirrel box feeders, which have a flip-top lid that the bushytails open themselves, are fine for feeding shelled corn. (See plans for building a squirrel box feeder on page 273.) Opening the lid will slow them down a bit so that they don't empty the entire feeder in just a few minutes. Plus, the very human look of the animals as they stand and use their paws and nose to wiggle open the lid makes for entertaining action at the feeding station.

Stock Up for Winter

Shop around for the best prices on whole corn and shelled corn. Rural feed stores usually beat bird-supply outlets by a mile. As usual, buying in bulk will bring you the best bargain. You can pay as much as $1 an ear for cob corn, or as little as $10 for 50 pounds—a winter's worth of feeding.

Keep a dozen ears or so in reserve in case of bad weather or increased traffic, but avoid buying much more corn than you can readily use within a few weeks or within a winter, if you live in a cold area. Because of its high oil content, corn is apt to turn rancid in warm weather. In my area, where winter temperatures usually stay below 40°F (sometimes well below!), the corn I stock up on in October is still fresh in February. Store your corn in a mouse-proof, squirrel-proof metal trash can.

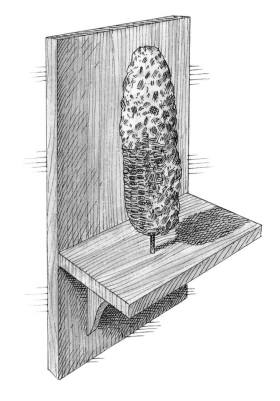

Recycle stripped corn cobs by spreading the cob with suet or peanut butter. Roll in nuts or other treats if you like. Then push the cob back onto its spike and watch for customers to arrive.

Commercial Corn Feeders

IN MY experience, the corn feeders you can buy are more complex, as befits their higher price, but I'm not sure that the birds notice the difference. Here's a rundown on what you'll find.

- One of the simplest is a wire coil into which you drop an ear of corn. Woodpeckers like to peck away at the kernels through the wires around the cob, and squirrels deftly extract the entire ear and carry it away to their cache in the trees.

- Spike feeders abound in various configurations, from single-ear platforms to holders for multiple ears. It's harder for a squirrel to pull free the cob when it's shoved onto a spike, so they generally eat in place at these feeders instead of doing the old snatch-and-scamper routine.

- The mini table-and-chair setup is deservedly popular (with both squirrels and their human ob-servers) and sells for $10 to $20 at bird-supply stores and home-town craft shows.

- Rotating feeders, which spin ears of corn like a carnival ride, will keep squirrels busy—and away from your high-priced seeds—for hours, plus they will give you a few good chuckles as you watch the determined varmints try to master the trick. Expect to pay $20 and up for a front-row seat at this squirrel carnival.

Cornmeal

Attracts doves, juncos, native sparrows, towhees, and other ground-feeding birds

HIGH IN FAT AND PROTEIN, cornmeal is the perfect foundation for bird-attracting recipes. It's impractical for feeding alone because it quickly absorbs moisture and becomes rancid if uneaten. You can try sprinkling cornmeal lightly over snow-covered ground for doves, juncos, native sparrows, towhees, and other ground-feeding birds.

Mix cornmeal with peanut butter to extend that expensive spread so that it serves more birds and slides down their gullets more easily. Combine the two at a 1:1 ratio and stuff into holes drilled in a section of 3- to 4-inch-diameter log. Use a heavy duty screw eye in one end of the log to hang it from a branch. This makes an easy feeder that's irresistible to chickadees, nuthatches, titmice, and woodpeckers.

You can also increase the proportion of cornmeal to peanut butter (approximately 2:1), and mix it with your hands until the mixture has the consistency of stiff cookie dough. The resulting "dough" is an ideal bluebird food to stock an open tray feeder. Experiment in your kitchen, combining cornmeal with one or more of the foods listed below in "Mix-and-Match Cornmeal Combos" to create custom-made treats that will appeal to many of your favorite feeder birds.

Mix-and-Match Cornmeal Combos

DEPENDING ON what you have around the house, you can whip up an array of treats by mixing cornmeal with a binding agent—something liquid or sticky—and other special tidbits.

Choose a binding agent from the first list to keep the treats sticking together, then add tidbits from the second list for extra bird appeal. Add enough cornmeal to the mix so that the end product is fairly stiff, like cookie dough, so birds can peck off small bits or pull out special tidbits without getting their head feathers greasy (which can inhibit the feathers' insulation qualities). Start with ¼ cup liquid fat to 2½ cups of cornmeal and 1 cup treats, and add more cornmeal if needed to stiffen the mix.

Binding agents: bacon grease, cool but still liquid; beef drippings; canola (rapeseed) oil; corn oil; peanut butter; peanut oil; suet, melted, cool but still liquid; sunflower oil

Special tidbits: acorn nutmeats, chopped; apples, chopped; bacon, cooked and crumbled; beef, cooked and finely chopped; currants; nuts, any kind, finely chopped; peanuts, chopped; pine nuts; raisins; suet, chopped

Watch your feeder birds' responses to each combination you try, and you'll quickly see which of your experiments finds the most favor with your feathered friends.

Cosmos

Attracts all kinds of seed-eating birds, such as cardinals, doves, goldfinches, sparrows

WE'RE SO USED TO THINKING of cosmos as a garden flower that it's hard to imagine it was once only a wildflower, splashing Mexico and the southern United States with warm orange, yellow, and pink blossoms. In the wild, as in the garden, this aster family member appeals to all kinds of seed-eating birds, from cardinals to doves to sparrows. Plant it in masses in full sun near your feeding station or outside your favorite window, where you can watch the crowds of birds that arrive to dine on its seeds. Look carefully to spot goldfinches, which blend in surprisingly well among the flowers and foliage. A bending stem is sometimes the only telltale clue to their presence.

Like other bird favorites, cosmos can stand all winter long in the garden. Even though this annual is killed off by frost, its ferny stems still provide shelter, and birds will work on its seedheads all through the winter months.

The seeds of both yellow, orange, or red cosmos (*C. sulphureus*) and pink, red, or white cosmos (*C. bipinnatus*) are yummy to birds. These heat-loving annual plants can take a long time to flower, a drawback in short-season areas, where they may just hit their peak when killing frost arrives. To encourage faster bloom, grow them in lean soil with no fertilizer.

Collect cosmos stems after the flowers go to seed and use them in outdoor wreaths for the birds. Some seed eaters will perch on the wreath to dine, while ground-feeding birds such as doves, sparrows, and towhees will congregate beneath the wreath, where they'll quickly clean up any dropped seeds. Birds are bound to miss some that fall to the ground, and those seeds will sprout the following spring to produce a new year's round of flowers and seeds.

A couple of dollars' worth of cosmos seed will yield a big patch of flowers. The seeds are especially popular with goldfinches and other seed-eating birds.

Crackers

Attract blackbirds, chickadees, crows, doves, jays, juncos, nuthatches, pigeons, titmice, sparrows, starlings, woodpeckers

POLLY WANT A CRACKER? Yep, and so do chickadees, doves, jays, juncos, nuthatches, titmice, sparrows, and woodpeckers. Feeder birds, including blackbirds, crows, pigeons, and starlings, quickly devour crumbled crackers.

You can offer commercial crackers of practically any sort at the feeder. Use your hands to break them into small bits that birds can easily nibble. Jays and starlings—and our rodent friends, including squirrels and chipmunks—will also snatch up whole crackers as a real prize. Serve crackers in small amounts because they quickly soak up moisture and become unappealing to all but the hungriest starlings.

For a quick and convenient way to use up bacon grease or beef drippings, crumble saltines into the liquid (but cooled) grease, and stir with a wooden spoon until the coarse cracker crumbs and pieces have soaked up the fat. Woodpeckers are particularly fond of these snacks at my feeders, with jays giving them stiff competition. Small native sparrows and juncos are quick to snatch up any yummy bits that fall to the ground during the larger birds' forays.

Putting out whole saltine crackers is also a good way to grab the attention of birds. When a frigid spell hits in early spring, I toss white saltines onto the ground. Hungry robins are quick to spot them.

> Woodpeckers are particularly fond of saltines crumbled into bacon grease or beef drippings.

Cranberries

Attract mockingbirds, robins, waxwings, Carolina wrens

OUR AVIAN FRIENDS don't appreciate the old-fashioned charm of cranberry garlands on the holiday tree. In my experience, birds rarely prefer these pretty fruits. When I switched from stringing cranberries to stringing grapes and dried cherries, the birds chorused their approval. Mockingbirds, robins, waxwings, and Carolina wrens all became regulars, pecking at the garland decorations until they were bare of fruit.

Fresh cranberries are so appealing to our eyes (and so reasonably priced) that you may want to experiment with the tastes of your own birds.

Birds do eat cranberries in baked goods, and I have discovered that mockingbirds and robins will turn to the dried cranberries at the feeder when no other fruit remains. One year the leftover dried cranberries in my fruit tray feeder enticed a migrating yellow-bellied sapsucker to stick around my area for 2 weeks.

I still scatter cranberries in my tray feeders now and then, especially in winter when natural fruit is scarce. But when it comes to handiwork with needle and thread, I've switched from cranberries to the more appreciated grapes. They are easier to string, too!

> Fresh cranberries are more appealing to our senses than to birds' tastes—they prefer grapes.

Crossbills

CROSSBILLS LOOK LIKE overgrown house finches, but there the similarity ends. These heavy-bodied reddish birds are indeed members of the finch family, but their slow, deliberate behavior is unlike the frantic flutterings of house finches, and their bills are the most bizarre among American songbirds.

A crossbill has a curved beak that looks more like a parrot's than a songbird's. The upper half of the pointed, conical bill crisscrosses the bottom, looking like a pair of misaligned scissors. This odd appendage gives the bird the perfect eating tool for its specialty: the seeds of pines, hemlocks, and other conifers. The bird holds open the scales of a cone with its strong beak, while it extracts the seed with its equally useful tongue.

Unpredictable is the rule when it comes to crossbills. Famed for their irregular jaunts as well as for their oddball bills, crossbills may stray far from their usual domiciles in winter. Although the **white-winged crossbill** usually resides in the pine woods of the North year-round and the **red crossbill** lives

Odd but efficient, the red crossbill's curved, overlapping bill gives these birds the perfect tool for extracting seeds from between the scales of cones.

in the North and West, in an irruption year the birds may wander as far as the Atlantic coast or the Southeast states in winter. (For more on irruptions, see Irruption Year on page 179.) It's an occasion when crossbills arrive at the feeder or in the yard. Their noisy eating habits are a wonder to watch, whether they're snapping sunflower seeds or ferreting seeds from a pinecone. Both species are very similar, with red males and yellow-olive females, but the white-winged crossbills sport a pair of bold white stripes on their black wings. If you ever get the chance to see the males of both species at the same time, you may notice that a red crossbill is a more saturated brick red than the pinker white-winged crossbill.

Crossbill Behavior

Crossbills usually travel in flocks, except during breeding season. They're gregarious birds and given to calling to each other while they fly or feed.

Crossbill acrobatics go along with their oddball eating utensils. Since conifer cones often dangle from the tips of branches, the birds are perfectly at ease maneuvering their bodies in an upside-down position to reach their dinner.

Like other northern finches, crossbills have a hearty appetite for salt. A salt block is a great way to attract their trade if your yard is short on pinecones or if you want to entice them to stay a little longer. Of course, if you have a brick house, you may want to reconsider this strategy because crossbills also relish the mortar between bricks. They seem to have quite a craving for the stuff, especially if it's old and crumbly. During an irruption year, I once watched a flock of 19 crossbills industriously pecking at the 100-year-old mortar of a historical bank building in Mt. Vernon, Indiana. They clung to the brick wall just a few feet from the rush of traffic, oblivious to everything but the task at hand: eating mortar. I wasn't at all surprised to see that corner of the building start to give way the following spring! Luckily, a new bank soon replaced it or who knows what the consequences of the crossbills' appetites might have been.

CROSSBILL FEEDER FOODS

- Pine nuts
- Salt
- Sunflower seeds

Crows and Ravens

EVERYBODY CAN IDENTIFY a crow. Big, black, and loud, crows patrol mall parking lots, feast in downtown restaurant dumpsters, and flock over open fields. Crows and their raven cousins figure largely in human legend as well. Every Native American tribe had its own name for these birds, and their avian intelligence often figured in myths and stories passed down through the ages.

Personality Plus

Crows are intelligent and playful. They tumble, dive, and swoop in the air together apparently for the sheer fun of it. They are also masterful thieves, snatching up any object that appeals to them. Although they are fearless, they are routinely wary and suspicious, and many have learned to stay beyond gun range from humans.

When I lived on the coast of Oregon, I watched ravens routinely steal fish from eagles and ospreys in mid-air or when perching. They would harass the eagle with loud cries and feinting attacks until the raptor dropped its prey, which the wily raven quickly snagged. Once the tables turned when a crow made the mistake of annoying a peregrine falcon that had just landed a duck. Without losing a wing beat, the big falcon turned on its attacker and dispatched him, too, with one lightning-fast strike of its legs and beak.

Big and Black

Biggest of the bunch, the **common raven** can reach an imposing 2 feet from beak to tail, as big as a great horned owl and bigger than a red-tailed hawk. Its strong wings stretch at least 4 feet wide. It's a year-round resident mainly from the Rockies to the Pacific, in the Far North, and much more rarely in the Appalachians. This bird has beautiful, glossy, jet black feathers. Its beak is big and thick, and it has a shaggy, almost swollen look at the throat that distinguishes it from the sleekness of crows. Its cries are low and hoarse. In the Southwest, the smaller **Chihuahuan raven,** which sports a white collar on the back of its neck that is visible when it dips its head, ranges in open farmland areas.

The **American crow** is a common bird over nearly all the country, except for a few arid regions of the Southwest. It is the largest of the crows at 17 inches. The more petite **fish crow** patrols along the eastern seaboard and Gulf, often in the company of American crows. Listen for its more nasal call to tell the two apart. In the Northwest, the appropriately named **northwestern crow** scavenges along the coast.

Feeder Behavior

Crows and ravens find their own food easily. They're omnivorous birds that take advantage of any banquet that presents itself, whether it's roadkill, ripe berries, grubs turned over by a plowing tractor, or stale hamburger buns at a fast food joint.

Usually crows and ravens keep their distance from human dwellings, stalking around the edges of the feeder area until hunger draws them closer. Smaller birds may disappear at first when crows or ravens arrive, but they soon return. The big birds routinely dine on the eggs and young of songbirds, but they pose no threat to adult birds. In fact, they can be a songbird's ally, setting up an alarm at the first sight of any danger.

Some people prefer not to entice these birds to their feeders, but I welcome them. They are fascinating to watch because they interact with each

Expect to be entertained when you offer new and different foods to a crow. The bird's quick wits are always evident, whether it is maneuvering strands of spaghetti into its beak or peeling a plastic wrapper from scraps scavenged from the neighborhood trash.

other more like humans than birds. You can almost watch the wheels turning in those bird brains.

Serve food to crows and ravens directly on the ground or in a low open tray feeder. If the birds are reluctant to approach your feeding station, lure them in by spreading eye-catching whole-kernel corn and tempting chunks of beef fat on the ground at the far end of your yard. Gradually move the offerings closer to your feeding area until the big birds are eating within view of your favorite window.

In winter, crows join together in large communal roosting areas that can include hundreds and even thousands of birds. Each morning they head out to forage for the day and return to rest in late afternoon. If the roost is in or near a town or city, the birds can become pests, upsetting trash cans, dirtying cars and sidewalks with droppings, and disturbing the peace with their loud, raucous voices. Some communities seek to dissuade the birds with noisemakers or the more permanent methods of poison or sharpshooting. The songbird laws don't protect these birds, and they often fall prey to target practice or end up as bagged birds during open hunting season.

CROW AND RAVEN FEEDER FOODS

- Bones with marrow or meat attached
- Bread and baked goods
- Corn, any kind
- Dog food
- Eggs, raw in shell, hard-boiled, or scrambled
- Leftovers
- Meat scraps
- Pasta, cooked
- Suet

D

Deer

BEAUTIFUL DARK-EYED BAMBI can be a real nuisance at the feeding station, causing just as much damage as he and his friends and family do in the garden. Instead of nibbling a mere handful of seeds over the course of the day, deer can vacuum your feeders to bare wood in just one short visit. And because bird-feeder design doesn't accommodate large animals, deer can damage the feeders as well as eat you out of 6 months' supply of birdseed.

If deer are only occasional visitors to your yard or if you enjoy watching them, you may want to set up a feeding station just for them. Of course, there's no way to put up a no-trespassing sign at other feeders. But by offering a bounty of their favorite foods, you may be able to keep them confined to an area apart from more fragile bird feeders. Corn, apples, and other goodies will keep them occupied. You can serve the food directly on the ground or in a sturdily built tray feeder. Deer will also regularly visit a salt block. Should deer run out of eats at their feeding station, they will devour millet, birdseed mix, and just about any other grain-based foods at your other feeders.

Keep in mind that deer are browsers. They nip off the twigs and tips of many garden plants and trees. If you invite deer to your yard, they may quickly become a nuisance and injure your treasured plantings. Unless you have a very large property where deer naturally dwell and can supply their food far away from favorite garden areas, it's probably best not to open the door to the potential problems they can cause.

To discourage deer permanently, you'll have to resort to the same methods

The first deer at your feeders can be a thrill, but Bambi quickly wears out his welcome by devouring pounds of seed at a time. Fencing is the surefire solution.

that gardeners use. The only fail-safe solution is a high fence around your yard. High plastic netting is effective and much less expensive than wire or wood, and its dark color blends in with the background so that you hardly notice it. (See "Resources" on page 348 for sources.) Tie strips of white cloth to the fence at first, so that deer don't blunder into it accidentally. A dog is also a great deterrent to deer. Some folks recommend other home remedies such as scattering bundles of human hair, hanging bars of soap, or spreading dried blood around the property—give them a try if you like.

An interesting low-tech solution to deer at the feeder is to fill your feeders with seed treated with capsaicin, the fiery stuff of hot peppers. Birds don't mind the substance in the least, but mammals are sensitive to the burning effects and will only eat pepper-coated seed as a last resort. The Birdseed (page 33) and Hot Peppers (page 162) entries have more details on capsaicin-treated seed.

DEER FEEDER FOODS

- Acorns
- American persimmons
- Apples
- Beech nuts
- Bread and other baked goods
- Cereal
- Corn
- Crackers
- Salt

Diary

By KEEPING A DIARY of feeder happenings, you'll soon have a record that allows you to compare menu choices and how they are affected by season or weather. You'll also have a better idea of what birds to expect at your feeder as the seasons progress. But apart from the educational data of a diary, keeping a daily or weekly bird-feeding journal is just plain fun.

My diary is a hodgepodge of all kinds of details. Some days, the entry is only a quick note of weather, plus a bare-bones list of which birds were eating breakfast at the feeders. On chattier days, the diary includes notes on behavior ("Tufted titmouse whistling 'Peter' as he approached feeder—spring must be getting closer"). I like to note plumage changes as birds brighten up for breeding season or switch to winter wear, and I often include quick sketches. When I dream up a new recipe, I note it in the diary along with the results! I tape in snapshots and clippings, too. On red-letter days when a fox sparrow or other special bird turns up, I switch to bright marker pens to highlight the occasion.

A bird-feeder diary is almost as good for daydreaming as a seed catalog. In the gray days of winter, I like to re-read my entries from late spring—I can almost hear the buzz of hummingbird wings and smell the oranges the oriole was eating then. And in sultry summer, reading about juncos scratching in the snow serves as a quick reminder of cooler days ahead.

> A bird-feeder diary is almost as good for midwinter daydreaming as a seed catalog!

Dog Food

Attracts blackbirds, crows, jays, mockingbirds, robins, thrashers, thrushes, starlings, Carolina wrens

MOISTENED DRY DOG FOOD is a fine facsimile for the natural soft foods eaten by jays, mockingbirds, robins, thrashers, thrushes, Carolina wrens, and other birds. Inexpensive brands, usually based on corn or other grain products fortified with protein are particularly serviceable. A shallow tray of such food placed at ground level will draw customers, especially in the wintertime when natural substitutes are scarce.

Moistened dog food is also the perfect decoy for luring blackbirds, crows, jays, starlings, and other plentiful, pesky feeder visitors away from more expensive foods for which they compete with less aggressive birds. Dry dog food, unsoftened by water, may also be tempting to chipmunks, squirrels, and other furry visitors.

To serve dog food, fill an old cafeteria tray or serving tray with the kibble, then add warm water—about one-third the volume of the dog food (experiment until you find the right amount of liquid). Aim for soft but not soggy dog food bites, so that birds can easily pick them up in their beaks.

Opossums and raccoons also appreciate dog food, and these nighttime visitors can extend your hours of viewing pleasure at the feeding station. Position a garden light or small spotlight so that you will be able to see the customers in the dark. A motion-sensor light is practical and energy-saving, and your after-hours dog-food diners will soon become accustomed to feeding in the pool of light it casts. (See Opossums on page 221 and Raccoons on page 237 for more about these mammals and their visits to your bird feeders.)

> Inexpensive dry dog food (usually based on corn) makes a fine substitute for birds' usual soft foods.

D

Dogwood

Attracts bluebirds, catbirds, flickers, grosbeaks, mockingbirds, robins, tanagers, thrushes, vireos, waxwings, woodpeckers, and others

IF YOU'RE LUCKY ENOUGH to live near a dogwood-filled forest, you can collect (with permission, of course) one of the best-loved bird foods for fall and winter feeding. Bluebirds, grosbeaks, tanagers, thrushes, vireos, waxwings, woodpeckers, and hosts of other birds adore red, shiny dogwood berries. Once a horde descends on a tree, a few dozen birds can strip it bare in just a few hours.

When you find a tree loaded with berries, gather a few handfuls into a resealable plastic bag and store them in the freezer. Later, string the berries to decorate evergreens or a discarded Christmas tree, or you can offer them in an open tray feeder. In winter, when the berries are long gone from local trees, bluebirds, catbirds, flickers, grosbeaks, mockingbirds, robins, and downy woodpeckers will adore the treat.

Because a dogwood tree tends to attract large flocks of robins, it's a good place to look for albinism, a fairly common occurrence among robins. Watch for birds with white feathers on wings, body, or head. You may even see an entirely white bird. (See Albinism on page 4 for more.)

Flowering Dogwood and Friends

Flowering dogwood (*Cornus florida*) is a superb small tree for a partly shaded site through Zone 5. Other lesser-known dogwoods are just as popular with birds, although they seem to be a well-kept secret among gardeners. Many species are available, including pale dogwood (*C. obliqua*) and redosier dogwood (*C. sericea*), two shrubby dogwoods that make fine windbreaks or cover strips at feeding stations and bear clusters of stemmed fruits that are eagerly stripped by birds. Native dogwoods are often sold at extremely reasonable prices by state departments of natural resources or through county extension offices.

Another good reason to experiment with lesser-known dogwoods is the unfortunate affliction known as "dogwood blight," which is shortening the lives of

Dogwood berries ripen in fall, tempting migrating tanagers and grosbeaks. You may not recognize the birds at first, dressed in their drab winter plumage.

flowering dogwoods in the wild and in the garden. This disease quickly saps the tree's vigor and can kill it within a few years. Flowering dogwoods that are already stressed by other conditions—drought, poor drainage, all-day sun—seem to fall victim more easily than plants in better sites and conditions. Nurseries are doing what they can to stop the spread of the problem from the eastern part of the country by selling uninfected trees that have passed inspection.

Because this dogwood is a beautiful asset to the yard and such a hit with birds, it's worth a try, but plant other species for backup. Settle *C. florida* in a partly shaded site, similiar to the natural open woods where it usually grows, instead of in the middle of your sunny yard. Amend the soil by digging in lots of humus, which you can make yourself from composted fall leaves or buy in bags. Water regularly when rain is scarce for at least the first 2 years after planting. Mulch around it to avoid damaging the bark with a lawn mower, which opens the way to disease.

Dogwoods of Distinction

MANY NATIVE dogwoods (*Cornus* spp.) bear fruit that attracts birds. Most of these North American natives are shrubs with casual growth habits and easily overlooked flowers, although the list also includes a beautiful ground-covering perennial and a western tree similar to the popular and showy flowering dogwood of the eastern states. Try a regionally suited choice from this list, or explore other natives in your area. A field guide to trees and shrubs will help you locate a suitable choice, or you can check with a nearby nature center or native plant specialist to get recommendations for your region.

Dogwood	Description	Range and Hardiness
Pagoda dogwood (*C. alternifolia*)	Deciduous tree, about 20 feet tall, or large shrub; also called green osier. It has a flat-topped, tiered habit like its pagoda namesake and creamy yellow flowers followed by black berries.	Eastern native; hardy to Zone 3
Roughleaf dogwood (*C. asperifolia*)	Large deciduous shrub with beautiful blue berries; a tall variety *C. asperifolia* var. *drummondii* may grow to the size of a small tree and has white berries.	Prairie native with range extending into the Southeast; hardy to Zone 6
California dogwood (*C. californica*)	Deciduous shrub with dark red bark and white berries; considered a hybrid (*C.* × *californica*) of western dogwood (*C. occidentalis*) and redosier dogwood (*C. sericea*) by some taxonomists	Western native; hardy to Zone 8
Bunchberry (*C. canadensis*)	Low-growing groundcover perennial with whorled leaves topped by typical flowering dogwood blossom followed by clusters of red berries	Native to northern North America; hardy to Zone 2
Flowering dogwood (*C. florida*)	Small deciduous tree with large white flowers on graceful branches and red berries in fall; avoid planting in areas where "dogwood blight" is prevalent (check with local cooperative extension office).	Native in the East to Southeast; hardy to Zone 5
Pacific or mountain dogwood (*C. nuttallii*)	Small tree similar to flowering dogwood (*C. florida*) but often has a greenish tinge to the creamy flowers; orange-red berries in fall	Western native; hardy to Zone 7
Pale dogwood (*C. obliqua*)	Deciduous shrub to 12 feet tall, of loose, open habit; great in hedges, mixed with evergreens; has clusters of small white flowers followed by white to pale blue berries	Native to eastern North America; hardy to Zone 4
Western dogwood (*C. occidentalis*)	Deciduous shrub or occasionally small tree; has white berries in summer; western counterpart of redosier dogwood	Western native; hardy to Zone 6
Redosier dogwood (*C. sericea*)	Deciduous, suckering shrub, ideal in a hedgerow or as an informal patch of shelter; good with a background of evergreens to show off the red color of young stems; 'Bailey' is a nonspreading selection. If you cut this back to ground level in early spring to encourage new shoots for good winter color, you'll sacrifice the clusters of small white berries that birds find appealing.	Native to eastern North America; hardy to Zone 2

Doughnuts

Attract chickadees, jays, titmice, and other feeder birds

AH, TO EAT LIKE A BIRD, consuming huge quantities of high-fat foods with never a care for extra calories! The supercharged metabolism of feathered creatures quickly burns a caloric intake that would make couch spuds out of us slower-paced humans. Doughnuts are just one of the fattening foods that birds can safely enjoy. They're favorites of chickadees, jays, titmice and other feeder birds.

Plain doughnuts or doughnut holes, without the coating of powdered sugar that is only an impediment to bird beaks, are the best choice for feeders. Your local bakery or doughnut shop may be willing to reserve any unsold plain doughnuts to sell to you at a reduced price. Ask for dense "cake" doughnuts rather than the yeast-raised glazed type.

Feed doughnuts in a wire suet basket or other container that allows birds to peck at them but prevents chunks from falling to the ground. You can also stick doughnuts on a spike nail, but be prepared for whole-sale thievery by jays, squirrels, and starlings. These birds may grasp the treat and fly away with as much of it as they can handle.

> Plain "cake" doughnuts, without a glaze or powdered sugar coating, are the best choices for birds.

Doves

QUIET COOING VOICES and gentle demeanor make doves a welcome sight at the feeder. We often observe these symbols of romance in pairs during the breeding season, which may last all year in warm-winter areas. In cold areas, or when not paired off for nesting, small or large flocks may show up at the feeder to partake of small grain or other feeder foods or to devour berries from backyard plantings.

In every part of the continental United States, you can hear the melancholy cooing of the **mourning dove.** This is the most common native dove, instantly recognizable by its extremely long, tapering tail. The **rock dove,** otherwise known and often scorned as the pigeon, is actually an introduced species that did not exist naturally in America; French explorers brought the bird to these shores almost four centuries ago.

The large **band-tailed pigeon,** which frequents western conifer and oak woods is a lesser-known native dove with a more limited range and a smaller population. When I lived on the coast of Oregon, it was always a surprise to come upon a band of "pigeons" feasting on red elderberry fruits. I thought of

Locally common in western woods, the band-tailed pigeon is big and beautiful. These birds often travel in small groups from one food source to another.

pigeons as city birds, and it took a while to become accustomed to the presence of this woods-loving species. In the Southwest and Texas, the **white-winged dove** is abundant here and there. Its flashy

D

The white-winged dove of the Southwest and Gulf states has a mournful cooing song. In flight, it flashes big white wing patches and white tail corners.

white wing patches make the bird easy to identify. The patches are visible as bars when the bird perches and appear as wide bands when the bird flies.

Two rarities, the **red-billed pigeon** of southern Texas and the **white-crowned pigeon** of the Florida Keys, may occasionally show up at feeders or in gardens in those areas.

Dove Behavior

Doves may look calm and relaxed when feeding, but they can take off like a rocket should they be-come alarmed—which is frequently. The birds seem to be particularly quick to react to any danger, real or imagined. When a group of doves is feeding, watch to see how birds take turns acting as sentry. Without a sound, they pass the duty from one to another, so that the ma-jority of the group can eat greedily while the ap-pointed bird keeps watch.

Doves are ground feeders, though they will visit a raised feeder if seed is not available at lower levels. They do best with a sturdy, open or roofed tray feeder, where their large bodies can find a se-cure place to stand and peck. Often they will glean dropped seed below high feeders. Offer seed in a low tray feeder or in small quantities directly on the ground. Doves are also quick to patronize a salt block.

If weeding is a garden chore you'd like to do less of—and who wouldn't?—encourage the presence of doves at your feeder and in your backyard. The birds consume massive amounts of weed seeds.

DOVE FEEDER FOODS

- Acorns
- Bread and other soft foods (rock dove)
- Bread crumbs
- Buckwheat
- Cactus fruits and seeds
- Corn, whole or cracked
- Elderberries (*Sambucus* spp.), fresh or dried
- Millet
- Milo
- Nuts
- Peas, dried
- Salt
- Weed seeds
- Wheat

Bygone Birds

HAD YOU lived east of the Missis-sippi River 200 years ago, you would have witnessed stupendous flights of **passenger pigeons**. They flew from feeding to roosting grounds in flocks numbering mil-lions of birds—so many that they reportedly made the sky turn dark for 3 days on end when passing.

Traveling in such large flocks, these birds were easy targets for hunters who shot and clubbed the birds for their meat.

As careless foresting and hunting to supply local markets took an early toll on the population, the expansion of the railroad brought further disaster to the species. Once the railroad could provide easy transportation east, the hunting of passenger pigeons increased in fervor. Although mass hunting stopped as the species declined in numbers and made the marketing less profitable, the re-maining birds did not reproduce sufficiently to resurrect the species. It is not clear why the final birds were unable to survive but the impact humanity had on the species was insurmountable.

Drawing Birds

EVEN IF THEY END UP looking more like Woodstock from the Peanuts cartoon strip than the cardinal in your tree, the pleasure you get out of drawing your feeder guests is the main reason for picking up a pencil in the first place.

There are other good reasons for drawing birds. When you want to identify an unfamiliar bird but don't have your field guide nearby, it takes virtually no artistic skill at all to make a basic bird shape. Then, you can label it with features you want to remember when you get back to a field guide: "about the size of a sparrow," or "two white bars on the wings," or "reddish brown under tail." You'll be surprised at how helpful such notes and sketches are when you try to identify the bird later.

I keep a drawing pad near my feeder window to capture the kinds and behaviors of birds that come to visit the feeder. A few quick lines and I have a record of how a tufted titmouse bends its body to whack open a sunflower seed or of how a robin leans back to pull out a worm. I note the date, and I have a record of who was there when, what they ate, as well as a pleasant visual reminder of their visit. Then I like to page through the notebook after a few months and relive those glimpses of bird life I was privileged to oversee.

The best way I have found to improve at drawing birds is to just do it. You don't need any special equipment: a pencil, eraser, and paper will do just

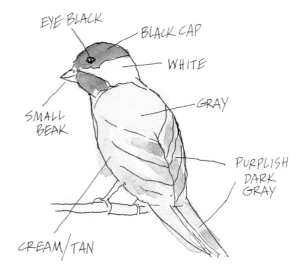

A quick sketch lets you "capture" feeder visitors for later ID, in case the bird doesn't linger. Note all the details you can on your drawing.

fine for starters. The more you draw, the more your sparrows will look like sparrows, and your jays like jays. You'll soon find yourself paying attention to the postures each bird typically assumes and to the way a leg bends or a wing unfolds. Drawing birds not only makes you a better artist, it also makes you a better bird watcher. It's also a soothing activity that leaves you feeling calm and refreshed.

Eagles

NEVER DISCOUNT THE POSSIBILITY of any bird at all showing up at a feeding station. Granted, an eagle is not apt to greet you unless you are regularly offering whole fish or ready-to-eat mammals, but unusual visitors do drop in. If you live in eagle country, such as the western states, a spread of unusual "feeder treats" placed far from the house may draw one of the big birds to your property.

If you have a poultry farm in your area, cheap chicken parts may draw the bird of your dreams. A chicken farm I frequently drove past years ago on my way to Hawk Mountain Sanctuary in Kempton, Pennsylvania, spread leftovers from the processing onto their fields. This unusual feeding station attracted dozens of red-tailed hawks, an occasional rough-legged hawk, and, lo and behold, sometimes a bald eagle! Here in southwest Indiana, where bald eagles gather along the Wabash and Ohio Rivers in winter, I came upon a young eagle sitting smack-dab in the middle of a four-lane highway, dining on a white-tailed deer that had met its fate in traffic. When I pulled my car off the road, the eagle glared fiercely at me for several minutes, then returned to his dinner.

Regal and deliberate, the bald eagle is not apt to become your everyday feeder guest—unless you live near water where the bird can find fish.

Eagle ID

Identifying an eagle is fairly easy because no other hawk approaches the size of these gigantic birds, which stand almost 3 feet tall with a wingspan approaching 7 feet. Only the turkey vulture comes close in size, but it tilts its wings in a V when soaring while both the bald and golden eagles hold their wings flat out, often with the feathers spread at the tips like our fingers.

The **bald eagle**, official symbol of the United States, ranges across nearly the whole country in winter, except for the Southwest. This huge bird usually sweeps its way over rivers and lakes and along coast-lines or sits perched near a body of water. That's because its main menu item is fish, rounded out with the occasional duck or small mammal (plus roadkill). In winter, bald eagles tend to gather in numbers at good fishing spots.

Golden eagles are less common than bald eagles, except in the West and Southwest, but they may occur anywhere in the country because their diet is more varied. They eat mostly rodents (rabbits, marmots, and prairie dogs) but they will take anything they can kill, including full-size antelope and deer.

When eagles are young, it's hard to tell the species apart. Both are dark brown with blotchy white showing beneath the wings and at the base of the tail. It takes eagles a few years to acquire either a golden sheen or a shining white head and tail.

EAGLE FEEDER FOODS

- Fish, uncooked
- Meat scraps, raw
- Poultry innards
- Poultry parts
- Suet, large chunks

Earthworms

Attract robins and other thrushes

ROBINS ARE THE NUMBER-ONE nemesis of these protein-packed wigglers, although other birds, including thrushes, may also dine on earthworms. A subterranean crowd of earthworms will thrive in healthy soil that is high in organic matter. Compost piles are also terrific worm habitat because these superb decomposers dine on decaying vegetable matter. Worms also favor mulched beds, with moist, dark soil protected by layers of chopped leaves, grass clippings, or other organic mulch.

Watch a robin search for worms in your lawn, and you'll gain new respect for the food-finding skills of birds. Experts once believed that the birds could hear the movements of the worms in their earthen burrows, but now it is known that a robin's-eye view is the perfect vantage point for actually seeing worms at work. As the robin cocks its head for a better look, it fixes the point of the worm. One quick beak thrust, a determined drag, and the worm is down the hatch. When you see a robin with a bill full of squirming earthworms, you know a nest is nearby.

Boost your earthworm population by avoiding toxic lawn chemicals and by layering as much organic matter as you can find on garden beds. Anything that is or was once plant material is

The quintessential early birds, robins prize juicy earthworms. Compost, mulch, and organic matter boost the wiggler population and make the hunt a cinch.

fair game, including grass clippings, straw, manure, cardboard boxes, pizza boxes, and newspaper. If your worms are in short supply, you can buy worms at a bait shop or from mail-order sources.

Eggs and Eggshells

Attract chickadees, crows, game birds, grackles, jays, juncos, magpies, purple martins, starlings, house and native sparrows, ravens

IF YOU YEARN FOR PURPLE MARTINS but have had no luck attracting these persnickety birds to your ready-and-waiting martin house, try eggshells. A scattering of crushed white shells on a low tray or directly on open lawn is extremely tempting to these birds and many others, from game birds to native sparrows and

chickadees. Eggshells supply the grit necessary to keep a bird's food-grinding gizzard in fine fettle, and they supply calcium in the diet. To prepare the shells for birds, use a rolling pin to crush the saved, dry shells between two sheets of waxed paper until the particles are moderately fine but not powder.

A parent bird engaging in nest cleaning may drop stray eggshells in your yard, or shell fragments may also tell the story of a less benign event. Some birds, including crows, grackles, jays, and ravens, prey on the young or eggs of other birds, stealing eggs from any nest they can find. They crack the egg to reach the nutritious yolk and white inside. It may seem cannibalistic, but eggs provide nutrients just like other foods do. In fact, many birds will gladly accept cooked eggs as part

> Eggs provide nutrients just like other foods do, and eggshells add needed calcium to a bird's diet.

of the feeder menu. Jays, magpies, house sparrows, and starlings favor leftover scrambled or hardcooked eggs and juncos or native sparrows may nibble on them as well. Offer the leftovers from your egg dishes in an open tray feeder or directly on the ground.

Evergreens

Attract many kinds of birds throughout the year

THE POPULARITY of blue spruces several decades ago was a real boon for birds. If you have one of these giant Christmas trees in your front yard (or smack against the front of your house), keep an eye on it at dusk and in bad weather, and you'll discover that it is a favored roost and nesting site for many birds. The dense branches and prickly needles keep the birds safe from skulking cats and hawks. In fact, it's landscape spruces that get part of the credit for the blanketing of America by the house finch. Using the trees for nesting sites, the birds managed to colonize the Great Plains, a last bastion between the western and eastern populations of the birds.

A chipping sparrow tends its nest within the dense, prickly branches of a needled evergreen. Broad-leaved evergreens also provide places to nest and roost.

Make an evergreen, or two or three, your first choice when adding plants to make your yard more bird-friendly. All evergreens provide shelter for birds, and most are also good food plants. Unlike deciduous plants, they offer birds year-round protection. They are perfect as windbreaks, which protect your feeding area from chilling gusts and blowing snow and rain. A hedge of evergreens offers exactly the kind of cover birds seek when moving from one place to another, as well as a gathering spot where they can hang out when not foraging.

Think Native

No need to look to Siberia or Japan for rare specimens: The best candidates for bird-attracting evergreens are right in your backyard. Native birds have evolved along with native plants that offer them food when they need it and appropriate shelter that stands up to local foul-weather conditions. From a gardener's point of view, native plants are also ideal.

You won't need to fuss with soil improvements, fertilizer, extra watering, or winter protection because the plants will thrive naturally in your climate.

Topping a long list of good evergreens is the pine, a genus that includes plants for almost every part of the country. Only in the treeless prairies and some deserts are native pines absent. Along with oaks, pines

(continued on page 92)

Native Evergreens for Birds

ALL EVERGREENS provide good bird shelter, and many are tops for food, too. Satisfy your landscaping needs and the food and shelter needs of local birds at the same time with some smart choices from among the many native evergreen species that are available.

Evergreen	Food for
Firs (*Abies* spp.)	Chickadees, Clark's nutcrackers, crossbills, grouse, magpies, nuthatches, sapsuckers
Manzanitas (*Arctostaphylos* spp.)	Evening grosbeaks, grouse, jays, mockingbirds, fox sparrows
Salal (*Gaultheria shallon*)	Blue grouse, spruce grouse, band-tailed pigeons, wrentits
Huckleberries (*Gaylussacia* spp.)	Bobwhites, catbirds, crossbills, pine grosbeaks, grouse, jays, orioles, quail, tanagers, towhees, wild turkeys
Hollies (*Ilex* spp.)	Bluebirds, catbirds, mourning doves, flickers, grouse, jays, mockingbirds, phoebes, quail, robins, sapsuckers, white-throated sparrows, thrashers, thrushes, towhees, wild turkeys, vireos, waxwings
Junipers (*Juniperus* spp.)	Bluebirds, catbirds, Clark's nutcrackers, crossbills, purple finches, flickers, grosbeaks, jays, mockingbirds, band-tailed pigeons, quail, robins, sapsuckers, Townsend's solitaires, starlings, thrashers, thrushes, wild turkeys, yellow-rumped warblers, cedar waxwings
Magnolias (*Magnolia* spp.)	Sapsuckers, towhees, vireos, woodpeckers
Bayberries, wax myrtles (*Myrica* spp.)	Bluebirds, bobwhites, bushtits, catbirds, chickadees, crows, flickers, boat-tailed grackles, grouse, meadowlarks, mockingbirds, phoebes, starlings, tree swallows, scarlet tanagers, brown thrashers, hermit thrushes, titmice, towhees, wild turkeys, vireos, yellow-rumped warblers, red-bellied woodpeckers, red-cockaded woodpeckers, Carolina wrens
Spruces (*Picea* spp.)	Chickadees, crossbills, pine grosbeaks, grouse, red-breasted nuthatches, pine siskins, cedar waxwings
Pines (*Pinus* spp.)	Bobwhites, chickadees, Clark's nutcrackers, brown creepers, crossbills, mourning doves, ground doves, house finches, purple finches, flickers, goldfinches, blue grouse, spruce grouse, grosbeaks, jays, juncos, magpies, nuthatches, band-tailed pigeons, pine siskins, yellow-bellied sapsuckers, brown thrashers, titmice, towhees, wild turkeys, myrtle warblers, pine warblers, red-bellied woodpeckers, Carolina wrens
Rhododendrons (*Rhododendron* spp.)	Grouse, hummingbirds (nectar)

An Evergreen Combo for the Birds and You

Think of an evergreen, and the first plant that comes to mind is likely to be a "Christmas tree"—a pine (Pinus *spp.), spruce (Picea *spp.), fir (Abies *spp.), balsam (Abies balsimea), or other conifer. These trees and their relatives have needlelike leaves, which may be short and prickly, like firs, or long and graceful, like pines. With few exceptions—including larch (Larix *spp.) and dawn redwood (Metasequoia glyptostroboides)—all conifers are evergreen.

But not all evergreens are conifers. The magnificent live oaks (Quercus virginiana) of the South and the West, the rhododendrons (Rhododendron *spp.) around your front door, and many other fabulous bird plants hold their leaves all year, making them invaluable for shelter from the storm. Their overlapping leaves work like roof shingles to keep rain from reaching the birds perched beneath the foliage.

A mixed planting of conifers and broad-leaved evergreens makes your yard look more interesting than a group of either kind alone. Combining the textures, shapes, and colors of these plants can be such a pleasure that you may find yourself with a new hobby as an evergreen connoisseur—or at least with a new garden bed for your collection. Keep in mind that, as with other shrubs and trees, an isolated specimen is less useful than a group of plants, both to birds and for garden appeal, although a mature pine or other evergreen will definitely attract birds by its sheer size and the bounty of food it produces. The plants listed for this garden will grow to fill a 30 × 40-foot space, so plan accordingly, or choose fewer plants (or more) to suit your space requirements.

PLANT LIST

1. Hemlocks (*Tsuga* spp.)

2. Oregon grape holly (*Mahonia aquifolium*)

3. Bayberries (*Myrica* spp.)

4. Bearberry (*Arctostaphylos uva-ursi*)

are favored as food by more birds and animals than practically any other plant. A long list of songbirds and game birds seek out the seeds from species such as pitch pine (*Pinus rigida*) and white pine (*P. strobus*) in the Northeast; slash pine (*P. elliottii*), longleaf pine (*P. palustris*), loblolly pine (*P. taeda*), and scrub pine (*P. virginiana*) in the Southeast; and lodgepole pine (*P. contorta*) and Ponderosa pine (*P. ponderosa*) in the West—and that's just a sampling from among 30-plus native species.

The evergreens at your local garden center may or may not include natives, but since local plants typically go unappreciated in their own backyard, it's more likely that the evergreens for sale will include rhododendrons, Chinese hollies (*Ilex cornuta*), and yews (*Taxus* spp.)—mostly nonnatives. It may take a bit of work to ferret out native plants for your area, but the extra effort is worth it. A privately owned nursery or garden center is usually happy to order plants for you. Or you can go to mail-order sources. Check also with the

Many birds seek out pines for their seed-laden cones. Some birds' beaks are specially adapted for extracting pine nuts from the cones.

cooperative extension office in your area: Many state offices sell native plants raised in their nurseries at bargain prices. Stick with natives that are adapted to your climate and your native birds, and you can't go wrong. Consult a reference book or local nature center for plant recommendations for your area.

F

Falcons

WHEN YOU ENTICE many smaller birds to your yard, you may be inadvertently issuing an invitation to birds of prey, which will gladly come to the party. Falcons are one of the types of raptors that may arrive to dine. Swift fliers, they are skilled at following the desperate twisting, turning flight of their avian prey, usually nabbing the bird in midair with a hard strike that snaps its neck.

Smallest of the falcons, and most likely to frequent a bird-feeder area, is the **American kestrel.** This elegant species has a streamlined body, long pointed wings, and snazzy black sideburns. Females are rich chestnut brown marked with subtle mottling. Males have blue-gray wings that set off the warm tones. About the size of mourning doves, these birds often perch on roadside wires and posts, where they keep a keen eye on the ground below for stirrings of grasshoppers, rodents, or small birds.

Its sideburns identify the elegant American kestrel, a small falcon. In summer, the kestrel eats grasshoppers and rodents; in winter, it targets small birds.

Falcon Behavior

The American kestrel's nickname is "sparrow hawk," which gives you a good idea of the size prey this bird will seek near your feeders. Juncos and other ground-feeding species are frequent targets, but any bird that lags behind its brethren when the hawk attacks may fall to its clutches. Although watching the food chain in action can be disturbing, take comfort in knowing that the force of the falcon's strike usually dispatches its prey instantly. The kestrel usually carries off its prey to pluck and eat elsewhere, generally on a high perch.

The dramatically large **peregrine falcon** was once so rare that it was unthinkable to consider it a possible threat to feeder birds. But now that reintroduction programs have brought peregrines back to the scene, the bird may occasionally dart through a backyard in the city or countryside to grab a feathered bite of fast food. While the kestrel seeks out small birds, the much larger peregrine goes for the big prey. In the wild, it's famed as the "duck hawk," but should it choose to focus on your feeder, it will seek pigeons, doves, and starlings for its main course—although it dines on smaller birds, too. The peregrine may devour its dinner on the ground, protecting its catch by drooping its wings to form a cloak or "mantle."

Interestingly, bird feeders in cities have the advantage for peregrine visits. Originally cliff dwellers in wild places, these big falcons have adapted to the "cliffs" of skyscrapers and other edifices in our American cities. As the peregrine population improves, city pigeons may become less of a nuisance.

FALCON FOODS

- Chickadees
- Goldfinches
- Juncos
- Mice
- Mourning doves
- Pigeons
- Quail
- Siskins
- House sparrows
- Native sparrows
- Starlings
- Voles

Fall Feeding

FALL USHERS in the prime season at backyard feeding stations. Migrating birds arrive from points north, stopping to spend a day—or three—restocking their bodies with the calories they burned on the long flight. Goldfinches and grosbeaks are among the early crowd. The yellow "wild canaries" are a sure bet to pack the perches of tube feeders filled with niger seed, while the grosbeaks are a distinct possibility for lunch-time customers at the sunflower tray. You'll want to make sure you have plenty of high-fat foods on hand for these hungry travelers.

Feeder visitors vary with the seasons. In fall, you are likely to be treated to visits from family groups or small flocks of blue jays and other species.

As birds that overwinter in your area move in, they'll spend a while foraging in fields and wild areas to feast on seeds before they settle into winter territories and become regulars at your feeding station again. When you spot the first tree sparrow at a feeder, it's a sure sign that the rest of the crowd won't be far behind.

What to Watch For

You may not recognize some of the birds at your feeders in the fall—at least, not at first. Many male birds change clothes after the spring/summer breeding season, taking on colors that are similar to the female's and a far cry from their bright breeding plumage. Leaf through your field guide to familiarize yourself with the fall dress of blackbirds, bobolinks, orioles, tanagers, and other birds. Also study the pictures of immature birds, which may be making an appearance at the feeders as well.

Many birds will visit your feeders in groups of the same species, instead of singly or in pairs, as is more typical in breeding seasons. As the weeks go by, you'll see the numbers of each kind of bird rise and fall as the migrants arrive and then depart.

As the weather turns cold, the traffic at suet feeders is likely to become a waiting line. Because suet feeders are so small and don't result in much litter, I put up as many as I can squeeze in.

Be sure to keep an eye on your garden as well as on your feeders in fall. Those gone-to-seed flowers and weeds you left standing are a prime target for migrating birds, as are shrubs and trees that sport bright berries. Ground-feeding migratory birds, such as blackbirds and sparrows, may sift through leaves and mulch in your garden in search of fallen seed.

One of my favorite fall activities is to listen to birds flying overhead at night. Many songbirds migrate under the protection of darkness to avoid hawks, which fly by day. If you listen carefully, you can hear their quiet calls and chip notes filtering from the sky overhead. When I hear many birds passing over during the night, I make it a point to be outside at the crack of dawn, even before the sun rises. That's when birds drop from the sky to find food and resting places for the day. One morning, my son and I watched dozens of Baltimore orioles

10 To-Dos for Fall

1. Thoroughly clean all your feeders. Repair any loose perches, weak corners, and other structural points; rickety feeders that may have held up to light summer traffic need to be in tip-top shape for the busy season.

2. Invest in new feeders: You can never have too many! Try buying a suet feeder, nut feeder, or another specialty type that you don't already have.

3. If you live in an area where freezing weather doesn't arrive until late fall, set up an oriole feeder for nectar-drinking woodpeckers and other larger birds.

4. Clean out your birdseed storage bins. Inspect remaining stored seed. If you find seed that's infested with insects, discard it on the compost pile. Stock storage containers with fresh seed, usually available at bargain prices after the farm harvest season.

5. Replace old suet with fresh blocks or chunks.

6. Freshen the mulch beneath your feeders. Spread a 2-inch thick layer of wood chips or bark mulch over the area where seeds and hulls usually fall.

7. Plant new shrubs and trees. Find spots for them near your

feeder area. Check the regional lists of bird-friendly trees and shrubs in Landscaping on page 184 to see which plants are recommended for your area.

8. Collect ripe berries of holly (*Ilex* spp.), sumac (*Rhus* spp.), and other shrubs, as well as weed seeds, flower seeds, and nuts and acorns for the feeders. It's fun to use these treats to bring birds such as waxwings out of the bushes for easier viewing when they visit your feeders.

9. Remove fallen leaves from birdbaths daily.

10. Set up a salt block to attract finches, siskins, and other birds.

and scarlet tanagers dropping like falling leaves into the shade trees of our small town. Within an hour, the berry-covered pokeweeds and dogwoods in my garden were filled with breakfasting birds.

Millet and Nectar for Fall Stragglers

The changing leaves of fall are the signal for me to make sure I have plenty of millet on hand. This is the season when native sparrows are moving through in droves on their way to southern wintering grounds. At first the heavy sparrow traffic is made up mostly of transients, but there are always a handful of birds that stay behind to spend the winter months in my neck of the woods. The related juncos arrive soon after the sparrows, reminding me that winter will soon be here. Both sparrows and juncos prefer the tiny golden seeds of proso millet, and with 100 birds or more clustering in open tray feeders and hopping about on the ground beneath, they go through a lot of seeds. Though a sack of millet goes a long way because of the small seed size, I lay in an extra 50 pounds to make sure I'm not caught short in fall feeding season.

Hummingbirds' tiny bodies need ample fuel for the grueling trip south and to keep them warm on chilly

nights. Early fall often brings many pairs of humming wings to the nectar feeders that I keep filled to the brim. Even at Thanksgiving time, a laggard may make an appearance.

Autumn marks the switch for birds from insects to seeds. Many male birds also change from bright breeding plumage to duller colors as fall arrives.

Fast Foods for Birds

Attract many kinds of birds

IT HAPPENS TO THE BEST OF US—it's the height of feeder season, the yard is filled with customers, and you realize the birdseed can is empty. I learned my solution at my mother's knee—ransack the kitchen for anything remotely edible! Stale bread, withered fruit, and peanut butter are all fine fill-in-the-gap foods.

Keep the food preferences of your feeder birds in mind as you scan the shelves. Human foods based on grains, meat, or fruits will also appeal to your bird friends. Look, too, for anything that has nuts in it. The last slice of lunchmeat, diced into small pieces, makes a treat for jays, Carolina wrens, and other insect-eating birds that will appreciate the protein.

I usually stoop to raiding the dog food supplies, too. You can soak dry dog food in warm water to moisten it, or crush it into crumbs. Sparrows and juncos are among the first takers of this offering.

Combine various ingredients in ways that make sense to the birds: Dry foods for seed eaters, soft foods for the birds that prefer a softer diet. Proportions don't have to be exact to be a hit. Use the recipes below as a starting point for your own creativity. Such impromptu stop-gap measures will keep your birds well fed until you can get out for supplies.

Like this pigeon, most birds must rely on you to visit the drive-through for them—or to provide another source of "fast food" to satisfy their nutritional needs.

RECIPE

Blenderized Breakfast

Make this nut meal to keep chickadees, nuthatches, titmice, and woodpeckers content.

INGREDIENTS

A variety of nuts

Bacon, crumbled (optional)

Pour almonds, peanuts, pecans, walnuts, or other nuts, or a combination of nuts, into a blender or food processor. Process briefly until nuts are finely ground but not liquefied into nut butter. Stir in crumbled bacon if available. Pour into open tray feeder.

RECIPE

PB&J for the Birds

Fruit eaters and peanut butter lovers alike enjoy these quick and easy mini-sandwiches. They may tempt bluebirds, chickadees, jays, mockingbirds, orioles, robins, woodpeckers, and Carolina wrens.

INGREDIENTS

Peanut butter, creamy or chunky

2 slices bread

Grape jelly

Cornmeal

Spread peanut butter thickly on one slice of bread. Coat a second slice of bread with grape jelly. Sprinkle cornmeal thinly onto the jelly and thickly onto the peanut butter. Press slices together to make a sandwich. Using a sharp knife, slice into ½-inch chunks. Spread in tray feeder.

Stuffing-Mix Stop Gap

This multipurpose blend will fill the bellies of blue-birds, chickadees, jays, mockingbirds, nuthatches, titmice, woodpeckers, and Carolina wrens.

INGREDIENTS

Stuffing mix or bread crumbs

Hamburger, fresh or thawed

Vegetable oil, such as canola, corn, peanut, safflower, or sunflower

Check your shelves and breadbox for stuffing mix or bread crumbs, either packaged or made from fresh bread. Pour into large bowl. Add as much thawed hamburger as you can spare. Add a liberal amount of vegetable oil, and mix with a gentle lifting motion to combine. Allow 10 minutes for the bread to soak up the oil. Serve in tray feeder.

Spaghetti Supreme

Instant breakfast for crows, jays, robins, or starlings.

INGREDIENTS

Spaghetti, dry or leftover cooked pasta

Vegetable oil, such as corn, peanut, or sunflower

Raisins, currants, or chopped dried fruit

Cook spaghetti per package directions, or use leftover cooked pasta. Pour in a liberal amount of oil. Toss to coat well. Stir in raisins, currants, or chopped dried fruit. Or drain canned fruit, chop, and add to pasta. Serve in low feeder or directly on ground.

Feathers

IF YOU HAVE EVER SNUGGLED under a down quilt, you already know one of the major benefits of feathers. These specialized structures preserve body heat, a vital factor for a creature whose temperature runs about 10°F hotter than our own. Snug in their personal down jackets, birds can tolerate extremes of cold that would have an unprotected body turning blue. Take a look at the chickadees or other birds at your feeder on a chilly winter day, and you will notice that they look like butterballs, with feathers fluffed. Trapping air between the feathers increases their insulation against outside temperatures. On hot days, birds can also raise and ruffle their feathers to release excess heat.

Even a quick glance at a bird will show you that feathers vary in shape and structure. Feathers closest to the body are soft and fluffy like bits of thistle-down, while the outer body feathers have a definite shape and give the bird its contour and color. The long, stiff feathers of wings and tail serve as steering devices and provide the sturdy support needed for flight. In some birds, the tail feathers are adapted for special needs, such as the rigid, pointed tail feathers of woodpeckers, which work as props to keep the bird secure against a tree trunk.

Watch your feeder birds after a bath or following a rain shower, and you will see they don't look wet for long. Aided by applications of oil that the bird applies from the preen (or uropygial) gland near its tail, the feathers shed droplets of water like a yellow rain slicker, quickly returning to a sleek or fluffy state.

To truly appreciate the marvel of a feather, take a close look with a magnifying glass when you find a dropped feather. You will see an intricate system of interlocking hooks, or barbs (and smaller barbules), that keep every bit of the feather in place. When you see a bird drawing a feather through its bill, it is realigning these barbs to restore its structural integrity.

> In winter weather, birds fluff up their feathers to trap an insulating layer of air against the cold.

Feeder Birds

CERTAIN BIRDS ARE so well adapted to taking advantage of bird feeders and so widespread in their range that you can expect to see them just about anywhere. Friendly chickadees, finches, loudmouth jays, and juncos crop up at feeders from California to Maine. Learning the names of the regulars is the easiest way to start bird watching. You will have the luxury of looking at a bird long enough to find it in a field guide, and you will have the pleasure of getting to know the personalities and behavior of different species.

The arrival of uncommon visitors is what makes feeding birds so much fun. At migration time in spring, unusual birds may stop over for a bite of fast food before they take to the skies again, or they may visit to restore their energy before settling down nearby. In southern Indiana, I can count on a few rose-breasted grosbeaks to stop for a share of sunflowers every spring, but I know they won't stick around to nest. About the same time, brilliant indigo buntings also arrive and siphon up tiny millet seeds for a few weeks before they disperse to nearby nesting grounds.

Fall arrivals are more predictable and provide just as much pleasure. In fall, the regular feeder guests grow by several species, as northern birds take up residence for the winter. When I spot the first white-throated sparrow or junco, I know it's time to check the weather stripping and get the house in shape for winter.

Winter storms can bring unexpected customers. During one blizzard, a great blue heron sailed into my feeding station, astonishing me and panicking the songbirds. A few years ago, my sister in Pennsylvania found a juvenile night heron perched like a big brown chicken at her tray feeder. A red-shafted flicker I found after a major snowstorm—some thousand miles off course—now resides in the specimen collection of the Museum of Natural History in New York. In inclement weather when natural pickings are unreliable or nonexistent, horned larks or snow buntings may come in from the farm fields, bluebirds may travel long distances from their usual sheltering hedgerows, and birds of prey may patrol or even sample some suet.

Cardinals, jays, sparrows, and others flock together at a winter feeder. In exchange for a meal, birds will give you hours of entertainment on a snowy day.

A bobbing head feather adds to the California quail's comical charm. They are frequent winter feeder guests throughout their western haunts.

The birds you can expect to host at your feeder will depend on your geographical location and what your wild surroundings are like. If your property adjoins or is near grasslands, you may get regular visits from dicksissels, meadowlarks, quail, or vesper sparrows. In forested areas of the Northwest, the varied thrush, towhee, and fox sparrow will be regulars. In forested areas of the Midwest, you will never see a varied thrush but the spectacular scarlet tanager may honor you with its presence.

Seed eaters are the best customers at feeders because the menu is tailored to their natural preferences. Their numbers include scores of interesting species, from grosbeaks to goldfinches to the curious crossbills. Sparrows alone can become an obsession: Trying to figure out which is which can easily use up several Saturday mornings! Woodpeckers are fond of feeders, too.

Many insect-eating birds, including flycatchers, robins, wood warblers, wrens, and others, also enjoy berries and soft foods such as suet, which may lure them to your feeding station, especially when hunger is strong and natural food is scarce. Don't expect to see strictly insectivorous birds at your feeder, however: Swallows and swifts, for instance, will not be interested in your offerings. No matter how delectable, feeder food just can't compete with insects on the wing.

Most Common Feeder Birds

With a few regional variations, the following birds are most likely to visit your feeders:

- Cardinals
- Chickadees
- Doves
- Finches, such as goldfinches, house finches, and others
- Jays
- Juncos
- Nuthatches
- House sparrows
- Native sparrows, such as song sparrow, tree sparrow, white-throated sparrow, and others
- Starlings
- Titmice
- Woodpeckers

Feeder Covers

AN OPEN, UNCOVERED FEEDER gives you a great view of the birds that come to visit. That's the good news. The bad news is that an uncovered feeder also gives soaring hawks a fine look at the smorgasbord of bird life below. And it exposes the seed—and the birds—to rain, snow, and wind. Uncovered feeders also give squirrels and other seed-hogs easy access to the seed you put out for your preferred feeder visitors.

Despite these drawbacks, open feeders are still my favorites, and they are highly popular with my feeder birds. But when rainy weather settles in come the fall, I add covers to some of the tray feeders so that birds can have a choice of dining *al fresco* or beneath an awning.

Blame It on the Wind

My feeder "roofs" are functional rather than beautiful, reflecting my limited carpentry skills. But they do the job. The simplest arrangement employs a slanted roof to block prevailing winds and weather. The angle of the roof also ensures that water and snow will run or blow off. I make it from a piece of plywood that I screw to the rear corners of the tray with easy-to-remove wing nuts. My most elaborate cover design stands above the feeder on stubby wooden legs of two different lengths, providing a slanted roof that shields the entire seed tray.

In times of desperation, when winter snows blow in and birds are frantic for food, I have resorted to stapling branches of spruce and hemlock to the edge

(*continued on page 101*)

A Pest-Preventing Wire Cover

Here's how to make a wire cover that will keep out both squirrels and large birds. A feeder that's covered in this way is a good place to offer dried fruit, chopped suet, nutmeats, peanuts, and other treats that would be quickly gobbled at open-access feeders.

MATERIALS

Enamel-coated wire mesh

Wire cutters

Heavy-duty work gloves

6-inch-wide scrap board for bending wire

Twist-ties (optional)

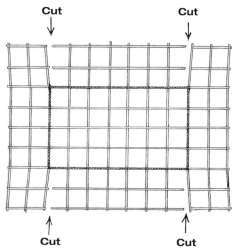

Step 1. Measure the inside dimensions of your open platform tray feeder. Buy a piece of stiff, enamel-coated wire mesh with a 1½-inch-square grid, such as that sold for garden fencing, that is 12 inches wider in both dimensions than your feeder measurements. For example, if your feeder is 12 inches × 24 inches, buy a piece of wire that measures 24 inches × 36 inches. Ask to have the wire cut to size at the store where you buy it; this timesaving step is usually free or less than a dollar.

Step 2. Using a pair of wire cutters, make two 6-inch-deep cuts, 6 inches from the left and right edges, on one long side of the piece of wire mesh.

Step 3. Repeat on the other long side.

Step 4. Don heavy-duty work gloves to protect yourself from scratches, and bend the wire to form a box shape, folding 6 inches along each edge toward the center. A 6-inch-wide board makes a good measuring tool and a useful edge to form the fold.

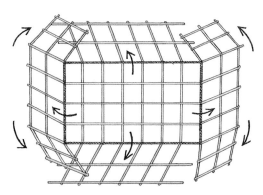

Fold to make an open-bottomed box.

Step 5. Using pliers, bend in the outer "flaps" to form the corners of your box. Lap the flaps over the corners to overlap the long edges.

Step 6. Fasten the corner flaps with twist-ties, or if the wire mesh has loose edges, by bending these wires around the grids.

Step 7. Push snugly into place inside the walls of your tray feeder.

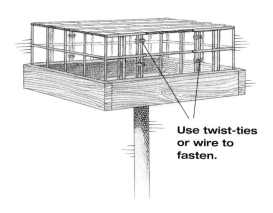

Use twist-ties or wire to fasten.

of the tray feeders on the side that faces the wind. The densely needled boughs cut the wind-driven snow much like an old-style roadside snow fence so that the feeder tray stays mostly clear of the white stuff.

No-Pest Covers

Another reason for covering feeders is to limit the kind—or size—of the visitors dining from it. A recent innovation in pest-preventing feeder design is deceptively simple—and highly effective. Wire-grid feeder covers snap into place over tray feeders, keeping out pest birds or pest animals, such as our favorite squirrels. Two styles are widely available. One includes a rigid grid that rests just above the surface of the seeds. It allows birds of all sizes to eat freely because their beaks can fit between the wires of the grid. The birds also appreciate the grid wires, which make ideal perches for feeding on the seeds below. But it's highly frustrating to squirrels.

The other style is also a wire grid, but this one is tall, raised several inches above the surface of an open tray feeder, with larger holes in the wire. Small birds easily fit between the wires to reach the feeder tray, where they can dine in peace. Larger birds, such as jays and starlings, are simply too big to squeeze in, so they are excluded. Squirrels, too, are denied entrance by the wire mesh. Both these feeder covers are fairly easy to fashion yourself.

Feeder Maintenance

THE WEAR AND TEAR OF BIRDS, squirrels, and weather takes its toll on feeders. Hooks may pull free, side boards may split, corners may come unglued. And accidents do happen—such as when your cold fingers drop the glass pane of a hopper feeder. Luckily, a little timely repair will usually save the day and give your feeder more years of useful life.

If you possess excellent carpentry skills and have a workshop full of craftsman's tools, go to it! Even if you're not a natural-born handyperson, you can still manage a number of basic feeder repairs. Here are my tools of the trade, useful even for a klutz like me for making quick feeder fixes:

Can of wood putty. This is great for filling cracks and holes where a hook has pulled free.

Putty knife. This tool's flat metal blade is useful for digging putty out of the can and applying it where holes and cracks need filling.

Screw-eye hooks. The screw-in bottoms of these handy gadgets require no tools at all to install, just a steady hand and a bit of pressure. I use them when a feeder will no longer hang from its original hook, usually because the wood has rotted around the old screw. A couple of eye hooks and a length of wire, and the feeder is ready to go again.

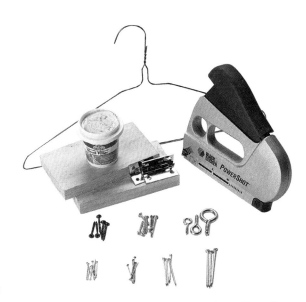

A few dollars' worth of repair tools and supplies will help you keep your feeders in working condition. These items are all handy to have on hand.

Wire coat hangers. A great source of new hooks and hanger material, coat hanger wire is flexible enough to bend into shape, yet strong enough to support a filled feeder. Double the wire for extra strength.

L-shaped metal hinges. I use these to reinforce corners that have pulled apart on feeders. Buy the largest size that will fit your edges, and screw them on with rust-proof screws.

Assorted screws and nails. It always helps to have some ready hardware when you need to do quick repairs. You can buy a prepackaged assortment, or assemble your own at a hardware store that sells loose nails and screws by weight. I prefer the latter, just because it's more fun to pick them out myself. Make sure you get weatherproof hardware that won't rust during wet weather.

A heavy-duty staple gun. You can do a lot with staples, and fast! I use my staple gun to rejoin corners that have pulled apart, attach a new side ledge, or hang a mesh bag of fat from a post. Staples are not a permanent fix for feeder repairs, although thanks to my procrastinating, they sometimes seem to be. Eventually it's best to replace these fasteners with screws or nails.

The friendly folks at my local lumberyard. When a feeder breaks, I remove the damaged side, top, or bottom, and take it to the experts, who are very willing to cut me a suitable replacement of the exact size I need. The cost is low, and the banter is always fun.

Replacing Glass

A broken hopper isn't the end of the line for a feeder as long as the rest of it is still in decent shape. Carefully remove the broken glass, and measure it exactly. Then check the Yellow Pages of your telephone book to find a business that cuts glass to size. Check whether the glass slides within a channel; if it does, take a piece of the original glass along when you go to order the glass so that they can match the thickness. Consider replacing the glass of a hopper feeder with clear, heavy-duty rigid plastic, which won't pose the danger of broken glass in case of another fumble-fingers accident.

Feeder Mounts

BIRD LOVERS EVERYWHERE cheered the introduction of black metal "shepherd's crook" poles for mounting feeders. Instead of digging a hole in the ground to sink a wooden post, or climbing into a tree to affix a dangling chain to a branch, we now need only step on the anchoring foot of a sturdy metal pole to sink it securely into the ground. And a shepherd's crook is not only easy to install, it is a good-looking addition to the garden as well.

Shepherd's crooks come in many varieties to suit your yard, your feeders, and your bird population. You can find single-armed models to hold a lone nectar feeder, tube feeder, or seed feeder. Double-armed designs will easily secure a pair of feeders. There are even crooks with multiple arms at the top to attach several feeders. If that's not enough, you can also buy add-on arms that secure onto the shaft of the pole for hanging additional feeders at various heights. Thanks to the popularity of these appealing

hangers, manufacturers have designed shepherd's crook feeders for more urban sites as well: There are short crooks that mount on deck railings, as well as hooks with heavy, flat, umbrella-stand bases for the patio.

Although I use metal hangers in my setup, I rely on wood posts to carry most of the weight—literally. Many of my feeders receive a lot of traffic, and the shepherd's crook, while strong, can sometimes tip with the weight of its customers. A wood post's solid heft supports tray feeders securely, and its brawn is well matched to the proportions of most seed feeders, looking solid and sturdy instead of puny beneath its burden. Wood posts also have a natural look that blends in with plantings and gives the feeding station a permanent feel. Because I like both looks for feeder stands, though, I do both, using some feeders on crooks and some on posts, and I even combine the two by mounting a hook on the side of a post.

Aim for Eye Appeal

Feeders are a focal point in the garden, drawing your eye as much as any carefully chosen garden ornament. Before you begin adding bird feeders willy-nilly, consider the overall look of your installations. Select the design of feeder mountings just as you would do with a piece of statuary. For tasteful good looks, keep it simple, and keep the following design concepts in mind.

Match proportions. Large feeders hanging from skinny poles or chains jar the eye because of disproportion. Match your feeders to their mounts according to their size and visual weight: A hefty horizontal feeder looks best securely mounted atop a good-size post; a see-through plastic dome or tube feeder is fine on a narrower pole.

Employ repetition. Use similar mounts, or those with complementary features, rather than mixing and matching different styles. Keep colors similar, too: Avoid mixing white and black poles, for instance. If you prefer a more formal effect than weathered wood, paint all posts black or green-black.

Think straight and solid. For the most unobtrusive arrangement, choose hangers and stands with straight lines and solid shafts, such as metal poles, long steel hooks, or wooden posts. A dozen feeders dangling from chains can make your backyard look junky.

Practice simplicity. It's easy to purchase and install shepherd's crook iron hangers, but a forest of black stands can have the same effect as a gathering of pink flamingos. I find that three black hangers is the limit for my midsize feeding area.

Mount in multiples. Think vertically as you design your feeder setup to avoid feeding station clutter. A single tall, solid wood post can support half a dozen suet, corn, or fruit feeders along its sides.

Go easy on the curves. Curved lines call for attention. Keep them to a minimum, or arrange them in a coherent way so that the eye travels naturally from one to the other rather than jumping about. Three curving iron hooks look better stacked in a vertical arrangement on

> Choose hooks and hangers to support the weight of seeds and squirrels as well as feather-light birds.

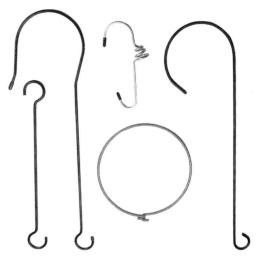

Use hangers and hooks to improve feeder access for you and birds. The small, coiled hook (*top, center*) lets you lift a feeder to a branch on a broom handle— no step-stool needed. Large hooks fit over thick branches, and the circular hanger keeps squirrels from knocking down a feeder.

the same side of a tall post than they do staggered at varying heights and positions around the post.

Hangers and Hooks

Most feeders are sold with a handle or hook on top for hanging. Examine this attachment before you buy to make sure it is sturdy and strongly attached with screws or bolts rather than staples. If a wood feeder is cracked at the point of attachment, pass it up. Look for one with a handle or hook that will hold up to heavy wear.

Also determine whether the feeder hanger will get in the way of refilling. If you have to jiggle the lid of the feeder to open it because of an intrusive handle, refilling will be a chore. Look for tube feeders with lids that slide up the bail of the handle, instead of those that have to be completely removed and replaced after filling; if you're prone to forgetting the gas cap on your car, you're likely to do the same with these feeders. I've pressed more than one mayonnaise-jar lid into service as a temporary replacement for the misplaced cap of a tube feeder.

You'll find a multitude of hooks and chains in hardware and discount stores, garden centers, bird supply shops, and other outlets. Keep stability in mind as you make your selections. Birds may be featherweights, but seed adds pounds to the weight of a feeder, and visiting squirrels can drop with force from nearby trees. Choose sturdy S-hooks that will support the weight of the birds, chain, feeder, and seed.

When purchasing your hanging equipment, go easy on the chain—swinging feeders waste seed. Niger, nectar, and small seeds can spill out easily with every sway of the feeder. Choose hooks and hangers that will keep your feeders as stable as possible. The longer the chain or the series of hooks, the more wildly the feeder will swing in strong winds or under the weight of arriving and departing customers.

Spilled food is not a problem for suet feeders, corn cob feeders, and fruit feeders, which hold food securely on spikes, in bags, or in wire cages. If you have a spot that requires lowering the feeder substantially so you can enjoy the view as your feathered friends feast, these are the feeders to suspend from wire, chain, or linked hooks.

No matter what arrangement you use for hanging your feeders, be sure they are within easy reach for cleaning and refilling. It's no fun to stretch for a feeder and have seed—or worse, sticky nectar—spill down your arm or neck.

A couple of mechanical devices that are simple to attach, widely available, and best of all, low-cost will prevent frustration with hanging feeders. Instead of unhooking your hanging feeders to refill them, or tipping them sideways to pour in seed, just attach them to a small pulley. The device will allow you to raise and lower feeders or retrieve them from a distance without stretching on tiptoes. If you use a chain or other long hanger with your feeders, invest a couple of dollars in a swivel hook to attach feeder to hanger. As the feeder turns in the wind or under the weight of birds, the swivel will prevent the chain from getting all wound up. If you can't find these labor savers in the bird feeder aisle, ask at a hardware store.

Creative Shopping

Arts and crafts shows are a great place to pick up interesting feeder mounts. Blacksmithing seems to be enjoying a comeback, and metalworkers are turning out lots of lovely styles of hooks and poles. There's a gamut of selections, from poles topped with a simple leaf shape or two to fanciful work-of-art designs with birds, hearts, and flowers—whatever suits your fancy.

Antiques shops, architectural salvage stores, and plain old junkyards are always fun to treasure-hunt in, too, if you want a bird feeder mount that functions as a garden ornament.

Feeder Placement

PUTTING OUT a spread for the birds isn't a purely altruistic gesture on our part: The payoff for us is the pleasure of watching the birds go at it. The life and color birds bring to the view outside the window is well worth the small investment in sunflower seed and other goodies. That's why the best place for your feeders is where you can easily see them. There's no point placing feeders far away from the house, unless they are supplementary stations meant to attract shyer birds that prefer to stay back, or unless you need more than one feeding station in order to accommodate an overflow crowd or a bunch of hungry squirrels or other feeder gluttons.

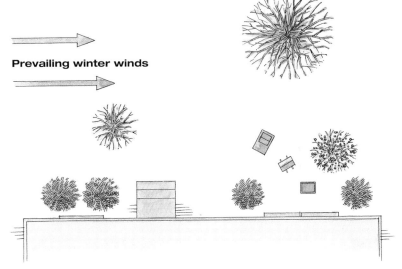

Prevailing winter winds

Choose feeder locations that offer a clear view of visiting birds and easy access for refilling. Enhance bird appeal with nearby plants for shelter.

Location, Location, Location

Deciding where you place your feeder may not be the simple decision you expect it to be. Here are some feeder placement matters for you to consider when you're choosing a location.

- Your view of the feeders
- Window dangers
- Sheltering plants for quick cover
- Height of feeders
- Prevailing winds
- Ease of filling

A Room with a View

Watching birds—and other feeder guests, such as squirrels and chipmunks—has a soothing effect on human observers. It's a great stress reliever, no matter what birds are part of the view. Whether you're watching house sparrows and city pigeons from an urban apartment, or chickadees and cardinals in the backyard of your suburban house, feeling calm and optimistic seems to be a very common "side effect" of watching birds.

When you place your feeders near a window in your house, you'll have a fine view of bird activity with or without binoculars. It's hard to get interested in feeder activity when the clients are just moving specks. But when the birds are near enough to see well, it won't take long before you and the other family members get into the habit of checking the feeder every time you walk by. You'll want to show each other unusual or interesting sightings, too, so be sure to allow plenty of room for friends and family to gather nearby.

Even family members who profess to be completely disinterested in watching birds are likely to undergo a change of heart, though it may take them some time to admit it. When my sister put up a feeder, her husband at first wanted nothing to do with it. He'd barely glance up as he walked by on his way to the living room. But within just a few short weeks, watching the birds had become a regular part of starting their day together.

Plan the position for your feeders according to how you spend your time in the house. If you wash dishes by hand, a feeder outside the window over the sink is in a perfect place. If your family gathers around the kitchen table for bagels and coffee, outside a window near the table is another excellent site. A multifeeder setup outside a family room window is another possibility. Just make sure there is clear visibility to the feeders from a sitting position and that there are comfortable chairs for viewing.

Plants in the Feeder Area

It takes much longer to lure birds to a feeder in the middle of a wide, bare lawn than to a feeder that is in a well-shrubbed area. Birds feel safer if there is cover near the feeder into which they can quickly retreat, should danger threaten. Visiting a feeder in the middle of a lawn is asking for trouble, from a bird's point of view.

A group of shrubs or a single conifer can provide enough shelter to make birds feel more comfortable. Flowerbeds, shade trees, vegetable gardens, ornamental grasses, and berry patches all contribute to a bird's sense of safety.

Be sure to keep an alert eye out for predators in this Eden, especially the ubiquitous house cat. Keep your own cats indoors, and chase away visitors or strays. (See Cats on page 57 for more ideas for pulling the welcome mat out from under a prowling kitty.)

High or Low

Birds such as chickadees and woodpeckers that spend most of their time in the trees are accustomed to eating at higher levels than birds such as towhees and sparrows that usually skulk about at ground level. That's why you will want to place your feeders accordingly.

Birds will adapt to feeders at unaccustomed heights if they are hungry enough. But your aim is to attract birds not only during winter blizzards, when the snow covers everything in sight. You also want to tempt birds to your feeders even when natural food—or the neighbor's feeder—is competing for their attention. Putting up both high and low feeders is an important way to make birds feel more at home.

Of course, seed will soon be kicked out of high feeders by foraging birds, so ground feeders like mourning doves and white-throated sparrows will still be able to find food at the level they prefer. But suet, corn, and other foods usually served in high feeders are often inaccessible to birds that stay near the ground or that lack the ability to cling to these feeders. A low tray near ground level is ideal for offering these foods to juncos, robins, and other low-level eaters.

Know Which Way the Wind Blows

Keeping warm and dry is a primary concern of birds because calories burned to stay cozy mean less energy to fuel other body functions. You'll want to put your feeder in a place protected from chilling fall and winter winds, and out of the line of driving rain and snow. Seasonal wind direction varies in different parts of the country, but in general, cold air tends to move from the north or northwest.

Block the path of prevailing winds with existing shrubs and trees or with newly planted windbreaks. Evergreens are best for the job because their dense foliage is effective in winter. You can also erect trellises of vines to cut the wind.

Keeping feeders clear of blowing snow can be frustrating. Feeder traffic is high during bad weather, and the hungry birds may be quickly reduced to pecking at a few small open areas of seed. The morning after a storm, birds will most likely be out and about before you are, and if deep or crusted snow covers their seed, they'll have a hungry wait until you help them out. In emergencies, you can erect temporary windbreaks of plywood or an old Christmas tree, which will break the force of

blowing snow so that at least a small area on the leeward side stays relatively bare of snow and gives birds access to the seeds within.

Easy Filling

Another reason to place feeders near the house is so that you don't have far to go to refill—which can be every morning during peak season. Keep in mind where the door of the house and the seed storage area are when you choose a feeder location. A short walk in summer may be an arctic trek come December.

If you live in an area of particularly bad winters, or if you know you will have difficulty leaping the drifts, consider a convenient windowsill-mounted feeder. One of the first types of bird feeders, these simple trays allow you to refill from inside the house by simply sliding open the sash and pouring in a fresh scoop of seed.

Feeder Problems

PESTS ARE THE MAIN PROBLEM at a feeder. Birds and animals can easily become nuisances, thanks to the abundance of delicious food there for the taking. Changing the menu to foods they find less appealing or changing the feeders to models that they cannot use are the best alternatives.

Feathered pests fall into two categories: bullies and hordes. Crows, jays, mockingbirds, and ravens are the bullies. They can wreak havoc with the gentle daily life of a feeding station. Apparently these birds missed their kindergarten lessons on learning to share because when they arrive at the feeder, all they see is "Mine, mine, mine!" They chase away less aggressive birds with raucous calls or threatening dashes. Mockingbirds can be especially irritating because unlike the other bullies, they don't leave the feeder when they're through eating. They stick around the feeder area, making life miserable for any other bird that dares to approach. The solution to bully birds is to add more feeders, especially models that prevent them from patronizing the feeder. In the case of a territorial mocking-

bird, you can empty the feeders altogether until the bird moves on, or you can set up other feeders at a location separated by a large visual barrier, such as a high fence or your house.

Bird pests that arrive in hordes are troublesome because they use up most of the feeder space as well as gobble much of the food. One starling at a time is not a problem. But when a dozen of them descend on your suet feeders, there's no room for a wren or nuthatch to get a bite. Blackbirds, which flock in fall and winter, can also arrive in multitudes. House finches, too, are well known for swarming a feeding station, although in recent years their numbers seem to be taking a slight downturn. Feeders with protective wire grids or cages, or with weighted perches, are highly effective at keeping at least some of your feeders free for the use of smaller birds. My solution to the hordes keeps everybody happy: I add more feeders or offer cracked corn, an excellent decoy food for blackbirds, well away from other feeders.

In the cute-but-furry department, we have the notorious squirrels, plus various pests ranging from tiny mice through hundred-pound deer. Dogs are highly effective deterrents for most furry pests. Squirrel-proof feeders will slow those varmints down or encourage them to stick to their own feeders. Better sanitation will discourage mice and other small rodents. Fencing helps keep out larger pest animals and is the only permanent solution for deer. Or, if you can't beat 'em, you might choose to enjoy them. Apples, corn, and other offerings served at a distance from the bird area are eagerly welcomed. Once the pests aren't raiding your feeders, you may enjoy watching them as much as you do the birds.

Feeders

FEEDER DESIGN HAS NOT CHANGED drastically since I began feeding birds some 30 years ago. There's a very good reason: The styles that worked well years ago still work today. The only major innovation I have seen in those years was the introduction of the tube feeder, an instant classic thanks to its sensible design, ease of use, and popularity with the birds.

Most seed feeders are simple constructions of wood, metal, or plastic that are built to last for years. Those with hoppers that dole out seed automatically are designed to hold a good quantity, so that you don't have to refill frequently. Other types of feeders are tailor-made for offering birds special treats other than the staple seeds.

Choosing a feeder is a matter of satisfying your needs and those of the birds you hope to attract. The birds that come to your yard will determine the types of food you offer, and the food, in turn, will determine which feeder(s) you use. You may need to exclude squirrels or even some pest bird species.

Baker's Dozen for the Birds

The selection of feeder types includes designs for serving just about any bird-attracting food you can imagine. Try some of these styles in your yard.

- Tray (platform) feeder
- Hopper feeder
- Suet feeder
- Tube feeder
- Stick-on window feeder
- Squirrel-proof feeder
- Caged feeder to exclude large birds
- Hanging plastic sphere feeder
- Nut feeder
- Corn feeder
- Fruit feeder
- Doughnut feeder
- Peanut butter feeder

Shopping Tips

Feeder prices vary dramatically from one supplier to another. Homemade feeders are usually the least costly, whether you make them yourself or buy them at nearby nature centers or other outlets for local craftspeople. Feeders of unusual, complicated design—such as gazebos—or those made to look like antique ornaments are the Cadillacs of the feeder business. In between, you'll find dozens of models priced affordably.

Shoddy feeders are no bargain. They'll fall apart when it's least convenient—usually just after you've filled them with the last of your seed supply. And squirrels will take advantage of lightweight and poorly constructed feeders by chewing through them with amazing speed or by dropping them to the ground to spill out the contents. Expect to pay $20 and up for a moderate-size, well-constructed feeder made of solid wood. Examine the feeder before you buy, and look for signs of good quality, such as these:

- Solid wood, not plywood

- Nails or screws at joints, not staples

- Sturdy screened bottoms in tray feeders (for drainage in wet weather and improved air circulation to prevent mold formation)

- Strong attachments for hangers

- Metal reinforcing around feeder holes to keep squirrels from chewing their way to the seed inside

Also be sure that the feeder you like is easy to open and fill. Remember that it won't be sitting on a convenient shelf when you refill—it will probably be swinging from a hanger or atop a post, and you'll be opening the feeder with one hand while you hold the container of fresh seed in the other. If you can do the imaginary filling job without frustration, take the feeder home with you. If it's tricky to handle in the store, it will likely be even more frustrating in

Simple, sturdy feeders generally are easier to fill and maintain than fussy styles. This quartet holds niger, nuts, suet, and loose seeds, satisfying all feeder birds.

your backyard on a cold, snowy day when you're wearing a pair of heavy gloves or mittens.

Size of Feeders

At least one of your feeders should be a large one that holds plenty of seed and plenty of birds. Otherwise, you will be spending an inordinate amount of time trekking to the feeder to refill.

A large, homemade tray feeder is the foundation of my feeding station. The big open tray provides abundant space for dozens of birds. They perch on the sides and scratch and peck in the tray itself. This feeder attracts both small seed eaters, such as finches and chickadees, as well as larger birds, including cardinals, jays, and grosbeaks.

Small-size feeders, such as the clear plastic kind that are attached to windows with suction cups, hold very little seed. I don't mind including small feeders in my feeding station because I enjoy the variety of shapes and sizes, and I like to watch which birds prefer the different models. Small feeders are fine for supplemental treats, but a flock of small feeders is not a suitable replacement for a large-capacity mainstay feeder.

(continued on page 112)

A Simple Roofed Feeder

With the aid of a few basic tools, you can turn out sturdy, long-lasting feeders of simple design at very reasonable cost, usually $10 or less. You'll need a solid work surface and a few tools. A jigsaw works best for cutting the curved sides of this feeder but, if cutting curves is beyond your carpentry skill level, you can make the sides straight instead.

Many nature centers offer feeder-making workshops, at which the process is taught step-by-step. Materials may already be cut to size, a nice advantage for the beginner carpenter. You can find plenty of plans for feeders in books at your library and in birding magazines. Or, if you're a more experienced handyperson, you may be able to reproduce a commercially made design in your own workshop by drawing some preliminary sketches and plans.

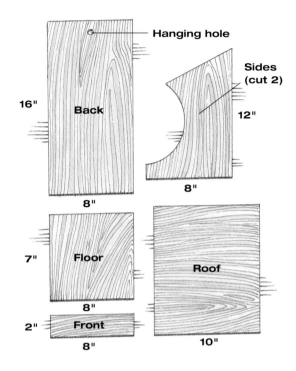

MATERIALS

½-inch plywood or other scrap lumber

Nails and screws, as needed

Caulk

Step 1. Cut (or have cut) the wood into pieces with the dimensions shown in the illustration. Be sure to cut two side pieces.

Step 2. Drill a hole in the center of the back piece, near the top, for hanging the finished feeder.

Step 3. Use nails or screws to attach the sides to the outside edge of the floor. Nailing the pieces together will speed assembly, but using screws will make a sturdier feeder. Predrill holes for screws, if needed.

Step 4. Fasten the front piece onto the exposed edges of the sides and floor.

Step 5. Attach the back piece to the exposed edges of the sides and floor.

Step 6. Put the roof on last, attaching along the top edges of the two sides and placing it as flush to the back piece as possible. Run a bead of caulk along the joint between the roof and the back to keep out water.

Step 7. Use the hanging hole in the back to mount your feeder on a likely post or wall where you can enjoy watching birds dining from it. No paint is necessary; in fact, unpainted, weathered wood is easier for the birds to grip.

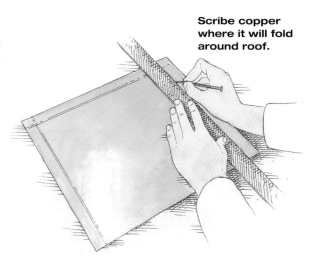

Scribe copper where it will fold around roof.

PROJECT

A Touch of Elegance

Why not create a truly handsome feeder that includes a decorative and functional copper-clad roof? Applying sheet copper to a feeder or birdhouse roof is not as difficult as it might seem; even a first-time craftsperson can achieve good results. You can make a homemade feeder fancy with the warm glow of copper, or you can gussy up a plain-Jane commercial bird feeder by covering its wooden roof with copper for a custom touch.

MATERIALS

Sheet copper, 28 gauge

Straightedge

Sturdy nail

Heavy-duty gloves

Pliers

Copper screws (optional)

Fine-grade steel wool

Polyurethane lacquer (optional)

Step 1. Measure the existing roof. Add 4 inches to the length to allow for bending copper around edges. *Note:* If the sides of the feeder extend to the roof, cut enough copper to cover only the top and edges of the roof, without bending around to the underside. To secure this type of roof, drill holes along top sides and insert short screws.

Step 2. Cut (or have cut) 28-gauge sheet copper to correct dimensions.

Step 3. To cover a flat roof, mark the dimensions of the actual roof area on the copper, using a straightedge to measure and a nail to scribe the marks on the metal.

Step 4. Position the copper along the edge of a worktable or straight-edged counter. Wearing gloves, bend the copper along the inscribed line. Repeat at inner line.

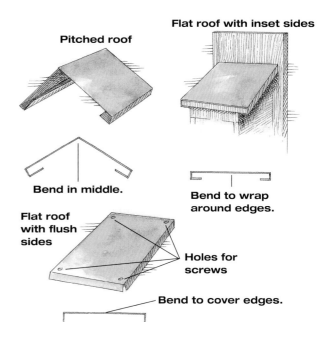

Pitched roof

Flat roof with inset sides

Bend in middle.

Bend to wrap around edges.

Flat roof with flush sides

Holes for screws

Bend to cover edges.

Step 5. For a pitched roof, bend the copper in the middle.

Step 6. Repeat Step 4 on other side of the copper sheet.

(continued on page 112)

Step 7. Slide the copper onto the roof. Tighten the copper around the roof's edges by squeezing with pliers, as necessary.

Step 8. Copper weathers when it's exposed to the elements, acquiring a soft green patina. If you want to keep its burnished metal color, you'll need to cover your finished copper creation with three coats of durable, gloss polyurethane lacquer. Before applying the polyurethane, sand the top side of the metal roof with very fine-grade steel wool to remove fingerprints and other blemishes; handle only at the edges of the metal after sanding. If you prefer a natural patina, leave the copper untreated.

(*continued from page 109*)

Feederless Feeders

One of the more interesting developments in the bird-feeding business isn't a feeder at all, in the usual sense of the word: It's a compressed block of food that makes its own feeder. At about 8 inches square, the blocks are a bit smaller than a salt block, and as an added benefit, they last a long time.

You can buy seed blocks made from sunflower, millet, and other favored seeds, or from a combination of corn, sunflower, and peanuts. Both mixtures appeal to birds as well as to squirrels, chipmunks, and other feeder visitors. Simply set the block on the ground, and it's ready to eat.

Compressed cornmeal, formed into a hard-packed cylinder for gnawing or pecking, is also available. The cylinder pushes onto a metal rod in a similar fashion to a corncob feeder. Although they cost more than corncobs, the cylinders are waste-free because all parts of it are edible, and longer-lasting, so you won't have to refill as often. They are also more difficult for squirrels to remove from the spike than a corncob, which means they won't disappear after a day or two. They're good for offering on decks or balconies.

The oldest type of feederless feeder has been around at least as long as I've been feeding birds—four decades now and counting. Though the price has gone up from the early days, "seed bells" are still a long-lasting bargain. They are made of birdseed mix or sometimes all sunflower seeds, packed tight into a molded bell shape. The bell accommodates only a single customer or perhaps two and is accessible to any clinging bird—chickadees, finches, nuthatches, titmice, and woodpeckers are the usual customers. Once the bell begins to acquire an irregular shape after weeks of nibbling, it may also be visited by less agile birds such as jays, mockingbirds, and starlings.

In the wintertime, I like to decorate the bare branches of the walnut tree in my side yard with seed bells. I vary the heights of the bells hanging from the branches, using heavy twine to attach them. To attach some bells to higher branches, I tie a generous length of twine to the bell, then knot the twine around a good-sized stone. I pitch the stone over the higher branches, retrieve the end of the string, remove the stone, and fasten the loose end of the twine to the bell.

Feeding Myths

FOLKLORE IS RAMPANT in the bird-feeding world, with myths being passed along over the backyard fence as well as through publications. When someone tells me that they've "always heard" that some bird "fact" is true, I don't believe it until I check into it myself. Thanks to the Internet, finding science-based information is a simple matter. I look for sites of reputable research institutions, such as the Audubon Society, Nature Conservancy, or university laboratories of ornithology. If you don't have access to a computer, a phone call to your

Red-dyed sugar water won't hurt your hummingbirds, but it won't help attract them either—the touches of red plastic on the feeder are enough for that.

local chapter of the Audubon Society or to a naturalist at a nearby nature center or state park can often yield the information you seek.

Here are some of the most popular myths that regularly make the rounds or are accepted as fact.

Adding red dye to hummingbird nectar will make the birds sick. FALSE. Some of us of a certain age may remember the red dye scare of a couple of decades ago, when a popular food additive was found to have carcinogenic effects in humans and was eliminated from processed foods and supermarket shelves. Perhaps that's where the hummingbird red dye myth originated. The truth is that there are no scientific studies that indicate a negative effect on hummingbirds from red dye. However, the rest of the truth is that colored nectar doesn't attract any more hummingbirds than clear nectar, as long as there's a bit of red plastic near the feeding ports. So why waste your time adding it to nectar? On the other hand, if you prefer the convenience of instant-mix commercial nectar products (which often include red coloring), there's no need to worry about killing off hummingbirds with red nectar.

Red pepper keeps squirrels from eating birdseed. TRUE. Birds aren't affected like mammals by the irritating capsaicin in hot peppers. Spraying your seed with pepper extract or buying treated seed will discourage squirrels strongly. In winter, when food is scarce, give squirrels their own feeder of untreated seeds, corn, and nuts, or they may overcome their aversion and eat the hot stuff anyway.

Clean feeders prevent disease. TRUE AND FALSE. Most instances of birds acquiring diseases at feeders are based on experiences of captive game birds or pets, which can't seek alternate food sources. I've noticed that my feeder birds don't bother with moldy seed; they simply fly off elsewhere to seek fresh food. An effort at good housekeeping is easy insurance. But the situation at feeders can also spread disease simply because of the unnatural gathering of large numbers of birds in a small place.

Should you spot a sick bird, take it as the cue to tidy up. Rake or cover hulls, and scrub feeders with a 10 percent bleach solution (10 parts water to 1 part bleach). If a few birds are showing signs of illness, empty your feeders so that the birds disperse and there is less chance of contagion. Take this opportunity to do your general housekeeping, covering the hulls and washing the feeders with a bleach solution to prevent the problem from spreading. After 1 or 2 weeks, restart your feeding program.

House finches are dying out because of eye disease. PARTLY TRUE. Those hungry hordes of house finches probably won't disappear anytime soon. House finch populations have dropped in many areas because of the spread of mycoplasmal conjunctivitis, a condition that effectively blinds the birds, after which they meet their fate from accidents, predation, or starvation. The disease is a bacterial respiratory infection that may occur in other species besides house finches. Although the disease spread dramatically at first, it appears to have tapered off, with perhaps up to 10 percent of house finches affected at any one time.

If I keep my nectar feeders up, hummingbirds won't migrate. FALSE. Birds migrate according to an internal timetable set to the hours of daylight, not because your food is too good to leave behind. Keep your nectar feeder up: After the bulk of hummingbirds depart, it can be a lifesaver for stragglers.

Don't throw rice at weddings or serve it at feeders— it will swell up in the birds' stomachs and kill them. FALSE. Rice is a big part of the diet of bobolinks, which regularly scour rice fields in the South. At the feeder, it's usually ignored in favor of other seeds. But if birds do eat it, there'll be no ill effects.

Hummingbirds migrate south by perching on the backs of flying geese. FALSE. I thought this old chestnut was dead and buried, but it seems to have come back to haunt us again. Although it may seem impossible, tiny hummers really do reach Central and South America under their own steam.

If I stop feeding the birds, they'll starve. FALSE, EXCEPT IN WINTER. But they may have a hard time for a while, until they locate other food sources. Do keep your feeders stocked in winter if you live in a cold area and if you don't have nearby neighbors that also feed birds. Low temperatures and a scarcity of natural food during a hard winter take a toll on birds, and a full feeder can mean the difference between life and death. If you're planning a winter getaway to the snowbelt, add extra suet feeders and top off the tube and hopper feeders before you go, or enlist the aid of a friend or neighbor to make sure your birds don't find the cupboard bare.

Feeding birds can change their natural habits. NO DEFINITIVE ANSWER YET. Feeders will never replace natural foods from a bird's point of view. I guess insects and wild seeds just taste better.

I am concerned, though, about the fast-increasing usage of nectar feeders by birds other than hummingbirds. After watching a downy woodpecker eschew suet and sunflowers day after day in favor of draining the sugar water dry, I couldn't help but wonder about the lack of balance in the bird's diet. Scientific research is just beginning on this question. If you worry about your birds' seeming addiction to sugar water, use nectar feeders without perches to limit access.

On the other hand, seed and suet feeders do make a difference in winter survival rates, and that is probably part of the reason why some birds are expanding their ranges. Evening grosbeaks, which used to move from the frozen Far North only in times of dire need, are much more common winter feeder visitors than they were even 20 years ago. Carolina wrens have moved in the other direction, spending winters several states northward of where they once drew the line. Several species of hummingbirds have shifted their wintering ranges, with some individuals of the species no longer trekking to Central and South America, but instead lingering in the South, where nectar feeders are abundant. The evidence could be circumstantial: Flowers have always bloomed year-round in the extreme south of this country. It's uncertain yet how big a part backyard feeders play in the expanding and changing ranges of American birds because other factors such as habitat loss, climate changes, and temporary weather conditions also play a part.

By the way, that story about swallows hibernating in the mud in swamps is a myth, too.

Feeding Stations

BIRD FEEDERS ARE like potato chips—one is just not enough. I guarantee that after you mount your first feeder, you'll soon be shopping for more. Additional feeders mean more birds, and a variety of feeders means a variety of birds. When you combine a cluster of diverse feeders, you create what is known as a feeding station: a place that birds of all kinds can come to satisfy their need for food.

The Basics

Seed feeders and suet feeders are the must-haves for any feeding station. They will supply the needs of nearly all birds that commonly visit backyards, from chickadees to jays.

Tray feeders are ideal for feeding a crowd. If you prefer to keep your seed protected and not in a help-yourself buffet, you can create more feeding room by adding more hopper-style or other enclosed feeders. Tube feeders are another good choice.

Suet feeders are always busy in winter, when this nutritious high-fat food provides ready calories to keep birds warm. Because suet feeders are small, you can provide several at your feeding station to accommodate more customers.

Special-Needs Feeders

To attract birds that don't depend mainly on seeds, you may decide to include other specialized feeders at your station. Fruit feeders and soft-food feeders that can hold doughnuts and other delights are a good place to start. Supplement these with nut feeders and corn feeders, and your feeding station will be ready to cater to just about any bird on the block.

Include several feeding devices on which to offer mockingbirds, orioles, and other fruit eaters their favorite treats. A simple nail spike feeder is perfect for skewering half an apple or orange. Small open trays are good places to pour a few handfuls of dried or fresh berries and grapes. And a plastic plant saucer makes a fine impromptu fruit feeder, since it won't absorb the juice.

Salt block

A mix of cover and open space creates ideal surroundings for a feeding station. Combine various feeders and ever-ready water—and make sure you have a good view.

Feeding Stations 115

To cater to bluebirds, provide a place in your feeding station to offer mealworms. You'll want a separate feeder for these bluebird favorites, where the shyer birds can dine in peace on their favorite treat. Position the bluebird mealworm feeder several yards from feeders frequented by aggressive guests, with an intervening shrub or trellis if possible. Or just let your bluebirds learn to share with other mealworm lovers, such as Carolina wrens.

Other Attractions

For a complete feeding station, make provisions for the other needs of birds. Grit, salt, and water will make your feeding station a one-stop shop for any bird. Clear an area for a salt block, protecting the soil beneath it and any nearby plants from leaching by lining the area with heavy-duty plastic. The shallow lid from a large plastic storage container is a good solution; cover it with a thin layer of wood chips to make it look better. Scatter grit or eggshells on open lawn, over bare soil, or in a low tray feeder.

Watching birds sip and splash in the bath is just as entertaining as watching them dine. Adding a birdbath or other water source near your feeders will accommodate birds and give you a great place to watch them bathe and drink. Keep the water far enough away from feeders to keep shells and other debris from falling in the bath. If your space is limited, a good solution is to hang a shallow basin from a hook or tree branch near a low, ground-level feeder.

Plants also add to the appeal of a feeding station, making it look more attractive to both you and the birds. Berry bushes, such as blueberries and sumac, along with other plantings that offer fruit, seeds, or insects, will satisfy the needs of birds for natural food that they can enjoy in every season.

A deck feeding station puts feeders nearby for easy filling in inclement weather. Use hull-less sunflower seed and tube feeders to reduce debris.

Field Guides

A FIELD GUIDE ILLUSTRATED WITH DRAWINGS, not photographs, is your best bet as a beginner. The classic Peterson's field guide, with separate volumes for eastern and western birds, is a great place to start. Clear drawings with arrows pointing out identification clues, such as wing bars or a notched tail, make it easy to separate one species from another. Birds are arranged by family, a great aid to learning the anatomical differences, such as shape of bill or wings. This will help you quickly peg any bird you see as a finch, say, or a blackbird—the first step to narrowing down an identification.

Although I learned many of my birds with the help of Peterson's, my favorite field guide is Golden Press' *A Guide to Field Identification of Birds of North America,* a book that covers all species found on this continent. The birds are shown in lifelike poses against a scrap of typical background: a yellow warbler on a willow branch, for instance—one of its favored haunts. The book's wide coverage was an eye-opener to me after my first few years with Peterson's narrower view. I knew the tufted titmouse from the Peterson's field guide *A Field Guide to Eastern Birds,* for example, but until I paged through the Golden guide, I had no idea that my little gray bird had such interesting western relatives. Another plus is that range maps are on the same page with the bird, unlike Peterson's guide, which sends you to an appendix of maps at the back of the book. I also like the informative text, which like all Golden guides, packs tons of interesting facts into very small spaces.

The Audubon series of field guides, illustrated with photos instead of drawings, is a book to add to your shelf for the pleasure of looking at its pictures and reading its well-researched text. But I find the photos, in which parts of a bird may be obscured by shade or vegetation, much more difficult than clear drawings to use for initial identification.

Choosing a field guide is a matter of personal taste and practical consideration. Consider these factors when you visit the bookstore.

How easy is the book to use? Pretend you have just seen a starling or robin for the first time. Try to find it in the field guide. If you fumble around or end up leafing through the book one page at a time, try another book.

How is it organized? If you're a visual person, choose a guide that has illustrations of each bird. If you prefer descriptions, focus on whether it clearly describes the birds' features.

How big and how heavy is the book? I like to carry my field guide in my pocket so I can whip it out whenever I hear or see an unfamiliar species. If the book is a convenient size to take along, you will identify birds more easily than if you have to wait until you're home to consult your bird book.

What does the book include? If you live on the water, choose a guide that will help you identify waterfowl. If you live in an area that gets extremely cold and your purpose is to provide foods for the birds you identify, make sure that information is supplied in the guide you choose.

What kind of binding does the book have? Look for a book that is stitched together at the spine, instead of only glued. Your field guide is going to get a lot of wear and tear. Select one that will last.

The Advanced Class

Once you've mastered the basics, you may want to graduate to the advanced field guides, which offer great help for figuring out the identification of shorebirds, wood warblers, and other frustrating species.

Familiarity with the birds themselves is just as vital as an advanced field guide in your backpack. The more time you spend watching birds, the more familiar you'll become with their behavior and their voices. I find that once I know the difference between the ways similar species sound and act, I'm not likely to be confused by variations in plumage. Referring to advanced field guides is a shortcut to spending hours in the field because they include notes on behavior that can help you tell similar species apart.

Finches

THE FINCH FAMILY is a large one that includes birds commonly called finches as well as buntings, cardinals, grosbeaks, siskins, sparrows, and others. Goldfinches also belong to the big finch family, but because they are one of the most common and widespread feeder birds, they warrant their own entry in this book. Except for the goldfinch, the birds that share the common name "finch"—the house finch, purple finch, Cassin's finch, and three western rosy finch species—have one obvious thing in common: The adult males all are blushing with beautiful rosy color.

The ubiquitous **house finch** is the most common of the four species. Once a California bird known as the linnet, its now coast-to-coast range is yet another example of humans interfering with nature. Traders sold it illegally as a cage bird during the heyday of canaries and other avian pets some 50 years ago. When federal authorities began closing in on East Coast pet shops, owners released the captives illegally. The species readily adapted to life on the opposite side of the continent, and the quickly expanding population met the West Coast birds that were simultaneously spreading eastward. The popularity of blue spruces in the home landscape made the once-treeless Plains bridgeable, encouraging the house finch's expansion. Be alert for color variations in the male house finches that visit your feeder. Some birds are orange or golden instead of reddish purple.

House finches can build to huge numbers at feeding stations. In recent years, the house finch population has decreased somewhat due to a wave of infectious eye disease called mycoplasmal

Look for the perky cap and deep raspberry color to distinguish the purple finch from its reddish relations. Females have a distinct white eye stripe.

It takes a sharp eye—or a careful ear—to separate the Cassin's finch of western conifer forests from its similar relatives. Its unique song offers positive ID.

conjunctivitis, which spreads quickly through the inbred eastern house finches.

Less invasive and often more welcome at feeders are two other similarly colored finches. In the West, **Cassin's finch** is fairly common, although it forages mainly in the wild and in backyard conifers rather than at feeders. The **purple finch,** most intensely colored of the three, breeds far in the North but winters south to the Gulf Coast and California. It is often confused with the house finch, although when the birds are side by side, it's easy to see that the purple finch is more brightly colored, with a distinctive eye stripe.

Females of these three species are streaky brown. The female purple finch sports a bold white eye stripe.

In the West, three species of rosy finches join the group. The **gray-crowned rosy finch** is most widespread. These birds are tinted with rosy pink over their brown bodies, and they wear a noticeable light gray cap with a black patch above the beak. The **black rosy finch,** an uncommon bird of western mountains, is dramatically dark in color with rose-colored wings and a gray cap. The **brown-capped rosy finch,** found in a very limited range especially in Colorado, is similar to the gray-capped but has a brown head. All three races live high in the mountains, nesting above timberline, although they come to lower elevations in winter. They are uncommon at feeders.

Finch Behavior

The red finches have lovely, warbling voices and sing loudly and often. Even the female house finch is renowned as a singer; she sometimes holds forth even when sitting on the nest. That beautiful song issuing from the tree canopy could very well be coming from a singing finch.

Often misidentified as a "purple finch," the house finch is so populous in some areas that it has become too much of a good thing.

When finches visit your feeder in quantity, they can forget their manners in a fight for the food. Keep squabbles to a minimum by providing plenty of feeding space where they can reach their favorite seeds.

Finches are big fans of salt. Provide a salt block to satisfy their craving for the mineral. Cassin's finches may not come for seeds at your feeder, but they are likely to visit a salt station. Gravel and grit also attract them.

In late winter, watch for finches sipping sap from broken twigs on maples, box elders, and other trees. House finches seem particularly fond of this treat. Addicted to nectar feeders, these birds may hog the perches at a hummingbird feeder for hours at a time.

FINCH FEEDER FOODS
▪ Bread crumbs
▪ Crushed eggshells
▪ Fruit (house finches)
▪ Millet
▪ Nectar (house finches)
▪ Niger
▪ Salt
▪ Sunflower seeds, any kind

Flax

Attracts buntings, goldfinches, purple and other finches

IF YOU'VE EVER POURED a premium finch seed mix into your feeder, you may have noticed a lovely volunteer plant growing nearby a few months later. Extremely delicate, with small needlelike leaves on a fine stem topped by a cluster of silky, sky blue flowers, flax is a beautiful garden flower as well as a favorite of finches. It also produces the fiber used to make linen fabric.

Flax seed is ultra-high in oil. Use the back of your thumbnail to press one of the flat, shiny brown seeds against a piece of paper and you'll see a greasy smear. That's great news for buntings, goldfinches, purple finches, and other small, high-energy birds, who seek out the high-calorie seeds to keep their active bodies stoked with fuel.

Most birdseed dealers sell flax seed only as part of a high-priced mix. Check with your closest feed mill or farm-supply store to see if you can buy the seed at bulk prices, which will save you a bundle when you make your own custom birdseed blends.

You could build a whole cottage industry around annual flax (*Linum usitatissimum*), which is simple to grow in a sunny spot. Besides fabric and birdseed, flax is also used to make thin paper—for Bibles, cigarette rolling papers, and old-fashioned onionskin writing paper. The seeds are pressed commercially to yield linseed oil and animal feed additives. But if you want to limit your plantation to birdseed, simply scatter the seeds thickly over prepared soil, press into the soil with a lawn roller, and wait for a field of blue flowers to appear. Let it stand in bloom, and as the flowers fade, it will attract birds for months.

The mission in life of an annual flower is to reproduce itself, and that means lots of seeds, since its roots won't survive a second season. But perennial flax species are also attractive to birds, even though their seeds aren't as abundant as those of most annual species. The plant most commonly known as perennial flax, *Linum perenne*, is a popular garden flower because of its graceful appearance and pretty

Silken blue flowers make flax a beautiful addition to the bird-friendly garden, but it's the shiny brown seeds that birds love. They're a goldfinch magnet.

sky blue flowers. Its clumps of wiry stems are clothed in delicate needle-like foliage. Like annual flax, its blossoms open in the morning and close by afternoon, except on cloudy days. The lookalike prairie flax (*Linum perenne* subsp. *lewisii*) of western North America has a slightly more robust look, as does the species *L. narbonense*, which is gaining popularity in perennial gardens.

If blue doesn't fit your color scheme, how about yellow flax, red flax, or white flax? With more than 200 species in the big *Linum* genus, there's a color to suit every garden. I adore the silky rose-red flowers of *L. grandiflorum*, another super-easy annual to grow in a sunny spot, and the finches and siskins adore its seeds. Golden flax (*L. flavum*) glows with warm color, but this perennial is tough when it comes to winter cold—I've seen it flourishing in Zone 4 gardens. Whatever flax you choose, be assured that the birds will approve.

Flickers

Is IT THE CALL or the flashy white rump patch that gives flickers their name? Before you decide, consider a third possibility: that these big, brown woodpeckers were nicknamed for the glimpse of bright color beneath their wings that shows only in flight.

Flickers may hold the record for bird nicknames. According to the definitive collection made by Frank L. Burns and published in the *Wilson Bulletin of Ornithology* in April 1900, there were once 126 names for the bird, including yellowhammer, goldenwings, partridge woodpecker, pigeon woodpecker, high-hole, harry-wicket, wake-up, and, my favorite, yawker bird.

A bird with that many names obviously was conspicuous in 1900, and it remains hard to overlook. Its loud, ringing "Wicka-wicka-wicka" call can be heard resounding through woods, across small town streets, and over country fields and golf courses. Besides their loud voice, these big, beautiful woodpeckers boast a white rump patch visible in flight that tells the world who they are from a distance.

The species known as the common flicker includes three races, or subspecies, which together provide a flicker for almost every corner of the country. All races have brightly colored undersides of wings and tail feathers that help distinguish them. In the eastern two-thirds, the **yellow-shafted flicker** flashes shining golden feathers with every wing stroke. Like the others, this race has a barred brown back, with a wildly spotted white breast and belly and a dashing slash of black across its throat. In the Southwest, the **gilded flicker**, also a yellow-winged race, rules the roost. In the West, it's

Unlike most woodpeckers, flickers wear brown feathers instead of black and white. They're named for the white rump patch that "flickers" when they fly.

the striking **red-shafted flicker** that prevails. Just to make things confusing, the ranges of the races overlap, and these closely related birds frequently hybridize. It's not unusual to see a flicker with the head markings of a yellow-shafted but the wing color of the red-shafted race, or any other combination you can think of. Red-shafted birds occasionally stray far eastward of their normal range.

Flicker Behavior

Unlike most woodpeckers, flickers don't stick to the trees. You will frequently see these birds on the ground, where they gobble beetle grubs or nip up ants. Lawns are attractive to them. A flicker or two or six often join the mixed flocks of starlings, robins, and other birds that settle on lawns in late summer and fall.

In breeding season, flickers can be a pain in the ears. Not only do they vocalize loudly, they also drum on resonant surfaces to mark their territories or to impress a mate. Flickers favor tin roofs and wood-sided houses as percussion instruments.

FLICKER FEEDER FOODS

■ Amelanchier (*Amelanchier* spp.) berries

■ Blueberries (*Vaccinium* spp.)

■ Bread and other baked goods

■ Grass seeds

■ Peanut butter

■ Peanut butter and cornmeal recipes

■ Suet

■ Sumac (*Rhus* spp.) berries

■ Watermelon

Flicker courtship is amorous indeed. If you see a female bird perched on a tree or pole, with two or more males below her, you can bet they are dueling for her attention. Taking turns, first one male will hitch up the tree toward the female, contorting his body and finally flashing his wings in an attempt to blind her with his suitability as a mate. Then the next bird gets his turn to impress. I have sometimes watched as many as five male flickers wooing a single female.

Starlings often take a liking to flicker nest cavities, sitting back while the woodpeckers do the excavating work and then attempting a hostile takeover when the nest hole is ready. If you hear flickers making a commotion, it may be the beginning of a fierce anti-starling defense of their home.

Flickers are a great reason to treasure the anthills in your yard or the trails of ants walking up and down tree trunks or to your nectar feeder. The big woodpeckers eat these insects like candy. Of course, when they finish chowing down on the ants at your nectar feeder, they may settle on the container for a long bout of sugar-water sipping.

Flickers are agile clinging birds that can use high-level feeders, low trays, suet cages, and nectar feeders (which tend to swing violently initially under their weight). In the parched Southwest, try putting out a half of a watermelon or chunks of the sweet fruit on a tray feeder to tempt the gilded flicker to visit your feeding station.

Eastern flickers boast golden yellow underwings, but salmon red identifies this western bird. Both subspecies may wander, so watch flying flickers closely.

In colder regions, flickers may stick around in winter instead of migrating southward if the weather is milder than usual. A hand-cranked meat grinder, which you can buy from catalogs or at country stores, especially in Amish or Mennonite areas, is the perfect accessory for winter flicker feeding. Use it to grind suet into hamburger-like consistency and spread in an open tray feeder to delight every lingering flicker in the neighborhood.

Male or Female?

LOOK CLOSELY at the heads of flickers with binoculars to learn to tell male from female and one race from another. All races and both sexes have a black throat swash.

Flicker Race	Sex	Head Cap	Red Nape	Mustache	Face	Underwing Color
Yellow-shafted	M	Gray	Yes	Black	Tan	Golden
Yellow-shafted	F	Gray	Yes	None	Tan	Golden
Red-shafted	M	Brown	No	Red	Gray	Salmon-red
Red-shafted	F	Brown	No	None	Gray	Salmon-red
Gilded	M	Brown	No	Red	Gray	Golden
Gilded	F	Brown	No	None	Gray	Golden

Flowers for Birds

Attract many birds at various times of the year

FOR THE MOST PART, gardeners choose the flowers they grow based on color and/or fragrance. But birds have an entirely different agenda when it comes to their floral favorites. If you want to use your flower garden to tempt birds into visiting your yard, look for flowering plants that provide edible seeds, useful nesting materials, or shelter for safety and nesting. Except for nectar-sipping orioles and hummingbirds, birds are uninterested in the blossoms themselves unless they attract small insects, another mainstay on the bird menu.

Flowering plants tempt birds with cover as well as seeds and nectar. Branching plants benefit birds seeking shelter. Insects add even more bird appeal.

More is better when it comes to bird gardens. A single potted plant won't attract much, if any, avian attention. But a wide bed with a variety of plants is bound to be a popular spot, thanks to the insects that live among the leaves, branches, and flowers. Those aphids you despise are a delicious appetizer to chickadees; your plump tomato hornworms are as desirable as prime rib to a brown thrasher. Even the Japanese beetles devouring your roses are appealing to foraging birds.

Flowers for Food

Keep in mind that a yard filled with flowers attracts zillions of insects, which are manna to birds. Even if you're growing flowers that don't yield seeds or fruits for bird dining, they'll still add something for hungry birds to munch on. Daisies (*Chrysanthemum* spp.), oregano (*Origanum vulgare*), yarrows (*Achillea* spp.), and other flowering plants that produce clusters of many tiny nectar-rich flowers are best for attracting the small insects that bring in the birds!

Foraging birds move fast, unless they're shelling seeds or sipping nectar, so you may not even notice the many songbird visits to your flower garden. Place a comfy bench or small tea table and chair near your flower garden and notice who comes to call, especially in early summer when nesting is at a peak and parent birds have hungry mouths to feed. You may spot bluebirds, catbirds, orioles, thrushes, towhees—in fact, any nearby resident birds—flitting from plant to plant for munchies on the move.

If you hope to grow seeds for your flock along with your flowers, start with the plants listed in "Annual Flowers for Birds" on page 126. Annuals are prolific seed producers and, therefore, a best bet where birds are concerned. Perennial flowers tend to be stingier with their seeds, but some are worthwhile from a bird's point of view. Take a look at "Perennial Flowers for Birds" on page 127 to see which "seedy" perennials to include in your birdseed flowerbed.

Flowering weeds are also great for the bird garden: common chicory, goldenrod, the dandelion-like hawkweed, and the tiny pink-flowered plants called knotweeds are just a few of the weeds that help feed the birds. (For more on weeds attractive to birds, see Weeds on page 327.)

Flowers for Nesting Material

Plant fibers and twigs are two top components of many bird nests. If you let your garden plants stand over winter, their stems will be weathered just right for birds to strip long lengths of fiber from them at spring nesting time.

Any perennial or annual flower with stiff, slim twiggy branches is a prime candidate for nesting material. If you can bring yourself to delay spring cleanup, you can watch birds collecting sticks or stringy leaves from many garden flowers, including bearded iris (*Iris* bearded hybrids), Siberian iris (*Iris siberica*), mallows (*Hibiscus* and *Malva* spp.), liriopes (*Liriope* spp.), and many others. If you prefer a tidy garden, collect the stalks of fibrous plants and pile them beside your compost pile or in view of a favorite window for orioles to harvest at nesting time.

Flowers for Shelter and Nesting Sites

A densely planted flower garden that features tall, branching plants as well as clumps of plants closer to the ground provides useful shelter to birds in your backyard. Lush flower gardens give birds a place to wait out rain and wind. If the flowers are near your feeders, birds can use the flowerbed as an escape route in case of predators or panic. Be aware that prowling cats may also use flowers near feeders as cover for sneaking up on birds. If cats are a problem in your yard, keep the flowers at least 6 feet from the feeders.

Birds that spend most of their lives on or near the ground may even become residents of your flower garden. Buntings, native sparrows, and common yellowthroats are the birds most likely to turn up because they aren't as shy as others when it comes to human interference. In relatively undisturbed corners, you may also find thrushes and towhees making themselves at home.

Ground-nesting birds like to snuggle their woven cups against a dense clump of grass or among thick

Composite flowers like this zinnia are made up of many small flowers, each of which produces a seed. A single zinnia seedhead can keep a goldfinch busy for an hour, as it cracks its way through the nutritious banquet, one seed at a time.

plant stems, where they're hidden from view. Flowers that grow into shrub-size plants or those that form thick colonies are ideal nesting sites for indigo buntings and the common yellowthroat. Song sparrows often nest among daylilies (*Hemerocallis* spp.) and in groundcovers, while white-crowned sparrows favor lupines (*Lupinus* spp.).

Designing Flower Gardens for Birds

Time to think like a bird again: When it comes to designing a garden, you'll want to provide protective cover and food first because these two work hand in hand to tempt birds into lingering in your yard. Begin by considering where birds spend their time in the wild and where they hunt for food naturally. Then apply those insights to your flower garden plan, keeping in mind what birds you want to attract:

- Robins and a few other birds, like grackles and starlings, appreciate a sparsely planted garden, with neatly weeded space between the plants because that gives them easy access to open soil for pulling worms and finding bugs.

- Grosbeaks, orioles, tanagers, vireos, warblers, and other birds that spend most of their time in the trees are lured to lower levels by abundant fruit or insects—their favorite foods. They prefer to stick close to cover, so make sure your flowerbeds form a corridor that leads to and from the safety of trees.

- Buntings and native sparrows are low on the food chain, so they spend most of their time in thick vegetation. In the wild, they stay in the brushy edges of fields and roadsides. In your flower garden, they'll appreciate plenty of taller, branching plants that mimic the shrubs in their wild habitat.

- Cardinals, catbirds, mockingbirds, and wrens aren't as shy as other songbirds because they're accustomed to living around people. But densely planted flowers of varying heights will keep them safe while they search for food in your garden.

GARDEN DESIGN

Birdseed Flower Garden

Seed-eating birds are, of course, accustomed to getting their seeds from plants as well as from bird feeders. This garden lets you cut out the steps of buying seed and putting it into feeders. Instead, grow a lush garden filled with these seed-producing flowers and enjoy the view: pretty flowers for you and plenty of seeds for your bird buddies. You can grow all of these annuals from seed started indoors in late winter or sown directly where you want your garden to grow.

PLANT LIST

1. 'Lemon Queen' sunflowers (*Helianthus* spp.)
2. 'Rosa' cosmos (*Cosmos bipinnatus* 'Rosa')
3. Bachelor's buttons (*Centaurea cyanus*)
4. Love-lies-bleeding (*Amaranthus caudatus*)
5. 'Vanilla Ice' sunflowers (*Helianthus* spp.)
6. Garden balsam (*Impatiens balsamina*)

Annual Flowers for Birds

ANNUAL FLOWERS are terrific bird plants because they produce ample amounts of snackable seeds. Think how many seeds are in a double-flowered zinnia—one seed per petal—and multiply by the dozens of blossoms a plant produces to get an idea of the bounty an annual garden brings for birds. Plant self-sowing annuals where their free-seeding ways won't turn them into perennial garden pests.

Flower	Description	Birds Attracted	Comments
Tickseed sunflower (*Bidens aristosa*)	Billowy, ferny-leaved plant to 4 feet tall and wide, with masses of fragrant yellow daisies that attract butterflies	Bobwhites, buntings, cardinals, chickadees, goldfinches, house finches, purple finches, other finches, pheasants, redpolls, siskins, sparrows, titmice	Self-sows abundantly; nice to fill a sunny hillside. Buntings and sparrows may nest at the base of a cluster of plants. Flowers attract many insects that bring in flycatchers, orioles, vireos, warblers, and other insect eaters.
Cosmos (*Cosmos bipinnatus, C. sulphureus*)	Tall, graceful plants with ferny foliage and flowers in shades of pink, white, or red-purple (*C. bipinnatus*) or yellow and orange (*C. sulphureus*)	Buntings, goldfinches, house finches, redpolls, siskins	Seeds ripen while other flowers are still blooming; look closely to see feeding birds. Self-sows.
Annual sunflowers (*Helianthus annuus, H. debilis*)	Tall, usually single-stemmed plants with cream, yellow, rust, or bi-colored flowers atop and along stem; *H. debilis* types are multibranching.	Cardinals, chickadees, finches, jays, titmice, woodpeckers	Plant at 2-week intervals for a steady seed supply. Cut some heads to save for fall and winter feeding. Self-sows.
Garden balsam (*Impatiens balsamina*)	Short, bushy plant with hummingbird-attracting flowers in pastel pink, lavender, and white	Cardinals, grosbeaks, hummingbirds, towhees	Self-sows. Watch for towhees scavenging fallen seeds beneath the plants.
Impatiens (*Impatiens wallerana*)	Familiar bedding and container plant with bright or pastel hummingbird-attracting flowers in all colors but blue	Cardinals, grosbeaks, hummingbirds	Perennial in mild climates
Marigolds (*Tagetes* spp.)	Ruffled, multipetaled or single flowers in shades of gold, rust, maroon, and yellow; ferny, aromatic foliage	Juncos, siskins, native sparrows	Not as popular as other annuals, but birds will visit them in winter when other seeds are scarce if you let the plants stand.
Mexican sunflower (*Tithonia rotundifolia*)	Eye-catching plant to 6 feet tall with zingy orange-red daisies that attract multitudes of butterflies and hummingbirds	Buntings, cardinals, doves, finches, hummingbirds, jays, sparrows, titmice, towhees	Look for birds both on the seedheads and at the base of the plants. Buntings and sparrows may nest beneath these bushy plants in an undisturbed garden area.
Zinnias (*Zinnia* spp.)	Fast-blooming favorites in sizes from dwarf to tall, with single or multipetaled flowers in rich, saturated hues and delicate pastels; all colors but blue	Buntings, cardinals, chickadees, goldfinches and other finches, redpolls, siskins, sparrows, titmice	Plant shorter varieties in front of tall types to hide ragged bottom foliage.

Perennial Flowers for Birds

PERENNIALS ARE rarely as generous as annuals with their seeds, although exceptions exist among members of the daisy family, which often produce a bumper crop. Some perennials make up for their sparse seed production by yielding bird-attracting fruits. When its spikes of black berries are ripe, the common groundcover liriope attracts bluebirds faster than a tray of mealworms.

Flower	Description	Birds Attracted	Comments
Jack-in-the-pulpit (*Arisaema trifolium*)	Three-part leaves grow below an unusual hooded flower that matures to a tight-packed cluster of glossy red berries; shade lover	Pheasants, gray-cheeked thrushes, wood thrushes, wild turkeys	Chipmunks will also nibble seeds. Pluck a few seeds to start in pots to expand your planting.
Purple coneflower (*Echinacea purpurea*)	Clump-forming plant produces many lavender-purple daisies with attractive raised golden centers	Buntings, finches, juncos, siskins, sparrows, towhees	Attracts butterflies and other insects, which may lure flycatchers and orioles to your garden. Self-sows moderately.
Perennial sunflowers (*Helianthus* spp.)	Tall, branching golden daisies that usually spread to the point of invasiveness by underground roots	Buntings, finches, juncos, sparrows, towhees	Plant in a natural meadow or wilder part of the garden where their aggressiveness won't swamp neighboring plants. Good with native grasses.
Liriopes (*Liriope* spp.)	Short, grassy clumps of foliage with spikes of purple or white flowers followed by black berries	Bluebirds, mockingbirds	Edge a bed or fill a shady nook with liriope to attract bluebirds from a distance.
Lupines (*Lupinus* spp.)	Dense spikes of pea-blossom–shaped flowers arise from clumping or sprawling plants; with nearly 200 native North American species, size, habit, and color vary widely.	Bobwhites, Clark's nutcrackers, quail, native sparrows, wild turkeys	All legumes, lupines included, are good food sources for game birds and some ground-feeding songbirds.
Buttercups (*Ranunculus* spp.)	Buttery yellow 5-petaled flowers spark clumps of deep green leaves; often spreading	Bobwhites, buntings, grouse, pheasants, quail, redpolls, sparrows, wild turkeys	Good for the natural garden or around the garden pool. Some species can be invasive; *R. constantinopolitanus, R. glacialis,* and *R. rhomboideus* are not overly aggressive.
Gloriosa daisy (*Rudbeckia hirta* 'Gloriosa')	Clump-forming biennial to perennial plant with tall stems of large daisies in buttery yellows and rich rusty browns; some bicolors	Buntings, cardinals, finches, juncos, siskins, sparrows, towhees	Self-sows moderately. Don't confuse with *Rudbeckia* 'Goldsturm', a sterile cultivar that rarely sets edible seeds and thus holds no interest for birds.
Goldenrods (*Solidago* spp.)	Plumes of golden flowers atop plants ranging from knee-high to shoulder height, depending on species	Prairie chickens, goldfinches, grouse, juncos, pine siskins, swamp sparrows, tree sparrows	Especially handsome combined with blue or purple late-blooming asters
Violets (*Viola* spp.)	Ground-hugging plants with usually heart-shaped leaves and dainty blue, purple, or white flowers	Bobwhites, doves, grouse, juncos, quail, native sparrows, wild turkeys	Wild turkeys scratch out and eat the tuberous roots of violets, while other species favor the seeds.

Flying Squirrels

IF YOUR BIRDSEED is disappearing overnight, the leading suspect may be a creature that flies in from the treetops. No, this isn't some unusual seed-eating owl that's emptying your feeders—it's a flying squirrel.

Nocturnal cousin of the chipmunk and ubiquitous squirrels, the flying squirrel is a gentle little creature with huge dark eyes—the better to see in the dark with, my dear. It is soft brown with a pale belly and an odd, flattened tail that looks as if it was pressed between the pages of a book. Folds of furred skin along the side of its body stretch open when the animal spreads its front and back legs wide, catching the air like a parasail as it glides downward from the trees.

Recent research indicates that flying squirrels may be even more numerous than our familiar daytime squirrels. Because they are rarely seen, they were once thought to be a rarity. But scientists have taken to the trees to find them and are still collecting data on flying squirrel populations.

The first flying squirrel I ever saw was rustling like a mouse in a box of peanut brittle on my kitchen counter. The rustling alerted my cat and me at the same time, but I investigated first. Instead of the mouse I expected, I met a fearless little animal—cute is the only word to describe it. It sat up on its hind legs and looked at me with bright button eyes. It didn't seem at all scared and was easily tempted to nibble daintily on some black walnuts I offered.

Once I knew I had flying squirrels in my neighborhood, I began looking for them at the feeder. Every night at about 11 P.M., two to five squirrels would arrive one by one, sailing in from the oaks (*Quercus* spp.) and tulip poplars (*Liriodendron tulipfera*). They'd sit in the open tray feeder of sunflower seeds and feast for an hour or so, then depart to look for acorns beneath the oak.

Look for flying squirrels at dusk, when they become active, often sailing across roads or from one

A nocturnal charmer, the flying squirrel is less of a glutton than its daytime kin. These tame mammals probably visit feeders more often than we realize.

large shade tree to another. The smaller type occurs from Maine to Minnesota, south to Texas and Florida; a larger subspecies ranges across the North; and a third type populates mountains from Canada south to California, Utah, and Tennessee. Flying squirrels make their homes in rotted-out knotholes or other cavities high in the treetops, or they may nest in dead snags and even bird boxes.

These squirrels are actually excellent gliders, since they are unable to achieve lift and thus don't actually fly. Observers have measured single glides of more than 150 feet starting from a perch 60 feet high. On the ground, flying squirrels are speedy runners. Although their habits are not fully known, they probably dine on bird eggs and perhaps nestlings as well as their favored acorns and nuts. The flying squirrels at my feeder also enjoy peanut butter, suet, raisins, grapes, and an occasional slice of apple.

Freezer Treats

Attract many kinds of birds

IT'S EASY TO STORE plenty of birdseed year-round, but soft foods such as bread and leftovers can pile up quickly, especially in summer, when the feeder traffic slacks off but the family keeps eating. I solve the storage problem by using my freezer. In winter, I'm always glad I did because I can pull out ready-to-feed freezer treats whenever the birds need extra food or a change of pace.

Resealable plastic bags in large and small sizes are my main storage containers. They let me see at a glance what's available, unlike rigid plastic containers that don't show the inventory.

Here's what's usually in my freezer:

- Cottage-cheese cups filled with suet or bacon fat

- Bags of chopped suet

- Bags of nuts, bought on sale

- A large bag of mixed crackers, stale bread, and other baked goods

- Bags of leftover fruit, or meat and egg scraps for making treats

- A stockpile of bird-appealing, hand-molded logs, balls, and cups of frozen food (see below)

Collecting Ingredients

Every day, I add bread crusts, cornbread crumbs, bagel remains, and any other grain-based products to a plastic freezer bag that I keep on the counter. When I wipe breakfast toast crumbs or the flour from rolling out pastry from my table or counters, I swipe the crumbs directly into the mixed bag.

I use another plastic bag when I'm cooking or serving fruit. Stray grapes, squishy blueberries, past-their-prime bananas, and apple cores all go in the bag. Meats, eggs, and fatty foods, like leftover meatballs, chicken skin, trimmed fat from roasts, bacon crumbles, and other goodies go in another bag when it's cleanup time. Nuts and peanuts, which are always precious because they're so popular and

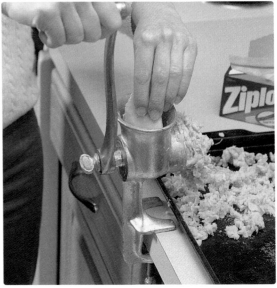

An old-fashioned meat grinder is the best tool for reducing chunks of suet to bite-size pieces for birds. Grind a big batch to stock your freezer for winter.

expensive compared to other foods, go in another bag. The last bag—for leftovers—comes in handy after the meal or when I periodically clean out the refrigerator. It feels great to toss that half-cup of cooked spaghetti or applesauce into a bag for the birds instead of watching it grow green mold in a hidden corner of the fridge.

The last big plastic bag in my freezer is a conglomeration of leftovers that I didn't bother sorting: stale cereal, sandwich crusts, pizza slices, meat drippings, old lunchmeat—whatever stray foods look like they might have bird potential. Anything based on grains, nuts, fruits, or meats is fair game. Don't overlook that last spoonful of soup or stew—chances are, it has something bird-edible in it.

Cookbooks usually have advice about what to freeze and what not to. In my experience, the reason for not freezing some foods is that the texture may change for the worse by human standards.

Birds aren't nearly so fussy. Unless you serve them something they don't eat at all—cooked green beans, for example—they'll gobble it up whether it's mushy or not.

The quick and easy way to serve this stuff is to merely dump it into an accommodating feeder, but that invites a few too many starlings, even for my tolerance level. If I'm trying to distract pesky birds away from the main feeding area, the dump-it method is appropriate. But usually I hoard my leftovers to make recipes that will attract the birds I treasure most: jays, woodpeckers, wrens, and the other smaller feeder customers. By combining ingredients to appeal to fruit, nut, or meat eaters, I can better target the beneficiaries of my kitchen cleanups.

Preparing Freezer Treats

In my house, bread and other baked products outnumber other leftovers by a huge margin. That should probably make me ashamed of wasting so much food, but instead it makes me feel as rich as Midas. As I watch the resealable bags pile up, I count my wealth in bread crusts instead of gold.

Because so many of my feeder friends welcome bread crumbs, I use my blender to whirl the frozen baked goods into coarse or fine crumbs. Chickadees, juncos, robins, sparrows, towhees, and their chums don't mind a bit that they're consuming crumbs of uncertain parentage. Was it a frozen waffle or an onion bagel? The birds don't care!

I invented my freezer treat recipes by watching what the birds at my feeders prefer to eat. So far, the only things that my birds usually spurn are raw or cooked vegetables, white rice, cheese, and other dairy products (although a friend swears that her mockingbird downs sour cream). Experiment with your own combinations. It's fun to get to know which blue-plate specials your regulars order most often.

Experimenting also comes into play when you're figuring out how much of a binding material, such as oil or peanut butter, you'll need to make your treats. Start with small amounts. You can always add more oil as you need it, but if you pour in too

much, you may have to sacrifice that loaf of crusty fresh bread to the mix.

Don't worry about mixing the ingredients thoroughly. Frozen foods clump together, and it's not necessary to have uniform-size small pieces. Just crumble any large lumps so that your mixture holds together better. If your treasure bags have frozen into a solid mass that you can't break up, partially thaw before using at room temperature or on the defrost setting in your microwave.

Serving Freezer Treats

I reserve my homemade treats for winter feeding, when low temperatures slow spoilage and feeder visitors are abundant. If you live in a mild-winter area, or if you want to serve your treats at other seasons, offer them in a tray feeder, where birds can snack on any bits that fall away.

In cold-winter areas, you can stick your treats onto spike-type feeders, such as you use for corncobs or orange halves. Densely packed loaves, logs, and balls will hold together as birds nibble or whack at them.

One of the big benefits of a freezer is that it makes serving fat-based foods much less messy. In summer, suet blocks and peanut butter can melt in the heat, wasting good food and staining your post or porch with grease. I've gotten in the habit of storing extra commercial suet blocks as well as homemade fat-based treats in the freezer for a few days before serving. Even in winter, the birds that eat them can still peck off bites of food no matter how hard it's frozen. And in summer, it lengthens the life span of these treasured treats.

You can fill plastic cottage-cheese or similar containers from any of your bags or a combination of frozen food scraps. Store in the freezer to serve anytime. Poke the containers onto big nails hammered through a board backing, so they remain securely in place while birds work at the contents.

Turn leftovers from your freezer into a smorgasbord of bird-tempting custom blends.

Woodpecker Favorite

This treat is tempting to chickadees, jays, nuthatches, titmice, and woodpeckers.

INGREDIENTS

2 parts from the bread bag

1 part from the meat bag

1 part chopped suet

½ part from the nut bag

   Vegetable oil (optional)

Pour into large bowl. Break apart chunks as necessary. Work ingredients with your hands until they are reasonably blended, and the mixture clings together. The suet will melt as you work, providing the binding agent. If mixture seems dry and crumbles instead of sticking together, add some peanut, walnut, or corn oil. Mold into balls or corncob-size logs. Serve on a spike feeder, or put in a mesh bag and hang from a tree branch.

Best for Bluebirds

High in fat and calories, this fruity mixture is tailor-made for bluebirds. It's a welcome meal for mockingbirds, thrashers, thrushes, and Carolina wrens, too.

INGREDIENTS

2 parts from the fruit bag

2 parts chopped suet

1 part from the bread bag

1 part from the meat bag

½ part cornmeal (optional)

Combine all ingredients. Spread on cookie sheet lined with wax paper. Refreeze until hard. Pour into large resealable plastic bags. Serve in an open tray feeder, especially after winter storms. *Note:* If fruits are particularly juicy, add ½ part cornmeal to mix.

Mockingbird Manna

Also favored by bluebirds, robins, thrashers, and Carolina wrens.

INGREDIENTS

2 parts from the fruit bag

2 parts from the bread bag

1 part chopped suet

½ part from the meat bag

½ part from the leftovers bag

   Corn oil or peanut butter (optional)

Combine all ingredients until partially mixed, using hands to break up any large clumps. Squeeze a handful; if it falls apart, pour in ½ cup of corn oil or peanut butter and mix again. Increase oil if necessary. Shape into low loaf shape, about 2 inches high, and serve in a tray feeder or on a horizontal spike feeder.

Starling Pleaser

Win the loyalty of crows, jays, magpies, and starlings with this treat. Mix in large quantity to make a big, long-lasting block that will keep these birds busy and away from your seed feeders.

INGREDIENTS

4 parts from the bread bag

2 parts chopped suet

2 parts from the meat bag

2 parts from the leftovers bag

1 part from the fruit bag

   Corn or peanut oil (optional)

Mix ingredients in a large bowl. Mold into a block or loaf, adding corn or peanut oil if necessary for binding. Serve directly on the ground, away from songbird feeders.

Fruit

Attracts many kinds of birds at various times of the year

A TASTE FOR FRUIT has made many birds less than welcome with commercial orchardists and backyard fruit growers. These folks must constantly protect their crops of apples, cherries, peaches, and other juicy fruits from the ravages of house finches, orioles, robins, and other fruit fanciers. "Ravages" is the correct word, too. Although birds eat small fruits such as cherries and grapes whole, they usually damage large fruits rather than consume them. The birds that descend on a tree use their sharp bills to stab the fruit and nip the flesh or sip the juice, leaving the rest to rot while they move on to another piece of fruit.

Fruits that taste good to us humans seem to be real bird pleasers, too. Juicy blackberries are plucked quickly by all fruit-eating birds.

This fondness for fruit gives backyard bird feeders another good way to tempt birds to feeding stations and the surrounding yard. Fruit on the tree will attract birds first because they naturally seek food in there. But in the off-season or when lured to the area by fruit trees, fruit-eating birds may soon move to the feeders.

Fruit at the Feeder

When fresh fruits are ripening in gardens and orchards, you won't have much luck getting birds to visit your feeders. They can pick sumptuous fruits at the height of ripeness in the shade of their leafy restaurant. I reserve most of my fruit offerings for midfall through winter, when the real thing is scarce. I do serve fresh oranges during spring, summer, and early fall in my oriole feeders, and I provide a year-round supply of apples, which feed squirrels as well as feeder birds.

You can feed fresh, dried, and even frozen fruits to birds. Take advantage of low prices at harvest time to lay in a supply for winter, when blueberries and many other fruits are worth their weight in gold at the supermarket. Resealable plastic bags make freezing a

Freebie Fruit

GET TO know the manager of your supermarket's produce department, and you'll tap into a great source for unusual feeder foods at little or no cost. Produce that is too far past its prime to go to food bank programs still has plenty of life left as bird food. Find out what days fruit is removed from the counters, then be sure to visit to collect grapes, oranges, grapefruit, apples, and other goodies for just pennies a pound—or even better, for free!

Ask at local farmers' markets to find out how the vendors dispose of their faded goods, too. The end of the last day of market is often a time when less-than-perfect fruit goes for rock-bottom prices. And, if you're lucky enough to gather more bargain fruit than you can use right away, store it in the fridge or freeze it in resealable plastic bags for future feeder filling.

Birds That Favor Fruit

PLANT A fruit tree in your yard, and you'll attract a bounty of birds when the crop ripens. It's not unusual to see dozens of species feasting on a fruit tree at the same time. Sling a hammock or settle a chaise longue near the tree for comfortable viewing. Many of these same fruit-fancying birds will also visit a feeder that offers fruit regularly.

- Blackbirds
- Cardinals
- Catbirds
- Chickadees
- Crows
- House finches
- Purple finches
- Flickers
- Great crested flycatchers
- Grackles
- Grosbeaks
- Black-headed grosbeaks
- Jays
- Kingbirds
- Magpies
- Mockingbirds
- Orioles
- Phainopeplas
- Phoebes
- Band-tailed pigeons
- Robins
- Sapsuckers
- House sparrows
- Starlings
- Tanagers
- Thrashers
- Thrushes
- Titmice
- Vireos
- Waxwings
- Woodpeckers
- Wrens

cinch. I freeze small fruits and cut pieces of larger fruits on wax-paper–lined cookie sheets first, then slide them into the plastic bags. That way, they stay separated instead of freezing into a solid lump that even a woodpecker would have a hard time hacking apart.

Apples, fresh, chopped, or dried, are one of the most widely popular fruits with birds. I like to put a few whole fresh apples on the ground beneath the feeders and watch how birds attack the problem of getting to the fruit. Usually it's a jay or starling that first punctures the tough skin. When the bigger birds move away from the prize, chickadees, juncos, and other small birds move in to get a bite of sweet flesh. You can easily dry apples in a warm oven or the microwave. Slice them into rings before drying. No need to remove the core or peel the fruit first. Children enjoy threading the slices into garlands for draping a fence, decorating a cast-off Christmas tree, or hanging down a post.

Serve large fruits on the ground, in tray feeders, or impaled on the spikes of fruit feeders. Scatter chopped fruits, dried fruit pieces, or small fruits in open tray feeders or directly on the ground once you have established a clientele.

Best Fruits for Birds

Any fruit, from apples to figs, cherries to cactus, will have its takers at the feeder or in the garden.

Apples, cherries, figs, and plums appeal to the largest variety of birds, but any fruit good enough for human consumption is good enough for the birds.

Birds also treasure wild fruits. Amelanchiers, hackberries, mulberries, sassafras, sour gum, and other trees that produce fleshy or juicy fruits are a guaranteed draw with many birds. As with other bird-attracting plants, regional natives will bring you plenty of customers because they are familiar to the birds. But both native and introduced species of mulberry are so popular with birds that even a single tree will bring great crested flycatchers, thrushes, vireos, and other unusual species winging from far away to feast on the fruits.

Growing Fruit for Birds

If you want to grow fruit yourself, choose varieties that thrive in your area and crops you will enjoy sharing if the birds let you.

Birds are much less fussy than we are. A few wormholes or brown spots are no drawback at all, and smaller fruits are just as welcome as giant specimens. That means you won't have to bother with thinning fruits so they attain the largest possible size, and you can dispense with sprayers and sticky traps to control pests. You don't even need to

(continued on page 135)

A Fruit Garden for Birds

Dwarf trees make it simple to add fresh fruit to your yard, even if it's a small offering. Most plants have pretty, fragrant flowers that look good in the garden, so you can integrate the fruit trees into your landscape plans just as you would any ornamental flowering tree. They provide clouds of bloom in spring—that attract insect-eating orioles and warblers—and later are absolute bird magnets when the crop ripens.

One fruit to beware of is the crab apple. Many hybrids have fruit that is apparently unpalatable. However, birds may feed on the fruit of some older cultivars and unimproved species varieties of these trees, available from native plant nurseries. Look around your neighborhood in winter, and you'll see crab apple trees bare of birds, weighted down by

their burden of fruit. If you decide to add a crab apple to your garden, visit the nursery yourself—in winter—and tag the trees that attract bird traffic.

If you're planting a whole area in fruit for the birds, fill in around fruiting trees with a few different types of berry bushes and a grapevine to attract the greatest variety of birds. Otherwise, mix fruit-bearing trees and shrubs into your landscape plantings to give them added bird appeal.

PLANT LIST

1. Serviceberry (*Amelanchier* hybrid)

2. Blueberries (*Vaccinium* spp.)

3. Concord grape (*Vitis* spp.)

4. Crab apple (*Malus* spp.)

prune—when your customers have wings, branches that are out of reach of an arm or a ladder are no problem at all. An elderly peach tree that I inherited along with my Indiana house attracts hordes of house finches, orioles, downy woodpeckers, and the occasional yellow-bellied sapsucker. The birds don't seem to mind a bit that the peaches are borne only at the very top of the tree and are usually so pocked with insect holes that each fruit is studded with oozing sap.

Dried Fruit

Store-bought dried fruit is too costly to make up a lavish part of your feeder menu, but birds treasure it as an occasional treat. Bluebirds, chickadees, mockingbirds, thrushes, titmice, and waxwings are all fond of fruit, whether it's fresh or dried. In winter, when wild or garden fruit is hard to find, such dried fruit offerings may draw birds that usually don't visit a feeder, such as catbirds, thrashers, and yellow-rumped warblers.

Serve dried fruit sparingly until you can gauge how rapidly your feeder birds devour it. Sprinkle a scant handful on a higher tray feeder for blue-birds, jays, and mockingbirds, or directly on the ground for robins and other low-level feeders. Nut feeders made of large-grid wire may be perfect for feeding fruit: Chop the pieces into a size that will fit between the holes of the wire. If you have time and patience, it's fun to fashion small life-like clusters of dried fruit to hang from shrubs or tree branches.

Dried fruit is a real bonus to have on hand when you concoct bird-attracting recipes, such as breads and muffins. (See Bread on page 47 for some easy fruit bread recipes for birds.) Chop the fruit into small bits and add to the batter before baking. You can also use chopped dried fruit in uncooked cereal or cornmeal mixtures. It is best not to add dried fruit to suet mixtures you cook up yourself. While it is true that many of the same birds that like suet also eat fruit, the fat is enough of a draw without squandering dried fruit. Also, the presence of the fruit within the fat may encourage birds to dig in deeply to reach the favored bits, greasing their feathers and decreasing the insulating properties that protect them from the cold.

Small Fruit for a Big Yard

IF YOU want to see every fruit-eating bird within, oh, ½ mile of your property, plant a mulberry tree. Birds can't resist the bite-size fruits, which grow in such abundance that they usually cover the ground beneath the tree in a purple blanket. That's one way to spot a roadside mulberry: The dark stain from squashed berries stains the road surface for a stretch of 20 feet or so.

The **red mulberry** (*Morus rubra*) and the **Texas mulberry** (*M. microphylla*) are the native species in America, but the intro-duced **white mulberry** (*M. alba*), brought to feed a fledgling silkworm industry, is also a common escapee along roadsides and woods' edges. **Black mulberry** (*M. nigra*), another introduced species, shows up wild here and there. Birds appreciate the fruit of all mulberries, and they will descend on the tree in huge numbers even before the fruit is completely ripe.

Birds are responsible for the spread of mulberries because they "drop" the undigested seeds wherever they get the urge. This method of plant distribution makes mulberries less popular with humans—thanks to the purple juice of the berries, the deposits leave very noticeable splotches wherever they land.

Mulberry trees may reach 80 feet tall. They were common door-yard trees in years past, when people welcomed the fruits for fresh eating and used them in jams, pies, and wine. The delicious fruit was well worth the occasional purple-splattered laundry on the line.

If you have a large property, a mulberry is the best bird fruit tree you can plant. The bird watching is excellent, as bluebirds, orioles, tanagers, vireos, and scores of other species arrive to dine. If you have a smaller yard or nearby neighbors, you should stick to a more well-behaved cherry tree.

Fruity Mix for Winter Birds

Make a batch of this dried-fruit and nut mix to tempt bluebirds, catbirds, purple finches, black-headed and rose-breasted grosbeaks, mockingbirds, robins, thrashers, and Carolina wrens into becoming regulars at your feeders. Dedicate a separate feeder to the food, so that the intended recipients feast upon it and it doesn't get kicked to the ground by nonfruit-eating sparrows.

INGREDIENTS

2 *cups raisins, golden or regular*

2 *cups dried cherries*

2 *cups chopped dried apples*

2 *cups chopped almonds, pecans, walnuts,*
   or other nuts

1 *cup chopped prunes*

1 *cup chopped peanuts*

1 *cup dried squash or melon seeds*

Recycle a window screen into an outdoor fruit dryer for a sunny summer day. Cut thin slices of apples or other fruits so they dry quickly; prop the screen so air circulates underneath.

To chop dried fruit more easily into beak-size bites, use a sharp knife, and dip it in cornmeal when fruit begins to stick to it. Pour all ingredients into a bucket or large bowl, and stir to combine. Store left-over mix in a brown paper sack in a cool, dry place until it's time to refill your fruit feeder.

Dry Your Own Fruit

DRYING YOUR own fruit is an easy project. Harness the power of the sun, the oven, or the microwave to turn fresh berries and thin-sliced apples, bananas, and other fruits into delectable bird treats. In an oven, a low setting—200°F or less—works best. The time it takes to dry sliced fruits varies, depending on the thickness of the slices and the juiciness of the fruits. Start with 30 minutes, then check the tray of fruit for dryness. This method may take several hours, during which you need to check the fruit often.

Because microwave ovens vary in power, you'll have to experiment to find the right timing. Try 2 minutes at low power to start; gradually add time in 1-minute increments, as needed. In summer, an old window screen makes an ideal fruit dryer. Arrange the fruit in a single layer, and cover it with a layer of cheesecloth to deter insects. If you are lucky enough to have a wood-burning stove, check country auctions or country stores, especially in Amish regions, for a "bean dryer." This large metal box holds water and provides a flat surface for drying fruit (or beans). Load the dryer with fruit and set on top of a burning wood stove for drying in the winter months.

G

Game Birds

"GAME BIRD" IS a common nickname refer-ring to birds that come to dinner—on a platter, with a side of savory stuffing. Plump-breasted quail, pheasants, grouse, and other meaty species face the brunt of hunting pressure nowadays, although in years past, hunters included robins and other songbirds in their list of quarry.

Modern game birds belong to the order Galli-formes and are called gallinaceous birds. The word is from the Latin for "domestic fowl," quite appro-priate as these birds resemble chickens. Their simi-larities to barnyard fowl include both appearance and behavior. Their rather long legs, with familiar chicken-type feet are adapted for fast running. A game bird can rocket away from a crouched hiding position in a heart-stopping burst of flight when nec-essary. Add the famous springtime courtship displays of strutting and crowing, and you can see how these birds are related to the good old chicken.

In forest and open areas scattered across North America, the **wild turkey,** largest of the game birds, pre-sides. Ben Franklin nominated this native bird for the symbol of America but the bald eagle won the vote, and the turkey continued to be a popular bird on the dinner table. The wild bird is unlike its ranch-raised rel-atives, butterballs on the hoof, so to speak. This is a wily and wary bird, seldom seen, thanks to its habit of skulking away from intruders. Only during breeding season, when the woods reverberate with its gobbling love calls, is it a likely target for hunters. In the wild, turkeys seek out acorns, fruit, and seeds, gathering in flocks to roost in trees after feasting all day. Like other game birds, it enjoys corn and other grains at the feeder.

Another game bird of the woods is the grouse, rep-resented across the country by five species that range mostly in the North and Northwest. These short-tailed, chickenlike birds roam about at ground level, picking up seeds and berries and nipping tender bits of vegetation. If you live near conifer forests, you may host the **blue grouse** and **spruce grouse** at your feeder year-round and the **ruffed grouse** in winter. In

You'll hear a bobwhite long before you see one, thanks to its name-saying call. Try mimicking the easy two-note whistle and you may start a "conversation."

summer, ruffed grouse, which also occur in the eastern mountains, move to clearings to forage. The well-named **sharp-tailed grouse** and **sage grouse** live in more open areas rather than forests. Look for sharp-tailed grouse in prairies and brushy areas of the northern half of the country. The sage grouse moseys through sagebrush regions of the West.

In the grasslands of the Midwest, **greater** and **lesser prairie chickens** once abounded. Their populations de-clined due to intense hunting—their tasty meat made them popular while their tame manners made them easy prey for hunters. The added pressure of habitat loss has made it difficult for the birds to reestablish themselves and today they are uncommon to rare. You probably won't see one at your feeder, but you can visit them on special reserves. Ptarmigans also won't partake of your feeder banquet, although they may come to nibble tender willow leaves if you live in the Far North or in the High Sierra, where the introduced and well-established **white-tailed ptarmigan** resides.

Far more common and wide-spread are quail, which wander about most areas of the West, and their relative, the **northern bob-white,** a bird that ranges in the eastern two-thirds of the country. Quail look like cute Walt Disney birds, with a silly curled feather bobbing over their heads and a fat, cuddly-looking body. **California quail** and **Gambel's quail** have adapted well to living with humans and are frequent feeder guests. In the mountainous West, the **mountain quail** strolls in woodlands and chaparral and in backyards nearby. **Scaled quail** and **Montezuma quail,** which lack the head plume, are the common quail species in the Southwest.

In various areas of the country, near open fields and hedgerows, you may find the **ring-necked pheasant,** an exotic bird with a ridiculously long tail, introduced from Asia. Pheasant populations wax and wane because the birds don't build up their numbers naturally in North America and are augmented by captive-bred birds released for hunting. Perhaps remembering the easy life on the game farm, pheasants are often quick to move into feeding stations near their natural haunts during the winter months.

Several kinds of quail visit western feeders. Although they look similar, their ranges and habitats are usually distinct. These California quail travel in flocks.

Game Bird Behavior

Watch game birds as they respond to danger, and you'll see they prefer to run away through camouflaging grass or brush rather than fly. But these birds can fly when necessary. If you ever make the mistake of stepping too near a well-camouflaged game bird in hiding, it will make your heart pound with a sudden blast of wings as it flies rapidly to freedom. Some game birds are unusually tame, showing little fear of your comings and goings around their feeding area.

GAME BIRD FEEDER FOODS

- Acorns
- American persimmons (*Diospyros virginiana*)
- Apples
- Bayberry (*Myrica pensylvanica*)
- Bearberries (*Arctostaphylos* spp.)
- Blackberries (*Rubus* spp.)
- Blueberries (*Vaccinium* spp.)
- Buckwheat
- Corn, on the cob, whole kernel, or cracked
- Dogwood (*Cornus* spp.) berries
- Dried peas and beans
- Grapes (*Vitus* spp.)
- Grass seeds
- Greenbrier (*Smilax* spp.) berries
- Milo (sorghum)
- Peanuts
- Pecans
- Pine seeds
- Raspberries (*Rubus* spp.)
- Rose hips
- Salal (*Gaultheria shallon*) berries
- Strawberries
- Sumac (*Rhus* spp.) berries
- Weed seeds, including dandelion, goldenrod, ragweed, and smartweed
- Wheat

Game birds are ground feeders. Scatter cracked corn or other foods directly on the ground for pheasants and turkeys. Quail will also dine from a low tray feeder. Planting a patch of buckwheat, milo, or corn is a good way to attract game birds, which will forage at ease among the sheltering stems. Most species, especially quail, also appreciate a low source of water. Conifers are a major attraction for grouse, which eat the needles and roost in them.

Game birds spend a good deal of time browsing on leaves and buds. What they eat depends on where they live. The grouse of northern forests dine on conifers and willows. The sage grouse fills almost 75 percent of its nutritional needs with leaves and flowers of sagebrushes (*Artemisia* spp.). If your property features regionally native shrubs, trees, and other plants, you have provided for grazing game birds. It's fascinating to watch the birds stroll through your yard, nipping off a leaf here, a bud there.

The habits of game birds differ from those of songbirds, although their needs for food and shelter are the same. Turkeys may visit singly or in family groups of a male, his assorted wives, and their collective offspring. Grouse are usually loners. Quail travel in groups called coveys and appoint a lookout to remain watchful while the rest of the group feeds.

Some game birds are famed as musicians and show-offs. Blue grouse, sage grouse, prairie chickens, and ptarmigans engage in booming contests, producing the sound by releasing air in a sudden huff through inflated sacs in their necks. Ruffed grouse also are percussionists deluxe—they fan the air with their stiffened wings, beating a fast rhythm and deep sound that reverberates like far-off timpani through the forest.

Although at first glance many gallinaceous birds appear to be mostly brown, the males have fabulously barred and striped tails that they strut as proudly as any peacock. Neck and head feathers also add to the display as the birds raise and lower them.

Springtime heralds the onset of courtship rituals, which look bizarre because of the male bird's exaggerated postures. Watch for displays and territorial battles between males. Listen for hooting, booming, crowing, and gobbling, too.

Ring-necked pheasant populations may rise and fall with the fortunes of the hunting season. Farm-raised game birds released for sport may visit at your feeder.

Wild turkeys are increasing dramatically in many areas. By day, the birds forage in woods and fields and may visit feeding stations. At night, they roost high in trees.

Goldfinches

The popular **American goldfinch** is one of the most common birds at the feeder, thanks to its continent-wide range and ability to adapt to varied habitats. Familiarity in this case breeds fondness, not contempt, perhaps because of the beauty of this perky yellow-and-black bird or because of its mannerly feeder habits. Give a goldfinch a tray of sunflower seeds or a tube of niger, and he and his cronies will contentedly crack seeds, with only an occasional flash of wings to betray a small squabble.

In the West and Southwest, the buttercup-yellow American goldfinch shares its habitat with the **lesser goldfinch**, who wears its yellow on the breast and belly, with a green or black back. **Lawrence's goldfinch**, a gray bird with small splashes of yellow and black, is another possible feeder visitor in dry areas of the Southwest and coastal Pacific.

Identifying female and immature goldfinches is a good test of birding skills, especially if more than one species ranges in your area. They are all generally olive green, washed with yellow, with faint wing bars. In winter, the males also lose their bright plumage, fading to drab greenish yellow. Around the time pussy willows bloom in my area, the males begin to regain

Easy to attract, sunny yellow American goldfinches may gather by the dozens at feeders in spring. They punctuate their flight with bursts of song.

their dapper black caps, bold black wings, and buttery yellow body feathers, although they definitely have a blotchy look for several weeks.

Sunflower and niger are the mainstays of a goldfinch's menu at the feeder, but they also enjoy other small seeds, such as millet. Weed seeds are a big attraction, which is a good thing to remember the next time you're muttering at your dandelions or burdock, two of their favorites. They will eagerly devour the seeds of many garden flowers, eating from standing plants or from stems you have cut and laid in a feeder tray.

Goldfinch Behavior

All goldfinches are gregarious types that travel in small flocks most of the year, except during nesting season. In areas where the species overlap, all three may intermingle. In the southern third of the country, goldfinches are mainly winter birds. In all other regions, except for the Far North, they are

GOLDFINCH FEEDER FOODS

- Aster (*Aster* spp.) seed
- Bachelor's-button (*Centaurea cyanus*) seed
- Canary seed
- Coneflower (*Echinacea* spp.) seed
- Coreopsis (*Coreopsis* spp.) seed
- Cosmos (*Cosmos* spp.) seed
- Flaxseed
- Goldenrod (*Solidago* spp.) seed
- Grass seeds
- Lettuce (*Lactua sativa*) seed
- Millet
- Niger
- Rapeseed
- Sunflower seed, especially black oil
- Tickseed sunflower (*Bidens* spp.) seed
- Zinnia (*Zinnia* spp.) seed

common year-round. During migration, your feeder population of these finches may swell into the dozens or even hundreds, filling nearby trees with their tinkling, musical voices.

If cleanliness is next to godliness, then goldfinches must be saints. Goldfinches are inordinately fond of birdbaths and other water features. Whenever it rains at my house, I can count on goldfinches showing up within minutes after the storm to splash and frolic in the puddled rainwater. They are daily visitors at the birdbath and even at my dogs' outside water dish. Unlike most of my bathing birds, goldfinches don't take long to abandon themselves to the joy of a bath. They remind me of 4-year-old kids in the tub, splashing and ducking their heads and throwing water everywhere.

The frequent chattering "conversation" of goldfinches is one of the reasons they are such a delight. They keep up a long stream of sweet, varied notes, occasionally punctuated by a querying "Sweeee?" that sounds exactly like the note my mother's pet canary used. Indeed, German immigrants who were familiar with the Old World songbirds quickly dubbed the bright American goldfinch the "wild canary."

Salt is another big lure for all three species of goldfinch. If they're not at the feeder gobbling seed, or splashing up a storm in the bath, they're apt to gather in a talkative group around your salt block. Supplying nesting materials such as unspun wool, cotton puffs, and down-lined milkweed pods is another good way to attract goldfinches.

Goldfinches can get feisty with each other, spreading their wings or making darting head gestures in a fit of pique over feeding rights. But they usually behave well with other species around their size, such as sparrows, and are quickly intimidated by larger birds, such as jays.

Gourds

IF YOU ARE LUCKY ENOUGH to have a long, hot growing season that lasts at least 90 days, invest a dollar or two in a packet of birdhouse gourd seeds. The fast-growing vines make an excellent quick cover to hide a chain-link fence or scramble up a trellis, and the night-blooming flowers, which unfurl their pristine white petals at dusk, attract interesting hummingbird-like sphinx moths.

At the feeding station, birdhouse gourds can be fashioned into utilitarian scoops and even impromptu feeders. Slice away until the gourd is shaped to suit your need. By the way, save the seeds you remove from the gourd: Put some aside to plant a new crop next year, and serve the rest to your feeder birds.

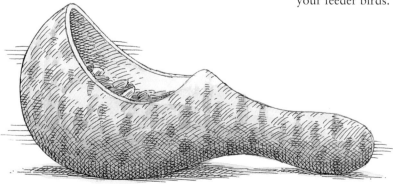

Birdhouse gourd vines produce enough gourds in a single season to supply a new home to a dozen birds. You can also turn them into sturdy birdseed scoops and feeders.

A Basic Gourd Bird Feeder

Birdhouse gourds got their name from their useful-ness as, of course, birdhouses. But they also make serviceable feeders. After the gourds mature (let the vines die back before you pick them), you can pick and dry them overwinter. Lay them in a warm, dry place and turn them weekly. If mold appears on the gourds, rub it off with a dry cloth. By spring the gourds should be dry (they'll feel much lighter) and are ready to become birdhouses and other handy items. Cut an opening, clean out the seeds, and hang a gourd as a feeder for several kinds of small-seed eating birds. Here's how to make your own home-grown bird feeder for your local bird friends.

MATERIALS

Dried birdhouse gourd

Wire for hanging

Feeder treats, such as nuts or sunflower seeds

A single gourd makes a fine freehanging house for wrens and chickadees, although it is not as quickly accepted as a nest box is. Purple martins, however, adore group gourd housing.

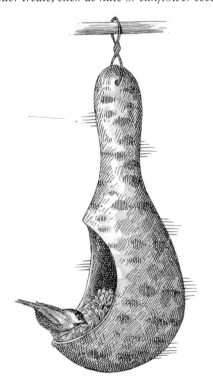

Step 1. Give the gourd a firm whack on the palm of your hand to loosen the seeds.

Step 2. Measure and mark the size of the opening with an indelible felt-tip pen.

Step 3. Carefully cut out the opening with a very sharp utility knife.

Step 4. Shake the gourd, opening side down, until most of the seeds have dropped out.

Step 5. Drill a hole through the neck of the gourd just below the stem, and insert a wire for hanging the feeder from a handy branch.

Step 6. Fill the feeder with nuts, sunflower seeds, or other treats. Birds will soon learn to seek its contents.

Grackles

GRACKLES COULD take first prize in an avian beauty contest, thanks to their sleek, svelte bodies, elegant all-black dress, and long, streamlined tails. But the harsh, squeaky vocalizings of grackles will make you want to run for the can of WD-40.

Like most other blackbirds, grackles fit in well with the changes humans have wrought to the natural landscape. They're opportunistic feeders, swallowing insects, seeds, and fast-food leftovers with equal delight. The **common grackle** is a universal presence in farmland, cities, and suburbia everywhere east of the Rockies. Like other grackles, this species wears a patina of iridescence on its glossy black feathers; variations in the flash of color determine whether the bird you're hosting is the purple or the bronzed. The common grackle has a keel-shaped tail—the feathers form a distinct V-shape, like the bottom of a boat. The **boat-tailed grackle,** a common species in Florida and along the Gulf and Atlantic coasts also has a keel-shaped tail. Longer than the common grackle by 4 to 6 inches, this is a big bird that can reach 16 inches from the tip of pointy beak to the end of the last tail feather. Another extra-large species is the **great-tailed grackle,** which stalks

The male common grackle's bright yellow eye shines against his black plumage like an 18K gold brooch. Grackles are among the bravest birds and will quickly come to the rescue when other birds need help.

about in the Southwest, sweeping its incredible tail like the train of a bridal gown. Both the boat-tailed and great-tailed show clear differences between the sexes. While the males gleam with purple iridescence over dramatic dark feathers, the females are soft brown to gray-brown. Most adult male grackles sport bright yellow eyes.

Grackle Behavior

Grackles don't always visit feeders because they fend for themselves extremely well. They prefer to eat at ground level, so you will often spot them beneath feeders. On the ground, they are a delight to watch, thanks to their strutting walk, extravagant tails, and often exaggerated body language.

Watch the grackles in your yard, and you'll see how varied a diet they enjoy. Practically anything edible goes down the hatch: caterpillars, grubs, snails, crayfish, beetles, mice, seeds, and other treats. Should you be visited by a large group of grackles at the feeder, offer cracked corn to keep these big birds busy and conserve your more expensive seed.

GRACKLE FEEDER FOODS

- Acorns
- Apples
- Bayberries (*Myrica pensylvanica*)
- Beech nuts
- Bread and other baked goods
- Corn, whole kernel or cracked
- Grapes (*Vitus* spp.)
- Leftovers
- Meat scraps
- Millet
- Milo
- Pasta, cooked
- Suet, chopped
- Wheat

Grapefruit

Attracts chickadees, house finches, mockingbirds, robins, starlings, and other birds

RUBY RED OR PALE GOLDEN, grapefruits are great additions to the bird-feeder banquet. Filled with their own luscious, juicy pulp, they may attract the attentions of chickadees, house finches, mockingbirds, robins, and other birds. Orioles may sample the flesh, though sweet oranges tempt these birds more easily. Emptied of their contents—by you or the birds—grapefruit rind halves make sturdy, simple minifeeders for filling with bacon fat, melted suet, or other offerings.

Grapefruit is also a suitable distraction for starlings, which may forsake the main feeder area for an offering of grapefruit halves in easy reach. You can put the halved fruit into wire baskets (a suet feeder usually fits), or impale a half grapefruit on a sturdy nail, either horizontally, for perchers such as starlings and mockingbirds, or vertically, for clinging birds such as chickadees.

Make feeder baskets from empty grapefruit halves by sticking a wire through the rind at three equidistant points, about ¼ inch from the top. Twist the wires together and suspend from a branch or shepherd's crook. Chopped apples, raisins, currants, sunflower seeds, or peanuts are good in grapefruit baskets. The edge of the rind makes a serviceable perch for lightweight birds such as chickadees.

> Impale a grapefruit half on a large nail for a juicy treat. Empty rinds make simple holders for suet, seeds, or other foods.

Grapes

Attract bluebirds, cardinals, catbirds, great crested flycatchers, grosbeaks, mockingbirds, tanagers, thrashers, thrushes, woodpeckers, wrens

GRAPEVINES ARE GREAT VINES, as far as birds are concerned. Like other rampant-growing vines, grapes offer good cover, shelter from the elements, and protected nesting spots. Their fruit is a favorite of cardinals, catbirds, great crested flycatchers, grosbeaks, mockingbirds, tanagers, thrashers, thrushes, woodpeckers, wrens . . . the list goes on and on. Their sweet-smelling flowers attract a myriad of tiny bugs—more fodder for foraging birds. And the peeling bark of their vines is easy for birds to strip and use for nest weaving.

If you didn't inherit Grandma's grape arbor, start your own on a strong trellis by planting a fast-growing, easy-care 'Concord' vine if you live in the North (Zones 5 to 8) or a muscadine if you are a southern gardener (Zones 7 to 9). In 2 years, you'll have a decent crop. Don't fret about pruning;

Wild grapes have bite-size fruit beloved by cardinals and other birds. Grapevines are likely to sprout from bird-deposited seeds around your feeding area.

just give the vine a haircut now and then to keep it in bounds. It'll bear fruit regardless of your pruning skill.

In the meantime, while your vine grows, get your grapes from other sources. Salvage any strays from your refrigerator fruit bin; birds don't mind bruised or withered fruit. Place single grapes in an open tray feeder for easy visibility, preferably in the soft-foods feeder so that grape lovers don't have to compete with seed eaters for feeder space.

Like other fruits, grapes attract the most attention from birds in fall and winter when natural fruit is scarce. But if you have fruit eaters such as bluebirds, catbirds, mockingbirds, or Carolina wrens nesting in or near your yard, you may enjoy a steady stream of customers to your fruit feeders through the summer, especially if there's no natural fruit nearby.

Since birds are creatures of habit, it's a good idea to put grapes in the same spot if you offer them regularly. Hook clusters of grapes on hooks or nails, or fasten them on branches of shrubs or trees. To prevent these watery, thin-skinned fruits from freezing fast to snow or frozen soil, freeze a supply of individual grapes in resealable plastic bags for winter use. After winter snow or ice storms, chop grapes coarsely (whole frozen grapes are too big to swallow), and scatter them on the ground for robins and other birds to scoop up.

> Add a cup hook to the end of your wooden feeder and hang clusters of grapes from it for fruit-loving birds.

Grasses for Birds

Attract many kinds of birds at various times of the year

IT'S FUN TO SEE where birdseed comes from, which is why I always let a few of the volunteer plants beneath my feeders grow to maturity. Many will turn out to be sunflowers, but the rest are sure to be grasses—planted by birds that dropped the seeds.

Without grasses, you and I and our bird friends would be mighty hungry. That bowl of cornflakes we crunch for breakfast, the bread that makes our lunch-time sandwich, and the millet that we pour in our feeders for the finches all come from grasses.

Of all the plants in the giant Gramineae, or grass family, grains like corn and wheat are the most useful to us humans, but birds and other wildlife appreciate almost every one of the hundreds of grass species. Next time you're yanking up a clump of crabgrass (*Digitaria* spp.), think of chipping sparrows and song sparrows, which adore the tiny, tasty seeds of your quick-crawling weedy enemy. (For more on weedy grasses that attract birds, see Weeds on page 327.)

Grass is golden where birds are concerned. Native species like this switchgrass produce abundant seeds and supply nesting material and good cover.

Volunteer grasses spring up from birds scratching in feeders or from tube feeders tilting in the wind. Millet (*Panicum miliaceum* and other species) is my top crop, thanks to messy eaters who kick the little tan seeds out of their feeders. You may get other grass volunteers sprouting around your feeders since some seeds eaten in the wild may survive the trip through a bird's digestive tract intact.

Plant a Grassy Garden

Young grasses all look alike at first—like a lawn that needs a haircut. But if you let them grow, they'll turn into a garden of birdseed: millets, canary grass (*Phalaris canariensis*), foxtails (*Setaria* spp.), milo (*Sorghum bicolor*), and wheat (*Triticum* spp.). If the look of a few stragglers under the feeders is less than appealing to you, plant a patch of grasses just for the birds as a complementary feeding station.

Choose a site in full sun, in average soil. Prepare the site as you would for a bed of annual flowers, by digging or tilling to a depth of about 6 inches. There's no need to add fertilizer: Grasses grow well on a lean to average diet of soil nutrients.

To keep your neighbors from turning you in to the weed police, make the area square or rectangular, which gives it a controlled look, and mark the planting with a metal plant label. Include a few clumps or a back row of native perennial grasses, such as switch grass (*Panicum virgatum*), to give the bed year-round substance. Sow separate swaths of the seeds of these annual grasses: millet, annual canary grass, and milo. If you have space, annual ryegrass (*Lolium multiflorum*), a common lawn-grass seed, is also appreciated by seed-eating birds. Keep the planting well watered while you're waiting for the seeds to come up. Don't worry about weed grasses that invade your plot: Chances are, their seeds will be just as eagerly sought as the ones you planted.

Grasses are fast-growing. By mid- to late summer, some of your plants will be pushing up seedheads loaded with grain. Let the plants ripen naturally to attract birds where they stand. Buntings, quail, siskins, sparrows, and other small-seed eaters will scratch about for dropped seeds or pull down seedheads all through fall and winter. Before the birds get all the bounty, cut a few handfuls of plants to save for winter bird feeding. Their long stems are easy to work into outdoor arrangements for the birds, or you can simply lay them in a feeder or on the ground.

A garden of grasses also attracts birds because the dense stems and clumps provide good cover. Use corridors of grasses, annual or perennial, to help birds move through your yard undetected by predators. Let your bird grasses stand over winter to continue serving as shelter. Robins, sparrows, and other birds will use the dried foliage for next spring's nest building.

Natives Work Best

Don't shy away from searching a bit to track down native perennial grasses for your garden: The payoff

---

A Trio for Shade

ALTHOUGH MOST grasses crave sun, several bird-attracting species thrive in shady places. If your yard features shade-casting trees where birds nest and feed, add a few of these grasses in the shady spots beneath them for bird food and interesting landscape texture.

In lighter shade, **hairgrasses** (*Deschampsia* spp.) create clouds of delicate seedheads, valued by birds in the cool mountain areas where the species originated.

Bottlebrush grass (*Hystrix patula*) is a great addition along shady paths, as a treat for songbirds and human visitors. Birds love the plump seeds of this easy-to-grow native grass, and kids of all ages enjoy stroking the whiskery seedheads, which look just like their namesake. When the seedheads are fully ripe, they shatter under the touch, which just makes things easier for the small songbirds that seek the seeds on the woodsy floor.

For pheasants, quail, and other game birds, **deer-tongue grass** (*Panicum clandestinum*) is just the ticket. This handsome plant has pointed, 1-inch-wide leaves that jut at angles from furry stems tipped by airy panicles of fat little seeds. All of these shade-tolerant grasses are native American plants.

for paging through those catalogs is more birds in your yard. Birds are accustomed to finding food from the grass species in their native range, so they'll soon seek out your planting. Blue grammagrass (*Bouteloua gracilis*), switchgrass (*Panicum virgatum*), little bluestem (*Schizachyrium scoparium*), and many other native grasses are chock-full of good birdseed.

Keep in mind that many birds travel over a wide range of country during their migrations, so unless you're trying to re-create a natural ecosystem, you don't have to limit yourself to a narrow region when you're choosing native grasses. The red-winged blackbird that seeks out the prairie grasses in your midwestern garden in fall, for example, may be gleaning seeds from subtropical species in his winter home in the South.

Although natives are tops with birds, weedy grasses that originally hailed from lands across the ocean have plenty of takers, too. There's no need to learn what every grass in your yard is—just watch whether birds eat it. I let grasses of any kind grow among the shrubs of a hedge or in a corner of the yard, or wherever I can sneak in a discreet weed patch without alarming the neighbors. Native sparrows and juncos especially appreciate a grassy patch gone wild, where they can forage all winter among the standing stems. Disguise your weed patch, if you must, by bordering it with a double row of zinnias—tall ones in the back, dwarfs in the front—for a tidier look and extra seeds.

> Ornamental or weedy, grasses offer seeds, shelter, and nest-building materials for many kinds of birds.

See "Resources" on page 348 for nurseries that feature native plants. You may also find native grasses at well-stocked local nurseries (ask if they will order them for you) or via Internet sources.

Grit

Attracts all birds

TEST YOUR TEETH on a kernel of dried corn, and you'll see why grit is a necessity for birds, which lack the dental structure needed to break down hard foods. Birds depend on a muscular organ called the gizzard where small stones and grit provide the abrasion necessary to break down their food into a digestible state. Birds frequently gather in flocks along roadsides to pick up the tiny stones and gravel they need to replenish their gizzards.

You can supply the much-needed grit near your feeders for your feathered friends. Washed, natural aquarium gravel is an ideal source of larger grit. Builder's sand, the coarse tan variety that you can find at any home-supply store, will serve their need for finer grade gravel. Crushed eggshells or crushed clam and oyster shells can also provide grit for birds.

Making grit is a great way to recycle those seashells you lugged home from the ocean—the ones that now reside in the drawer or on the back porch, unloved and out of sight. That 2-ton tool in your driveway is a quick way to smash seashells: Just drive back and forth over them a few times, then sweep them up and put at the feeding station. Or you can give last summer's souvenirs a few good whacks with a hammer. I slip my clamshells into a thick, stretchy sock or wrap them in an old hand towel before hammering away, to prevent sharp bits from flying into my eyes.

Offer grit on a flat, vegetation-free area of your yard or on top of a large flat rock, near the feeders where birds can easily find it. Choose a raised area so that rain puddles don't submerge the grit. Keep the supply replenished year-round.

> Birds fill their gizzards with grit and small stones to make up for their lack of teeth.

G

Grosbeaks

GROSBEAKS GET their name from their big, conical bills. Among the largest members of the finch family, these birds have beaks that rival the cardinal's in size and seed-cracking power.

Two mostly northern species and three more southerly and westerly species give us a full spectrum of grosbeaks. In the North and the West, the yellow, olive, and black **evening grosbeak** patrols conifer forests, moving southward irregularly to land at feeding stations. The rosy red **pine grosbeak** joins its yellow counterpart in spruce and fir forests and also sweeps southward, though more rarely than the evening grosbeak. In the eastern half of the country, particularly in the northern quadrant and in mountains southward, it's the striking **rose-breasted grosbeak,** with his brilliant crimson throat, snowy belly, and black-as-coal upper parts, that fills the niche. Across the southern half of the country, look for the beautiful **blue grosbeak.** This cobalt-colored bird, with touches of rust on its wings, dwells in hedgerows and other brushy areas and farming country. In the West, the vivid golden orange **black-headed grosbeak** patrols open woodlands. Females of all species wear dowdy dress of varying shades of olive- or grayish green or brown.

A male rose-breasted grosbeak in spring finery is one of the most beautiful birds in America. His relatives are just as colorful in other hues. Tempt them down from the treetops with sunflower seeds.

Except for the blue species, grosbeaks are birds of the canopy, spending much of their time over our heads. It's a real occasion when these large and beautiful birds move into feeding stations or stop at a birdbath or other water feature.

Grosbeak Behavior

At first glance, an evening grosbeak may remind you of a big goldfinch, but that's where the similarity ends. Unlike flighty, fast-moving goldfinches, which

GROSBEAK FEEDER FOODS			
■ Acorns	■ Corn, whole kernels or cracked	■ Elderberries (*Sambucus* spp.)	■ Virginia creeper (*Parthenocissus quinquefolia*) berries
■ Blackberries (*Rubus* spp.)	■ Crackers	■ Figs (*Ficus carica*)	■ Wheat
■ Cherries, fresh or dried	■ Dogwood (*Cornus* spp.) berries	■ Sumac (*Rhus* spp.)	■ Wild grapes
■ Common ragweed		■ Sunflower seeds	

panic at every opportunity, grosbeaks are slow-moving birds, as deliberate in their motions as parrots, and often almost tame. Big and bold-colored, they are a real treat at the feeder, although their appetites match their body size. When a flock of these birds descends on your sunflower seeds, they can make short work of what seemed like an abundant stash of seeds. They eat wherever they find food: at a high feeder, low feeder, or tube feeder, or on the ground. They generally don't seek other feeder foods if you supply plenty of sunflower seeds. They are also fond of salt.

Grosbeaks are adept at acrobatic maneuvers. You may spot them hanging upside down like parrots while they dine on the seeds of catalpa trees or the buds of maples and other trees. One of the best tricks I've seen grosbeaks do was to capture the seeds of jewelweed (*Impatiens capensis*) from the plant without exploding the hair-triggered seeds.

Listen for the pretty, warbling songs of grosbeaks in your yard. Their call notes—the "Pink!" of the rose-breasted, the chirp of the evening—are another clue that grosbeaks are in the area. If you are lucky enough to host grosbeaks at your feeder, watch for the eye-catching splashes of white in most species' wings as they arrive or leave. The birds are unusually "confiding," as birders say, showing little fear of humans. In fact, an evening grosbeak was the first bird

The black-headed grosbeak resembles an oriole, thanks to its vivid coloring. But the big conical bill reveals its true identity.

I hand-tamed: It readily accepted a palm full of sunflower seeds when I very slowly approached it at the feeder. Pine grosbeaks, like other birds of the Far North, are the most unafraid of all their kin. It's easy to snap close-range pictures of them as they feed on seeds in a tray or berries in your yard.

Groundcovers

Attract fox sparrows, thrushes, towhees, and other ground-dwelling forest birds

IF YOU HAVE A LOVELY SWEEP of green lawn beneath your feeders, either you're not much of a success at bird feeding, or you're stocking your feeders with waste-free seeds. With all the traffic at a feeding station, the surrounding area will soon look less than perfect, thanks to all those little bird feet scratching among the seeds and shells that they drop.

Many feeder keepers don't mind the accumulation of debris beneath the feeder, but if you prefer a neater look, there's an easy solution: Cover the ground directly beneath the feeders, in about a 3-foot-diameter circle, with wood chips or other coarse mulch. (See Mulch on page 211 for details.) To make birds feel at home as they approach and exit the feeders and to cut down on maintenance, I plant an oasis of groundcovers extending from the mulch to the shrubs and other plants that border my feeding station. I've noticed that fox sparrows, thrushes, towhees, and other ground-dwelling forest birds seem much more comfortable about approaching the feeder when they can move from clump to clump of vegetation rather than travel over barren lawn grass.

It helps to think like a bird when choosing groundcovers for around your feeding area. The criteria for bird-appealing groundcovers are a little different from the usual things that we people look for in a groundcover:

■ Instead of a continuous, dense, low-growing effect—the typical groundcover look—aim for plants separated by a few inches of open space. Or try a continuous sweep of plants that have room for birds to move beneath their branches.

■ Choose plants for food value as well as appearance, to get more use out of the planting.

■ Deciduous groundcovers are often preferable to evergreen, unless you live in a mild-winter area. By the time the plants make their reappearance in spring, you'll welcome the fresh greenery to hide the winter debris.

Choose groundcovers that do double duty as both cover and food. Bearberry forms mats of evergreen leaves decorated with bird-appealing berries.

Room to Move

Birds have a hard time moving through the thickly tangled stems that groundcovers such as periwinkle (*Vinca minor*) produce. They prefer plants like Allegheny pachysandra (*Pachysandra procumbens*) that are tall enough and erect enough to allow passage between their stems. My birds also avoid ground-hugging cotoneasters (*Cotoneaster* spp.) and junipers (*Juniperus* spp.); the birds tend to travel around the plants rather than through them. But birds welcome those groundcovers with higher branches and a few inches of open space beneath them and soon establish favorite routes under the sheltering branches.

Great Groundcovers

Many low-growing plants bear excellent crops of bird food on their stems and branches. Low-growing blackberries (*Rubus* spp.), blueberries (*Vaccinium* spp.), and other ground-hugging fruits draw in birds

that rarely visit a feeder, including tanagers and thrushes. I'm not a big fan of liriope (*Liriope spicata*), but when I found an armload of the plants on the local yard waste dump, I planted them in my shady front garden near the feeder. I was happy to find out that the black liriope berries that ripen in late summer are a magnet for bluebirds, which visit for a week or more to pluck the fruit.

A top-notch berry for bird appeal and groundcover use is one so common, it's probably already growing in your vegetable garden or, if you're lucky, in nearby wild places: the common strawberry (*Fragaria* spp.). Plant any variety you like, including native wild strawberries, and birds will be sure to brighten your yard.

In a sunny spot, ornamental grasses can cover the ground with a natural meadow look. Since ornamental grasses can be costly to buy, I like to experiment with native grasses and grasslike sedges that I import from other places in my yard or from the property of friends and family. Many species that aren't well mannered enough or well known enough for the nursery trade are perfect for birds. Three of my favorite finds are purple love grass (*Eragrostis spectabilis*), a delicate beauty with

Groundcovers for Birds

THESE PLANTS are easy for birds to navigate through. Many have tempting fruits or seeds for birds, too, and some can be used as nesting material.

Groundcover	Bird Use
Bearberry (*Arctostaphylos uva-ursi*)	Travel corridor, berries
Bunchberry (*Cornus canadensis*)	Travel corridor, berries
Strawberries (*Fragaria* spp.)	Travel corridor, nest site, fruit
Wintergreen (*Gaultheria procumbens*)	Travel corridor, berries
Huckleberries (*Gaylussacia* spp.)	Travel corridor, fruit, nest site
Junipers with branches at least 4 inches off the ground (*Juniperus* spp.)	Travel corridor, berries, nest site
Liriope (*Liriope spicata*)	Travel corridor, berries
Partridgeberry (*Mitchella repens*)	Travel corridor, berries
Allegheny spurge (*Pachysandra procumbens*)	Travel corridor, nest site
Mayapple (*Podophyllum peltatum*)	Travel corridor
Smartweeds (*Polygonum* spp.)	Travel corridor, seed
Chickweed (*Stellaria media*)	Travel corridor, seed, edible leaves
Blueberries dwarf or low-growing (*Vaccinum* spp.)	Travel corridor, fruit, nest site
Violets (*Viola* spp.)	Travel corridor, nest site
Clump-forming grasses such as fescues (*Festuca* spp.), switchgrasses (*Panicum* spp.), prairie dropseed (*Sporobolus heterolepsis*)	Travel corridor, seed, nesting material
Ferns such as maidenhair fern (*Adiantum pedatum*), cinnamon fern (*Osmunda cinnamomea*), interrupted fern (*O. claytonia*), polypody ferns (*Polypodium* spp.), and Christmas fern (*Polystichum acrostichoides*)	Travel corridor, nest site

clouds of airy flowers in fall; deer-tongue grass (*Dichanthelium clandestinum*), a shade lover with leaves that remind me of bamboo; and wood sedge (*Carex sylvatica*), a liriopelike evergreen species in my area.

It's amazing how fast your opinion of weeds will change once you consider their potential as bird-attracting groundcover plants. If you can bear the thought, you may find you get as much delight as I do in the ultracommon dandelion (*Taxacum officinale*). I actually removed the lawn grass and sowed a solid patch of dandelion around my feeding station in the sunny backyard. This perennial stays green most of the winter, then brightens March with its flowers. I don't mow it down when the flowers are done because it draws indigo buntings, goldfinches, white-crowned sparrows, and other great birds to its charming—yes, really!—puffs of seed.

I also pamper any plants of henbit (*Lamium amplexicaule*), purple dead nettle (*Lamium purpureum*), and common chickweed (*Stellaria media*) near the sunny-site feeders. Like most annual weeds, these rarely stay in one place for long, but every few years I'm rewarded by a big, beautiful patch of purple by the feeders. Sparrows and other birds nibble the fresh leaves and also eat the seeds.

Before you go out to buy groundcover plants, look around your yard and think creatively. An ideal groundcover may be right under your nose—or foot.

G

Ground Feeding

IF THE DOVES, juncos, quail, sparrows, and towhees at your feeders had their druthers, they would want their food as close to the ground as possible. These birds are ground feeders that in the wild typically scratch seeds from the soil or pick insects from leaf litter. Although they will adapt to using bird feeders at the usual waist-high setting, they will eagerly accept food offered closer to or directly on the ground.

Commercial feeder manufacturers have accommodated these birds by adding low-level tray feeders to their product lineup. You can find them at bird-supply stores or in catalogs such as those listed in "Resources" on page 348. You can also make your own short-legged tray feeder. Four equal lengths of 2 × 4, each about 6 to 12 inches long, will make a stable set of legs for a low-level feeder. Nail a leg onto each corner of an existing tray feeder, driving the nails down through the tray and into the top of the 2 × 4. For the sake of appearance, orient all four legs in the same direction.

A large rock with a concave surface also makes an ideal bird feeder for ground-feeding birds. Quail, in my experience, take to such a setup immediately. You can also rest a plastic plant saucer or an old platter on a stack of bricks.

Pouring seed or other food directly on the ground can lead to problems for birds because the food may quickly turn moldy in wet weather. Although wild birds I have watched will not bother with moldy seed, it can cause problems if any do ingest it. They may suffer health problems such as aspergillosis, a

When you're hosting a large flock, it's simple to scatter seed on the ground. If seed gets wet and moldy, birds will avoid it unless there's no alternative.

serious fungal infection that can quickly spread through birds feeding at spoiled grain. Spreading seed directly on the ground can also encourage the visits of mice and other rodents, who will creep out to take their share of the feast.

Keeping these caveats in mind, you can still feed birds on the ground if you follow two basic guidelines: Feed small amounts at a time, so that seed does not accumulate and spoil or attract vermin, and remove any seed that gets wet. During winter snows, when feeder visitors increase dramatically, I often handle the overflow by pouring seed onto an area of packed snow protected by a windbreak of evergreen boughs or by a piece of slanted plywood. I also put out bread and other baked goods on the ground so the small birds and robins can get their share without fighting the competition at the feeder.

Hand Feeding

TAMING WILD BIRDS to take food from your hand or your hat brim is easier than it looks. The only tool you need is patience. Bad weather helps, too, because hunger is a big incentive for birds to get over their natural fear of humans. Winter is the best season to tame birds. The morning after a snowstorm or ice storm, you can have birds eating out of your hand—the only "feeder" available—in as little as half an hour. In summer, when birds can turn their backs on the sunflower seed and snitch caterpillars from your garden, it takes much longer to entice them to eat out of your hand.

Once birds are regulars at your feeder, they will probably be waiting for your arrival in the morning to refill their dishes, especially if you stock feeders at about the same time each day. Should a brave chickadee or other bird come close, offer it a handful of seed before you fill the feeders. It may surprise you by accepting it immediately or after just a few minutes of standing patiently and quietly.

I have found walnut kernels a real temptation for taming birds: Chickadees, jays, nuthatches, titmice, and woodpeckers have eagerly eaten them from my hand. To hand-tame cardinals, goldfinches, purple

Nothing compares to the thrill of hand-feeding a wild bird. With a week or so, you can coax one of the fearless species, like this chickadee, onto your fingers.

finches, evening grosbeaks, and pine siskins, I use sunflower seeds. I find crossbills, red-breasted nuthatches, and redpolls, which visit infrequently from the Far North, almost fearless; these birds will often immediately take a seed from my fingers if I approach them slowly at the feeder. For bluebirds and mockingbirds, a handful of enticing crumbled peanut butter and cornmeal dough is the key.

Have 'Em Eating out of Your Hand!

YOU CAN train feeder birds to eat out of your hand by becoming a regular presence there yourself, a process that takes about a week. Time your visits for early morning, when birds are hungriest after a night without food.

Start by emptying all feeders but one—a basic open tray model. Fill that feeder, then pull up a lawn chair near the feeder, about 3 feet away. Dress appropriately for the weather and sit still. Your guests, which probably headed for the hills when you arrived, should return in less than half an hour. Remain sitting quietly while they feed for another half hour.

Repeat the procedure the next day, but this time position the chair directly beside the feeder. Again, sit and wait while activity returns to normal and the birds accept your presence.

The third day, rest your hand in the feeder, with a tempting handful of nuts or sunflower seeds in the palm. Don't worry if birds eat the seeds around your hand but not those in it; just stay still and nonthreatening.

The fourth day, empty the feeder and repeat the offering on your palm. You should get at least one taker—generally a chickadee or titmouse. Nuthatches can also be among the first to approach.

Continue the sitting posture for another day or two, until birds freely visit your hand. Then dispense with the chair, and try standing at the feeder. Once a few friendly birds accept you as a new walking feeder, they may alight on your shoulder to ask for food as you stroll the yard. Be sure to carry some of their favorite seeds or nuts in your pocket.

Harvesting Seed

BEATING THE BIRDS to the best seeds in your garden can be a challenge because they're monitoring the ripeness of the maturing seedheads even more often than you are. Thus, the presence of seed eaters such as goldfinches at your sunflowers, zinnias, or other seed-bearing plants is a sign for you to start collecting if you intend to put aside any ripe seeds for later feeder use.

Harvesting seeds before they are completely ripe helps you beat the birds. Many seeds continue to ripen even if harvested from the plant when green. In general, look for seedheads that have filled out with plump green seeds that are beginning to turn to yellow. These seeds usually will dry to a ripe golden or brown color even if removed from the plant.

If you intend to use seedheads in wreaths, swags, or bundles, allow long stems when picking. Otherwise, you can snip individual clusters into a large brown paper sack. To separate the seeds, tightly close the sack and shake briskly, causing the ripe seeds to fall free from the seedhead. Pour off the seeds into containers for later use.

If you are picking seeds that are not fully ripe, spread the seedheads in shallow cardboard trays in a dry place protected from birds and rodents. Cardboard trays for shipping soda cans are available at convenience stores or supermarkets and will do the trick. An unheated garage is perfect. Check the seeds daily, and when they are ripe, transfer the seedheads and any fallen-out bits to paper bags to shake off the seeds as described above.

Many flowers and weeds lend themselves to seed collecting. It's fun to observe which birds prefer

When sunflower heads start to droop, harvest quickly if you want to save the seeds for future bird feeding. Once the seeds are dry, store them in a rodent-proof container.

which seeds when you offer them later at the feeder. Here are some easy ones to get you started:

- Amaranths
- Ragweed (if you're not allergic to it!)
- Safflower (*Carthamus tinctorius*)
- Lamb's-quarters
- Chicory
- Cosmos (*Cosmos sulphureus, C. bipinnatus*)
- Purple coneflower (*Echinacea purpurea*)
- Sunflower, annual
- Garden balsam (*Impatiens balsamina*)
- Lettuce
- Marigolds
- Dandelions
- Zinnias

Hawks

WITH EYESIGHT sharper than any other bird, hawks are supremely well adapted for their job of feathered predator. They can catch motion and discern a grasshopper from a 30-foot utility pole or zero in on a junco while soaring high overhead. If you have a feeding station patronized by daily crowds of birds, it is likely to catch the attention of a hawk in the area. Hawks usually seek out feeding stations in winter because the pickings are a lot easier at this literal bird buffet than in the wild.

First, consider it a compliment if a hawk comes to visit. Its presence means your yard is teeming with birds. Then admire the cool beauty of these creatures. Whether your visitor is a large, heavy-bodied red-tailed hawk of the *Buteo* genus; a streamlined, sharp-shinned hawk representing the *Accipiter* clan; or a small, slim American kestrel, a widespread member of the genus *Falco*, your meat-eating guest has its hunting skills honed to a fine art. No member of the hawk family wastes energy getting a meal, though methods of catching prey differ. Buteos include the nationwide **red-tailed hawk;** the **red-shouldered** and **broad-winged hawks** of the eastern half of the country; and the southwestern **zone-tailed hawk.** They usually hunt from a perch, spying on surroundings until they spot a rodent, insect, reptile, or bird. Accipiters are swift and agile fliers. The **sharp-shinned** and **Cooper's**

A soaring Cooper's hawk makes smaller birds dive for cover—and for good reason. Birds top the menu for this agile flier and its lookalike cousin, the sharp-shinned hawk.

hawks, found across the continent, and their larger brother of the north, the **northern goshawk,** generally drop from the sky to snatch a bird, a habit that once earned them the nickname "blue death." The once-rare **peregrine** and **prairie falcons,** and their smaller falcon kin, the **American kestrel** and the **merlin,** are the fastest fliers in the hawk family and loath to let a bird escape once they have spotted it. They may fly through a feeder area to see what they can scare up.

Hawk ID

Figuring out what hawk is terrorizing your bird feeder isn't as easy as it may seem. Hawks vary widely in their plumage as they mature; males and females also may have different coloring. Mottled coloring rather than the clearly defined areas of solid brown or other hues shown in your field guide are the hint that you're looking at a youngster.

HAWK FOODS

- Suet, large chunks
- Meat scraps, raw
- Poultry scraps, raw
- Mice
- Voles
- Squirrels
- Pigeons
- Game birds
- Songbirds
- Starlings

It helps to learn the flight patterns and general sizes of the hawks in your area. The big buteos—red-tails, red-shoulders, and a few others—are extra large size birds; they may flap or soar. Accipiters like sharpshins and Cooper's hawks are slim, trim birds with longer tails and narrower wings, but the real clue is their flight—it's a distinctive pattern of a few flaps followed by a spread-winged glide. Falcons are fairly easy to recognize, thanks to their pointed wings, as sharp as a Russian scimitar. Keep your binoculars handy if a hawk becomes a regular. Over the winter feeding season, you're sure to get a fix on it.

Protecting Feeder Birds

You may want to discourage a hawk from returning once you witness his first meal at your feeder. Even if you find the food chain in action a fascinating sight, you may wrestle with the question of whether it is ethical to lure potential prey to your yard. You can usually give the hawk the hint by withholding seed for a week. By that time, smaller birds will have stopped flocking to the area and will have dispersed to wilder haunts, and the hawk may move on to look for another concentrated gathering of birds.

Of course, if the hawk arrives in the middle of severe cold or snow, you'll be sending your dependents out to face a food shortage if you withhold seed. That may be as fatal as a hawk strike. If this is the case, serve songbirds their meals beneath a sheltering tree or shrub, where they can instantly find cover and protection. In winter, I surround my feeders with discarded Christmas trees for quick and portable cover.

Hawks are not always hunting for birds at your feeder. Most species also relish mice, rats, and other rodents. Tell your squirrels—or not!

Hawk Behavior

If a hawk drops in, pull out the binoculars and take a close look. The strong beak, built for tearing flesh, and the tightly gripping talons are marvels of form-fits-function. Hawk plumage is also beautiful through binoculars, exhibiting subtle bars and streaks. Take a look, too, at the color of the eye; some species have a piercing yellow orb, while others gleam blood red.

In winter, a red-tailed hawk may claim a feeder as its private diner, preying on daily guests. If your feeders seem suddenly birdless, look for a perched hawk.

If you are feeding large hunks of suet or meat scraps to your feeder birds, you may find hungry hawks tearing at the meal during cold weather or storms, when their natural food is in hiding or locked in ice. Should the hawk make a kill at your feeder, watch to see where it goes so you can observe how it devours its prey. The plucking process is fascinating, and so is the most favored first bite—often the head. If you feel squeamish at the thought, take comfort in the knowledge that these birds of prey usually kill their intended meals instantly.

It's not cruelty that causes hawks to prey on birds—it's just a natural step in the food chain. The only unnatural part is what we do—encourage smaller birds to gather in concentrated numbers at a feeding station. The hawk is just doing its job.

H

Hedges and Hedgerows

Attract many kinds of birds at various times of the year

BACK IN THE DAYS before monster combines and tractors the size of a small house, farmers kept hedgerows along the edges of their fields to provide homes for game birds, rabbits, and other wildlife. As farming became big business and clean fields the norm, hedgerows disappeared, eliminating precious habitat and prime nesting sites.

Recreate those farm hedgerows on your own property, and the numbers of birds that visit and reside at your place will increase dramatically. The same mix of plants that worked in the old days—basically whatever came up and survived in the strip of land next to the fence—is ideal today, but it fits best into a more relaxed landscape.

I think of a hedge as a row of a single type of plant—flowering shrubs or berry bushes, for instance—and a hedgerow as a multilevel mix of both planned and unexpected delights. More formal or better-planned hedges with fewer types of plants will also supply shelter, but they aren't nearly as appealing to birds as a hedgerow's casual, jumbled mix of young trees, shrubs, vines, weeds, and grasses.

Diversity Makes the Difference

Diversity brings in the birds. In a mixed hedgerow, seeds and fruits ripen at different times, providing months of tasty food. Various insects are attracted to different plants, so that those birds that seek aphids can find beetles, too, and those that prefer caterpillars can eat their fill. An assortment of plants also supplies a variety of nesting sites, so that your hedgerow can host shrub-dwelling catbirds, branch-building robins, and ground-nesting sparrows all at once.

A little laissez-faire also helps a hedgerow appeal to birds. Keeping a hands-off approach lessens the intrusions of your disturbing presence into possible nesting territory. No self-respecting bird will build a nest where the gardener is always fussing around with hedge clippers or string trimmers. Declaring a moratorium on weeding or string trimming around the woody plants also creates a dense undergrowth of weeds and grasses—plants that are perfect from a bird's eye view because of their bounty of seeds.

Although it can be difficult at first to change your standards from manicured garden to dirty-fingernails natural, you'll find a big payoff, not only in birds but also in the amount of interest the hedgerow holds. You can watch as wildflowers take hold and retreat, as blackberries or roses move in, as tree seedlings sprout and grow—the whole story of succession in one small strip of plants. You'll also find a whole world of fascinating creatures besides birds, from beetles and praying mantises to tree frogs and deer mice.

Include a Few Evergreens

For year-round use and unbeatable shelter in rainy weather, be sure to include a few evergreen shrubs and trees in your hedge. Look for those that supply berries or cones, including Oregon grape hollies (*Mahonia* spp.), hollies (*Ilex* spp.), and conifers, or suit your own sensibilities and plant whatever evergreens you like. Rhododendrons and azaleas (*Rhododendron* spp.), camellias (*Camellia* spp.), magnolias (*Magnolia* spp.), and other broadleaved types are as useful as needled evergreens for nesting and shelter.

For instant usefulness to birds, invest in a few good-size evergreens that already sport the dense branches that appeal to birds. From the time they're waist-high, hemlocks (*Tsuga* spp.), upright junipers (*Juniperus* spp.), and spruces (*Picea* spp.) are highly appealing to shelter-seeking birds, and they are usually available at a reasonable price. Evergreens that grow more slowly are usually priced accordingly: Plants that fit a limited budget are apt to be small in stature. In addition to instant-utility plants, you may want to include pines (*Pinus* spp.) and other evergreens that have open branches when young and gradually fill out with age.

Starting a Hedgerow

Experimenting with the combinations for a hedgerow makes an entertaining game. The best part is that there is no wrong way. I like to include a few basic types of plants in the row, and then let nature take over and fill in or weed out the rest. Native plants that can tough it out among the competition are best for a hedgerow. To start this great bird area, begin with a selection of excellent bird plants,

arranged in any order you like. That's all you need. The bare spaces will soon be filled in, as birds drop seeds of vines and creepers; squirrels bury nuts and acorns; and weeds, grasses, and wildflowers sprout from the soil. Consider using these plants:

- A few nut trees, like pecan (*Carya illinoinensis*), shagbark hickory (*C. ovata*), and butternut (*Juglans cinerea*)

- Native fruit trees, such as wild plum and wild cherries (*Prunus* spp.)

- Hazelnuts (filberts) (*Corylus* spp.)

GARDEN DESIGN

Creating Hedges

Hedges are useful as windbreaks around the feeder area, and they provide corridors of safety for birds as they travel about your yard or to neighboring properties. Annual sunflowers and several other good bird plants make almost-instant hedges that can tower 6 feet or taller in a single season. Other hedges are a long-term proposition, starting small and gradually filling in over a period of years. Whether you plant one or both types, choose plants for the hedge that will supply birds with food as well as shelter, if possible. Exercise your creativity by combining plants in a sort of linear garden, or plant a row of all the same kind.

ONE-SEASON HEDGE PLANTS

Love-lies-bleeding (*Amaranthus caudatus*)

Tall amaranth (*Amaranthus* spp. and cvs.)

Tickseed (*Bidens aristosa*)

Sunflowers (*Helianthus annuus, H. debilis*)

Mexican sunflower (*Tithonia rotundifolia*)

Indian corn (*Zea mays* var. *indurata*)

Popcorn (*Z. mays* var. *praecox*)

Corn (*Z. mays* var. *rugosa*)

Tall zinnias (*Zinnia elegans* cvs.)

A hedge of annual plants such as corn (1), Mexican sunflowers (2), amaranth (3), and branching sunflowers (4) provides plenty of seeds for birds to eat and creates a quick and colorful privacy screen for your yard.

- Berried shrubs, including spicebush (*Lindera benzoin*), highbush blueberry (*Vaccinium corymbosum*), and arrowwood viburnum (*Viburnum dentatum*)
- Hawthorns (*Crataegus* spp.)
- A few evergreens such as white fir (*Abies concolor*), eastern red cedar (*Juniperus virginiana*), or white spruce (*Picea glauca*)
- Native vines, such as clematis species or greenbriars (*Smilax* spp.)
- Sumacs (*Rhus* spp.)

You can also simply stop mowing a strip of lawn at least 10 feet wide and let succession take its course. At first, you'll have tall grass. Then tough weeds and wildflowers will show up, such as Queen-Anne's-lace (*Daucus carota*) and curly dock (*Rumex crispus*). Within about 3 years, expect to see blackberries (*Rubus* spp.), goldenrods (*Solidago* spp.), and asters move in, along with tree and shrub seedlings. As the trees gain height and the shrubs increase their girth, they'll crowd out the weeds everywhere except along the open sides of the hedgerow.

PERMANENT HEDGE PLANTS

Serviceberries (*Amelanchier* spp.)

Ceanothus (*Ceanothus* spp.)

Hazelnuts/filberts (*Corylus* spp.)

Box huckleberry (*Gaylussacia brachycera*)

Hollies (*Ilex* spp.)

Spicebush (*Lindera benzoin*)

Wild cherries and plums (*Prunus* spp.)

Sumacs (*Rhus* spp.)

Currants (*Ribes* spp.)

Native roses (*Rosa* spp.)

Blackberries (*Rubus* spp.)

American elderberry (*Sambucus canadensis*)

Hemlock (*Tsuga* spp.)

Blueberries (*Vaccinium* spp.)

American cranberrybush (*Viburnum trilobum*)

A combination of shining winterberry holly (1), sumac (2), and elderberry (3) will ensure a steady level of bird activity around your yard.

Hollies

Attract bluebirds, catbirds, mockingbirds, robins, thrushes, waxwings, Carolina wrens

EVERY DAY IS CHRISTMAS for the birds when holly berries are ripe. Once a flock of robins or waxwings or other berry eaters discovers a holly, they'll return day after day until every berry has gone down the hatch. Barely pausing for breath, the birds gulp down the fruit so efficiently that you can see your precious winter decorations dwindle while you watch.

That appeal is exactly why you'll want to add holly berries to the menu at your feeding station. Once the bluebirds, catbirds, mockingbirds, robins, thrushes, waxwings, or Carolina wrens discover your berries, you can count on daily visits until the branches are bare.

Plant shrubs and trees near the feeding area for the long-term payoff. While you're waiting for your plants to bear fruit, offer your birds branches of holly you've begged, bought, or, um, borrowed. Holly branches are beautiful in winter window boxes or stuck in those big clay pots that were too heavy to haul indoors. Thanks to their shiny evergreen foliage, which stays fresh outdoors for weeks in cold weather even without water, they look good even when their accents of red berries are long gone.

Finger-pricking holly leaves may be unwelcome to the human touch, but to birds, they're a boon. A sleeping berth in an evergreen holly means an undisturbed night's rest for birds because cats and other predators are reluctant to brave the spiny foliage. Migrating flocks of robins often take cover for the night in large, dense American holly (*Ilex opaca*) trees, while sparrows may use smaller shrub-size cultivars.

Most of us think evergreen when we hear the word "holly," but deciduous species hold great appeal for birds, too, especially for bluebirds, which seem to find these berries irresistible. Unlike the evergreen hollies, some of which can grow to 100 feet tall, deciduous hollies (*Ilex verticillata* and hybrids) are shrubby plants that grow only about 6 to 8 feet tall. They're perfect for planting in groups or in the mixed border outside the window by your favorite easy chair. With any luck, they'll bring hungry bluebirds to within easy view. Deciduous hollies also thrive in much wetter conditions than their evergreen cousins, as well as in average garden sites. In the wild, they often grow along roadside ditches or watercourses, where the soil is downright boggy at times. If you have a wet area in your yard where the soil is slow to dry out after winter snow or rain, try a deciduous holly.

I've had good luck with every "unimproved" species of holly I've tried—as far as bird appeal, that is—but I've discovered that some cultivars and hybrids seem to be unpalatable to birds, perhaps for the same reasons that some crabapple fruits hang on the branches without a bird ever looking twice at them. If birds snub your hollies, try another type!

Evergreen hollies are hardy to USDA Zone 5; deciduous types thrive as far north as Zone 3.

Berries by the Branch

STORE-BOUGHT holly branches carry a hefty price tag between Thanksgiving and Christmas, but after New Year's, the bottom pretty much drops out of the market. That's the time to swoop in for bargain berries! Visit florists, garden centers, and supermarket floral departments soon after Christmas—before they pitch their stock—and you'll probably be able to pick up berried holly branches for a cut-rate price (or even free!).

Holly berries remain appealing to birds for weeks after the branches are cut, especially in cold weather. Lay the loose branches in an open tray feeder, or use floral wire to attach the branches to a post for a faux holly tree. If you acquire an abundance of holly branches, you can strip the berries and refrigerate them in resealable plastic bags for feeding all through winter. Be sure to remove branches of prickly leaved evergreen holly once the birds are done with the berries; fallen holly leaves can be an unpleasant surprise should they wind up in your flowerbeds.

Honeysuckle

Attracts catbirds, hummingbirds, mockingbirds, robins, thrashers, thrushes

THINK LANGUID summer nights, heady fragrance, and a hummingbird's delight—that's honeysuckle, a must for hummingbird lovers. Some species grow as vines while others are large shrubs, but all bloom for several weeks, drawing long-beaked hummingbirds to their deep, nectar-filled blossoms, which are not only sweet but pretty, too. After the blossoms come berries, eagerly devoured by songbirds like catbirds, mockingbirds, robins, thrashers, and thrushes. Songbirds may nest or take cover in both shrub-type and vining honeysuckles, which makes them ideal plants to add to your feeding station area.

Hummingbirds and honeysuckles are a natural combination. The tubular blossoms evolved with hummingbirds to ensure pollination needs are met.

That's only half the story of honeysuckle. Some imported species of these plants have become thugs in the American landscape, burying native vegetation with their thick vines and bushes. Japanese honeysuckle (*Lonicera japonica*), the familiar white- and yellow-flowered vine, is the worst culprit, but some foreign bush honeysuckles have gone wild, too. Ironically, the problem-causing honeysuckles are non-native plants imported to North America to provide food and shelter for wildlife. Unfortunately, the experts forgot to consider what would happen when birds and animals spread the seeds far and wide.

Stick to all-Americans like the well-behaved trumpet honeysuckle (*Lonicera sempervirens*), and you won't have to worry about the plants taking over your neighborhood when you turn your back.

Six Native Honeysuckles

NO MATTER where you live, there's a great native honeysuckle waiting for you to invite it home. Check native-plant nurseries like those listed in "Resources" on page 348 to find some of these home-grown beauties:

White honeysuckle (*Lonicera albiflora*): Shrub with white or creamy flowers and orange berries; native to the South

Arizona honeysuckle (*L. arizonica*): Shrub with bright orange flowers and red berries; native to the Southwest

Yellow honeysuckle (*L. flava*): Shrub with yellow flowers that turn orange; red fruit; native to the Southeast

Chaparral honeysuckle (*L. interrupta*): Twining shrub, evergreen, with yellow flowers and red fruit; native to the Southwest

Twinberry (*L. involucrata*): Shrub with yellow or red flowers and purplish black fruit; native to the Pacific Northwest

Trumpet honeysuckle (*L. sempervirens*): Vigorous vine with brilliant red flowers with yellow inside; small red berries and evergreen foliage; native to the East and South

Hopper Feeders

Hopper feeders are feeders with built-in seed storage. These handy devices dole out seed as quickly as it disappears from the surrounding tray, so that you don't have to bother with daily refills. (As you might imagine, this is especially helpful during the winter months.) The seed is stored in a covered container that shelters it from rain and snow; a slit or other small opening at the bottom allows the stored seed to run out and fill the tray as your guests empty it out.

Not only do hopper feeders save you time, they also guarantee that fresh seed is available to birds even when you aren't around to refill. In winter, you don't have to tromp through the snow so that the birds can dine at their early breakfast table—let the hopper do the dirty work while you catch a few more winks snug under the covers. If you plan to be away on vacation during peak feeder season, a hopper feeder will allow you to leave with a clear conscience because your birds will still find plentiful food while you're gone.

There are many readily available designs of hopper feeders. You can buy lightweight, clear plastic models or huge, heavy metal or wood constructions that hold up to 10 pounds of seed. Fill the feeder with whatever seeds your birds like best: millet, sunflower, or a mix.

Because hopper feeders are more complicated in structure than simple tray feeders, they are also more expensive. Expect to pay from $30 to $75 for a well-made hopper feeder. These feeders are worth the ini-

Built-in storage reduces refilling chores with these feeders. Weighted models like the one at right block out seed-gobbling squirrels and heavy-bodied birds.

tial investment, though, because you and your bird friends will be using them for years.

Limited feeding space is the only drawback of hopper feeders. The storage area often takes up most of the space, leaving only a narrow ledge for birds to eat from. They can't accommodate nearly as many customers at one sitting as an open tray feeder. Some designs compensate for this by attaching a wider tray area beneath the hopper.

Tube feeders, which also hold seed in a storage compartment, are usually considered a separate "species" of feeder; you'll find details on them in the Tube Feeders entry on page 306.

Hot Peppers

Attract western sparrows, quail, and other birds

The small flat, round seeds from hot peppers (*Capsicum annuum* var. *annuum*) pack a powerfully hot punch to human taste buds, but many birds eat them with impunity. Western sparrows, quail, and other birds that hail from the desert Southwest may sample pepper seeds. Birds of other regions may enjoy them once they become familiar with them.

A plethora of hot peppers are available for home gardens. All do well in well-drained soil in a sunny location, but the plants need a long growing season to produce their best. Any variety will work for birdseed.

It's best to allow the plants to stand in your garden for a self-serve buffet. Birds will find the seeds during the fall and winter. Harvesting and cleaning the peppers—which can produce prodigious crops—can be a painful procedure unless you are extremely careful. If you want to clean the fruits to free the seeds, be sure to wear thick rubber gloves to prevent the irritating capsaicin from contacting your skin. Most important, do not rub your eyes or touch unprotected skin once you have begun to work. The burning chemical contaminates your gloves and the slightest touch can easily transfer the chemical to bare skin.

Hot pepper extract may help deter squirrels from the feeder. You can buy commercially treated birdseed, or spray the seed yourself with a commercially produced extract. You can also try brewing your own pepper spray by soaking hot peppers in water (again, exercise great caution). Results of treated birdseed have been unpredictable; but if squirrel-proof feeders don't discourage your furry friends, you may want to conduct your own backyard trials.

> Many birds eat hot pepper seeds with impunity, while an extract may deter squirrels from feeders.

House Sparrow

HOUSE SPARROWS, a species imported from England, arouse extreme ire and have done so for decades. "The English sparrow among birds, like the rat among mammals, is cunning, destructive, and filthy," huffed the authors of *Birds of America*, published in 1942. There's no doubt these birds can be pests. However, house sparrows, released in large flocks in the early 1850s, arrived here by invitation, not by choice. I find it hard to fault the bird for its adaptability. Its success shows that this species can survive under circumstances where other birds fail.

In urban areas, industrial wastelands, and even suburban developments, the decline of native birds is primarily caused by our own species. When we alter the natural landscape, we destroy the habitat needed by our less adaptable native birds. Once the less adaptable tanagers and orioles disappear, the go-with-the-flow house sparrows move in. By building a bird-friendly yard, you can help prevent the evolution of a world where house sparrows dominate their habitats completely. As long as our native birds are thriving, I trust they'll give house sparrows a run for their money.

Familiar to most Americans and almost as widely despised, the house sparrow has several habits that secure its reputation as an undesirable. Most important from the view of our native birds is its habit of nesting

Noisy house sparrows are a familiar presence across America. They rarely range far from our own dwelling places, so they'll be first at the feeding station.

in cavities. Nothing is more frustrating than trying to keep house sparrows from claiming that bluebird box you just put up in the backyard. Every March, I exhort my bluebirds to put up a fight for their home, but they yield without much fuss at all, turning over the

The Bright Side

HOUSE SPARROWS do have some appealing traits. In a Boston city neighborhood, I watched a couple scattering bread crumbs for a flock of house sparrows. When I asked why, they told me the birds were best friends to their fruit trees and vegetables. "After they eat the bread, they eat the bugs," they told me, smiling at the noisy brown birds at their feet.

House sparrows have a big appetite for pests, which helps to compensate for the grain and fruit they destroy and all the new shoots of garden lettuce they nip off. They help control outbreaks of alfalfa weevils and cutworms. They also have a fondness for Japanese beetles, snapping them up by the dozens from garden plants, and they dine on other garden pests, including caterpillars and aphids.

The species generally stays near human habitat, so they don't compete with woodland birds or birds of wide open spaces. Those that live in the country forage for grain in the fields, but they rarely venture far from the farm buildings.

In areas where humans have crowded out most native birds, house sparrows will still visit the feeder, so that even the most city-bound resident can enjoy watching birds.

---

keys to sparrows after as little as half an hour. Although there are reports of sparrows destroying nests and young of other birds, in my experience, the occupation usually consists of the sparrows simply perching near or on the house. I have seen the sparrows poke their heads in the hole, but I have never seen beak-to-beak combat. The intimidation alone is apparently enough to bully bluebirds, purple martins, wrens, and other species out of house and home.

House sparrows are also notorious for their less-than-appealing personal habits. They seem to argue with each other constantly, fighting vociferously over food, elbow room, or females. They prefer to live near humans, where they hang around in noisy groups, making themselves at home just about anywhere, including city streets, farmyards, and suburbia. At night, they join together in large flocks, which means droppings whitewash their favored roosts. Unlike many songbirds, house sparrows are casual in their choice of mates. Instead of forming a lifelong pair bond, the male bird pursues as many females as possible. Though house sparrows are related to the superb Old World builders known as weaver finches, these imports lack the dexterity of their talented relatives. House sparrows settle for messy, sprawling nests that usually trail telltale strips of grass, plastic, or paper trash.

House Sparrow Behavior

Short-tempered house sparrows are quick to fly into a frenzy. At the feeder, you'll see them shouldering aside others of their kind or engaging in open-beaked combat. I sometimes encourage the quarrels by tossing out half slices of bread. Like crows, gulls, and other aggressive types, the house sparrows argue for possession, flying back and forth after the "lucky" bird that first nabbed the prize. Often the bread changes beaks several times before the birds finally rip it into pieces and devour it.

House sparrows travel in groups, and they're a loud-mouthed bunch, constantly chirping or squawking. If you keep a tray feeder stocked with cracked corn, millet, bread crumbs, and other house sparrow favorites, you can decoy the birds away from your other feeders, so that the less aggressive songbirds can eat in relative peace.

Watch for courtship displays, in which males approach a female with drooping wings. Vicious battles between males may punctuate these performances, and they may end with a group of males in hot pursuit of the harried female.

HOUSE SPARROW FEEDER FOODS

- Birdseed mix
- Bread and other baked goods
- Corn, cracked
- Crackers
- Doughnuts
- Fruit, fresh or dried
- Leftovers
- Millet
- Milo
- Pasta, cooked
- Suet, chopped
- Sunflower seed, black oil
- Wheat

Hummingbirds

A NECTAR FEEDER IS ALL IT TAKES to bring hummingbirds to your yard—or window or balcony. These amazing creatures, the smallest birds in North America, connect the color red so exclusively with food that they will investigate any red object they can reach. This may be the new feeder you just put up, your child's red wagon, or the handle of your pruners sticking out of your hip pocket!

Hummingbirds are strictly an American phenomenon. Imagine the wonder European explorers felt when they first saw the brilliant, insectlike birds. Their colors are unbelievably gorgeous, their flight so swift it's hard to follow, and they are the only bird anywhere with a reverse gear.

Go West, Young Bird Watchers!

Eastern hummingbird watchers have good reason to envy their counterparts in the West. Only one hummingbird species, the ruby-throated hummingbird, regularly visits and nests east of the Mississippi River. Travel westward and you'll encounter at least 14 breeding species, plus other hummers that may be sojourning from points south. In prime hummingbird-watching areas, especially in the Southwest, folks have turned hummers into a tourist business. They open their homes as guest houses so that visitors can spend as long as they like watching the fantastic birds at feeders and at flowers. When I watch

Hummingbirds are unbelievably beautiful. Males sport brilliant metallic colors on their throat (and sometimes head), like the neon pink of this Anna's hummingbird.

a hummingbird feeder with other hummer enthusiasts, whether it's at a bed-and-breakfast or behind plateglass at a nature center or park, I always think of fireworks. The crowd reaction to these feathered bursts of color will remind you of the Fourth of July— "Aaah! Ooh! Oooo!" You'll naturally join the admiring chorus. What else can you say when a

---

How Hummingbirds Fly

ALL BIRDS can fly forward, and some birds can hover for a short spell, but only hummingbirds can zip into backward flight, too. This is possible because their wings actually flip over on each stroke when hovering or going backward, so that the leading edge, which remains facing front in

other birds, works in either direction. Hummingbirds also work their wings from what would be our shoulder joint, instead of flapping them at the elbow and wrist joints like other birds. To really appreciate the fantastic mechanics of a hummingbird's wings, try it yourself:

Step 1. Hold your arms out with thumbs forward so your arms are slightly ahead of your shoulders.

Step 2. Now swing your arms so that they point backward, while rotating your arms at the shoulders so that your thumbs face back.

Step 3. Repeat, so that thumbs again are facing front as you rotate your arms and bring them forward.

Step 4. Now do it 70 times a second. Hey, you're a hummingbird!

bright purple, green, and bronze-colored mite zips by at 60 mph?

Of course, it's the hummingbird watchers in the Andes who are luckiest of all. In Central and South America, particularly in the mountains, hummingbirds appear in an incredible diversity—more than 300 species! Some have long, streaming tail plumes like a scissor-tailed flycatcher; others sport colors so fantastic you'd think a jeweler had fashioned the bird from gold and gems for some discerning emperor.

If you can't get to South America soon, plan a trip to Ithaca, New York, to see the

Hummingbird flight is a miracle of anatomy, thanks to adaptations that allow motion in any direction. This black-chinned hummer shows the art of hovering.

amazing splendor of more than 100 species of hummingbirds. A remarkable collection of specimens assembled more than a century ago adorns the wall of the headquarters of Cornell University's Sapsucker Woods Laboratory of Ornithology. The birds are absolutely unreal in their beauty, their colors shifting like an opal as you move a step to the left or right before the wall-mounted case. Ornithologists have not identified all of the specimens. Some experts believe that at least one hummingbird in the collection is actually an invention of the taxidermist who mounted the birds—created from an assemblage of parts and feathers from various species. The label on one of the 100 birds reads the "beautiful hummingbird," a title that could easily apply to all.

Practical and Pretty

Hummingbirds and American flowers complement each other perfectly. The birds pollinate blossoms with tubular bases, which hold their nectar so deep that insects and butterflies can't reach it. As the hummingbird probes the flower with its beak and tongue, its head becomes dusted with pollen that the bird then transfers to the next flower it feeds upon.

Where hummingbirds abound, tubular flowers do, too. In western North America, these specialized

blossoms open on a schedule that coincides with the movements of hummingbirds. As the tiny birds move up from Mexico, they follow a wave of flowers northward, like Hansel and Gretel following a trail of bread crumbs. When an unseasonable, lingering cold delays spring blooms, the birds stay put temporarily until the flowers again unfold before them. In summer, when hummer populations are at their peak, western penstemons and salvias—two favored hummingbird flowers—are in high gear, too.

A Rainbow of Hummingbirds

Why aren't hummingbirds brown or gray? You certainly don't need iridescent feathers to pollinate a flower, as any sphinx moth can attest. It's a wonderful mystery and a delight to us feeder watchers, who can appreciate the marvels of hummingbird hues from just inches away.

Like any iridescent object, hummingbird feathers appear dark, or black, unless a shaft of light illuminates them. The first time I watched western hummingbirds congregating around a feeder, I thought I was looking at 20 birds of the same species—and none of them would take your breath away. The feeder was in shadow, so the birds appeared only as dark, indistinguishable silhouettes, some slightly smaller, some slightly larger. When the sun came out, I was awestruck.

Except for a few species, only the males boast brilliant colors. Females are green, with paler bellies, and they are very difficult to identify by species. The most vivid patch of color on the male bird's body is at the throat. These feathers, called gorgets, are the first key to a quick ID of a hummingbird species. If you live in the East, you've probably already noticed the vivid scarlet pink throat of the well-named **ruby-throated hummingbird.** Take a peek through binoculars to fully appreciate the brilliance of the shining feathers as the bird moves and the light hits its gorgets.

Moving west, hummingbirds begin to appear in greater variety. One of the most widespread is the **rufous hummingbird,** a beautiful rust-colored bird with bright orange gorget. The rufous is a wanderer and occasionally delights easterners with a brief appear-ance, although it nests only in the West. The **black-chinned hummingbird** is a common species in western mountains, although it nests as far east as Texas. If you're looking at a hummer in bright light and its throat remains black, this is your bird; a violet-purple throat band below the black will underscore the ID. In the Rockies, it's joined by the **broad-tailed hummingbird,** a very close relative of the look-alike eastern ruby-throated hummingbird. Tiny and less common, the **calliope hummingbird** has a throat that looks striped, as the bird fans its bib of purple gorgets against a white underlay. The smallest hummingbird, the calliope measures only 2¾ inches from stem to stern—and that includes its long bill! One of the most glorious birds is **Anna's hummingbird,** a Pacific coast species, whose head is almost entirely neon pink, like a fluorescent highlighter pen. **Costa's hummingbird** visits and nests in southwestern deserts, where the bright red flowers of the ocotillo are a favorite nectar source. It sports a purple head

Hummingbird I.D. at a Glance
LOOK AT the throat gorgets to identify male hummingbirds at a glance.

Hummingbird	Gorget Color
Allen's	Orange-red
Anna's	Hot pink
Black-chinned	Black
Blue-throated	Cobalt blue
Broad-billed	Blue blending to green
Broad-tailed	Ruby red
Buff-bellied	Green
Calliope	Purple streaks against white
Costa's	Purple
Lucifer	Purple
Magnificent	Rich bright green
Ruby-throated	Ruby red
Rufous	Orange
Violet-crowned	Pure white
White-eared	Emerald green, purple under bill

and a bib of gorgets that it can fan out like a fur collar.

Less common hummers include **Allen's hummingbird,** a bird with a red-orange throat and ruddy tail, and the perfectly named **violet-crowned hummingbird,** whose rich purple cap contrasts with its pure white throat. The **magnificent hummingbird** is a mixture of deep green and bright spring green crowned with royal purple. The **blue-throated hummingbird** is a beauty with cobalt gorgets and golden green belly. These two large southwestern species are giants among the clan, checking in at 5 inches plus.

Spikes of outward-facing tubular flowers are tailor-made for the habits of hummingbirds like this broad-tailed, which will visit each nectar-bearing blossom.

Hummingbird Behavior

Hummingbird behavior is as intriguing as the birds themselves. First there is the miracle of their flight—the quick slip into reverse, the tireless hovering, the changes in direction as speedy as a science-fiction spaceship. At courtship time, you'll see even more astounding flight patterns because hummingbirds depend on aerial dances to help woo a mate. It's Darwinian, of course: Any bird that's a superlative flier carries the necessary genes to ensure the progeny has what it takes for hummingbird survival. These courtship flights are spectacular. The male bird swings in pendulum arcs or does loop-de-loops and figure-8s for the female, who pretends to be blasé on her perch. The whistling noise of the air streaming over or through his wings, the chittering of his cries, and the flashing of his colors in the sun make a terrific performance to watch.

HUMMINGBIRD FEEDER FOODS

- Nectar
- Small insects attracted to butterfly fruit feeders
- Small spiders in crannies of feeders

Although hummingbirds don't sing, they do vocalize. Many have distinctive squeaky or ticking notes, and, of course, there's the buzz that gives these birds their name. The rufous makes a loud whine with its wings when diving; the broad-tailed produces a shrill whistle like a cheap metal flute.

The more you watch hummingbirds go about their daily activities, the more interesting things you'll see. These tiny birds also fuel their bodies with the protein from insects, so you may spot them snagging little bugs out of the air or from flowers. A ruby-throat I hosted regularly patrolled the garden, delicately picking itty-bitty insects from spider webs. The spider did the work of netting them, and the hummer snatched the spoils.

Believe it or not, hummingbirds do have feet. Don't feel silly if you had your doubts—early observers thought the same thing and even put the birds into a scientific classification whose name means "no feet."

Although hummingbirds are perfectly at ease hovering at a perchless feeder, they also make good use of perches while they drink. Keep in mind that perches also make the feeder more accessible to other sugar-water drinkers, a habit that is rapidly increasing among songbirds and woodpeckers.

Watch your hummingbirds when they leave the feeder, and you'll see they typically move to a perch to sit for a spell. These birds have the highest metabolism of any North American animal, except perhaps the shrew. That means they have to eat almost constantly during daylight hours. They intersperse periods of filling their bellies with brief resting periods from sunup to sundown.

Hummingbirds visit nectar feeders from the time of spring migration—which can be as early as February, depending on your location—through departure in fall, as late as November. Here in southern Indiana, I associate hummingbirds with federal income taxes: They both are due on April 15. Like other birds, hummingbird arrivals and leave-takings cleave to a schedule that usually varies by only a few days. Unlike seed eaters, hummingbirds are more at the mercy of the weather, which can retard the blossoming of the plants they depend upon for food along the migration route. If it's a late spring and nectar flower buds open late, hummingbirds may arrive up to a week after I expect them.

I get my feeders out early and leave them hanging until cold weather threatens to freeze the sugar water. Straggler birds are not unheard of, and a feeder that's still filled can be a literal lifesaver. In the several years I've lived in the Midwest, I have twice hosted hummingbirds in December. They stayed for a week, restoring their depleted energy reserves; then they bravely headed south.

At the feeder, hummingbirds can be hogs. These birds are among the most combative of any feathered species. They often claim a food source and defend it viciously against all comers. Don't be surprised if only one bird at a time visits your nectar feeder. Others may want to partake but the territorial first arrival may prevent them. I fill my yard with a half-dozen nectar feeders to accommodate more birds—for their nourishment and my pleasure.

Flowers for Food

The reason sugar-water feeders are so popular is that the solution tastes like flower nectar. Before bird feeders, hummingbirds depended on the nectar held

The male Costa's hummingbird sports a bib of violet purple with feathers that extend beyond its head. This little beauty roams around southwestern desert areas.

within blossoms to fuel their fast little bodies. Even with hummingbird feeders on every block, they still rely on flowers for food.

Flowers attract plenty of hummingbird traffic, especially if they're red. Red-orange and some shades of pink also get their attention. Once a hummingbird is in your garden, though, it will sip nectar from any suitable blossom, no matter what color the flowers. You'll want to place your nectar feeders in or near a flowerbed, so that you can enjoy longer hummingbird visits and watch the birds feed and behave naturally.

Color is foremost in grabbing the initial attention of a hummingbird. Once you've attracted one, choose flowers that are tubular in shape, with petals flaring from a long throat, such as honeysuckle, salvia, and bee balm, to keep the bird visiting. Flowers that really tempt hummingbirds also offer plenty of elbow, er, wing room. They often hold flowers arranged in spikes or clusters at the tips of stems. The spike of a salvia, for instance, holds the individual flowers arranged around the stem, with leaves below, so that hummingbirds can circle the blossom and sip from every flower without working in crowded quarters.

A Patio-Side Hummingbird Garden

The list of good hummingbird flowers is a very long one, with lots of possibilities no matter where you live. Be sure to include some native plants, which offer their nectar-rich blossoms at the times hummingbirds most need them. Wild columbines (Aquilegia canadensis, A. formosa) bloom in time to greet spring migrants, and Texas sage (Salvia coccinea) feeds fall migrants. Create a colorful drift of these hummingbird staples next to your patio or deck, and you'll enjoy hummingbird activity all summer long.

PLANT LIST

1. Butterfly bush (*Buddleia davidii*)

2. 'Enchantment' lily (*Lilium* 'Enchantment')

3. Blue or white annual or perennial salvias, such as *S. × superba* 'May Night' or *S. farinacea*

4. 'Lady in Red' Texas sage (*Salvia coccinea* 'Lady in Red')

5. 'Casablanca' lilies or other similar-size white cultivar (*Lilium* 'Casablanca')

I like to mount nectar feeders on my porch and stick them on the window at my desk, and I also use potted plants to bring the birds in close. Red-orange impatiens and fuchsias flourish on my shady front porch and ensure that I'll see a hummingbird almost every time I glance out the window while working.

Some friends have strung thin wire between the posts of their porch near their hummingbird feeders. It encourages the birds to perch in a colorful row, right by the feeder, as they rest between drinks.

If your feeders run dry, the birds may remind you by hovering outside a window or near the feeder

when you go outside. You can easily train hungry hummingbirds to drink nectar from a small bottle such as test tube you hold in your hand. They will also fearlessly sip from a flower you hold out to them. Once they learn to accept food from you, you can get them to sip nectar from the palm of your hand. Be forewarned—it tickles!

Neat Nesting

At nesting season, you may see hummingbirds gathering spiderwebs in their bills, for use in gluing their nest together. They also collect tiny bits of lichen for camouflaging the outside of the nest, which looks exactly like a natural knot as it hugs a tree branch. Hummingbirds are not poster birds for a committed relationship. Males will mate with any female that allows it. Females seek males only to fertilize their forthcoming eggs, then live a life as single parents, building the nest and raising the young alone. Should you discover a hummingbird nest, you'll love the way a mother bird sits with only her belly in the cup and her long bill extending over the side. When the young fill the nest, they will often sit with their beaks pointing skyward, perhaps so they don't stab each other.

Hummingbirds do sit still—more often than you think. This lucifer hummingbird has dined and now perches before feeding again, a habit it will repeat all day.

Migration-Time Multitudes

Depending on where you live, you may notice that the number of hummingbirds at your feeders and in your garden increases as summer turns to fall. That's a sure sign that migration is hitting its stride. If you live near the middle or at the southern end of a migration route, you will likely be blessed with dozens or even hundreds of hummers. These visitors will create a constant hum in your yard as they single-mindedly fuel up for the next leg of the trip.

Lucky-13 Hummingbird Flowers

YOU WILL attract hummingbirds if you plant these attention getters around your nectar feeder or in containers on a porch or balcony to bring hummingbirds near where you can observe them. Hummingbirds can't resist them!

- Wild columbines (*Aquilegia canadensis, A. formosa*)
- Butterfly bush (*Buddleia davidii*)
- Trumpetvine (*Campsis radicans*)
- Delphiniums (*Delphinium* spp.)
- Impatiens, red-orange–flowered cultivar (*Impatiens wallerana*)
- Cypress vine (*Ipomoea quamoclit*)
- Gilia (*Ipomopsis* spp.)
- Cardinal flower (*Lobelia cardinalis*)
- Bee balm (*Monarda didyma*)
- Penstemons (*Penstemon* spp.)
- Red-flowering currant (*Ribes sanguineum*)
- Red-flowered salvias, such as pineapple sage (*Salvia elegans*); red salvia (*S. splendens*, any cultivar); and Texas sage (*S. coccinea*)
- Mexican sunflower (*Tithonia rotundifolia*)

H

Whether flowers or plastic, red and red-orange colors grab a hummingbird's attention. This beauty is the magnificent hummingbird, also known as Rivoli's.

The holes on nectar feeders are positioned for easy access by this hovering ruby-throated hummingbird, the only one commonly seen east of the Mississippi.

Multiples of hummingbirds do gather around a single good food source in nonmigration times. Flowering trees are famous for attracting dozens of hummingbirds, but unless you look up, it's easy to miss them. Check out the next red-flowering buckeye, horsechestnut, or mimosa you come across—it may be swarming with hummingbirds.

During fall migration, hummingbird populations can build to astounding numbers. In southeastern states, where ruby-throated hummingbirds gather strength before jumping across the Gulf of Mexico, it is a common and wonderful sight to see hordes of hummingbirds at any likely food source. I have seen them zooming up and down city streets in Pensacola, Florida, sampling every window box and flower garden and even investigating red bathing suits on the beach. I once counted 85 hummingbirds in one city block, and the birds went almost entirely unnoticed by the tourists on the street! One burly fellow walking across an oceanfront parking lot had a red bandanna hanging from his back pocket, and a hummingbird was following close behind like a friendly dog panting at his heel.

Hummingbirds can feed without perching, but they'll perch if they can. A plastic antibee guard covers the feeding hole beside this rufous hummingbird.

I

Icicles

FINDING WATER CAN BE a tricky proposition in cold winters, when all natural sources have long frozen over and ice-free birdbaths are few and far between. Yet birds still manage to satisfy their thirst. Icicles are one way to sip a bit of liquid. A tufted titmouse that was a regular client of my feeding station for years (he was identifiable by a white wing feather) also routinely visited the long icicles that spiked the eaves of my log house. Thanks to the warm sun of the southern exposure, the icicles began dripping at their tips by 11 A.M. and continued until the sun sank in late afternoon. The titmouse would perch beneath the longest icicle, which was just a few inches from a porch post, and stretch his neck to sip droplets from the end of the icicle. I've watched house sparrows do the same trick, and I'm sure other birds have perfected this technique.

In late winter, when sap is rising in the trees but the nights are still cold, icicles quickly form when passing street traffic or storms break a branch tip. On sugar maples, box elders, and other trees in the maple family, these "sapcicles" have a faintly sweet flavor, which may be what makes them appealing to the birds that gather nearby when the icicles begin to melt. I've watched blue jays, house finches, and even a yellow-bellied sapsucker help themselves to the natural sweet treat on a February or March morning.

> When natural sources of water are frozen over, sipping from icicles is a way for birds to get needed liquid.

You can't do much to encourage the formation of icicles, but you can keep an eye out for birds that may be getting a drink from these winter decorations.

Identifying Birds

GETTING TO KNOW THE NAMES of your guests is vital so that you can brag about your feeder to other enthusiasts! Of course, identifying your birds also makes it easier to learn about them from reference books or other birders and to keep records and participate in data-gathering feeder counts sponsored by research organizations. Knowing the names of your diners even makes you a smarter shopper: Many birdseed mixes are labeled according to the birds they are intended to attract.

To figure out who's who, you can compare live birds to a field guide, using the shape of the bill and the color of the plumage to key the bird to its picture. Or make a quick sketch (no ability required!), writing notes on colors or other features that may help you find the bird in a field guide (see Field Guides on page 117 or "Recommended Reading" on page 352)—a useful technique if the bird isn't lingering at a feeder, or if it's an unusual one you haven't seen before.

Curved beaks   Straight beaks   Seed beaks

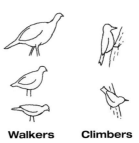

Walkers   Climbers

Use your field guide to familiarize yourself with the bills and body shapes of various bird families, so it's easier to narrow down the choices at identification time.

Insects

Attract many kinds of birds at various times of the year

PRACTICALLY EVERY BIRD EATS INSECTS—if it weren't for birds nabbing insects out of the air, off the ground, and from the bushes, insect populations would skyrocket in no time. Some birds eat more insects than other birds. The purple martin, which loops through the air, bill agape, scoops up thousands of flying insects, from dragonflies to mosquitoes, every day. One observer measured a full quart of cucumber beetle wing covers in a single nesting compartment of a martin box!

Even birds that depend mostly on seeds, such as native sparrows, also consume huge quantities of insects. You may even begin to appreciate starlings when you realize that they enthusiastically devour ants, millipedes, spiders, and wasps—and countless Japanese beetle grubs.

Because of their appetite for insects and arachnids, such as spiders and ticks, attracting birds to your yard means better health for your plants. Birds work tirelessly all year to glean insect eggs, young, adults, and cocoons from their hiding places among foliage, in bark crevices, or under leaf litter on the ground. Watch any bird, as it moves about your yard, and its insect-searching behavior will be evident.

An Insect for Every Taste

As with feeder foods, birds also have their preferences when it comes to insects. We owe this knowledge to the painstaking work of tireless researchers who have spent years counting, one by one, the individual insects contained in bird stomachs (now there's an interesting occupation to consider).

Other observers keep count by watching the process in action. A brown thrasher feeding young carried 247 grasshoppers, 425 mayflies, 237 moths, and 103 cutworms, plus smaller numbers of many other insects, to its brood in a single day.

It's fascinating to try to figure out who's eating what in your own backyard. You can learn a lot just

Nature's balancing plan works superbly: When the insect tide swells in early summer, even seed eaters like this field sparrow switch to an insect diet.

by watching birds at work. If a bird lingers at a plant and is obviously picking off insects, go find out what it's eating. You may discover that the bark is teeming with ants, or that tiny green caterpillars are looping their way through the leaves. When I saw a vivid blue indigo bunting making repeated forays into a clump of ornamental grass, I investigated and discovered scores of young grasshopper nymphs walking up the leaf blades. I quickly retreated so the bunting could finish its work.

Of course, birds make no distinction between so-called good bugs and bad bugs. They don't care if a sphinx moth caterpillar is chomping your precious tomato foliage or a wild catalpa tree: To a bird, that caterpillar is just a nice big bite of protein. Still, if you are an absolute arachnophobe, it's nice to know that hummingbirds, native sparrows, and wrens are on your side, nipping spiders out of their webs and hiding places with dexterity. Of course, those same spiders are important predators of insects in the garden, including many pests.

Don't bother trying to figure out what birds to attract to get rid of specific insects. While you will surely appreciate the efforts of grosbeaks in eating potato bugs, all bird efforts are vital in the grand scheme of things. Natural life is a balance, and birds help keep it that way.

Prime Time for Insects

In summer many birds use insects as a main staple of their diet. There are caterpillars and other delectable tidbits everywhere you look, and birds take full advantage of such easy pickings. Later, when seeds ripen and insects become scarce, finches and other seed eaters return to a seed-based diet.

Early to midsummer when nesting is at its peak, many insects are reaching their highest populations. That dovetails nicely from a bird's-eye perspective because there is abundant protein-packed food available just when nestlings need it most. Nestling birds aren't capable of cracking seeds or eating tough-skinned fruits with their tender bills, so parents seek bite-size bugs to stuff in their hungry mouths. By the time the young birds have left the nest and are

Here an ant, there an ant: Like other birds, this female Bullock's oriole is pest control on the wing, keeping insects from taking over your yard.

learning to hunt on their own, insects fill every nook and cranny of the yard and in wild places.

Birds quickly arrive on the scene when insect populations reach enormous cyclical highs. When

Each One Seeks One

EACH BIRD species has its particular way of searching out this favored food. Here are a few ways birds have evolved to seek this important protein-packed item of their diet:

- Nuthatches hitch their stubby-tailed bodies from the crown of a tree down its trunk, keeping a sharp eye and a sharper beak at the ready in case they spy any choice morsels under flaps or in the cracks of the bark.

- Brown creepers spiral up trees from the base to the branches, affording a view of any insects overlooked by nuthatches on their way down.

- Woodpeckers drill into trees, probing with their long tongues to extract larvae or adult insects from the wood.

- Robins patrol the lawn, heads cocked alertly as they look for earthworms to betray their presence.

- Kinglets and warblers are in constant motion about tree tops, fluttering through the foliage in a supercharged game of find-the-insect.

- Bluebirds, flycatchers, and kingbirds find a comfy perch to survey their domain, poised for instant flight after passing prey. Hawks often behave similarly.

- Grackles and thrashers use their bills to whip aside leaf litter and other debris on the ground to find the six-legged treasures hidden there.

- Native sparrows do a two-legged, hop-front–scratch-back movement that loosens the surface of the soil so they can find insects (as well as seeds).

Who Eats What—Birds and the Bugs They Love

BIRDS ARE opportunists that eat the insects found in their native habitat: Birds of the grassland eat grasshoppers; birds of the treetops dine on caterpillars; birds of the air eat whatever happens to fly by. Here are a few of the top insect and arachnid menu items of some common birds.

Bird	Favored Insect Food*
Red-winged blackbird	Beetles, caddis flies, cankerworms, gypsy moth and tent caterpillars, grasshoppers, grubs, mayflies, moths, spiders
Yellow-headed blackbird	Alfalfa weevils, beetles, caterpillars, grasshoppers
Eastern bluebird	Beetles, crickets, grasshoppers, katydids
Mountain bluebird	Beetles, weevils
Western bluebird	Beetles, crickets, grasshoppers
Indigo bunting	Aphids, beetles, cankerworms, cicadas, grasshoppers, mosquitoes, weevils
Painted bunting	Cankerworms, caterpillars, crickets, flies, grasshoppers, spiders, wasps, boll weevils
Cardinal	Aphids, beetles, caterpillars, cicadas, crickets, grasshoppers, leafhoppers, codling moths, scale insects, spiders, termites
Black-capped chickadee	Caterpillars, codling moths, codling moth caterpillars, insect eggs, spiders
Flickers, all races	Ants
Common grackle	Ants, beetles—Japanese, June, and others—sphinx moth caterpillars, cicadas, earthworms, flies, grubs, grasshoppers, boll weevils
Black-headed grosbeak	Bees, beetles, cankerworms, codling moth caterpillars, flies, grasshoppers, scale insects, spiders, wasps
Evening grosbeak	Beetles, spruce budworm, cankerworms
Rose-breasted grosbeak	Colorado potato beetle and other beetles, cankerworms, tent caterpillars, gypsy moth caterpillars, grasshoppers

gypsy moth caterpillars marched their armies into the woods at my house in Pennsylvania some years ago, their archenemies were close behind. Although I had never before hosted a nesting pair of cuckoos, these large, long-tailed birds (both yellow-billed and black-billed species) moved in within a week. Aided by orioles and blue jays, they devoured countless fuzzy caterpillars. Even an outbreak of aphids can mean a bonanza for neighborhood birds. The Carolina chickadees in my southern Indiana yard regularly patrol for these soft-bodied plant pests, and I've even seen ruby-throated hummingbirds taking aphids from infested stems. Of course, sometimes there simply are too many insects for the birds to control, as with serious gypsy moth outbreaks. But for day-to-day suppression of insects, birds provide efficient, effective control.

Insects Affect Travel Plans

Migrant songbirds that retreat from cold areas for the winter months are often birds that depend mainly on insects. Swallows, martins, and swifts, which catch insects on the wing, are among the earliest to move southward. They can't take any chances of a sudden cold front wiping out their sole food supply.

Unfortunately, spring weather is full of surprises, and purple martins are sometimes caught by a late-season cold snap after they have already started nesting. Your local bait shop can be the key to their

Who Eats What—Birds and the Bugs They Love—*Continued*	
Bird	**Favored Insect Food***
Blue jay	May beetles and other beetles, tent caterpillars, gypsy moth caterpillars, grasshoppers, spiders
Junco	Ants, beetles, caterpillars, spiders, wasps, weevils
Black-billed magpie	Flies, grasshoppers, maggots, ticks
Yellow-billed magpie	Ants, bees, beetles, grasshoppers, wasps
Northern oriole	Caterpillars, especially hairy ones such as gypsy moths and tent caterpillars
Orchard oriole	Ants, aphids, beetles, cankerworms, caterpillars, crickets, grasshoppers, mayflies
Robin	Earthworms; also beetles, cicadas, grasshoppers, termites, many others
Chipping sparrow	Ants, leaf beetles, caterpillars, grasshoppers, leafhoppers, spiders, weevils
Song sparrow	Ants, army worms, beetles, cutworms, grasshoppers, ichneumon flies, wasps, many others
White-crowned sparrow	Beetles, caterpillars, flies, mosquitoes, spiders
White-throated sparrow	Ants, beetles, flies
Plain titmouse	Aphids, true bugs, leafhoppers, scale insects, many others
Tufted titmouse	Mainly caterpillars
Downy woodpecker	Carpenter ants, click beetles, spruce beetles, wood borers, tent caterpillars, cicadas, moths, nut weevils, pine weevils, many others
Hairy woodpecker	Mostly larvae of wood borers, plus others, including large stag beetle
Pileated woodpecker	Carpenter ants, wood-boring beetles
*Includes earthworms and arachnids, such as spiders, which are not insects	

survival: $5 worth of mealworms, offered in an open tray feeder, fills a lot of martin bellies.

Most flycatchers, orioles, tanagers, vireos, and warblers migrate early, too, long before frost creeps in to still the insect life. These birds can supplement their diet with berries, fruit, and sometimes seeds, so a few hardy souls may linger into winter. These stragglers are one reason why soft food can be so valuable at your feeding station. When a sudden snowstorm surprises a lingering catbird or flock of robins and they can't find their usual fare, they welcome a handout. Ground suet, bread, special recipes, or other soft foods can mean the difference between life and death.

Seed-eating birds such as finches and juncos make less dramatic long-distance flights in fall because their natural food is available in nearby climates that may be only a few hundred miles south. Crows, jays,

and woodpeckers may not move on at all, being able to find food in any weather.

No Special Sauce, Please

Birds are our best allies in restoring the balance of insects in yard and garden. When grasshoppers begin to peak in late summer or when caterpillars hatch in hordes on my young oaks, I don't fret because I know the insect-eating birds won't be far behind. In 40 years of gardening, I have never lost a plant to insect pests, thanks to my feathered helpers. (I do occasionally handpick pests that can threaten food crops like squash or tomatoes seemingly overnight.)

Pesticides disrupt the natural equilibrium of your yard. Although your goal is to get rid of a particular pest when you reach for a bottle of pesticide, you are probably also killing off populations of other insects.

Loss of these insects makes it harder for your backyard birds to find the insects they need. Chemicals may also have adverse effects on birds directly; DDT was rightfully notorious for causing thin eggshells that wouldn't support the weight of parent birds, as well as other dangers. Chemicals such as diazinon—only a few years ago a common ingredient of "green lawn" treatments and still in use on golf courses and other places—may also have serious repercussions for bird health, as well as for humans and pets.

Keep your yard free of pesticides, and let the bird crew do the work of keeping insects in balance. After all, they've had a few million years of practice.

A catbird eats hundreds of insects a day and stuffs even more bugs into the beaks of its demanding nestlings. Pesticide use can spell slim pickings for insect-eating birds and their young.

Internet Resources

THE INTERNET MAKES being a bird watcher easy and fun. Shopping for anything bird-related is simple, whether you're buying a field guide, a sack of seed, or a squirrel-proof feeder. You can also shop for bird-related travel needs, from a cruise to the Amazon to bed-and-breakfast accommodations in prime Arizona hummingbird territory.

But even better than armchair shopping are the human-based resources you'll find on the Internet. Chat rooms and Web sites will put you in touch with other folks who've experienced the same problems you have. Whether you want to learn more tricks for deterring squirrels or just enjoy the comfort of commiserating with other birders besieged by the charming varmints, you will find likely sites to visit and people to "talk" to. You can also hook up with bird watchers in your area and farther afield to share sightings or plan trips.

Serious research sites are also available on the Internet, with the latest information about such topics as species of special concern, hummingbird feeding how-tos, and just about anything else you can think of.

Because Internet addresses change frequently, it's best that you do your own exploring to avoid the frustration of visiting a recommended site and finding it no longer in service. Use the search feature of your Net browser to type in the subjects that interest you most. Then just follow your instincts or Web-site links to get connected. "Audubon Society" is a good place to begin your search.

You can contact bird watchers in your area and farther afield to share bird sightings or plan trips.

Irruption Year

DEDICATED BIRD WATCHERS and backyard bird feeders get mighty excited when they hear reports of boreal chickadees, crossbills, purple finches, pine and evening grosbeaks, red-breasted nuthatches, redpolls, pine siskins, and Bohemian waxwings filtering in from other bird-feeding friends. The presence of large numbers of these birds, which make their homes in the cold stretches of the Far North, is a cause for celebration in more southerly climes, where they are rare.

Although a few of these birds may turn up each year at feeders, a true irruption year involves a massive relocation of these species, making them common guests at feeders far south of their normal range. Irruptions are thought to occur when the natural foods—mainly tree seeds, including those of pines, spruces, birches, and maples—fail to yield a good crop. Rather than face starvation, the birds fly south, where they find a true feast awaiting at feeders stocked with a constant supply of sunflower seeds.

It may be the popularity and abundance of backyard feeders that have influenced the movements of some northern birds, particularly evening grosbeaks. Once a rare sighting, these big golden birds have now become a much more common sight at winter feeders.

Another northern bird, the magnificent and huge snowy owl, also flies south irregularly when its rodent prey is unusually scarce. Like its northern relatives, this bird may show up in unlikely places far removed from its usual isolated haunts. I have seen snowies perched on utility poles in city neighborhoods, on split-rail fences in suburban lots, and in the wide-open spaces of airports, which are some-

Evening grosbeaks are an unexpected pleasure at the feeder. Once straying from their far northern homes only during irregular irruption years, they now make more frequent feeder visits.

what similar to their tundra habitat. With their beautiful white plumage and large, unblinking golden eyes, they are a memorable sight. Like the smaller birds of the Far North, the giant owls are unusually trusting of humans, much less apt to flap away than our typical owl residents.

Other northern birds of prey, including great gray owls, rough-legged hawks, goshawks, and northern shrikes, may also move south in an irruption year caused by rodent scarcity. They seem to adapt quite well to whatever rodents or other prey are available, instead of their usual diet of lemmings and voles.

Jays

JAYS ARE SMART and loud, two traits that they put to good use to clear the decks at a feeding station. With a raucous scream, they announce their approach, sending other birds scattering in alarm. Once settled on the feeder, they are usually not aggressive toward the other birds that quickly return to the feeders. For three winters, I hosted a junco that apparently figured out that the jay was all bark and no bite and so refused to budge from the feeder tray. Unfortunately, when the jay swept through one day crying "Thief! Thief!" in earnest because of an approaching hawk, the junco kept cracking seeds calmly. A few seconds later, all that was left were a few gray feathers floating to the ground.

Don't let that sweet look fool you—blue jays are loud, aggressive, and practically fearless. Watching them at the feeder is like having a front-row seat at the circus.

The only eastern representative of the clan is the **blue jay,** a crested bird with beautifully barred wings and tail and a white belly. In the Rockies and westward, **Steller's jay** takes over. This bird is darker than the blue jay, shading from bright blue to almost black, and lacks its white accents. Three crestless jays also roam the West: the **scrub jay,** a blue, white, and gray bird that skulks in thickets; the **gray-breasted jay,** blue on the back, which travels a small area of the Southwest; and the **pinyon jay,** a stubby-tailed blue-gray bird of the West that looks more like a starling at first glance. In the North and the Rockies, the soft-colored **gray jay,** or camp robber, is a familiar sight.

Jay Behavior

Members of the crow family, jays rank as geniuses among the birds. Instead of keeping beak to the grindstone like most other species, these bright birds make time for play. Jays are fond of shiny objects, which they may snatch and hide or use to play can't-catch-me. Teasing is a big part of their games. They pester crows, hawks, and owls, and they can be unmerciful with pets.

Once I watched a blue jay spend the better part of a morning playing "chase" with my dog, who was lounging near the feeders. The bird would alight near Blackie, and when the dog ran in pursuit, the bird took off with a flash of wings and a loud cry. Over and over, the jay repeated the maneuver, until the dog finally gave up and sulked.

Beautiful as well as impudent, jays are fascinating to watch at the feeder. If you host a crested species, take note of how that feathered cap predicts the jay's behavior. When it's stiffly erect, the bird is on the alert and when it's lowered, peace reigns. They pal around in groups when not raising a family, and feeder forays are often dash-in, dash-out affairs.

The cops of the bird world, jays instantly sound the alarm when they perceive danger. They will harass birds of prey, snakes, cats, and other predators.

They stay just a fraction out of harm's way with perfectly timed daring dives. It's always worth investigating when you hear jays making a fuss. The same songbirds that rely on jays to sound an alarm may also occasionally be victims of jays themselves. Jays are fond of eating bird eggs and nestlings. When you spot a robin or other typically docile bird pursuing a jay, you can be sure the jay has been out a-hunting.

Jays indulge in detective work, investigating any unusual objects, which means they will be one of the first birds to sample new foods at the feeder. These big birds also cache food, including nuts and acorns, which they often bury under leaf litter, contributing unwittingly to the growth of young trees that sprout from the seeds they "plant." The sunflowers that sprout in odd places around your yard may well be the work of jays, who typically fill their beaks with seeds, then fly off to crack them one by one or hide them for a rainy day.

During nesting season, other birds may chase a Steller's jay, thanks to its habit of raiding nests for eggs or young. Notice its large, expressive crest.

JAY FEEDER FOODS

- Acorns
- Amelanchier (*Amelanchier* spp.) fruits
- Bread and other baked goods
- Corn, any kind
- Crackers
- Eggs, hard-boiled or scrambled
- Fruit, fresh or dried
- Grapes
- Mealworms
- Meat scraps
- Nuts
- Peanut butter
- Peanuts
- Suet
- Sunflower seed, any kind

Although most jays are boisterous birds, all species become extremely secretive in nesting season. Their mating rituals are quiet, bobbing dances and soft love songs, and they approach and exit the nest site with great stealth.

Jays use their perfectly designed bill for whacking open hard shells. They can chisel open nuts by splitting them along the seam or peck into an acorn to get to the meat. At the feeder tray, you will often see them cracking sunflower seeds gripped in their feet. Corn of any kind and sunflowers are top staples on the feeder menu with jays, but they also are quick to sample many other treats.

A gray back and thin white "eyebrows" distinguish the scrub jay, a crestless western species, from the gray-breasted jay with no stripe and a denim-colored back.

Juncos

SOFT-COLORED, SOFT-VOICED JUNCOS are mostly winter visitors at feeders, arriving in early fall and lingering until spring. Many of us know them as "snowbirds," partly because their arrival makes us think of winter and partly because of their coloring, which combines the gray of a cloudy sky with a snowy white belly. We separate juncos into two species, the **dark-eyed**, which has several sub-species or races, and the **yellow-eyed**, a rusty-backed bird of forests of the Southwest. The **slate-colored junco,** one of the dark-eyed variants, ranges across most of the country in winter when it leaves its breeding grounds in the Far North. This is the classic gray-above and white-below bird. In the western mountains, the **gray-headed junco** joins the slate-colored subspecies. This dark-eyed race has a splash of rusty red on its back, like the similar yellow-eyed. The **Oregon junco,** which shows up across the western half of the country in winter, also breeds in some western mountain areas. This is a beauty among the quiet-colored juncos, with a showy black hood, chestnut back and sides, and snow-white belly. Another variation, the **pink-sided junco,** wears a gray hood. Several other races may appear in limited ranges, such as the **white-winged junco** of the Black Hills and southern Rockies. Female juncos of both species look much like their mates, but they may be paler and brownish with occasional streaking on their back, breast, and head.

JUNCO FEEDER FOODS
■ Bachelor's-button (*Centaurea cyanus*) seeds
■ Birdseed mix
■ Bread crumbs
■ Cosmos (*Cosmos* spp.) seed
■ Cracker crumbs
■ Grass seeds
■ Millet
■ Peanut butter, offered at a low height
■ Pine nuts
■ Suet, chopped, offered in a tray feeder
■ Weed seeds
■ Zinnia (*Zinnia* spp.) seed

Mirroring wintry sky above and snowy ground below, the slate-colored junco is one of the most widespread winter feeder birds. It seeks seeds such as millet.

Junco Behavior

In most areas, the juncos at our feeders are on vacation. They flock together in small or large groups, rarely visiting one at a time. Their short, conical beaks mark these birds as members of the finch family. Like their relatives, the sparrows, they prefer to feed on the ground, although they will visit higher feeders. Offer small seeds, particularly millet in a low tray, directly on the ground, or in higher feeders to please these winter visitors.

Listen for the twittering sounds of juncos, which they use for companionable conversation. They also sound distinctive chips when alarmed or as a scolding when they are feeling crowded at the feeder.

Most of us who host juncos at our feeders tend to take them for granted until one day we wake up to find that they have moved on. I keep a weekly feeder count on my wall calendar so that weeks don't slip by before I realize that the juncos have gone. Just as the arrival of my snowbirds portends winter, their departure means frost is a thing of the past.

Kinglets

HYPERACTIVITY IS the hallmark of tiny green kinglets, which rarely sit still. These quick, jerky birds flit nervously among tree branches or at feeder hangouts. Both species are olive green, and it can be difficult to distinguish between the two. If a bold dark stripe over the eye decorates the bird's head, you're watching a **golden-crowned kinglet,** who wears a pretty yellow patch on the top of its head. A wide-eyed look characterizes the **ruby-crowned kinglet,** which has a white-rimmed eye and no stripes on the head. You'll have to look closely to see the colorful patch of head feathers that gives this bird its name. Both kinglets range across the United States, with the ruby-crowned nesting farther southward than the golden-crowned. In breeding season, they stay in the northern third to half of the country and in western mountains. In winter, the golden-crowned ranges across most of the country, while the ruby-crowned stays in the southern third and in the warmer west. Females lack the red patch on their heads, although the female golden-crowned kinglet does wear the yellow cap.

It's tough to glimpse the spot of head color on a ruby-crowned kinglet—these tiny birds rarely sit still. Move in for a closer look: Kinglets are unafraid of humans.

Kinglet Behavior

The tiny dark bills of these birds indicate that they eat mainly small insects and their eggs and larvae, which they seek in their endless forays through the trees. They also sip sap and eat some small berries. In winter, kinglets hang out with mixed flocks of other gregarious birds, including chickadees, brown creepers, nuthatches, and titmice. When such a company visits your feeder area, the kinglets may nibble some soft food or small berries, but their favorite feeder food seems to be sugar water. They have become common fall-through-spring visitors at my "hummingbird" nectar feeders.

Kinglets don't seem to fear people, so get close for a good look when these birds stop by. Watch for the frequent wing-flicking movements of the ruby-crowned, which will soon allow you to identify this dynamic kinglet at a distance.

Although kinglets are similar in appearance and habits, their voices are very dissimilar. The golden-crowned's fuzzy, high-pitched call is pitched just below those inaudible dog whistles. They also sing a louder song at times. The ruby-crowned species is a virtuoso singer, with a lovely melody that rings so loudly, you can't believe it's coming from such a tiny body. Both belong to the old-world warbler family, which also includes the hyperkinetic gnatcatchers.

KINGLET FEEDER FOODS
■ Elderberries (*Sambucus* spp.), fresh or dried
■ Nectar
■ Persimmons (*Diospyrus virginiana*)
■ Raw hamburger bits
■ Suet, finely chopped
■ Sumac (*Rhus* spp.) berries

L

Landscaping

BIRDS DON'T CARE HOW GOOD your landscape design skills are. As long as your yard supplies them with food, water, shelter, and a safe way to move about, they'll happily spend hours there. But a yard with bird appeal should also look good to our eyes.

The hardest part about landscaping is remembering that plants come last. If you can control your buying and planting urges, you'll wind up with a garden that beckons to you and to birds.

Whether you like the straight edges, right angles, and controlled plantings of a formal style, or the casual plantings and curving lines of an informal or naturalistic garden, you can take steps to build in bird appeal. Remember that birds are more likely to take up residence in an area that is relatively undisturbed. If you can keep at least part of your yard undisturbed, or nearly so, with low maintenance or naturalistic plantings, birds will soon build nests in the hedges, shrubs, and trees. Beds of groundcovers and shrubs, meadow gardens, and woodland gardens all supply welcoming bird habitat.

Lawn areas are useless to most birds, except for robins, grackles, and a few other species, so you'll want to minimize the grass and focus on the plantings. Choose plants that offer food or year-round shelter as well as beauty to your yard. Instead of a traditional yew (*Taxus* spp.), for example, try a hemlock (*Tsuga* spp.), which will soon be bearing nutritious cones. You don't need to obsess over this point, though, because birds will find plenty of insects on whatever plants you fill your yard with.

Avoid using pesticides. The insects they kill might have been dinner for a bird, and their effects on bird health may be detrimental. Pest outbreaks are usually minimal in a garden that's filled with birds. It's their job, after all, and they're very good at it. If you need to help out, do so by handpicking or using barriers like floating row covers to protect your crops.

No matter what style of garden suits you, plan your bird-friendly landscape step by step:

10 Landscaping Tips

1. Vary the topography of a flat yard by adding berms, walls, or sunken areas. The changes in surface height will make your yard more interesting, and it will seem bigger, too. Also vary height by including trellised vines and arbors, which will supply more bird plants in a small amount of space.

2. Plant shrubs and young trees in groups. Three dogwoods or hollies planted together are more visually appealing—and more bird appealing—than isolated specimens.

3. Include broad-leaved and needled evergreens for textural contrast and four-season greenery (and bird shelter).

4. Experiment with native plants to supply food, nesting materials, and shelter that birds are familiar with.

5. Install birdhouses, with entrance holes custom-sized for your favorite birds. Natural wood boxes will soon mellow to gray, blending in with the background instead of standing out like sore thumbs.

6. Place the feeding station in the most accessible site. It's no fun lugging birdseed through winter snowdrifts.

7. Add the sound of running water to your yard, and give yourself a nearby sitting spot to enjoy the water music and the sight of birds at the bath.

8. Plant a shady garden in layers as in a natural woodland: tall trees, smaller trees or large shrubs, small shrubs, ferns and wildflowers, groundcovers, leaf mulch. It will offer a more appealing habitat.

9. Tie garden areas together with sheltering shrubs or beds so that birds can move safely through your yard.

10. Untidiness is a virtue in bird gardens. Let some weeds stand to entice small-seed eaters. Delay cutting back garden plants until late winter, so birds can shelter among their stems.

Step 1. First, decide on the best area for a permanent feeding station, a site where you will have a clear, close-up view from a favorite room of the house. Install the feeders, so you can have the pleasure of watching birds while you work on the landscaping.

Step 2. Next, plan for permanent features: water garden, fence, patio, play space, paths. Sketch their locations on paper. Install these "hardscape" features as time and money allow, but be sure to reserve the spaces you allotted for them. The space that's left is what's available for planting.

Step 3. Invest in trees and shrubs before you go whole hog on the flowers you're dying to plant. Woody plants take longer to grow than perennials and annuals, so every extra month in the ground is important. They also anchor the landscape design.

Step 4. Plant tall-growing ornamental grasses and hostas next. They also carry a lot of visual weight in the landscape and are permanent garden partners that need a few years to reach their potential. Add groundcovers around shrubs and tree groupings to make them look more cohesive as well as to cut down on maintenance and avoid unnecessary disturbance to resident birds.

Step 5. Finally, the moment you've been waiting for. After all the permanent foundation plants and features are in place, add the beauty of flowers. Plant perennials, then fill in with annuals, if desired. (If you hunger for color long before this step, fill containers with colorful annuals and use them as accents in the developing garden.) Mulch the beds and feeder area to cut down on bird-disturbing maintenance chores like weeding and dragging around a watering hose.

GARDEN DESIGN

A Wild Corner for Birds

When it comes to landscapes, birds prefer things on the casual side. In fact, the less tended an area is, the better, where birds are concerned. Naturalistic plantings provide the features that bring birds winging in for a visit and invite them to stay awhile. The plants in this garden offer food, shelter, and nesting sites and will make an especially pretty picture in the fall when the asters and goldenrod bloom and the sumac turns bright red. Watch for cedar waxwings dining on rose hips; these handsome fruit lovers don't often visit feeders but will come to your yard if there's fruit on-the-branch.

PLANT LIST

1. Staghorn sumac (*Rhus typhina*)

2. Wild rose (for example, *Rosa setigera*)

3. Canada goldenrod (*Solidago canadensis*)

4. Big bluestem grass (*Andropogon gerardii*)

5. New England asters (*Aster novae-angliae*)

6. Fescue (*Festuca* spp.)

7. Foxtail grass (*Setaria* spp.)

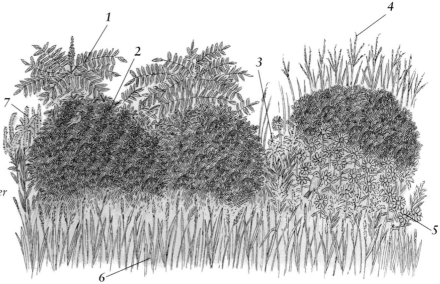

Native Woody Plants for Birds and Gardens

SELECTING NATIVE woody plants for the foundation of your garden will make your area's native birds feel right at home: They are already familiar with the shelter and food such plants supply. Inventories of birds' eating habits point to native plants as a prime source of year-round food. The suggestions on this list combine prime bird appeal with good looks in the garden. All will slip into a naturalistic or informal landscape with ease; most of them can also be used in a more controlled garden, except for the free-spirited colony-forming plants. Use these native trees, shrubs, and vines to create a garden that will welcome birds year-round with food, shelter, and nesting sites. In addition to the uses listed below, remember that birds will seek insects from any of these plants year-round, so that even when your plants are young, they will attract birds.

EAST

Include some of these plants in your garden if you live anywhere from New England to Wisconsin and south to Virginia.

Plant	Description	Nonfood Uses
Spicebush (Lindera benzoin)	Graceful large shrub to small tree with yellow flowers studding bare branches in early spring, golden fall foliage and red berries in fall; host plant for spicebush swallowtail butterfly	Nest sites
Northern bayberry (Myrica pensylvanica)	Suckering shrub with deciduous to semi-evergreen foliage and whitish berries	Nest sites; shelter
Virginia creeper (Parthenocissus quinquefolia)	Fast-growing vine with 5-part leaves that turn crimson in fall; clusters of dark blue berries	Nest sites
Pines (Pinus resinosus, P. rigida, P. strobus)	Evergreen conifer trees, fast-growing when young; develop craggy character with age	Nest sites; shelter; nest material (needles)
Wild cherries (Prunus pensylvanica, P. serotina, P. virginiana)	Super fast-growing small to large trees with small fruits that may be bitter, tart, or sweet, depending on species	—
Oaks (Quercus alba, Q. coccinea, Q. palustris, Q. rubra, other species)	Stately deciduous shade trees of several species; classified generally as "white oaks," with rounded-lobe leaves, or "red oaks," with leaves whose lobes end in points	Nest sites
Sumacs (Rhus copallina, R. typhina)	Colony-forming shrubs or small trees bearing pinnate foliage with beautiful red color in fall and dense clusters of fuzzy berries	—
Elderberries (Sambucus canadensis, S. pubens)	Large multistemmed shrubs bend under a heavy load of deep purple-black or bright red berries	Nest sites
Eastern hemlock (Tsuga canadensis)	Densely branched needled evergreen, valuable even when young as shelter; bears diminutive cones	Shelter; nest sites; nest material
Wild grapes (Vitis aestivalis, V. vulpina, V. labrusca, V. riparia)	Fast-growing vines that clamber up trees or over fences	Nest material (bark); nest sites

SEASON FRUIT IS AVAILABLE   ▉ SPRING   ☐ SUMMER   ▨ FALL   ▩ WINTER

Native Woody Plants for Birds and Gardens—*Continued*

SOUTHEAST
Landscape your southeastern or southern garden with these plants.

	Plant	Description	Nonfood Uses
■■	**Hackberries** (*Celtis laevigata, C. occidentalis*)	Large trees with curious warty gray bark and a bounty of small fruits	Nest sites
□■	**Dogwood** (*Cornus florida*)	Graceful deciduous tree with white flowers followed by red berries	Nest sites
■	**Persimmon** (*Diospyros virginiana*)	Small tree with open branches, often slightly drooping, with unusual brown flowers and astringent fruits that turn sweet after frost	—
■■	**Southern wax myrtle** (*Myrica cerifera*)	Suckering shrub with evergreen foliage and whitish berries	Nest sites; shelter
□■	**Black gum** (*Nyssa sylvatica*)	Tree with brilliant glossy red fall foliage that hides small deep blue fruits	Nest sites
■■	**Oaks** (*Quercus laurifolia, Q. marilandica, Q. nigra, Q. virginiana, other species*)	Stately deciduous shade trees of several species; many evergreen in this region	Nest sites
■■ ■	**Pines** (*Pinus echinata, P. palustris, P. rigida, P. strobus, P. taeda*)	Evergreen conifer trees with long or short needles	Nest sites; shelter; nest material (needles)
□■ ■	**Wild grapes** (*Vitis aestivalis, V. rotundifolia, V. vulpina*)	Fast-growing vines that clamber up trees or over fences	Nest material (bark); nest sites

MIDWEST
Try these plants from east of the Rockies through Illinois.

	Plant	Description	Nonfood Uses
■■	**Hackberries** (*Celtis laevigata, C. occidentalis*)	Large trees with curious warty gray bark and a bounty of small fruits	Nest sites
■■	**Hollies** (*Ilex decidua, I. glabra, I. verticillata*)	Evergreen and deciduous shrubs and trees with attractive form and bird-magnet berries	Nest sites; shelter
■■	**Cedars** (*Juniperus scopulorum, J. virginiana*)	Evergreen-needled conifer trees with abundant pale blue berries on female plants; be sure to plant at least 1 male tree with your females if wild cedars are scarce in your immediate area.	Shelter; nest sites; nest material (bark)
□	**Wild cherries** (*Prunus pensylvanica, P. serotina, P. virginiana*)	Super fast-growing small to large trees with small fruits that may be bitter, tart, or sweet, depending on species	—
■■	**Oaks** (*Quercus imbricaria, Q. macrocarpa, Q. marilandica, Q. stellata, other species*)	Stately deciduous shade trees of several species; most deciduous; some evergreen	Nest sites
□■ ■	**Riverbank grape** (*Vitis riparia*)	Fast-growing vine that clambers up trees or over fences	Nest material (bark); nest sites

SEASON FRUIT IS AVAILABLE   ■ SPRING   □ SUMMER   ■ FALL   ■ WINTER

Native Woody Plants for Birds and Gardens—*Continued*

WESTERN MOUNTAINS AND DESERT

Plants on this list suit gardens from the Rockies to the Cascades and into the Southwest.

Plant	Description	Nonfood Uses
Serviceberries (*Amelanchier alnifolia, A. utahensis,* other species)	Usually suckering or colony-forming shrubs or small trees with a cloud of white spring flowers and deep blue fruits in summer	Nest sites
Arizona madrone (*Arbutus arizonica*)	Small to medium-height tree with white to pink nectar flowers followed by small orange-red fruit	Shelter
Manzanitas (*Arctostaphylos glauca, A. patula, A. pungens*)	Shrubs or small trees with beautiful smooth red bark, evergreen foliage, and small fruits	Shelter; nest sites
Cedars (*Juniperus occidentalis, J. scopulorum, J. utahensis*)	Evergreen-needled conifer trees with abundant pale blue berries on female plants; be sure to plant at least 1 male tree with your females if wild cedars are scarce in your immediate area.	Shelter; nest sites; nest material (bark)
Prickly pears (*Opuntia* spp.)	Cacti with flat oval pads linked together into jointed "branches"; showy, waxy flowers followed by red and yellow fruits	—
Spruces (*Picea engelmanni, P. glauca, P. pungens*)	Short-needled evergreen trees with dense branches	Shelter; nest sites
Pines (*Pinus cembroides, P. flexilis, P. contorta var. latifolia, P. ponderosa*)	Evergreen-needled conifer trees	Shelter; nest sites; nest material (needles)
Quaking aspen (*Populus tremuloides*)	Small- to medium-height tree with glossy leaves that tremble in the breeze; tasty winter buds and catkins in spring	Shelter
Mesquite (*Prosopis juliflora*)	Medium-height tree with fragrant yellow flowers from spring to late summer, highly attractive to bees; seeds in summer and fall	Shelter
Oaks (*Quercus chrysolepis, Q. emoryi, Q. gambeli, Q. utahensis,* other species)	Stately deciduous shade trees of several species; many evergreen in this region	Shelter; nest sites
Buckthorn or redberry (*Rhamnus crocea*)	Medium to large shrub with dense branches, spiny foliage, and red fruits	Shelter; nest sites
Wild grapes (*Vitis arizonica, V. californica,* other species)	Fast-growing vines that clamber up trees or over fences	Nest material (bark); nest sites

SEASON FRUIT IS AVAILABLE — SPRING — SUMMER — FALL — WINTER

Native Woody Plants for Birds and Gardens—*Continued*

PACIFIC NORTHWEST

Gardeners in coastal Oregon, Washington, and northern California can have fun experimenting with these plants.

Plant	Description	Nonfood Uses
Firs (*Abies concolor, A. magnifica, A. nobilis,* other species)	Short-needled evergreen conifer trees with dense branches	Shelter; nest sites; nest material (needles)
Red alder (*Alnus rubra*)	Quickly spreads into dense thicket of small trees; avoid planting where roots can invade neighbor's yard. Good for a naturalistic wet site. Bird-tempting buds, catkins, and seeds	Shelter; nest sites
Alders (*Alnus sinuata, A. rhombifolia,* and other spp.)	Pretty, colony-forming small trees but invasive in limited-size residential yards; check if neighbors are agreeable before planting.	Nest sites
Manzanitas (*Arctostaphylos glauca, A. patula, A. pungens*)	Shrubs or small trees with beautiful smooth red bark, evergreen foliage, and small fruits	Shelter; nest sites
Dogwoods (*Cornus californica, C. nuttalli, C. occidentalis*)	Small trees or shrubs with white spring flowers followed by delectable fruits	Nest sites
Salal (*Gaultheria shallon*)	Shiny-leaved evergreen shrub to small tree spreads by roots into dense colonies; good as groundcover; waxy flowers followed by black fruits	Shelter; nest sites
Pines (*Pinus contorta, P. jeffreyi, P. monticola, P. ponderosa,* other species)	Short- or long-needled evergreen conifer trees	Shelter; nest sites; nest material (needles)
Douglas fir (*Pseudotsuga menziesii*)	Tall needled evergreen conifer excellent for cover even when young; cones contain small, winged seeds	Shelter; nest sites
Oaks (*Quercus agrifolia, Q. chrysolepis, Q. douglasi, Q. garryana,* other species)	Stately deciduous shade trees of several species; many evergreen in this region	Shelter; nest sites
Elderberries (*Sambucus caerulea, S. callicarpa, S. melanocarpa*)	Large multistemmed shrubs bend under a heavy load of black, blue, or bright red berries	Nest sites
Blueberries (*Vaccinium spp.*)	Small to large deciduous shrubs, good understory plants for shady garden; sweet dark blue to blue-black fruit	Shelter

SEASON FRUIT IS AVAILABLE ▪ SPRING ▫ SUMMER ▫ FALL ▪ WINTER

Larks

IF YOU LIVE NEAR the wide open fields that larks inhabit, you may find the birds showing up at your feeding station, particularly after winter storms. The North American birds called larks belong to two separate families. The **eastern** and **western meadowlarks,** two nearly identical-looking species, are not truly larks but are classified in the blackbird family. Both have a chubby, short-tailed look, very similar to a starling in silhouette. They wear vivid deep yellow from throat to belly, slashed with a broad black band across the upper breast. Their backs are mottled and streaked brown and white, the better to blend in with grassy fields where they dwell. Fine points of plumage, such as a yellower cheek, distinguish the two species, but I depend on their songs to tell them apart. The eastern bird gives forth in melancholy, downward-slurring whistled phrases, while the western has a loud and beautiful fluting song.

The **horned lark** is the only native North American member of the true lark family (the Eurasian skylark has been introduced in British Columbia). This slender bird is brown above, white below, with a finely detailed head pattern of black sideburns and breast swash and a yellow face that is striking through binoculars. Tiny feather tufts form the decorative "ears." Their delicate tinkling voices often

The horned lark spends nearly all its time earthbound in open fields and grasslands. But at courtship time, it soars into the sky with ethereal song.

trill over fields across America in all seasons, although the birds themselves are hard to see except when in motion.

Lark Behavior

It's hard to tell whether a lark lives up to its "happy" reputation, but you will undoubtedly be smiling should one of these birds show up at your feeder. An unusual visitor is always a delight to get to know. In the wild, these species are practically invisible thanks to their camouflage, but at the feeder they are standouts. All feed on the ground, so offer grain and seed in low feeders or directly on the ground.

LARK FEEDER FOODS			
■ Bayberry (*Myrica pensylvanica*)	■ Millet	■ Suet, chopped, served at ground level	■ Weed seeds, such as pigweed, common ragweed, and common lamb's-quarters
■ Canary seed	■ Milo		
■ Corn, all types	■ Native grass seeds	■ Sunflower seed, black oil	
■ Lawn-grass seeds	■ Oats		■ Wheat

Lawns

Attract blackbirds, flickers, grackles, robins, starlings

YOUR LAWN IS a great place for backyard parties and outdoor games, but do wild birds like lawns? My answer is: They're not prime bird habitat, so don't go to the trouble of maintaining a lawn just for the birds' sake. But if you have a lawn in your yard, chances are, you'll spot several kinds of birds foraging there.

Lawn Birds to Watch For

Robins are the number-one bird visitor to lawn areas. The open space gives them plenty of room to hop about and the close-cropped grass gives them a good view of the worms they seek.

Flickers appreciate a lawn where they can scour the area for ants. Worms, grubs, beetles, and other lawn delectables also appeal to some bird species.

Flickers are another common lawn bird. These big brown woodpeckers hunker down on the grass near anthills, picking off the inhabitants by the beakful. When ants swarm in a dense mound, or when the winged adults leave the ground in search of mates, don't reach for the ant spray: Flickers and other ant-eating birds are likely to show up for the feast.

You may not appreciate starlings chowing down at your feeders, but you'll love the way they gobble white grubs, which are the larval stage of Japanese beetles and other pests. Starlings stalk about lawns in search of grubs, stabbing their long pointed beaks deep into the soil to extract the delectable morsels. (Blackbirds and robins also grab grubs.)

While flickers, robins, and starlings are the most common birds you'll spot on or around your lawn, there are others to watch for as well.

- Killdeers and roadrunners, which chase after their insect prey, appreciate the open space of lawn as a happy hunting ground. They'll scoot after grasshoppers, lizards, beetles, and other bites of living bird food.

- Grackles spend much of their time stalking about open areas looking for insects or eating seeds. When they're at work on your lawn, you can get a good look at the iridescent sheen on their elegant black plumage. You may also spy red-winged or yellow-headed blackbirds, rusty blackbirds, or other blackbirds hard at work on your lawn.

- Horned larks or meadowlarks may visit your lawn if your yard adjoins open wild country. These birds prefer a more unkempt grassy area than the typical lawn, but they may deign to go slumming in your clipped grass if the insect pickings are abundant.

- Bluebirds and flycatchers that live in or near your yard may flutter over your grass as they hunt down butterflies, moths, and other flying insects. Border your lawn with flowerbeds to attract these types of food-on-the-wing, and supply a few wooden posts to serve as perches for the insect-hunting birds.

- Swallows and swifts, which won't visit a feeder, skim over open areas of lawn to collect flying insects. It's fun to lie back in a hammock and watch them swooping overhead.
- Even hummingbirds find something to like about a lawn: They use the unobstructed space to indulge in show-off courtship stunts, where they swing and swoop and dive through the air like buzzing mini-airplanes.

Lawn Care for Bird Watchers

Dousing your lawn with pesticides or herbicides may give you picture-perfect grass, but using these chemicals will also decrease the bird life in your backyard. Birds won't come hunting if all the bugs are belly-up after a drenching with chemicals! So instead of spraying, let the birds keep the pest population in balance. Part of the reason that insects reach pest proportions in a lawn area is because it's an unnatural environment. Single-species plantings of lawn grass don't occur spontaneously in nature. If your lawn is plagued with ants, Japanese beetles (*Popillis japonica*), June beetles (*Phyllophaga* spp.), and other lawn pests, it may be time to downsize that grassy expanse.

As for lawn weeds, keep in mind that many weeds may host caterpillars that birds view as delectable treats. During nesting season, catbirds, orioles, robins, and other songbirds may scour your less-than-perfect lawn, looking for fritillary caterpillars on the violets that have infiltrated your grass, or picking off buckeye caterpillars (*Junonia coenia*) from plantain (*Plantago major*) leaves. Should your lawn be blessed with a crop of dandelions (*Taraxacum officinale*), you'll find the puffy seedheads are a favorite treat of indigo buntings, white-crowned sparrows, and other native sparrows.

Less Lawn Means More Birds

Robins and other lawn-appreciating birds don't need an acre of mown grass to feel at home. A smaller patch suits them just fine. If you want a greater diversity of birds to visit, plan on reducing the size of your lawn. The birds will be happy, and you will be, too, because you'll spend less of your precious time on monotonous lawn care.

If you make a large lawn drastically smaller, any killdeers in residence will probably desert you for bigger open spaces. But blackbirds, flickers, grackles, robins, and (sorry!) starlings will still come visiting. The insects they seek are plentiful in plantings of flowers and groundcovers, too.

A Balanced View

OPEN AREAS of lawn are a double-edged sword for always-vulnerable birds: They give birds a clear view of your neighbor's stalking kitty, but they also make songbirds sitting ducks for predatory hawks dropping from the sky or for fast cats who've mastered the rushing attack.

The only way to solve this dilemma is to take a hint from the birds themselves. Spend a few hours watching the birds on your lawn, and take note of their behavior. You can expect to see your lawn birds pause frequently to look and listen. (Sometimes groups of birds seem to appoint a lookout who watches for danger on behalf of the group.) But if the birds seem restless and edgy, ready to startle into panicked flight at any instant, that's a sign that the birds feel unsafe and need more cover nearby. A few shrub groupings, a hedge, or a wild corner can make your yard come alive with bird life.

Watch for predators that visit your yard, too, when you're deciding how much lawn to leave. If the neighbor's kitty frequently comes calling, help your birds avoid her clutches by siting birdbaths and feeding areas in open areas of lawn. Kitty will have a much harder time catching birds if he has to cross 20 feet of clipped lawn grass to reach them. If your problem is hawks, not cats, give your birds as much cover as possible. Speedy hawks win easily in life-or-death pursuits with songbirds when they can zoom across large, wide-open lawn areas.

As the plant diversity of your yard increases, so will the bird population. You may not have as clear a view of your robins as you once did, but instead, you'll hear song sparrows and catbirds singing in the hedges and goldfinches calling among the flowers.

You'll probably want to set aside enough lawn to play ball with the kids, toss a frisbee for the dog, or entertain your summer party guests. The rest of the turf can go! Here are some ways to painlessly reduce the size of your lawn:

- Plant a hedge along the perimeters. As always, choose plants that offer good sheltering places and food: shrubs with berries, evergreens, and even statuesque annual flowers all do the trick. A 3-foot-wide strip of sunflowers down the edge of your yard will save you at least two swipes of the mower while supplying plenty of birdseed-on-the-stalk.

- Break up large areas of lawn by planting a group of shrubs, a bed of groundcovers, or a corridor of flowers of varying heights.

- Add another bird-feeding station to your yard and cover the area beneath it with wood chip mulch.

- Replace an area of lawn grass with a prairie or meadow garden. Plant it with native grasses that thrive in your region and sturdy wildflowers, such as bee balm (*Monarda* spp.) and perennial sunflowers (*Helianthus* spp.), that have spreading roots and can hold their own without coddling. Sow seeds of annual flowers for added color.

- Create a new water feature, whether it's a simple clay-saucer birdbath balanced on a rock or a triple-tier waterfall. Once you add water to your yard, you'll find that you can't help but create a garden around it. A few clumps of rushes, some spiky red cardinal flowers—before you know it, you've got another garden beckoning to the birds.

> If you want a greater diversity of birds to visit your yard, reduce the size of your lawn.

Lean-Tos

IN A DISCREET AREA OF MY YARD, beside the foundation of my house, I keep a motley assortment of emergency supplies for winter feeding: sections of plywood of various sizes, lengths of 2 × 4s, stacks of bricks, and even a few concrete blocks. At Christmastime, salvaged evergreen boughs also get added to the pile. This is my lean-to construction collection.

When winter snows blow in, I erect emergency lean-tos to protect feeding areas from the brunt of wind and blowing snow. Lean-to feeding areas are much appreciated by ground-feeding birds, including doves, pheasants, quail, towhees, and sparrows. In my area, cardinals also make good use of them. In areas with hot summers, lean-tos also create welcome shade and break the force of dry summer winds.

Construction is simple: Just lean a piece of plywood at about a 45-degree angle, tilted so that prevailing winds sweep up and over its surface. The specific angle of your lean-to is less important than the comfort of your intended guests: If birds feel penned in under a shelter, they'll avoid it. Use bricks and blocks to help hold the plywood in place, and prop up the contraption with sections of 2 × 4s so that the shelter doesn't collapse and conk birds on their heads.

If you live in an area of frequent snows, you don't need to disguise your lean-to because the white stuff will take care of that. But if the snow won't cooperate, try my trick of stapling evergreen boughs to the plywood. Arrange branches so that their tips drape over the top edge of the board, which gives it a more natural look. Pines, spruce, hemlock, magnolia, bayberry, and other evergreens work well.

> In a pinch, you can even use a pizza box held in place with a brick to make a temporary wind block.

Leftovers

Attract blackbirds, chickadees, jays, mockingbirds, robins, thrashers, wrens, and many others

THAT PLASTIC CONTAINER in the back corner of the refrigerator may hold the makings of a fine meal for your feeder birds. Many "human" foods are chock-full of the fat and carbohydrates that birds crave. Like other unfamiliar foods, leftovers may linger for a few hours until birds are brave enough to sample them. Seasoned scavengers such as crows, jays, magpies, pigeons, house sparrows, and starlings are usually the first clients. Thus food scraps are an excellent food for distracting these birds from other feeder areas. Bluebirds, robins, mockingbirds, woodpeckers, and other birds may also welcome leftovers depending on whether the offerings are animal-, fruit-, or grain-based. If the birds don't eat your leftovers, squirrels or nighttime opossums and raccoons may enjoy them.

Too stale? Too much? Pass leftovers along to chickadees and others, which will peck off the good parts. A tray feeder lets the cleanup crew work freely.

Leftovers for Lunch

IF YOUR family's not into leftovers, try feeding them to the birds—the leftovers, not the family! Here are some "people" foods that may find favor with your feathered friends.

Food	Where to Serve	Birds Attracted
Cooked corn, on the cob or kernels	Drain any liquid and spread on low tray feeder.	Blackbirds, crows, jays, mockingbirds, starlings, woodpeckers
Fruit pies or fruit pastries	Empty suet feeder	Bluebirds, chickadees, mockingbirds, orioles, starlings, titmice
Fruit salad or canned fruit	Drain any liquid and spread on raised tray feeder.	House finches, mockingbirds, orioles, starlings, thrashers, Carolina wrens
Green salad	—	Not appealing to most birds; house sparrows may nibble a small amount.
Lasagna and other pasta dishes with sauce	Directly on ground or on shallow plastic tray low to ground	Crows, jays, magpies, starlings
Meat scraps, any kind	Empty suet feeder	Chickadees, crows, jays, magpies, starlings, titmice, woodpeckers, Carolina wrens
Quiche	Directly on ground	Chickadees, crows, jays, magpies, starlings, titmice
Sandwiches	Tray feeder or directly on ground	Chickadees, crows, jays, magpies, mockingbirds, robins, starlings, titmice
Withered or bruised apples and other fruit	Raised tray or spike feeder	House finches, mockingbirds, orioles, starlings, thrashers, Carolina wrens

L

Lettuce

Attracts purple finches, goldfinches, pine siskins, native sparrows

GOLDFINCHES ARE SO FOND of lettuce seeds that they used to go by the name "lettuce birds." In your bird-friendly backyard, you can plant lettuce to attract not only goldfinches, but also purple finches, pine siskins, and native sparrows.

Living Lettuce-Seed Feeders

Lettuce (*Lactuca sativa*) is a prolific seed producer. This simple-to-grow salad plant zooms to the flowering stage and produces seed stalks as soon as the weather warms up. Plant successive crops in a sunny spot, and you'll have a ready-made goldfinch feeder right through frost. Lettuce seeds are reluctant to sprout when temperatures climb over 80°F; to overcome this problem during the heat of summer, put the seeds in the fridge for a week before you plant them.

Although finches will eventually find even a single isolated lettuce plant, you'll have better luck if you plant a block of lettuce, either near other goldfinch-attracting plants (such as cosmos) or near your regular finch feeder area. Any variety will do the trick, but leaf lettuce matures much faster than head lettuce. Be sure to plant your lettuce where you'll have a good view of the birds as they come to feast upon it.

Wild lettuces are worth considering, too. Be forewarned that they often have slightly prickly leaves and the flowerstalks may reach 7 feet tall, with open clusters of tiny daisies at the top. The most common, *Lactuca scariola*, is a widespread weed from Europe and is probably already trying to colonize some bit of open space in your yard. Another worthy wild lettuce is telegraph lettuce (*L. floridana*), a 3- to 6-foot-tall species crowned with small dusky blue flowers in summer to fall. Check a wildflower field guide to find out what grows in your area and get to know the plants so you can encourage a few in your yard. No matter what species your lettuce is, seed-seeking goldfinches will love it.

Let your lettuce bloom, and you'll see its floral resemblance to other members of the vast composite family, which includes asters, sunflowers, and other daisies whose seeds birds love.

Buying and Saving Lettuce Seed

Purchased lettuce seeds are generally too pricey to pour into the bird feeder as a regular meal. For an occasional treat, buy untreated seed at bulk prices from local hardware stores, farm and garden supply stores, or mail-order seed catalogs, and fill a niger tube feeder with the tiny, lightweight seeds.

It's much cheaper to save seed from your own lettuce patch. Just clip the seed stalks into a brown paper sack, and store them in a dry place until you're ready to serve them to the birds. Lettuce seeds are surrounded by fluff, but there's no need for you to clean the seeds if you feed your home-grown seeds in a tray (not tube) feeder. Birds are adept at sorting out seed from fluff, and any seeds that manage to drift from their grasp will yield a nice crop of volunteer lettuce plants to produce seeds for next season.

Liriope

Attracts bluebirds, mockingbirds

I USED TO SCORN LIRIOPE (lilyturf) as too boring for my garden. The only reason I tried it was that I found a truckload of the grasslike groundcover pitched on a pile at the county waste dump. The indestructible perennials were still alive and growing, even though most of them were upside down.

Anything that determined deserved a home, I figured, and I had just the spot: a strip of dry shade beneath sugar maples where even hostas sulked. I carted the thick mats of liriope home, ripped them into smaller pieces, and used them to fill in along my sidewalk. Grateful for the reprieve, they rewarded me with fresh growth and a beautiful burst of lavender-blue flowers a few weeks later.

When the liriope flowers ripened into black berrylike fruits, I found out what a prize my rescued plants really were. A pair of eastern bluebirds, which usually strayed no farther than the hedgerow bordering the farm fields near my house, braved the town traffic to settle on the spikes of black berrylike liriope fruits. In fact, the only thing in my garden that bluebirds like better than liriope is the berries of deciduous hollies.

A No-Care Groundcover

Liriope muscari is tough as nails and thrives in sun or shade through Zone 6. Its thin, strappy, dark green leaves look like lush grass and reach about 1 foot tall. The spikes of lilac-blue flowers appear

Liriope is a tough groundcover, and when its berries ripen in late summer, bluebirds can't resist flying in to feast on them.

above the foliage in late summer. Liriope is a plant-it-and-forget-it groundcover or edging plant that shrugs off drought, disease, humidity, and pests. If your yard is within a ¼ mile of bluebird habitat, don't turn up your nose at this commoner. Liriope may be just what you need to lure those beautiful birds right to your doorstep.

M

Magpies

ONCE YOU SEE A MAGPIE, you'll never forget it. This striking crow-size bird resembles a harlequin in sharply contrasting patches of black and white. If you're close enough and the light is right, you'll catch a beautiful iridescent sheen of blue, purple, and green on the bird's magnificently long tail, which streams out behind it in flight like the tails of scarlet macaws of the Amazon rain forest.

But pretty is as pretty does, and magpies, despite their beauty, are tough customers. They are bullies and, like crows and ravens, have a strong taste for meat, whether it's carrion, rodents, or songbirds and their nestlings. Years ago, ranchers killed thousands of these western birds because of their unsavory habit of picking at still living but defenseless livestock, either newborn, sick, or just branded.

Magpies have unpleasant voices as well as uncouth eating habits. Their loud, harsh cries echo wherever these big birds dwell.

The **black-billed magpie** is by far the most widespread species; it ranges winter and summer across the West, venturing barely into the Southwest. In a small strip of the far West, the **yellow-billed magpie** joins its relative.

Magpie Behavior

Magpies aren't all bad. Most of their diet consists of insects, and they eat zillions of grasshoppers every season. They are intelligent birds and are as fond as crows are of playing with shiny objects or with each other.

Keep magpies occupied at the feeder with any leftovers you can scrounge up: old ham bones, cold pasta, meat loaf, bread—they'll eat practically anything. Be sure to serve the magpies' food far from the seed feeders, so that your smaller birds can eat undisturbed. These bright birds quickly learn the feeder-stocking routine and may be waiting when you come on your morning rounds. They are also rewarding to hand tame. Great at pest control, magpies will gobble up any mouse that dares show its whiskery face.

If magpies are a feeder nuisance you'd rather do without, switch to feeding seed in weight-operated feeders that deny them access, or in tube feeders. See the Nuisance Birds entry on page 217 for other ways to discourage them.

Bold patches of black and white adorn the magpies of the West. This one is the black-billed species, which builds humongous, highly visible nests.

MAGPIE FEEDER FOODS
■ Amelanchier (*Amelanchier* spp.) berries
■ Apples
■ Blueberries and other small fruits
■ Bones
■ Bread and other baked goods
■ Cereal
■ Corn
■ Figs
■ Grapes
■ Leftovers
■ Meat scraps
■ Suet
■ Wheat

Mealworms

Attract bluebirds, purple martins, robins, yellow-rumped warblers, woodpeckers, Carolina wrens

THE SIGHT OF SQUIRMING, segmented whitish tan larvae may make you squeamish but mealworms are a four-star meal as far as bluebirds are concerned. A simple open tray feeder stocked with a single layer of these wiggly critters can make bluebirds a regular presence in your yard.

What's so appealing about these undeniably homely creatures? They're packed with protein! Birds that eat caterpillars, grubs, and earthworms include mealworms in their diet. Woodpeckers of all sorts, purple martins, Carolina wrens, and yellow-rumped warblers may also dive into the feeding frenzy at a mealworm buffet. Robins, too, enjoy a generous helping of the nutritious larvae.

I make sure that I keep a few containers of mealworms on hand in late winter and early spring, when the capricious weather may clamp down on migrant martins or bluebirds that are already nesting. The larvae give them a ready source of critical food when no natural insects are on the wing because of chilly or rainy weather.

Mealworms are the larvae of meal beetles (also called darkling beetles) that are pests in granaries and other grain storage places. You can buy mealworms at reasonable prices at a local bait shop or through mail-order sources such as those listed in "Resources" on page 348. Start small with your mealworm ranch, making the initial offering to your birds and keeping any extras in the refrigerator in a securely closed container.

If you find you're feeding every bluebird within a mile, you can buy in quantity or grow your own. A plastic 5-gallon bucket with a secure lid makes a great home for mealworms. Fill it with a few inches of cornmeal for the larvae to eat, add an initial small container of mealworms from a bait shop, and you're in business. Put a damp paper towel on top to supply moisture. The insect larvae will mature in the container and reproduce, giving you an expanding colony for feeder fodder. Your crop will do better if

If you long to see bluebirds at the feeder, lure them with mealworms. Keep the mealworm feeder filled and enjoy the bluebirds that fly in to dine.

you toss in a piece of lettuce every few days to keep their environment slightly moist.

If you don't fancy a mealworm farm in your home, ask a bait shop owner if he or she will raise the critters in quantity for you. If you assure them of your patronage, the shop owner may agree.

Other grubs may also appeal to your bluebirds and other larvae-eating birds. In southern Indiana, late spring and early summer are marked by the appearance of two big beetles. May beetles emerge from the soil in May, followed a few weeks later by iridescent green June beetles. Both spend their formative months as unappealing whitish grubs in the soil.

One year, I dropped some grubs into a lidless box. I intended to raise them indoors so I could watch them transform into beetles, but the bluebirds who'd been watching had other ideas. As soon as I moved to the far end of the row, the pair swooped from their birdhouse and gobbled up the hapless grubs.

M

Melons

Attract cardinals, doves, grackles, jays, nuthatches, sparrows, titmice, woodpeckers

SPITTING WATERMELON SEEDS across the yard at family picnics is about the most any of us do with melon seeds. Usually we scrape them out into the compost bucket without a second thought (until a cantaloupe vine comes sprawling out of the compost next summer).

It wasn't until a friend visited me from Kuwait, bearing gifts of crunchy toasted cantaloupe and watermelon seeds, that I realized I was throwing away a healthy snack every time I scraped out a melon. That's when I started saving my melon seeds by scooping them into a colander, rinsing with a strong spray from the hose, and pouring them onto my patio table to dry in the sun.

One morning I scared up a pair of cardinals from the table, and when I went to investigate, I found a pile of cantaloupe-seed hulls, each with the meat neatly removed. That's right—birds like melon seeds, too. Cardinals, doves, grackles, jays, nuthatches, sparrows, titmice, and woodpeckers eagerly devour the dried seeds of any melon: cantaloupe, honeydew, watermelon, or fancy French 'Charantais'.

If you want to add melons to your feeder menu, you'll find that the seeds dry fast and easily on old window screens supported on lawn chairs. Wash seeds in a colander before spreading them out on a screen, and crumble clumps occasionally as they dry to keep them from sticking together. If you want to save the seeds for fall and winter feeding, cover them with a single thickness of cheesecloth to keep birds out while the seeds dry. Pour the dried seeds into brown paper bags and store them in metal containers.

If you buy a melon in winter, wash the pulp off the seeds in a colander, shake off excess water, then spread the seeds on a section of newspaper, and dry on top of the refrigerator or another warm place. Turn the seeds daily to prevent mold. Or you can save time and just scrape the fresh seeds into the feeder for birds to sort out themselves.

> Little more than annoyances to us, melon seeds make a welcome treat for seed-eating birds.

Mesh Bag Feeders

MESH BAGS ARE ONE OF THE EASIEST and most convenient feeders, both for you to make and hang, and for birds to visit and feed from. When fishnet stockings went out of style along with go-go boots, I grieved slightly, but I'm glad to see that they're making a comeback in some areas—not because of the style involved, but because their flexible mesh makes great bird feeders. If you have some old ones lying around the house, cut them into large sections, tie one end, and voilá! mesh bag feeder, ready to be filled. If you happen not to have a pair handy, substitute the plastic mesh bags used to hold onions, potatoes, and other products that you buy at the supermarket.

Mesh bags make great impromptu feeders when the need arises. You can fill them with suet, nutmeats, peanuts, sunflower seed, raisins, or anything else that won't fall out between the holes in the mesh. And it's easy for birds to slip their beaks between the strands and pick out the delicacies you serve them.

No-Mess Mesh

Making a mesh bag feeder couldn't be easier: Just stuff the bag with food, tie off the top, and hang it by a string. Don't be afraid to fill the bag to bulging; the plastic net is tough and resists tears, and the suet or nut pieces peeking out between the cracks will quickly alert the birds to a new food source. As an added bonus, they cost virtually nothing when you use a recycled bag (or, of course, those old stockings). Still, commercial dealers have gotten into the act by offering already filled mesh bags. You may choose to buy some for the convenience they offer— no filling, no tying, just hang on a nail or hook and they're ready for customers. I have invested in thistle mesh bags just so I could have the empty bags to refill later. Their mesh is finer than the bags I find at grocery stores, so I can fill them with a wider variety of smaller feed items; although they are sold as disposables, I reuse them several times.

Unfortunately, mesh bag feeders are popular with squirrels, cats, and raccoons as well as birds. Without much effort, larger animals can tear open the mesh to get at the food inside. To counteract this somewhat, I tie long strings to the bags for hanging, which does slow down the thieves a bit. The string adds to the entertainment value, too: One night I watched a determined coon pull a bag up by reeling in the string hand over hand. I figured he deserved his prize of suet after that ingenuity.

Cheap and effective, a feeder made from a plastic mesh bag filled with fat will delight your suet customers. Recycle an onion bag to make this feeder.

Mice and Rats

AMONG THE MANY FURRY RODENTS that visit your bird-feeding station, mice and rats may show up for their share of the handouts, particularly if you allow seed and other food to lie on the ground. When these undesirable guests begin to arrive, it's a clear signal to improve your feeder housekeeping.

Traps are the quickest and most reliable way to eliminate a rodent problem. Forget the old-fashioned whack-'em traps; they'll get rid of your mice and rats, but they can also snag a bird or flying squirrel. Use only live box traps that allow the animals to enter but not leave. You can find plastic or metal models at discount stores, hardware stores, bird-supply shops, and home-supply outlets, or you can order them from catalogs, such as those listed in "Resources" on page 348.

I depend on multimouse traps, which can accumulate a night's worth of small rodents in a single large box, instead of the one-at-a-time traps that require resetting night after night. I take my mice to a wild area far from my home to release them. Rats are larger and smarter and may be harder to catch than mice. Wear heavy leather gloves when releasing rodents from the traps to avoid rat bites and protect yourself from disease. Keep the traps away from your face to avoid breathing in any contaminants—scientists believe the deadly Hanta virus spreads through the air. Wash your hands thoroughly with antibacterial soap after handling the traps, and avoid touching your face before you clean up.

To prevent rodent problems before they start—and once started, they multiply fast—practice good sanitation around the feeder area. Avoid feeding birds on the ground, and shovel up spilled seed regularly. Letting your cat prowl at night is an excellent preventive (but keep Kitty indoors during nesting season). Opossums, raccoons, foxes, and coyotes may also catch and eat mice.

Though you want to control your mouse and rat populations quickly, you may soon attract owls while the pests are in residence. Screech owls, which live even in cities, are better mousers than any cat you've ever had. Larger owls, such as the great horned owl and the barn owl, make quick work of rats in both towns and rural areas.

Little dramas play out at the feeding station when small animals creep out to dine on spilled seed. Silent and swift, owls are fond of a midnight snack of mice.

Migration

THE FIRST TIME I LOOKED DOWN from an airplane window, I suddenly understood how it must feel to be a migrating bird. After a long night of flying, navigating by starlight or magnetic instinct or with rivers and mountains as guides, the breaking dawn would illuminate for the birds the very same oases I was seeing far below my soaring jet. Islands of trees announce loud and clear that here is safety, food, and shelter.

From the air, the shade trees in an old neighborhood look just as appealing as a natural forest. Understanding this made me realize why migrants drop out of the sky in large numbers in spring and fall to seek sustenance, even in city neighborhoods.

It's only a short flutter of the wings to reach a hospitable feeding station or berry-filled backyard once the migrating birds are in your neighborhood. Whether they've alighted in a nearby natural area or

Rose-breasted grosbeaks at the feeder are one of the grand surprises migration may bring. As birds stream north in spring, they may refuel far from their homes.

just down the block, migrants will soon show up at your well-stocked feeder, since eating is the number-one order of business on these long trips.

Birds migrate north in spring, once insects and other foods are available on their breeding grounds. In fall, they reverse the process, heading south when short days signal the onset of winter cold and the forthcoming lack of food.

Migration Patterns

Nearly all birds that depend mainly on insects and nectar—the hummingbirds, orioles, thrushes, vireos, and warblers—commit to the long haul. These long-distance flyers travel 1,000 miles or more to reach a region where their favored foods will be abundant.

Goldfinches, jays, and other birds that depend on more varied or more easily available foods may go for just a short jaunt. They travel a few hundred miles to what must seem like greener pastures, so to speak. The birds they replace may similarly travel a short distance southward. Unless you live in the northern extreme limit of these birds' range, you will have what seems like all-year residents of these species. In fact the birds you host in winter may be different individuals from those that dine at your feeders in the summer months.

Not all birds migrate. Some stick around all year, showing up at the feeder with their families in summer and stopping by singly in wintertime. Most titmice and woodpeckers follow this pattern.

Migration Means New Birds

After months of feeding the same old reliable cardinals, chickadees, jays, and woodpeckers, it's a real treat to host somebody new and different. That's why bird watchers get so excited by the arrival of migrants at the feeder.

In spring, a grosbeak, an oriole, or a tanager passing through may grace your feeder. In fall, you can welcome back the native sparrows and juncos that bring life to winter bird feeding. Of course, the birds you see during and after migration will depend on where you live. If you're near the northern end of the route, you will get most of your unusual visitors in spring, when northern-nesting birds return. If you're at the southern terminus, orioles, robins, and other long-distance travelers may swamp your feeders in winter. If you live somewhere in the middle of the migration route, you'll get to welcome great birds both coming and going.

Tailor your feeder menu to the needs of the migrants you expect to see, or add new foods quickly once they arrive. Fruit, suet, peanut butter, bread crumbs, and mealworms are popular with orioles, tanagers, thrushes, and other travelers that eat mostly insects. These delicacies may entice them to linger a little longer at your feeding station. They will also come to drink and bathe in fresh water, especially if you add a drip device so the birds can hear the water from a distance.

Red-Letter Days

KEEP TRACK of the arrivals of new birds at your feeder, so that you can anticipate them next year. And try—although it's harder than you might think—to jot down the date, or a close approximation, when birds leave your area.

Migration schedules are almost like clockwork: In 35 years of keeping notes, my records show deviations of usually only a day or two in arrival dates. Barn swallows in southern Indiana, for instance, always show up on or close to my birthday, April 25.

I keep a bird calendar a year in advance, so I can mark the expected arrival dates of birds. When I turn the page to the new month of April, for example, last year's arrival of indigo buntings, rose-breasted grosbeaks, and scarlet tanagers will be clearly marked. I love anticipation!

Many local chapters of the National Audubon Society ask members for their observations of migration comings and goings. If you don't already belong, join the club and ask if they have a list of past records. That way, you'll know when to expect the first junco or say goodbye to the last oriole.

Feeder Observations

You certainly will notice the absence or appearance of migratory birds at your feeder. But if your area is host to the same species summer and winter, it's often hard to tell whether you're looking at the same birds or their seasonal replacements, since all birds of a feather tend to look pretty much alike. That's why it helps to pay attention to the small details of the birds at your feeder. If you notice an individual with a distinctive call or unusual albinistic coloring, for example, you will easily be able to distinguish it from the rest of its kin and thus gauge its seasonal movements.

Much of migration is still a mystery. But bird-banding efforts and other observations add more details to the picture every season. Your contribution of data, through local bird counts and Project Feederwatch, are a big aid to the science of bird travel. See Banding on page 11 and Bird Counts on page 23 for more details on how you can help.

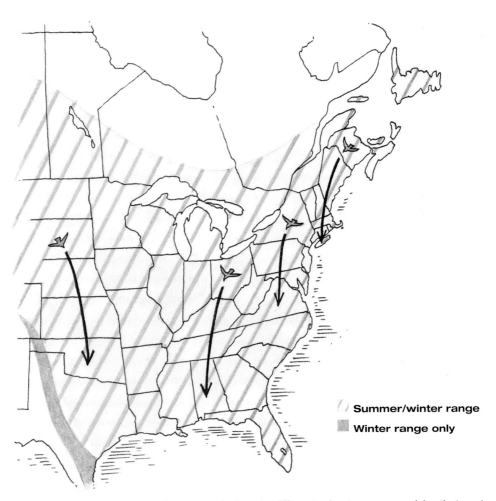

Summer/winter range

Winter range only

The blue jays you see in your yard all year may belong to different migratory groups. A jay that nests in Canada may spend its winter break in New York, while the New York jay takes off for Virginia. The migration paths shown here are from actual bird banding records.

Millet

Attracts buntings, doves, finches, juncos, pheasants, quail, siskins, native sparrows, towhees, varied thrushes, Carolina wrens

MILLET IS A BEST BUY in birdseed. Although 50 pounds of millet costs about 50 percent more than 50 pounds of sunflower seed, a sack of tiny, dense millet seed holds millions more seeds than a sack of bulky sunflower. That means you can feed a lot more birds with a sack of millet than you can with a sack of sunflower.

Any Millet Will Fill the Bill

Several species of grass yield the grain commonly called millet. Most belong to the genus *Setaria*, while one "millet" hails from the *Panicum* genus—*P. miliaceum*, better known as broom corn. German millet (*Setaria italica*), also called foxtail millet, Italian millet, or Japanese millet, is the most widely available. This annual grass shoots up like a rocket, reaching 5 feet in height, with stout seedheads that may stretch almost 1 foot long! You don't need to become a millet expert to make your birds happy: They will eagerly eat any millet, no matter what botanical name the parent plant goes by.

By the way, millet is good food for people, too. It's a dietary staple in countries such as India, Korea, and China.

A Real Crowd Pleaser

Pour some millet in a tray feeder or even right on the ground, and it will quickly attract buntings, doves, finches, juncos, pheasants, quail, native sparrows, towhees, siskins, and Carolina wrens. In the Pacific Northwest, the gorgeous orange-and-blue varied thrush is another big fan of millet.

Millet is a good choice for year-round feeding. When winter snow or ice storms make it hard for birds to find food, even bluebirds and robins will readily eat millet. During spring migration, another time when fast fuel is at a premium, scarlet tanagers may stop at your feeder for a few quick mouthfuls of millet.

Millet is a common ingredient in birdseed mixes, but you can also buy the seed plain, by the pound or in bulk, in case you'd rather make your own custom blends or if you want to feed birds at a bargain rate.

Millet seeds are small and round and may be golden tan or reddish brown, depending on which plant species the seeds came from. Birds eat both colors of seed with alacrity, but the white proso millet will bring them to a new feeder faster because it's easier for the birds to see.

A Millet Garden for Birds

MILLET IS an annual grass that's simple to grow in any sunny spot. In fact, it's probably growing beneath your feeder already! (See Grasses for Birds on page 145 for more on volunteer millet.) Grow a garden of millet, and your birds will thank you by gracing the seedheads of the grasses all through fall and winter. Any seeds that drop will be welcome fodder for doves, juncos, quail, native sparrows, towhees, and other ground-feeding birds.

The easiest way to grow a millet garden is to simply sow some birdseed. Or you can plant a sampler of varieties from specialty catalogs. I like to sow millet seed purchased from bird-supply stores because it's fun to see what kind of millet it will turn out to be. My favorite surprise was the crop I got from planting sprays of long, arching millet seedheads that I found at a cage-bird supply store. This pendant variety of Japanese millet

(*Setaria italica*) turned out to be the most ornamental grass in my entire garden!

A crop of millet will mature 6 to 10 weeks after planting, so you can plant it anytime in spring or summer. Prepare the soil as you would for a bed of annual flowers, removing existing vegetation and loosening the top 4 to 6 inches of soil. Scatter the seed thickly, cover lightly with soil, and water with a sprinkler or hose sprayer. Keep the soil moist until the millet is up and growing well, usually a matter of a week or two.

Milo

Attracts doves and some game birds

MILO IS THE SEED OF LAST RESORT for most feeder birds. If you've ever found an uneaten collection of hard, round, reddish seeds among the hulls of sunflower and other seeds at your feeders, it's milo. When other seeds are there for the taking, birds will kick milo out of the feeder or leave it untouched in the tray. Only doves and some game birds seem to favor milo seeds.

Why do seed mixes contain milo if birds won't eat it? Because it's cheap and relatively big, so it's a popular filler in low-priced mixes. If you want to feed milo to game birds like pheasants or wild turkeys, buy it separately from a feed store. Save your birdseed budget for a good-quality seed mix that contains seeds songbirds *like* to eat, such as millet and sunflower.

Milo is also called sorghum (the plant's botanical name is *Sorghum bicolor*); commercial farmers raise sorghum for syrup production. Milo is an annual grass that's easy to grow in your own backyard, where it may attract doves, pheasants, quail, wild turkeys, and other birds that forage among the stout, cornlike stalks. The seed has a hard coat so it lasts through winter. Plant milo in the spring, as you would corn, after the soil has warmed. Prepare the soil as for any annual and scatter the seed thickly—

Milo, or sorghum, seems to be more attractive to red-winged blackbirds and other birds when it's on the stem. At the feeder, the seeds usually go uneaten.

or plant in rows if you prefer. Cover lightly with soil, and wait for the flush of vigorous green shoots. Don't worry if weeds crop up: The milo can hold its own, and birds will enjoy the weed seeds, too.

Mimicry

AS A SENSITIVE TEENAGER, I was appalled to hear a distinct "wolf whistle" issuing from an apartment window every afternoon when I walked home from school. I ignored it for several days until I couldn't stand it anymore. Looking up toward the open window and cupping my hands, I shouted "Stop it!" at the top of my lungs. To my surprise, a friendly woman pulled aside the curtain and invited me to come up and meet my harasser.

The flirt turned out to be her pet myna bird. The bird was pleased to have an audience and immediately ran through a repertoire that included sailor-worthy expletives as well as assorted whistles and a maniacal laugh.

The myna, an old-world species, is close cousin to our introduced common starling, one of the most gifted mimics in the North American bird world. The only other birds that have a real knack for copycat sounds are the well-named "mimic thrushes"—the catbird, the mockingbird, and thrashers (particularly the brown and California)—and several members of the crow family.

Like the starling, skilled mimic thrushes can imitate dozens of other bird species, from bob-whites to blue jays, along with dog barks, gate squeaks, coyote howls, hawk screams, and frog croaks. They also have their own songs, which can be beautifully intricate and sweet. Don't be surprised to hear them switch from song to raucous mimicry in an instant.

Crows and their relatives, including jays, magpies, and ravens, readily adopt other sounds as part of their vocal repertoire. Birds of these species that were kept as pets learned to mimic human words, as well as the usual laundry list of bird calls, animal noises, whistles, and mechanical sounds.

Why some birds have a knack for imitation is unknown. Other than humans, they are the only animals that imitate sounds not part of their natural language. (By the way, it is an old wives' tale that splitting the tongue makes a bird "talk" better.) Some individuals are much more gifted than others. Members of the crow family are the Mensa club of the bird world. Some are intelligent enough to perform well at human tasks, such as counting and memory games. It's fun to try to teach wild birds of these species to imitate a distinctive whistle of your own. If you frequently whistle for your dog, you may have already served as inspiration!

> Starlings, catbirds, mockingbirds, and crows are gifted mimics that can copy a wide variety of sounds.

Mockingbird

AMONG SONGBIRDS, mockingbirds are the bullies on the playground. Like a 6-year-old who hasn't learned to share, this big gray bird flies in to a feeder proclaiming it "Mine! Mine! All mine!" and causing milder-mannered birds to scoot out of the way and head for cover.

Despite their hoggish habits at feeders, mocking-birds are a valuable ally to other birds. These seemingly fearless birds will charge after any threat to their families, whether it's a cat, hawk, squirrel, or snake. If another bird sounds an alarm call, the mockingbird is first on the scene to investigate and pitch in. Their long sharp beaks, which they don't hesitate to use, are excellent weapons for driving off climbing snakes. Augmented by flashing white wing patches and a harsh, loud voice, a mockingbird in battle mode is fearsome enough to drive even a trespassing human away.

Although they also have their own original music, mockingbirds get their name from their remarkable

Mockingbirds sing sweetly on summer nights, but they defend their home and food aggressively. They often perch conspicuously overlooking "their" territory.

ability to imitate other birds' songs. That's why a mockingbird from the eastern United States sounds very unlike a western mockingbird cousin.

Listen to a mocker in Arizona, and you'll hear songs of local birds like Scott's oriole, scrub jay, and plain titmouse. In Pennsylvania your mocker is likely to imitate a Baltimore oriole, blue jay, and tufted titmouse.

It's not just birdsong that mockingbirds mimic. If your garden gate has a nice loud squeak, or if your neighbor whistles for his dogs daily, you may hear those variations worked into a mockingbird's theme song. This talent makes it easy to recognize your own neighborhood mockingbird.

Mockingbird feeder

Chopped apples

Cup hooks with grapes

Separating feeding stations by shrubs or a hedge or placing separate feeders on opposite sides of the house is the only way to deter a mockingbird from driving all other birds away from your feeders.

Mockingbird Behavior

Mockingbirds have high-voltage personalities, which makes them fun to observe. Look for threatening displays of drooped, outspread wings and tail, which the birds use to scare insects out of hiding or to chase snakes away. Listen for them singing on summer nights, often from a rooftop or antenna. Their "whisper song" is a tender, quiet warbling from a hidden perch that's audible only for a short distance.

Since mockingbirds eat just about anything, you can't just switch the food in your feeders to discourage a territorial bird. When a mocker claims your feeder, the best thing to do is put up another

feeder on the other side of a hedge, fence, or the building. The obstacle may prevent the mockingbird from claiming that one, too.

If a territorial mockingbird patrols your yard, you might try teaching it some tricks since you will be spending plenty of time together (you filling the feeder, the mockingbird watching you). When I began whistling a jaunty three-note phrase every time I set out its favorite foods, only a few weeks passed before the bird began imitating my "soup's on" call. When nesting season began and the bird left my yard, I still occasionally heard that whistle when I took a walk.

MOCKINGBIRD FEEDER FOODS			
▪ Bread and other baked goods	▪ Crackers	▪ Hamburger, raw	▪ Mealworms
▪ Cereal	▪ Dogwood (*Cornus* spp.) berries	▪ Hawthorn (*Crataegus* spp.) berries	▪ Meat scraps
▪ Chopped suet	▪ Fruit, fresh or dried	▪ Holly (*Ilex* spp.) berries	▪ Millet
▪ Corn, all types	▪ Grapes	▪ Leftovers	▪ Oranges

Mold

MOLDY SEED IS A FACT OF LIFE. When dry seed absorbs moisture from dew, rain, snow, or errant sprinklers, mold can quickly set in because of the lack of air circulation at most feeders. In my experience, birds do not eat bad seed, but keep in mind that moldy conditions can, at worst, set the stage for bird illnesses or, at least, ruin a perfectly good tray, hopper, or tube of seed.

To prevent mold, keep seed dry. During the rainy season, use feeders such as tube feeders with enclosed seed storage or roofs. Or feed sparingly, filling open feeders with only as much seed as the birds will down that day. Birds eat wet seed readily, so even if it rains during feeding hours, they will still devour the offering. Before refilling your feeders, scoop out any leftover wet seed or wet hulls to keep fresh seed dry longer, and serve seed in a very shallow layer. Also, look into using tray feeders with wire bottoms to help seed stay fresh. These feeders drain away excess water and allow air to circulate around the bottom of the seed.

If accumulated seed on the ground begins to mold, rake mulch over it to bury it. I find that in extended periods of wet weather, dropped seeds will sprout before they get moldy, giving me a pleasing fresh green carpet beneath the feeders.

> Tray feeders with wire bottoms drain away water, let air circulate, and help seed stay fresh.

Moles

MOLES ARE GRUB EATERS and earthworm eaters. They are not interested in your birdseed, but your feeder area may attract them if the moisture-holding layer of sunflower shells and other debris attracts the prey they seek. Other than occasionally pushing a plant out of the ground as they burrow along, they are harmless.

Moles are fantastic diggers, thanks to their huge scooping paws, which look like the business end of a steam shovel. They are so proficient at their digging that you may think your yard is hosting a horde of moles, when in fact it's only a single animal. Flatten the tunnels by walking on them.

Voles, which are more closely related to mice than to moles, also burrow, but their tunnels are smaller and usually not raised. These animals can be highly destructive to fruit trees and ornamentals because, like mice, they eat bark. Vole populations can build to enormous numbers during cyclical population swings, during which years the hawk and owl population also rises—voles are a staple food for birds of prey.

Shovel-like front feet and tiny eyes mark the mole, a tunneler extraordinaire. Moles may tunnel near the feeder, where worms are beneath the seed hulls.

Morning Glories

Attract hummingbirds

MORNING GLORY fans will be pleased to learn that the vines are also great for providing quick covers for birds near a feeding station. The vines grow thick and fast, making a tangle where birds can easily take refuge. A trellis of morning glories is just the thing to shelter your feeders from hot summer winds and to give feeder birds a quick hideaway when danger threatens.

A trellis of morning glory vines is terrific next to a birdbath, too, because the trellis gives wet-feathered birds a safe place to preen. Hummingbirds like morning glory flowers, too, so I like to hang a hummingbird feeder from a trellis covered with morning glories.

Morning Glory Choices

Fast-growing annual morning glory (*Ipomoea tricolor*) can brighten a garden just about anywhere. Choose a sunny garden spot for your trellis, and plant the seeds next to it in spring after danger of frost is past. If summers are short in your area, start the seeds indoors about 3 weeks before the last spring frost date. Otherwise, the vines may not have time to produce flowers before fall frost kills them. Morning glories grow well in containers, too, so you can let them wrap around an upper deck railing or twine along a window frame.

Hardy morning glories are even better than annual morning glories for providing cover for birds. Weird but wonderful "man-of-the-earth" (*I. pandurata*) thrives through Zone 6. Its white flowers are splashed with red-purple middles and look like any pretty morning glory; but below the earth, this perennial vine grows enormous tubers that once were used as food by Native Americans.

Large morning glory flowers may tempt a passing hummingbird, but for continual hummer traffic, plant one of the small-flowered red species. Cypress vine (*I. quamoclit*) is a delicate climber with soft, feathery leaves that look like the foliage of cypress or

Morning glories greet each day with fresh new faces and climb quickly to cloak a trellis or fence. The tubular flowers are practically magnetic to hummingbirds.

dawn redwood. Let it ramble about the perennials in your beds, or grow it on a trellis. Red star morning glory (*I. coccinea*), with thick, heart-shaped foliage, is a more vigorous plant that grows best on a trellis or fence. Both will buzz with hummingbirds all summer long. Cardinal climber (*I.* × *multifida*), a hybrid of these two species, is just as irresistible to them.

All of the red morning glories flourish in containers. I sometimes plant cypress vine seeds in windowboxes and give the plants string to climb so they can frame my windows with flowers that lure hummingbirds right to eye level.

Mosquitoes

Attract many species of insect-eating birds

THE WHINE OF A MOSQUITO may send you searching for the swatter, but to birds it sounds like the dinner bell. Buntings, martins, native sparrows, swallows, and swifts include these prolific, widespread, and generally slow-moving insect pests in their diets. Many other bird species will also snap up a passing bloodsucker.

People have long considered purple martins excellent mosquito controllers, but there is some disagreement about this reputation. Mosquitoes tend to be most active in the dim hours before sunrise and after sundown, when most martins are snug in their high-rise houses. Martins are probably not prone to seeking out mosquitoes, but any of these insects in the air naturally get swallowed along with beetles, flies, and other flying food when the birds are flying.

It's the smaller insect-eating birds, not purple martins, that shine as chief mosquito catchers. When I walk the trails at a nearby bald-cypress slough in southern Indiana, a crowd of excited blue-gray gnat-catchers gathers in the branches overhead. In constant motion, they zip after the mosquitoes that accompany me through the wetlands. Native sparrows, thrushes, and wood warblers are also quick to grab a passing mosquito. In the marshes and other wet areas where mosquitoes breed en masse, mallard ducks, phalaropes, and many kinds of sandpipers feed on these pests.

You certainly don't want to breed mosquitoes to attract birds. Exercise common sense in mosquito control by emptying stray water-filled containers (such as old tires or forgotten buckets) that may serve as breeding sites. Don't overlook the rain gutters, as clogged gutters can support large numbers of larvae. The birds in your yard will do their best to keep up with the natural mosquito population and keep your outdoor experiences itch-free.

> Purple martins may not deserve their reputation as mosquito eaters. The birds are abed when mosquitoes are active.

Moths

Attract many species of insect-eating birds

SHHH, DON'T TELL THE MOTHS, but these winged insects and their eggs, caterpillars, and cocoons make superb bird food. Bluebirds, flycatchers, orioles, phoebes, robins, and dozens of other species make moths a staple in their diets. In winter, the tough fibrous cocoons of many moth species, from the giant cecropia to the common woolly bear, are targets for chickadees and titmice, which work industriously to tear open the tough silk and get at the meaty morsel within. Eggs and egg masses of moths are a big hit with nuthatches, woodpeckers, and other guardians of the trees. Moths on the wing make a quick snack for any bird near enough to grab a bite. Even screech owls seek out moths, particularly the large, fat-bodied giant silkworm moths, such as the cecropia.

A garden free of pesticides will support a wide variety of moths. With 10,000 species fluttering around North America, your yard is apt to include more moths than you can count. The moth world is incredibly varied. Species range from pesky tent caterpillars and codling moths to the throngs of nondescript tan and gray moth species that feast on lawns, shrubs, trees, and other plants. The translucent jade-green luna moths and beautiful underwing moths, which hide vivid red or yellow, black-striped hindwings under camouflaged forewings, contribute to the diversity. Because nearly all moths are night fliers, you won't actually see many of them, but your bird friends will find them, hiding during daylight hours on tree bark, beneath leaves, or in other concealed places.

Adding native plants—trees, shrubs, vines, grasses, flowers—to your yard is the best thing you can do to boost your moth population. Not only will the extra vegetation give moths more places to seek shelter, the plants will also serve as suitable hosts for the caterpillars, which have evolved along with our native plants and are often finicky in their tastes. Naturally you will want to avoid the use of pesticides, including BT (*Bacillus thuringiensis*), which kills leaf-eating caterpillars—which is most caterpillars! Also avoid planting genetically engineered corn or other crops that include BT in their genes.

Should you see a caterpillar inching along, wish it luck. In a yard full of birds, many moths are destined to wind up as someone's dinner.

Eastern tent caterpillar

Gypsy moth

Hungry beaks snatch moths up at all stages, from egg to caterpillar to cocoon. Even night-flying winged adults aren't safe—owls also eat moths.

Mulch

WITH ALL THE BIRD TRAFFIC at a feeder area, it can be tricky to keep the ground below feeders looking good. I cover the area with wood chips, which I get free from the utility company or from tree trimmers, who are happy to have a place to conveniently dump a truckload. If you don't have storage space for large quantities, you can buy bags of wood chips at the garden center. Chips are long-lasting, and their color and texture provide excellent camouflage for dropped seeds, hulls, and bird droppings. When the layer of mulch begins to look shabby, turn it over with a hoe and expose fresh stuff, or spread another inch or two over the top.

If you choose to plant under your feeders instead, avoid flowers, which soon look bedraggled, thanks to birds perching on their stems or scratching among their roots. Instead, go with a hardy groundcover such as Virginia creeper (*Parthenocissus quinquefolia*) or bearberry (*Arc-*

tostaphylos uva-ursi). These groundcovers are generally tougher than flowers and hold up better to high traffic—from both boots and bird feet.

Beware of Sunflowers

All those sunflower seeds your birds are cracking their way through will soon give you inches of hulls beneath your feeder. It looks like it would make good mulch, but don't spread it around treasured plants. Like the black walnut tree, sunflowers are allelopathic—their hulls contain chemicals that inhibit the growth of plant competitors. I even avoid adding sunflower hulls to my slow-burning compost pile, for fear of aftereffects in the garden. Instead, I rake them onto a ground sheet and drag the pile to a discreet corner, where I pile the hulls until the worms and other natural decomposers turn them back into earth. You can also leave the hulls in place beneath your feeders, if you like their appearance.

N

Nectar

Attracts hummingbirds, orioles, and dozens of other species

MIX NECTAR FOR ALL SUGAR-WATER drinkers at a ratio of 4 parts water to 1 part sugar. Boil the water so that it melts the sugar when you mix the two together, or try my trick of using superfine sugar, an instantly dissolving sugar available at supermarkets and restaurant supply stores. The superfine sugar dissolves instantly in cold water with just a quick stir. I mix my nectar in 2-cup batches to fill my most-used feeder perfectly. I pour ½ cup of sugar into a 2-cup liquid measuring cup, then add water while stirring until it is a shade over the 2-cup marking to allow for the displacement of the dissolved sugar.

Prepackaged nectar mixes are fine for feeding hummingbirds and orioles, but much more expensive than mixing it yourself. If you want to eliminate the inconvenience of boiling water to melt granulated sugar, switch to superfine as I do.

You can use a slightly weaker homemade solution of sugar water, but avoid making it stronger. Too high a concentration of sugar may taste delicious, but it is not necessary to attract birds, and some ornithologists believe it may have negative effects on the birds' health if continued long term.

Adding red dye to attract hummingbirds is probably harmless, but totally unnecessary. They birds will suck up the sweet stuff just fine once they locate the feeder—and they won't forget where

Nectar is a favorite of orioles as well as hummingbirds. Add a feeder designed to accommodate these perching birds, so that it's easier for them to get a sip.

they found it. Hummingbirds are loyal feeder visitors, returning every few minutes or at least every day to the same food sources. If the feeder isn't emptied within a week, clean it and refill with fresh solution. Once hummers become regular visitors, you may find you need to refill feeders every day or even more often!

Other Nectar Sippers

MORE THAN 60 species of birds—besides hummingbirds!—have been seen snitching a sip of sugar water from nectar feeders. Check your feeders frequently to see who's visiting yours. The most common non-hummingbird guests are orioles and house finches, with woodpeckers close behind. Also look for these bird species:

- Cardinals
- Chickadees
- House finches
- Purple finches
- Goldfinches
- Black-headed grosbeaks
- Rose-breasted grosbeaks
- Jays
- Orioles
- Tanagers
- Titmice
- Warblers (13 species and counting)
- Downy woodpeckers
- Hairy woodpeckers
- Red-bellied woodpeckers
- Red-headed woodpeckers

Nectar Feeders

HUMMINGBIRDS ARE THE number-one customer of nectar feeders and the number-one reason that we put them up. Getting these incredible birds into the yard is as easy as filling the feeder and hanging it in the garden. Because hummingbirds cover nearly all of America (they're scarce in the North, however), you're sure to attract customers within a week, if not almost instantly. As soon as a passing hummingbird spots your feeder, it'll be over to investigate.

Orioles are also famed for their attraction to sugar water. With the proliferation of backyard feeders, the behavior is becoming more common among orioles than it once was, and the birds seem to be quicker to accept a nectar feeder as a food source.

House finches, warblers, woodpeckers, and a laundry list of scores of other species are also making increasing use of nectar feeders. No specialized feeders are on the market yet, but the birds are agile at accessing even a model without perches. To prevent wasting your nectar solution, hang an extra feeder with perches for these birds to prevent it from tipping and spilling the liquid when the heavier birds fly in for a landing. Because I worry about my non-hummingbird guests getting a balanced diet (some of them will hog the feeder for hours at a time until it is drained dry), I keep a large feeder with perches for these nectar drinkers, and alter the nectar mix by replacing 1 part of the water with 1 part unsalted beef

Nectar feeders include two basic designs: the vertical bottle and the horizontal "flying saucer." Clear is best; it's hard to tell when opaque feeders are empty.

broth, to supply protein that the birds would be ingesting in a normal diet.

Choosing a Nectar Feeder

Easy cleaning is the main priority when you shop for a feeder. Sugar water can mold quickly, so you'll need to swab out the feeder before every refill. Make

Keeping Nectar Feeders Clean

THE BEST way to save time cleaning a nectar feeder is to buy a well-designed feeder in the first place. Since you'll most likely be cleaning and refilling the feeder every few days for months on end, you'll save yourself a lot of frustration by choosing a product that is fast and simple to disassemble,

with unobstructed access to all parts of the feeder.

Check the accessories aisle of a local bird-supply store or a specialty catalog like those listed in "Resources" on page 348 for brushes that will make cleaning your feeder easier. At a cost of only a few dollars, these small, flexible brushes are a bargain because they'll save you hours of time over the nectar

season. Regular bottle brushes, available in any discount store and many supermarkets, work well for cleaning the main reservoir of nectar feeders. Pipe cleaners are also handy for snaking grime out of the feeding holes of nectar feeders. If you use plastic snap-on devices to deter bees at the feeder holes, use an old toothbrush for a quick cleanup across their grids.

sure the feeder model you like comes apart easily and allows you to get into all those nooks and crannies without using sleight of hand.

Horizontally oriented feeders, with the drinking holes above the solution, are available in very easy-to-clean models that separate into halves that are as simple to wash as a salad plate. Vertically oriented feeders, the most commonly available, are more difficult to clean because only the cap comes off. Buy yourself a bottle brush to make the job quick and easy.

Make sure the feeder is not opaque. Artsy ceramic feeders may be pretty, but you won't be able to tell when the sugar water is getting low. Of course, if hummingbirds zip in, then immediately leave, you'll get the hint.

If this is your first nectar feeder, choose one with lots of red plastic to grab the attention of passing hummingbirds. Install all first-time feeders in an open area, where birds can easily see them. Once you have regulars at the feeder, you can move it to another part of the garden. You can then also replace the tacky, big red feeder with one that just has a discreet dab of red to mark the spot.

A jumbo nectar feeder reduces refills if you're hosting thirsty orioles or hummingbirds. They're handy in late summer, when migrating hummers arrive in droves.

Niger

Attracts house finches, purple finches, goldfinches, pine siskins

GOLDFINCHES ARE the big customers for niger seed—it's their absolute favorite at the feeder. The birds seem to spot a new tube feeder as soon as it's hung, and they'll quickly investigate to see if it's filled with niger. House finches, purple finches, and pine siskins also adore niger.

Niger also goes by the name "thistle seed," but how it got the name is a mystery because the seed comes from a daisylike plant that's native to Africa. It's not a thistle at all. Perhaps the name came about because goldfinches love niger and they also adore real thistle seed. Whatever the reason, it's caused lots of bird lovers unnecessary worry that

they might be spreading a plague of pest plants while feeding their birds. Rest easy! Whether you call it niger or thistle seed, niger is perfectly safe to feed to birds, and it won't create a weed problem in your yard.

Making the Most of Niger

Niger is costlier by the pound than most other birdseed, but a little goes a long way unless you're hosting hordes of finches (which can happen during migration, when hundreds of goldfinches settle at a well-stocked feeding area). Serve niger in a tube feeder for the least amount of waste. Invest in a feeder with heavy metal trimmings to add weight, so that it doesn't swing crazily at every breeze and dump your expensive seed all over the ground.

House finches can become feeder hogs when you feed niger. You can buy feeders with perches above the seed holes to discourage them. Acrobatic goldfinches just reach upside down to eat from these feeders, but the less acrobatic house finches can't reach the seed. In many areas of the country, though, house finches have become just as adept at handling upside-down perches as goldfinches are. Until a truly house-finch-proof feeder comes along, you may as well fill a regular tube feeder with niger for the house finches and hope they take the easy route and leave the other feeder to the goldfinches. If not, at least you're boosting the odds of having an available perch when a hungry goldfinch comes a-calling.

A Goldfinch Bonanza

You can put niger in hopper and tray feeders, but you'll inevitably lose some of the seed. Wind sends the tiny seed sailing, but at certain times of the year, I think the results are worth some lost seed. During the goldfinch migration season in March and April, I spread a thin layer of niger in my open tray feeders. At first, the seed will attract a handful of goldfinches. The next day, 20 birds will show up, and within a couple of weeks, I'm feeding 200 or 300 goldfinches every

Offer niger in small amounts or in a tube feeder to avoid wasting this pricey seed. Most small birds, like this common redpoll, eat niger, but goldfinches love it.

day! If I only put out tube feeders, they'd quickly desert me. I don't mind going over budget on niger for a few weeks: The payoff in goldfinches is worth a million bucks at least. And when I wake up one morning to find the whole kit and caboodle has moved on, I know the resident house finches will quickly clean up any leftovers from my extravagance.

The Source of Niger

NIGER SEED comes from a yellow daisy named *Guizotia abyssinica*. The last part of that mouthful of a name, *abyssinica*, tells us that the niger plant hails from the ancient land of Abyssinia, which we know today as Ethiopia.

Niger seed is heat-treated to prevent germination because, although it's not a thistle, it does spread like a weed, sowing itself by the zillions. An occasional niger seed may remain fertile, so if you find an unfamiliar branching plant bearing a bouquet of yellow daisies near your feeder, you may find yourself

the proud owner of a genuine specimen of guizotia.

In hot, dry areas like California where farmers grow the plants to produce seed for the birdseed industry, niger may escape cultivation and sprout along roadways and in other empty ground, making the western finches mighty happy.

Night Singers

OWLS, OF COURSE, ARE OUT and about at night, and herons may squawk nocturnally. You will often hear killdeer shrilling their "Kill-eeee!" calls as they fly in the dark. But when it comes to song-birds, nearly all of them limit their performances to daylight hours, with a few exceptions. The mocking-bird is the most well-known exception to this rule. Fond of singing night or day, the mockingbird's vir-tuoso performances often take place from a chimney, rooftop ridge, or roof-mounted satellite dish.

Now that most people sleep with closed windows and air conditioners humming, mockingbirds have a much smaller audience than they did on lazy summer nights when a screen was all that stood between the singer and the listener. If a mocker is residing in your neighborhood, it's worth throwing up the sash on a June night to revel in the romantic concert. Of course, if you have to listen to a mockingbird whistle night after night, holding forth in the wee hours of the morning, you may be less than enchanted by the bird.

Other members of the mockingbird family, in-cluding the catbird and thrashers, may occasionally sing at night. But most other birds are sound asleep once darkness falls. If you happen to hear a quick, short burst of song from a cardinal, robin, sparrow, or other bird, the bird was most likely disturbed on its nest or at its roost. Oddly enough, birds sometimes break into a line of melodic song when they are roused unexpectedly from sleep, instead of the alarm or distress call you'd expect.

Modern lighting "improvements" have had a huge effect on night-singing birds. In my small town, birds once slept soundly through the nighttime hours, even with white-bulb streetlights dotting the streets and backyards. But once the white lights were replaced with yellowish ones that cast a much greater light, the birds no longer slept soundly until natural break of day. Now robins begin singing at 2:00 A.M., and car-dinals, wrens, and others aren't far behind. In cities, starlings may twitter all night long, even though they're perched for rest in communal roosts.

There's something romantic about a songbird on a warm summer night. Throw open your window in June or July to hear a mockingbird's moonlight serenade.

You may also hear bird voices at night during spring and fall migration. Listen closely on a quiet night for soft cheeps and twitters overhead, beginning a few hours after sunset and continuing into the early hours of the morning. As I listen to the conversations overhead, I like to imagine the determined wings flying through the night and wonder where they've been and where they're going. Once in a while, I'll rec-ognize a call note of a thrush or warbler, but usually the voices aren't recognizable. March through early May and August through September are the best times to hear long-distance travelers on the wing at night.

Nuisance Birds

Too MANY, TOO OFTEN, too piggish, too messy: Any or all of those traits can land a bird on the Most Unwanted List. House finches, house sparrows, pigeons, and starlings in cities are usually branded as nuisance birds. Some feeder hosts also revile crows and jays because they can monopolize a feeder and deter other birds. A mockingbird can gain a place for itself here, too, should it decide to claim a feeding station for its sole use.

If you live in a very urban area, you may cherish the house sparrows, pigeons, and other "pests" at your feeder, since other birds are few and far between. But if nuisance birds have been frustrating you and your other feeder guests, there are a few possible solutions to help you regain control.

You can minimize the effect of nuisance birds at your feeders by taking advantage of their eating habits. Pigeons and house sparrows would rather eat cracked corn or chick scratch than sunflower seeds and niger, so I fill a welcoming tray feeder with the cheap stuff, where they can sit and peck contentedly. I also keep a decoy "starling table" at a far side of the garden, where I pile stale bread, leftover pasta, apple cores, and other food scraps that these birds adore. A big bowl of moist kibble dog food keeps them occupied for hours, as does the remains of your Thanksgiving turkey or a big ham bone.

The drawback to this open-handed approach is that the birds may pass the word, so that you end up with an ever-growing flock of pests. Because I enjoy watching their antics as they eat and quarrel over who gets the biggest piece, I don't mind an increase in the number of birds that visit.

If you want to pull the welcome mat out from under your starlings and pigeons, turn to pest-proof feeders. Tube feeders will discourage them, as will suet feeders that hold the fat on the underside where these birds can't get to it. Weight-sensitive feeders that slam the door on larger birds may also do the trick. Offering only large, gray-striped sunflower seed is another tactic that often works because the

Pigeons are enjoyable feeder guests—in moderation. But like other nuisance birds, they usually bring an ever-growing number of friends on subsequent visits.

birds can't crack the shells easily. But limiting the menu to that seed will make buntings, native sparrows, and other small seed eaters unhappy.

It's hard to discourage house finches because their favored foods are also tops with goldfinches, grosbeaks, and other desirable birds. Tube feeders with perches above the holes instead of below, so that the birds must eat upside down, may work. Be warned—in some areas, house finches, although initially discouraged by these feeders, soon learned how to contort their bodies to get a bite.

Since you can't teach a mockingbird to share, you'll have to resort to camouflage. Install other feeders where the mockingbird can't see them or can't get to them quickly to chase away visitors. Tube feeders are easily portable and will keep your finches satisfied until the mocker tires of its game. See Doves on page 84, Finches on page 118, House Sparrow on page 163, or Starling on page 274 to learn more about specific nuisance birds.

Nuthatches

If I had to choose my favorite feeder bird, nuthatches would be at the top of the list. I never tire of watching these svelte, acrobatic, dapper-dressed birds as they swivel up and down tree trunks or feeder posts and whack open seeds with their sharp pointed bills. All nuthatch species have gray-blue backs and very short, stubby tails. Largest of the clan is the **white-breasted nuthatch,** which ranges summer and winter across most of the country except for some areas of the Plains and Southwest. With its clean black-and-white markings, this bird looks like it's dressed for a formal dinner dance.

"Cute" best describes the three species of smaller nuthatches. The **red-breasted nuthatch,** a northern and western nester, fans out across most of the country in winter. The adorable **pygmy nuthatch,** a gray-capped bird, lives in areas of the West, especially in pine trees. The diminutive **brown-headed nuthatch** ranges across the Southeast and up the Atlantic coast.

Nuthatch Behavior

You'll enjoy watching the contortions of nuthatches at your feeder. These birds are climbers, whose job in nature is to glean insects, eggs, and larvae from between bark crevices; the design of their bodies is perfect for the job. They move up and down surfaces in jerky steps, clinging closely to the support, and typically working upside down—head down, tail up. Watch when another bird sounds an alarm call, and you'll see the nuthatch freeze to its

The white-breasted nuthatch is the largest of these often upside-down birds. Once called nuthacks, they are named for the way they hammer open nuts.

perch, transforming instantly into what looks just like a bump on a log.

Notice the difference between chickadees and nuthatches when they feed. Chickadees secure the seed in their feet to peck at it, while nuthatches wedge it into a crevice to hammer it into smaller bits. That dagger bill can be a self-defense aid, and

NUTHATCH FEEDER FOODS			
■ Corn, whole or cracked	■ Nuts	■ Rapeseed	■ Virginia creeper (*Parthenocissus quinquefolia*) berries
■ Elderberries (*Sambucus* spp.)	■ Peanut butter	■ Suet	
	■ Peanuts	■ Sunflower seeds, any kind	■ Wheat
■ Milo	■ Pine nuts		

nuthatches don't hesitate to make threatening gestures with it. Watch for lowered or spread wings, too, as signs of aggression.

In winter, nuthatches often roam backyards and wild places with chickadees, creepers, kinglets, and titmice searching for food. Whether they're eating acorns or sunflower seeds, they are energetic at their work, pecking vigorously at hard-shelled foods. Often they stuff seeds and other morsels into crevices for a later meal. Sunflower seeds will keep them busy at the feeder, but a variety of other treats, especially peanut butter, nuts, and suet also tempt them.

Nuthatches are the perfect birds to practice your hand-taming skills on. They are surprisingly unafraid of humans and very easy to approach if you walk slowly and quietly. The red-breasted species is the tamest of the tribe, in my experience. I've walked up to them—even in the wild—with an outstretched handful of nuts and had them eating out of my palm in less than 10 minutes!

The diminutive red-breasted nuthatch may visit sporadically during migration or linger all season long. Nuthatches take a seed or nut and fly off to eat it.

Nuts

Attract chickadees, jays, nuthatches, titmice, woodpeckers

BIRDS ARE JUST CRAZY ABOUT NUTS, but these meaty little morsels carry a hefty price tag at the store. At $5 a pound and up, walnuts, almonds, pecans, and other nuts can break the bird-feeding bank in a big hurry. Still, a spread of nuts in the feeder is guaranteed to attract wonderful chickadees, jays, titmice, woodpeckers, and, of course, nuthatches. And nothing works as well as nuts for hand taming these same birds. (For a nearly foolproof method to tempt birds to feed from your hand, see the Hand Feeding entry on page 153.)

You'll find the best prices on nuts through food co-ops, at health-food stores, and in the bulk foods aisle of your grocery store, where you can fill a bag with your selections. At the grocery store, packaged nuts are often put on sale in time for Christmas baking. Unsalted, uncoated raw nuts are best. In other words, buy the plain raw almonds, not the sugar-coated, pastel-colored dessert variety.

Nuts contain a lot of oil, which can turn rancid in warm weather or room-temperature storage. Should your stockpile of nuts go bad, pour them into a feeder and let the birds decide for themselves whether or not they're past the eating stage. When I filled my feeder with English walnuts that tasted terrible to me, the chickadees, jays, nuthatches, and woodpeckers made quick work of them. If birds scorn them, squirrels may still be interested. I never waste anything that looks like it may still have possibilities. Wild birds seem to know instinctively not to eat anything that will harm them.

Go on a Nut Hunt

If your budget isn't in the Bill Gates league, there's an easy way to acquire lots of nuts for nothing, plus develop a new family tradition at the same time: Go back to your hunter/gatherer roots. In the old days, before "No Trespassing" signs sprouted like mushrooms on most wild lands, gathering sweet beechnuts, mealy chestnuts, hard little hickories, melt-in-your-mouth butternuts, and all kinds of good stuff in the shell was a wonderful family ritual for fall. No matter where you live, there's bound to be some kind of wild nut trees within picking distance.

Many suburban and country roads are still dotted with fine nut trees, and others grow in fields, hedgerows, and woods. You'll have to search out the tree and get permission to pick the nuts (offer to share 50–50 any bounty you collect, and most landowners will jump at the offer). Don't gather nuts without asking permission first—an altercation with an unhappy landowner will make the family outing memorable, and not in a good way!

Storing and Feeding Whole Nuts

Birds love all types of nuts. Plastic grocery sacks are perfect for collecting. Because nuts vary in the ease—or difficulty—with which they part from their shells, keep different kinds of nuts separate for easier cracking when you're ready to feed. After the expedition, spread your booty in shallow cardboard boxes in an airy, dry place—the garage is perfect. After the hulls have dried (or fallen off, in some cases), pour the nuts into mouse-proof containers for storage.

Birds welcome nuts year-round, but save most of them to feed in cold weather, when birds most need

High-fat nuts help birds replenish the extra calories they burn just keeping warm in winter. To keep costs down, offer nuts in a feeder that blocks larger birds.

high-fat, high-calorie foods. To give the birds a treat, fill a tube sock with nuts, hold the end closed, and give a few good whacks with a hammer. Empty the sock into a tray feeder and sit back to watch the birds.

For more information about nuts for birds, see the Walnuts entry on page 316. Peanuts are actually legumes, not true nuts; you'll find lots of info about them in their own entry on page 228.

Grow Your Own Nuts

MOST NUT trees need from 5 to 7 years to bear their first crop. That may seem like a long time to us impatient gardeners, but the young trees will offer benefits to birds even before they bear. Their branches provide nesting places, their foliage and bark hide nutritious insects, and they add to the inviting cover your yard supplies to birds. Choose whatever nuts appeal to your family's taste: Once your tree begins bearing big crops, you'll have plenty of nuts for eating as well as bird feeding.

Nut trees grow into statuesque shade trees, but remember that they will drop nuts! Birds will clean up the meats, but they won't take away most of the shells, especially those of hard-shelled hickories and black walnuts. If you aren't sure you want to rake up fallen nuts year after year before they become sharp obstacles to bare feet or lawn-mower blades, think twice before you plant a nut tree. Of course, if you have a good population of squirrels, they'll do most of the cleanup.

Fallen nuts are really a problem with chestnut trees, whose nuts are surrounded by hulls as spiny as a hedgehog. They are painful to handle without stout leather gloves and a most unpleasant surprise to encounter when you're weeding or doing other garden maintenance.

O

Opossums

ANCIENT AND adaptable, the opossum, or possum as it's familiarly called, is one of my favorite animals. It's such an oddball, and so homely, you have to love it. Hunched and thickly furred with long gray hair, the opossum has a sharply pointed, whiskery face, naked ears, and pink feet and hands that are adept at grasping. Its thick, ratlike tail wraps around tree limbs to help the animal climb. Our only North American marsupial, the opossum raises its young for the first few months of life in a pouch on its belly, just like a kangaroo.

The nocturnal opossum is one of America's most primitive animals. But its small brain is perfectly capable of zeroing in on your grape arbor or feeder.

Opossums are widespread in cities and in the country from Iowa east and south and along the western coast. Once they discover a feeding station, they often become frequent visitors, with a taste for just about anything edible. They will happily dine on suet, seeds, and soft foods. An occasional dinner of birds' eggs may also be on the menu, along with persimmons and carrion. Cat food is also a favorite. If you often keep a bowl of pet food outside for your cat or dog, don't be surprised to find an unusual-looking "kitty" dining at it in the late evening. An opossum is usually so slow to take take alarm—one of the most primitive animals, it is not known for its quick-wittedness—that it may quietly continue eating for the second or two that it takes you to realize that this "cat" isn't what you first thought.

Active throughout the year, opossums are slow-moving and apt to play dead if a threatening growl and hiss don't stop an attacker. These interesting animals are nocturnal, so you may not even realize you are hosting one unless you find their distinctive star-shaped tracks around your feeder area or discover small, oval droppings in a tray feeder.

The opossums I've observed are more like night owls in their habits. They arrive to visit my feeders well into the night, usually between the 10 o'clock news and the late-night talk shows. I was astonished when I discovered that they may also be out and about on frigid nights. Their pink ears, feet, and tail, completely bare of the thick, soft fur that covers their bodies in a densely insulating layer, seem like they would freeze stiff in winter. But although many opossums do take to their den for a long winter's nap, some intrepid individuals stay on the prowl.

In spring, you may get to witness the never-to-be-forgotten sight of a mother opossum and her brood. The mouse-size youngsters cling securely to her back and sides, hanging on to her fur for dear life as she moseys along. As they grow bigger, they become more active and athletic and frequently hop down to explore when she stops to dine. One quick warning hiss from Mama, though, and they clamber back onto her body as fast as their stubby legs can carry them.

O

Oranges

Attract bluebirds, cardinals, mockingbirds, orioles, robins, starlings, woodpeckers

A BIRD WITH A SWEET TOOTH—now that I can identify with! The fructose in oranges (and some other fruits) is apparently what tempts orioles and house finches to oranges offered at the feeding station. These birds are also fond of sugar water served in nectar feeders. Cardinals, mockingbirds, robins, starlings, woodpeckers, and if you're lucky, bluebirds also will partake of oranges.

Commercially made orange feeders make it a snap to serve a fresh halved orange to your guests. You can also make your own feeder from a scrap of wood and a stout nail. Mount the feeder horizontally on a deck railing or flat-topped post, or hang it vertically: The birds will reach the orange either way.

You can feed oranges year-round with good results. Spring migrant orioles, just back in breeding territory or just passing through, are often quick to home in on an orange feeder. If you haven't had orioles at your feeding station before, be patient. It may take the birds a while to find the fruit. Replace the orange as necessary if patrons are slow in arriving.

Orange fruit brings orange feathers! Bullock's oriole and other species are attracted by fresh orange halves. Provide a perch for the bird to grip.

Orioles

A FEW SHORT YEARS AGO, an oriole at the feeder was a rare sight. Now the birds seem to have learned that feeding stations mean food, and they honor many delighted feeder-keepers with their visits. Except for the Gulf and Atlantic coasts, orioles are a spring-through-fall treat as they move far southward in winter. Nectar and fruit are the big draws for these birds.

Although their bright colors belie it, orioles are members of the blackbird family. The most common species is the **northern oriole,** which embraces the eastern Baltimore race and the western Bullock's race. Both are bright orange and black, with the Bullock's sporting big, flashy white wing patches, and

the Baltimore wearing a full black hood. In the Southwest, another orange and black species, the **hooded oriole,** ranges the trees. It has an orange hood and a black throat and breast. The **Altamira, streak-backed,** and **spot-breasted orioles** are three other bright orange-and-black species of very limited range. Sporting brick red rather than bright orange, the **orchard oriole** abides in the eastern half of the country. A common bird of the Southwest, **Scott's oriole** is vividly yellow and black. The uncommon **Audubon's oriole,** also yellow and black, occasionally ventures into southern Texas. In nearly all oriole species, females are olive green with a warm but faint wash of bright color.

In the East, the Baltimore oriole represents the species known as the northern oriole. It eats mainly insects, often gleaned from flowering trees.

The Bullock's race of the northern oriole ranges across the western states. The white wing patch is a sure way to identify this flashy bird.

Oriole Behavior

Color is the first thing you'll notice when an oriole visits your feeder. Its plumage is bright enough to spot from afar as the bird makes its way to your buffet. But you probably will have to look up to see an incoming oriole. These are arboreal birds, which means they stay mostly in the trees. If shade trees dot your yard, you can watch the birds use them for stopping points as they fly from one place to another. As they move about at feeders or in foliage, orioles often adopt a slinky posture, with head and body lowered, moving sinuously.

Once they reach your offering of oranges or suet, two top favorites, orioles may spend many minutes enjoying the food. They also welcome birdbaths and other water features. If you are camping in the Southwest in summer, set a shallow skillet of water at your campsite and you may lure a Scott's oriole as your guest.

Orioles aren't as fast to find a nectar feeder as hummingbirds, but be patient. If you live in a mild-winter area, plant agaves and aloes around the nectar feeder to help catch the attention of these birds, which also occasionally visit flowers for the sweet stuff.

ORIOLE FEEDER FOODS			
■ Amelanchier (*Amelanchier* spp.) berries ■ Apples ■ Berries, especially mulberries (*Morus* spp.), blackberries (*Rubus* spp.),	blueberries (*Vaccinium corymbosum* and *V. angustifolium*), and huckleberries (*V. ovatum*) ■ Corn, cracked or whole-kernel	■ Elderberries (*Sambucus* spp.) ■ Figs (*Ficus carica*) ■ Nectar (use a feeder with perches) ■ Oranges, halved	■ Peaches ■ Pears ■ Peas, fresh, dried, or frozen ■ Suet, chopped

PROJECT

Quick and Easy Oriole Feeder

Orioles are birds with sweet, um, beaks. This easy-to-assemble feeder is sure to bring them in to satisfy their taste for sugary foods. Mount the feeder on a post where the ants it may also attract won't become a problem. Place it near a water source, so you can hose off any grape jelly residue from time to time.

MATERIALS

Quart jar lids

12- to 18-inch length of 1 × 6 lumber

Small nails

Several large nails

Grape jelly

Orange halves

Step 1: Nail a few lids to the top side of the board, using small nails that don't protrude to the other side.

Step 2: Drive a few big nails through the bottom side of the board so they protrude between the jar lids.

Step 3: Lay the board flat atop a fence post, and nail it in place with the lids and nail points on top.

Step 4: Fill the lids with grape jelly and impale halved oranges on the protruding nails.

Step 5: Find a spot for viewing your feeder as the orioles fly in for a treat.

Ornithology

ORNITHOLOGY, THE SCIENTIFIC STUDY of birds, takes its name from *ornis*, the Greek word for "bird." Ornithologists work in various areas. Some work with the physical understanding of this feathered animal. Others are dedicated to the science of classification, or taxonomy, which examines the genetic and evolutionary heritage of birds, from the first fossil records in stone to the present day, in order to arrange them by genus and species. Much work is being done today in ornithological studies of ethology, or bird behavior; ecology and distribution; and applied ornithology, the science of birds' relationships with humans, of which conservation is a major concern.

Because birds are such a vital part of the web of life, some bird scientists work to develop ways that we average folks can help out our native species. Studies are conducted and research is carried out on all aspects of bird life, and this information translates into practical advice and products for the everyday bird watcher. You'll find birdhouse designs, feeder plans, and even the contents of seed mixes that trace their roots to scientific studies that determined their attractiveness to birds.

Much of what is known about which bird eats what is thanks to ornithologists, who spent hours dissecting birds and inventorying the contents of their stomachs. I can't imagine having the patience to count—let alone identify—parts and pieces of grasshoppers, mosquitoes, worms, weed seeds, or other food items, so I'm very grateful to the scientists who did.

Reading about old-time ornithologists is always interesting. Often, their research is fascinating and has practical implications as well. Even John James Audubon himself was an experimenter of sorts; once he played with a least bittern, the smallest species of heron, only robin-sized, to see how narrow a gap the bird could fit between. A space of 1½ inches between upright books in his library was adequate for the bird to pass through, he noted in his journals, although he omitted telling us just which books formed the gateposts. Today, when constructing nest boxes for birds, this information is good to have at hand so we know what size openings are appropriate for each species.

Modern ornithologists work on any questions that still need answers and investigate new problems that crop up. When the unusual disease called West Nile encephalitis showed up for the first time in America, ornithologists became involved because the disease is carried by birds, then transmitted by mosquitoes to humans.

Most research takes place today at universities and other institutions, although amateur observations are still solicited, such as the data collected during regular bird counts or through Project Feederwatch (see page 23). If you are interested in a career in ornithology, check with a local college or university or browse the Internet or your public library for more information on getting an education or career path opportunities in this field.

> Much of the information about which bird eats what is known thanks to ornithologists.

Owls

IT'S NOT THE OFFERINGS YOU PROVIDE in your feeders that will bring owls to your yard—it's the rodents that scurry around at night, picking up dropped seed. Owls are the number-one enemy of mice, rats, voles, and other small furry creatures. Their huge eyes are very keen even in the dimmest light. Their unbelievably sensitive hearing, almost as good as sonar, can pick up the sound of sneaky little paws from far away. As if that's not enough to stack the deck, owls also fly on silent wings, thanks to special feather adaptations that eliminate the noise of the air stream passing over them.

The songbirds, squirrels, rabbits, chipmunks, and other denizens of your yard will not thank you for attracting owls. Both larger species, such as the **barred owl, great horned owl,** and **spotted owl,** and small owls, such as the **burrowing owl, screech owl,** and even the tiny **saw-whet owl,** are just as satisfied to snatch a sleeping or nesting bird as they are a rodent. Almost any bird you can think of is on the owl menu, from diminutive hummingbirds to hefty Canada geese. The avian guardians of the bird

Large but hidden ear openings and extra-large eyes give owls a hunting edge. This northern saw-whet owl, just 7 inches tall, is one of the smallest and tamest.

kingdom—crows, jays, and ravens—are quick to make a commotion when they happen across a roosting owl. What they're really saying with those loud alarm calls is "Murderer!"

Owl Behavior

Owls can see perfectly well in daylight, but most species only come out at night. Some species are crepuscular, preferring the twilight at dusk and dawn, while others are nocturnal, hunting only after dark. The short-eared, barred, pygmy, snowy, and hawk owls often hunt by day.

When they're not on the wing, owls roost in trees, often in conifers, well hidden from the harassments of crows and jays. Because of their mottled brown plumage, owls are almost impossible for our weak human eyes to spot casually. If you follow a group of cawing crows or screaming jays, you may find an owl is the object of the hubbub being raised.

Because owls fly on silent wings and dispatch their prey without a squawk, you can't depend on the sound of the hunt to alert you to their presence. But there are a couple of sure ways to find out if you have owls in the neighborhood. First, sit outside at night and listen for owl calls. When you hear a far-off hooting or whinnying, imitate the call; the bird will often come closer to investigate its supposed compatriot. Or try playing a recording of owl calls at night in nesting season. For owls, that begins much earlier than songbirds—sometimes in January.

Late January to early March is a good time to try getting a response to recorded calls. Carry a portable tape or CD player outside and play a single species' call, starting with a common owl such as the screech, barred, or great horned. Click the recording off and wait a few minutes, then repeat the call. If nobody answers your recording after half an hour, try the voice of another common species.

OWL FOODS
■ Bats
■ Chipmunks
■ Flying squirrels
■ Game birds
■ Mice
■ Moths
■ Rabbits
■ Skunks
■ Songbirds
■ Voles

Chances are, you may never know that you have an owl regularly patrolling your yard. One giveaway, however, is the presence of owl "pellets," the compressed bundles of feathers, bones, and other inedible parts that owls cough up after they eat. If you can set aside your squeamishness and pull apart a pellet with tweezers, you will find a fascinating record of the owl's last meal.

P

Peanut Butter

Attracts bluebirds, chickadees, jays, nuthatches, starlings, titmice, woodpeckers, Carolina wrens

IF YOU POLLED THE BLUEBIRDS, chickadees, jays, nuthatches, titmice, woodpeckers, Carolina wrens—and let's not forget the starlings!—at your feeder, they would tell you that peanut butter is a perfect food: It's ultrahigh in fat and full of protein, which makes it a super food for cold weather feeding, when birds need extra calories, and a real treat any time of the year.

There are two drawbacks to feeding peanut butter: Because it's so popular, it can get expensive as a regular menu item, and it can be messy, leaving grease stains on wood posts or trees or even melting in bright sun.

It's easy to overcome these challenges. Birds aren't fussy about brands, so buy the cheapest peanut butter you can find. I like to use chunky style rather than creamy because picking out the nuggets of peanuts slows the consumption—while one bird pauses to swallow the peanut, another can grab a quick bite. Besides, I know from my own long history with peanut butter that it can be difficult to get down the hatch, although I've never noticed birds having difficulty with either creamy or chunky peanut butter.

To stretch your peanut butter, mix it with cornmeal, a low-cost product that's readily eaten by the same birds that enjoy peanut butter. Start with a mixture that's heavy on the peanut butter side, and over a period of days, work more cornmeal into the offering until you find a ratio that the birds seem to enjoy.

It's best to offer peanut butter or peanut butter mixtures in small amounts to prevent your treasured treat from being devoured before your eyes by starlings and squirrels and other rodents. Put out only what the birds will eat in an hour or so. You can always renew the feeding later.

Making your own peanut butter (or any true nut butter—almond, filbert, or walnut) is a fun project, especially with kids, who will get a whole new perspective on their favorite spread. Simply pour roasted peanuts, which you can buy in bulk in the generic-foods aisle of some supermarkets or at health-food stores, into a blender or food processor and grind until the peanuts turn into, well, peanut butter. Stop when the mix is still coarse, for chunky blend, or pulverize until it's creamy smooth. If you have long, hot summers, you can grow peanuts yourself from seed. It's fascinating to see the plant "peg" its stems to the ground and fun to dig the harvest from the soil later.

Peanut Butter Feeders

My simple homemade peanut butter feeder consists of a scrap of bark-on lumber that I picked up from a local sawmill. I nailed the wood to a porch post for a permanent feeder. All I do is smear the peanut butter directly onto the bark with a small spatula (or butter knife). The crevices and rough texture hold it in place and provide a good grip to woodpeckers and other customers. When I noticed that juncos, sparrows, and other small birds gathered beneath the feeder to pick up any dropped bits, I decided to cater to them, too. I made a similar feeder and hammered it horizontally to the bottom of my wood feeder post, so the peanut butter is just a couple of inches above the ground.

For neat peanut butter feeding, use a section of log drilled with cavities for holding the stuff. This is the perfect vehicle for birds that feed at relatively high feeders, such as chickadees, titmice, and woodpeckers. It also prevents those mobs of starlings that may attack if you serve peanut butter in an open tray. Birds that stay low to the ground also enjoy the nutty treat. Serve them in a low, wire-bottom tray feeder tucked under conifers or shrubs, where it is less visible to starlings. If starlings or jays do become pesky, put your peanut butter in a tray feeder protected by a wire cage that allows small birds access but blocks larger species and squirrels (see Feeder Covers on page 99).

> Birds aren't fussy about brands, so buy the cheapest peanut butter your store offers.

Peanuts

Attract chickadees, jays, juncos, nuthatches, sparrows, titmice, woodpeckers

PLUMP, MEATY PEANUTS MAKE a nutritious mouthful for many of your regular feeder birds. Chickadees, jays, nuthatches, titmice, and woodpeckers are all peanut appreciators. Other visitors, such as juncos and sparrows, may nibble smaller peanut pieces, but their beaks are generally too small to get a grip on a large kernel.

Grow 'Em or Buy 'Em

Peanuts (*Arachis hypogaea*) are not true nuts; they're the underground tubers of the peanut plant. You can actually grow peanuts in your garden, although if you live in the northern half of the country, you'll need to choose fast-maturing varieties. You plant peanuts in the spring and harvest in the fall when the plants' leaves turn yellow.

Of course, you can also buy peanuts to feed to your birds, and that's what most people do. Check the bulk-food bins at supermarkets or health-food stores for bargain-priced peanuts—they may cost less than those sold especially for bird feeding. Unsalted peanuts, either in or out of the shell, are the best choice for birds, although birds will also gobble the salted variety. That extra heavy dose of sodium won't harm your birds, but be sure water is freely available to slake their thirst. Roasted and raw peanuts seem to be equally popular.

Whichever type of peanuts you feed, be sure to buy fresh stock. Old peanuts may be rancid and unpalatable. Examine peanut pieces sold for bird food carefully before you buy: They may contain a high proportion of a bitter-flavored part of the peanut that is discarded by peanut-butter manufacturers. Look for very small elongated pieces: the bit of the peanut that lies between the two meaty halves and forms the tip of the kernel. These bits may be chopped up in the processing and hard to recognize. When in doubt, try a taste yourself. If the peanuts taste good and nutty to you, your birds will devour them like kids at a ballpark.

A male red-bellied woodpecker extracts peanuts from a wire mesh feeder filled with this highly favored food. Most feeder regulars eagerly eat peanuts year-round.

Foil Peanut Thieves

One way to outsmart squirrels and chipmunks (who also love peanuts) is to be stingy: Dole out a handful of peanuts at a time on fall and winter mornings, when the feeders are hopping with birds. Your presence should send squirrels scurrying, which is just enough time for the birds to swoop in and grab a nutty snack. By the time the squirrels return, all that's left of the peanuts will be a tantalizing aroma.

You can make your own squirrel-resistant peanut feeder by covering a shallow tray feeder with a piece of strong ½-inch wire mesh. Squirrels may still spend hours trying to wrest the wire from the wood, and their presence will discourage birds. If that is the case, invest in a sturdy "large seed" feeder made of metal, with a heavy-duty wire cage surrounding a central tube feeder. The wire allows birds easy access to the peanuts but blocks squirrels from reaching the tasty treats.

P

Pears

Attract bluebirds, catbirds, house finches, mockingbirds, orioles, robins, thrashers, thrushes, wrens

CATBIRDS, HOUSE FINCHES, MOCKINGBIRDS, orioles, robins, thrashers, wrens, and other fruit-eating birds have a definite sweet tooth. Even though many of these birds may not be regular visitors to your feeders, you can use sweet, soft pears to entice them to a feeding station. Homegrown or store-bought will do, as long as they're ripe.

Place pears directly on the ground for robins. For other birds, offer pears on a platform mounted on a post or in a tray feeder, about 3 feet high. Place the feeder near sheltering shrubs or a hedge so that these somewhat shy birds can feel safe while they eat. Slice the pear in half and offer it cut side up.

Fall migration time and winter in areas where these birds live year-round are the best times to offer pears. Natural fruits are abundant at other seasons, and unless the birds are already regulars at your feeder, they probably won't be interested. If a major snow or ice storm blankets your area, pears can be a lifesaver for birds that can't get to their natural foods. At times like these, you can even offer canned pears. Chop the fruit into small pieces so the birds can eat even if it freezes.

Plant a 'Bradford' Callery Pear for Birds

'Bradford' pear trees (*Pyrus calleryana*) are beautiful in bloom, striking in red to purple fall color, and tempting to bluebirds, thrushes, and other songbirds when their tiny fruits ripen. On the downside,

A 'Bradford' pear's fragrant flowers attract small insects that invite bug-eating birds to dine. Robins, thrashers, and others enjoy the fruit that comes later.

'Bradford' pear trees tend to have problems after about 10 years: They drop limbs, crack down the middle, or keel over in storms. 'Chanticleer' is considered a sturdier, longer-lived callery pear.

You may find a callery pear for $25 or less at discount garden centers in early spring, a small price for 10 years' worth of better backyard bird watching.

Bird Watching at a Callery Pear

ALMOST AS common as forsythia, callery pear trees are favorites for backyard birds. Here's why.

■ Dense, leafy growth makes the trees a favorite roosting spot, at night or during rainy weather.

■ When the trees are in bloom, the cloud of white blossoms attracts swarms of tiny insects, great fodder for orioles, tanagers, vireos, wood warblers, and other bug-eating birds, which makes a callery pear in the backyard a hot spot for at-home bird watching.

■ Fall brings ripening fruit, which look more like tiny, hard cherries than pears. Great news again for backyard bird watchers: The fruit ripens just as flocks of bluebirds, robins, thrushes, and waxwings are passing through in search of sustenance.

Peas

Attract blackbirds, cardinals, crows, doves, grackles, grosbeaks, grouse, jays, quail, pheasants, English sparrows

FRESH PEAS ARE ONE of the delights of a home vegetable garden, and dried peas are a favored food for doves, grouse, quail, pheasants, and large songbirds, including cardinals and grosbeaks.

Raising Peas for Birds

If you live near game-bird habitat, you can grow peas for fall and winter food right in place. A planting of peas will provide long-lasting food for foraging quail and other game birds, but growing peas for birds is a slightly schizophrenic process. In order to provide a bountiful harvest for birds when the peas mature, you'll have to discourage other birds from eating the seeds at planting time. Blackbirds, crows, grackles, jays, and English sparrows have an uncanny knack for finding a newly planted pea patch (I think they must hide and watch). To prevent them from robbing the seeds, cover the planting with floating row covers or straw.

If you have the space to plant a truly large area—a quarter-acre or more—of peas or other wild bird food, get in touch with your local cooperative extension office. They can supply the details you need to grow a successful crop. Unless you have plenty of free time and determination and lots of muscle, you'll need farm equipment such as a plow or tractor to do the planting and tending of such a quantity.

For a "large" backyard planting of, say, a 5-foot-wide 100-foot row, or for a smaller patch, prepare the soil as for any annual plant: Remove vegetation, turn the soil, and rake to a moderately fine texture. Scatter pea seeds thickly over the bed, and cover with enough soil so that the tempting, light-colored seeds don't grab the attention of blackbirds, which will be happy to devour them before they sprout.

Rural feed stores sell pea seed in bulk at prices reasonable enough to plant a large area—1,000 square feet will take around 10 pounds of seed. Combine the pea seed with corn seed at a ratio of 1 pound peas to 5 pounds corn, and you'll provide more food plus a built-in trellis of cornstalks for the peas to climb. In a smaller yard, try covering a fence or planting a hedge of fast-climbing pea vines, and let them dry and ripen in place. The birds will find the seeds without any further effort from you.

Feeder Peas

Many suppliers treat pea seeds with chemicals, so be sure to ask for untreated seed when you purchase your peas. You'll have to look a little harder for untreated bulk seeds, but they are available. Check mail-order sources such as those listed in "Resources" on page 348, or ask at local seed suppliers, especially Mom & Pop hardware stores in rural areas or at farm supply stores. Or you can try planting a plastic bag of dried soup peas from the supermarket! (Be sure to use whole peas, not split peas, which won't germinate.)

At the feeder, birds often overlook dry peas in favor of the ever-popular sunflower seeds and other

---

Legumes for the Birds

PEAS AND beans belong to the plant group called legumes, which also includes perennial flowers and even some shrubs and trees. Nearly all game birds like to eat a variety of legume seeds. Partridge pea (*Cassia fasciculata,* also known as *Chamaecrista fasciculata*), a pretty yellow-flowered perennial legume, is a particular favorite of quail. It's easy to add to this perennial to your wildflower meadow or prairie garden, where it will add late-season color and winter-long food. Partridge pea is hardy to Zone 5. It may bloom the first year from an early sowing, but it usually requires two full seasons to perform; if you live in Zone 3 or 4, you can take your chances and try it anyway, mulching deeply with fall leaves to help it live through the winter deep freeze.

offerings. If you scatter a handful of dry peas among a tray of black sunflower seeds, the eye-catching white seeds may draw the attention of woodpeckers.

Another way to encourage wild birds to shift to eating a new food like dried peas or small dried beans is to wait until the feeders are almost empty and then put out about a cupful of the peas in place of the sunflower seeds that would normally fill the feeder. Once the birds get a taste for the new food, usually within a day, you can return to the regular food and mix the dried legumes among them.

You also can place dry peas in a low tray feeder or directly on the ground for doves, pheasants, and other ground feeders or in open tray feeders for cardinals and grosbeaks.

Garden "Peas" for Birds

Other plants in the same family as peas—the legumes—produce pea-like seeds that birds also find appealing. The pretty pink blossoms of redbud trees, for instance, are distinctly pea-flower-shaped, and you may see chickadees and titmice working at the overwintering seedpods. The seed heads of clover and vetches are favored by game birds, native sparrows, and doves. Lupines, both native species and splashy garden cultivars, are just tasty peas in showy disguise. Though eating lupines can cause problems in livestock (the infamous loco-weed is a lupine), golden-crowned sparrows and other birds eat the seeds of these pretty ornamentals with impunity.

Photographing Birds

YOUR FEEDING STATION is the perfect setup for taking pictures of birds. The birds are accustomed to visiting the spot, so you know you will always have subjects handy. Although you can snap your shots through a window, you'll get clearer pictures outdoors.

Either set up a blind (see page 22) from which to photograph, or get the birds used to your presence by using a good dose of patience. If you sit quietly near the feeder, the birds will eventually accept you—with luck, in less than an hour—and return to feeding as usual.

Getting a Good Photo

Most beginners' bird photos look the same: a lot of sky, a lot of plants, and a tiny speck of bird. You need to get very close to a bird to get a good shot—either by actually being very near to the bird yourself, or by using a powerful lens. Combining the two will get you incredible close-up bird shots.

Read the fine print on those extreme close-up shots we drool over in magazines, and you'll see they were usually shot with a 400mm lens or larger. Big lenses like this are expensive. If you aren't ready to invest hundreds of dollars (or thousands) in a close-up lens, finagle yourself into the nearest position to

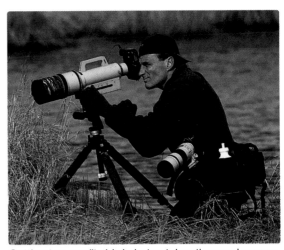

Getting top-quality bird photos takes time and money. High-power lenses and other gear add up. But snapshots can be worth it, if you get close to your subject.

your subjects you can find to make up for your lack of equipment. You may find that if you are reasonably close, you can get perfectly satisfying shots from an automatic point-and-shoot 35mm camera with a zoom lens. Ever-improving digital photography lets you adjust elements of a less-than-perfect photo.

P

Photogenic Tricks

Birds are high-energy creatures, and you will need to be quick to capture them on film. Start by aiming your camera at feeder birds, which usually stay put in the same general area long enough to focus on.

It's fun to document the birds that come to your feeder, but you don't want every shot to look the same: Cardinal at the feeder, goldfinch at the feeder, junco at the feeder gets boring in a hurry. For more interesting shots, it helps a lot to vary the settings and to aim for the most natural-looking background you can find.

Turning the area around your feeding station into a naturalistic landscape will help get you some great bird pictures. Instead of a bevy of quail eating from a tray feeder, you can catch them sidling through grasses or perching on a rock. A towhee or fox sparrow looks much better scratching among leaf litter than rooting around in 2 inches of old sunflower hulls.

An easy trick for getting natural-looking photos is to hide the bird food. Smear peanut butter on the back of a dead branch "planted" at the feeding station, and snap the titmouse or chickadee as the bird alights. Sprinkle millet at the base of a rock or among clumps of grass to get pictures of feeding doves, juncos, and sparrows.

Natural-looking water features also lend themselves to appealing bird photos. Chiseled-out or naturally concave rocks, waterfalls, or the shallow edges of garden pools are pretty places to shoot bathing or drinking birds. If you do photograph a bird in a pedestal-type birdbath, aim for an extreme close-up that catches the bird and the splashing water but cuts out as much concrete as possible.

Locating a nest on your property can also bring you some fine bird photos. Do not get so close that your presence alarms the birds; if you hear warning "Chip!" notes, back off a bit until the parent bird calms down. With luck, you catch the parents bringing food or fledglings leaving the nest.

Patience Is Key

Bird photography takes time and patience. The longer you spend with camera at the ready, the more likely you are to find something worthy to shoot. Keep in mind that birds take the "early bird" adage to heart: They're out and about early in the morning, with peak activity at the feeder going strong until about 10 A.M. Bird activity dwindles during midday (unless the weather is cold or a storm is coming in) and picks up again in late afternoon, a couple of hours before sunset. Take advantage of these times of increased activity, and be ready with the camera.

> Turn the area around your feeding station into a naturalistic landscape for better bird photos.

Pinecones

Attract many kinds of birds at various times of the year

ONE OF THE sloppiest bird-treat projects is also the most successful: Smear a pinecone with peanut butter, and you're guaranteed to draw in hungry birds from chickadees to woodpeckers. Even without the peanut butter, pinecones attract birds because they hide a multitude of tasty seeds.

You're probably familiar with pignolia or pine nuts, the plump, pale yellow-to-tan seed of the pinyon pine (*Pinus cembroides*), used in pesto and other recipes. Birds love these uncommonly large pine nuts (they're expensive, though), but the tiny, lightweight seeds of many other pinecones—as well as cones from other types of evergreens—are also popular with foraging birds (and squirrels). Tiny cones, like those of the hemlock, attract little birds like chickadees and titmice. Bigger cones draw in crossbills, grosbeaks, and larger jays. Crossbills depend so heavily on pinecones that their beaks have evolved as custom-made tools for quickly scissoring seeds out of cones.

P

Plant a "Pinecone Tree"

Spruces, hemlocks, firs, balsams, and other conifers all bear cones, and we commonly refer to all of them as "pinecones." Winged seeds flutter from the cones when mature, but birds will often descend on these trees and extract the seeds before they fall. Native conifers are an excellent choice for your landscape because they're well adapted to the climate and local birds are accustomed to feeding on the cones.

Plant conifers from spring through early fall so that they have time to settle in a bit and grow new roots before the ground freezes. These trees can be pricey, especially larger specimens. To help protect your investment, plant in late spring to early summer. Most conifers stay green and healthy-looking in cold weather, regardless of their condition. Once the weather warms, it can take several weeks for a tree that failed over winter to show signs of decline, so it could be late spring before you see browning needles. If your nursery's 1-year guarantee runs from June to June, you'll know by then if you need a replacement.

In addition to their popular seeds, conifers provide a safe haven for roosting and nesting birds.

Any conifer will attract birds to its sheltering branches. Hemlocks are one of the fastest to bear cones. A single mature conifer has great bird appeal, but a group planting is even better because of the greater cover it provides.

Predators

LIFE IS TOUGH when you are a feathered package of prey. With hungry cats creeping through the bushes and high-flying hawks patrolling overhead, it's no wonder birds are so jumpy and alert. Danger can come from any direction when they least expect it. Crows, jays, owls, raccoons, and snakes are also a threat to nestlings and parents at the nest.

Making your feeding area safe from predators is a matter of life and death for birds. If cats prowl your yard, discourage them. Keep your own felines indoors; they will soon become accustomed to it. If stray cats or neighbors' cats are a problem, chase them away whenever you see them. Clapping your hands, running toward the cat, or squirting it with water (warm weather only, please) may solve the immediate problem, but the attraction of birds is so great that the cats may return when you're not watching.

A fence may deter cats, especially if they are trapped within it and can't get out quickly when you are chasing them away. But a dog is your best defense against cats. Dogs rarely chase birds because they are usually unsuccessful at catching them; dogs are also easier to train to stay away from the feeding station.

To give your feeder birds a fighting chance against hawk attacks, provide dense cover near the feeding area. A hedgerow, bramble patch, or group of shrubs provide safe places to hide. You will also want to supply safe access routes to and from your feeders and about your property. Plant a hedgerow-like corridor of trees, shrubs, grasses, or other vegetation to keep birds hidden from sight as they move through your garden. Be sure to include a few evergreens in the mix, so that birds can seek shelter year-round and safe nesting sites in spring.

Preferred Foods

SUNFLOWER SEEDS, MILLET, and other feeder staples are the meat and potatoes of most birds' diets. They'll eat them day in and day out, just like your dog downs its bowl of dry kibble, because the offerings are abundant and readily available. But birds also have their preferences—the foods they seek out first, at the feeder or in the wild.

When acorns and beechnuts ripen, for instance, birds will desert the feeder in favor of these natural foods. The juicy fruits of a mulberry tree (*Morus* spp.) will also divert the attention of feeder birds that may have come to your place to pick up raisins or other fruity offerings. Ragweed (*Ambrosia artemisifolia*), lamb's-quarters (*Chenopodium album*), dock (*Rumex crispus*), and dandelion (*Taraxacum officinale*) seeds as well as holly (*Ilex* spp.) berries all have their fans. Watch the action in your yard, and you'll see that your gone-to-seed zinnias or the fuzzy thistles you overlooked in the garden draw a bigger crowd of finches than even the most expensive tube feeder of niger.

Your birds aren't being disloyal by spurning your offerings and turning to wild foods. They're only doing what comes naturally. Each species has its preferences, learned through ages of evolution. They seek the seeds, nuts, nectar, or fruits of plants that best supply the nourishment they need in the natural world.

Spring and summer insects are probably the biggest magnet for birds of all types. These high-protein niblets are everywhere during warm weather, and birds take advantage of the bounty. Soft-bodied insects are also the ideal food for nestlings, which can't crack the seeds in your feeders. When insect life is at its peak, feeder traffic drops off dramatically. Birds don't need to travel to seek sustenance, as they do in wintertime when insects are few and finding wild seeds requires effort. Don't feel discouraged when feeder traffic slackens in late spring. Just bide your time and the birds will return. Meanwhile, keep the feeders filled with a small amount of seed and other foods and the birdbath brimming with fresh water. Your friends haven't deserted you—it's just that after a winter of dry food, a succulent caterpillar is too tantalizing to ignore.

Individual Preferences

Many species preferences are easy to determine—goldfinches prefer niger and sunflower seed over other feeder foods, and woodpeckers seek suet with a side order of sunflower seed. Birds usually go first to feeder foods that most closely resemble their natural diet. But birds also display regional and individual preferences. The cardinals at your feeder may adore safflower seed, while a few hundred miles away the red birds are reaching for cracked corn.

It's fun to experiment with new foods at the feeder. Keep track of how quickly your birds take to the new foods and which birds eat what. One red-bellied woodpecker that visits my feeders scolds me if I forget to have his ear of corn ready, while his compatriots ignore the corn in favor of feeders filled with suet and sunflower seeds.

You can even do a semiscientific test of bird tastes by adding dividers of wood lath to an open tray feeder. After partitioning the feeder, serve only one kind of seed in each section. I depend on the eyeball method to tell me which foods are most popular. It's easy to see at a glance that sunflower disappears fastest and that milo is the last on the list. For the sake of fairness, I set up both a high tray feeder and a low tray feeder for this test because often the birds that feed on or near the ground prefer a different menu than those that eat at higher feeders.

> Use preferred foods to increase the odds that a particular bird species will visit your feeders.

Think of lists of preferred foods, like the one on the opposite page, as the standard menu of your bird café. Then add daily specials and watch the takers.

Bird Preferences at the Feeder

EXPECT YOUR feeder birds to head first for the preferred foods on this list. But birds enjoy occasional variety in their diet, too, and will eagerly eat other foods. They also nibble other edibles when their favorites are lacking, or when a jay or other disruptive bird is keeping them away from their favored foods. Bird "tastes" may also vary from one individual to the next, with one of your titmice heading for the suet while the other visits the sunflower seeds. Check the specific bird entries in this book for suggestions of other foods to offer your favorite guests.

Bird	Most Preferred Foods	Also Highly Enjoyed
Bluebirds	Mealworms, peanut butter	Suet, berries, bread and baked goods, raisins, fruit
Cardinals	Sunflower seed	Safflower seed, fruit, millet, bread and baked goods, fruit
Chickadees	Peanuts, nutmeats, peanut butter, suet	Sunflower seed, bread and baked goods
Doves, pigeons	Millet	Cracked corn
Finches	Niger, sunflower seed	Millet, pine nuts, peanuts, birdseed mix, suet
Goldfinches	Niger, sunflower seed	Millet, flax, canary seed, suet, chopped peanuts, birdseed mix, grass seed
Grosbeaks	Sunflower seed	Fruit, suet, millet, safflower, bread and baked goods
Jays	Nutmeats, peanuts	Sunflower seed, suet, corn, bread and baked goods
Juncos	Millet	Sunflower seed, cracked corn, bread and baked goods, nutmeats, chopped peanuts
Kinglets	Suet	Bread and baked goods
Mockingbirds	Fruit	Bread and baked goods, suet, sunflower seed, millet, birdseed mix
Nuthatches	Nutmeats, suet, peanut butter	Sunflower seed, corn
Orioles	Nectar, oranges	Grape jelly, fruit, suet, softened raisins
Pheasants	Cracked corn	Millet
Quail	Cracked corn	Millet
Roadrunners	Meat scraps	Suet, leftovers
Robins	Mealworms, berries, fruit	Suet, bread and baked goods, raisins
Native sparrows	Millet	Suet, bread and baked goods, sunflower seed, canary seed, grass seed
Tanagers	Fruit, suet	Millet, mealworms, bread and baked goods
Thrashers	Fruit	Birdseed mix, millet, sunflower seed, suet
Titmice	Peanuts, peanut butter, nutmeats	Sunflower seed, suet, bread and baked goods
Towhees	Millet	Sunflower seed, cracked corn, bread and baked goods
Woodpeckers	Suet	Sunflower seed, nectar, fruit
Wrens	Peanut butter, suet	Bread and baked goods, fruit

P
Pumpkins and Squash

Attract cardinals, jays, nuthatches, titmice, woodpeckers

THE NUTTY INNARDS OF PUMPKINS and squash are delectable to many seed-eating birds, including cardinals, jays, nuthatches, titmice, and woodpeckers. These vegetables usually produce a generous quantity of seeds, providing a ready source of free bird food to add to your feeder offerings.

Pumpkins and squash are fall and winter crops, which is perfect timing because that's when feeders are at their busiest. Preparing the seeds is easy, as long as you don't mind a little mess. It's best to work outdoors, so you won't have to worry about picking up slippery seeds from the kitchen floor, and you can easily dump the scooped-out flesh onto your compost pile after you separate it from the seeds.

Processing Pumpkin Seeds

Use a large, sturdy, sharp-edged spoon to scrape out the seedy part of the pumpkin or squash into a colander. Run the colander under a strong spray of water to help dislodge clinging bits of squash fibers. Then spread the seeds, separating them as much as possible, on an old window screen to dry in the sun. You can also spread them out on a sheet of wax paper on your picnic table.

If you are working indoors, you can dry the seeds in your oven set at a very low temperature of 175° to 200°F and check for dryness every 5 or 10 minutes. With apologies to my feathered friends for an insensitive choice of cliché, I usually kill two birds with one stone by drying squash and pumpkin seeds at the same time I'm baking dinner or dessert. I spread the wet seeds on a metal cookie sheet or pizza pan, and set it on top of the rear burner of my electric stove–where the heat from the oven escapes. Long before the oven dish is done baking, the seeds have been turned, dried, and poured into storage bags.

Don't waste those pumpkin seeds! Toast some for yourself and dry the rest for birds in the fall and winter feeder. Squirrels and chipmunks enjoy them, too.

Turn the seeds with a spatula occasionally to speed the drying process. When the seeds are dry, store them in a paper grocery bag in a cool, dry place. If you have a big hoard of seeds, put the bag or bags into a closed metal container, such as a pretzel tin, to keep rodents from raiding the stash.

Like other unusual foods, the seeds may sit unnoticed in your feeder for a few days before birds begin to sample them. Scatter a few of the light-colored seeds in an open tray of black sunflower seeds to help the birds spot them more easily.

Chipmunks, squirrels, and other furry feeder visitors also delight in eating pumpkin and squash seeds. If you have separate feeders for squirrels and other wildlife, add these seeds to the menu. You'll enjoy watching how they pick up the seeds one by one in their small paws to nibble away the shells.

R

Raccoons

THE NIGHTLIFE at your feeding station can be just as entertaining as the daytime activity, especially if you are hosting raccoons. These common and intelligent animals thrive in residential areas as well as rural surroundings.

At the feeder, raccoons aren't particular. They adore a feast of corn but also eat sunflower seeds, fruit, and soft foods. Dog food, cat food, and leftovers are welcome treats. Raccoons relish suet and a visiting 'coon may open your wire suet feeder with its dexterous black paws and make off with an entire block.

A water source will give the raccoons in your neighborhood another incentive to visit your yard. They are quick at catching fish and frogs, and they may also carry food from your bird feeders to the water to "wash" it before eating it.

These carnivorous animals also catch mice at the feeder area. They may nab nestlings or eggs from wild birds' nests as well. Protect your nest boxes by using metal predator guards on the posts beneath them. In most areas, raccoons hibernate in the dead of winter and breed when they wake up from their seasonal sleep.

Like many feeder visitors, raccoons are often regular in their habits, visiting the feeding station at about the same time each night. Put out a fresh supply of whole-kernel or cob corn before dark, and check hourly to see if you have visitors. In my yard, they usually show up from around 9 to 10 P.M.

Unfortunately, raccoons are susceptible to rabies, which can quickly spread through wild populations. The disease is particularly prevalent in the East but can crop up anywhere. To play it safe, avoid getting too close to the animals, no matter how cute they are. Hand feeding can lead to a nip from an overly enthusiastic eater, and that's a risk you don't want to take. Because raccoons are nocturnal, spotting one in broad daylight is a signal that the animal is likely to be sick. Keep away from such an animal or from a raccoon that

A raccoon performs a highwire act while trying to get his paws on the seeds in a tube feeder. Enjoy the antics of these cute-but-wild critters from a distance.

is walking unsteadily or stiffly, walking in circles, or falling down.

Raccoons are strong and determined animals, and if they visit your feeding station only to find no accessible food, they'll do their best to make it accessible by tearing apart feeders with their dexterous paws and sharp teeth. I don't argue with them: I provide easy-access corn, apples, and pizza crusts to keep them content and to give me the pleasure of watching them—from a safe distance. I do like to play with my raccoons by challenging their agility. Once I hooked a toy ladder to a hanging feeder stocked with highly aromatic canned cat food. You should have seen those bandits stretch to grab the dangling ladder, then climb to their reward.

Rain

A LITTLE RAIN DOESN'T BOTHER BIRDS. During a rain shower, you'll see birds at your feeders, cracking seeds and nibbling suet, giving an occasional shake to flick water from their feathers.

When rain intensifies, or if there are gusty winds or lightning, birds wait out the storm in the shelter of densely branched trees and shrubs. To make sure birds will feel at home in your yard no matter what the weather, be sure they have a spot to take shelter from heavy rain. If your yard is very open, try planting a couple of bushy junipers (*Juniperus* spp.) or camellias, hollies, rhododendrons, or other broad-leaved evergreens to provide some quick shelter.

Bathing in the Rain

Rain is a vital source of water for birds. They'll gather at puddles of rainwater to drink and bathe. Smaller birds, including warblers and hummingbirds, may even splash in a thin film of water trapped on a leaf. If hummingbirds frequent your garden, watch their behavior when it starts raining—you may see them drinking from or splashing on a leaf.

Keeping the Kids Dry

To birds on the nest, rain is a danger to eggs and young ones because water can quickly chill them. The parent bird uses its body to offer protection from the raindrops, spreading its wings to cover the nest by a tent of feathers. I once saw a pair of robins protecting their young during an extra-heavy downpour. The female was sitting in the nest, and the male was perched on the rim with outspread wings, as if chivalrously holding an umbrella for her. Not all birds are as ingenious, and you may find dead nestlings in your yard after a heavy rain—the force of the downpour can dislodge them from the nest. Nests themselves may also fall out of the tree or other site, especially if wind accompanies the rainstorm.

Checking for Wet Seed

At the feeder, especially tray feeders and hopper feeders, rain means wet seed. Check your feeders after the weather clears, and remove any wet seed so that it doesn't turn moldy or ruin new seed that you add. Suet and whole corn cobs can stand up to rain; they will dry out without damage. If the wet weather is prolonged, however, even cob corn may rot, and tube feeders may accumulate moisture inside that causes seed to clump up and decay. You may need to compost the spoiled food and replace it with fresh.

Surviving Little or No Rain

In the arid Southwest, and in other places, such as the Northwest, where rain is scarce or nonexistent for months at a time, birds have evolved to take advantage of water wherever they can find it. Morning dew is a treasured source of water, but like puddles and streams, dew also disappears when rain fails to fall and air and soil become parched. But the biggest sources of liquid refreshment for desert birds are succulent plant parts and living food. Fruits are eagerly sought, for their thirst-satisfying juice as well as their food value. Prickly pear, cholla, and barrel cactuses are good places to bird-watch when their colorful fruits ripen and lure quail and other birds to the feast. Other plant parts also contain water. California and Gambel's quail seek out the juicy leaves of chickweed and the western weed called filaree, while the Montezuma quail uses its feet to scratch out bulbs of nut grass. Insects, snails, lizards, and other invertebrates add more water to the diet.

Where rain is scarce or during a drought, a regular source of water is even more attractive to birds than the most carefully selected banquet at the feeder. Birdbaths and water features will have a steady stream of customers. To ensure room for all, place shallow clay saucers or other impromptu bird-baths at ground level throughout the yard, so your birds can quench their thirst or freshen their feathers.

> If birds begin to avoid feeders that still contain food, check to see if the seed is wet or spoiled.

Raisins

Attract bluebirds, catbirds, mockingbirds, robins, woodpeckers, Carolina wrens, and other fruit eaters

RAISINS ARE AN INEXPENSIVE fruit choice for feeder birds, but it may take a while before birds readily accept these dried grapes. Instead of sprinkling them in a feeder, start by incorporating them in a mix of other soft foods that bluebirds, catbirds, mockingbirds, robins, woodpeckers, Carolina wrens, and other fruit eaters enjoy. I like to keep a small open tray feeder just for these customers, where I can experiment with various foods and recipes to see which one gets the most takers. The birds, too, become accustomed to visiting this feeder for their treats, which means they're quick to sample anything I put there.

Birds seem to accept golden raisins, which are made from white (green) grapes, more rapidly as a new feeder food, perhaps because they are more visible than the dark kind. To lure birds to a raisin handout, I combine either light or dark raisins with chopped suet, or add the fruit to a mix of peanut butter and cornmeal. Raisins are also easy to add to any bird-bread recipe. I sometimes chop dried cherries and raisins and fill empty grapefruit halves for a treat that delights waxwings. In winter snows, I scatter dark raisins on the ground, where robins and the occasional brown thrasher or catbird eagerly snap them up. It's fun to keep track of who samples your raisins: Kinglets, rose-breasted grosbeaks, or yellow-rumped warblers may enjoy the fruit alongside the usual clients.

For the best bargain, look for raisins in bulk bins at the grocery store or at health food stores, where they usually cost much less per pound than commercial-brand boxes. Store extras in your refrigerator.

> Birds seem to go for golden raisins (made from white grapes) more rapidly than the dark kind.

Rapeseed

Attracts buntings, doves, finches, sparrows, towhees, and others

RAPESEED IS A POPULAR INGREDIENT in seed mixes for both pet birds and wild birds. It's the tiny round seed of a European mustard (*Brassica napus*), and it's also called canola—it's the source of the canola oil sold for cooking. In the Midwest and Canada, you can spot fields of rapeseed from great distances—acres of yellow blossoms that glow like pure sunshine.

Rapeseed is very easy to grow. It sprouts vigorously in just about any soil and needs hardly any care. It also self-sows sparingly to generously (depending on how many seeds the birds overlook). A dense patch of rape will delight buntings, doves, finches, sparrows, and other birds that seek small seeds. I like to scatter some rapeseed in my flowerbeds, where its yellow blossoms add a cheerful touch and attract butterflies as a bonus. In fall and winter, foraging fox sparrows, towhees, and other birds diligently scratch beneath the plants to gather dropped seeds.

Rapeseed is very high in oil content, which makes it an ideal seed for cold weather feeding when extra calories are exactly what's needed. You can buy the seed, for bird feeding or for planting, from rural feed stores as well as some mail-order catalogs. Offer rapeseed in tube feeders, trays, or hopper feeders, or use it as an ingredient in your own custom birdseed mixes. Combined with millet and canary seed, it adds to an appealing menu for goldfinches, purple finches, and other small birds.

> Rapeseed gets its name from the Latin *rapa*, meaning "turnip."

Rare Birds

NEVER DOUBT YOUR EYES when you see a bird that "shouldn't" be dining at your feeder. The most unusual visitors will drop by now and then at a feeding station. Stray birds that typically range hundreds of miles from your home may show up. A red-shafted flicker arrived one winter at my Pennsylvania feeder, many miles from its Midwest haunts. Species that you'd never dream that you'd host may also turn up, perhaps drawn by the presence of other birds. I've had a great blue heron at my feeding station during a March snowstorm. The giant bird stood before my high tray feeder, scything its beak through the millet while sparrows and juncos pecked around near its long-toed feet.

It's always fun to alert a birding hot line when an unusual visitor shows up at your feeder (see Birding Hot Line on page 30). Of course, be prepared for slow-moving vehicles near your house as other birders try to get a glimpse of your rare bird. You can also call a local nature center and your local chapter of the National Audubon Society to report your finding, which may turn out to be significant. When a least bittern, a tiny heron the size of a robin, showed up at a small pond just down the road from my Pennsylvania house, it turned out to be only one of a scant handful of sightings in the county—ever.

Rare birds can arrive anytime, but I've noticed that most of my more unusual guests show up after winter storms. When a deep blizzard struck in early spring one year, a dickcissel, a meadow lark, two horned larks, and a blue grosbeak joined my regular feeder clients. These birds would never typically visit a small town bird feeder but empty bellies had driven them in from outlying farm fields.

If you spot a bird at your feeder that you can't find in a field guide, take a photo if possible. Also jot down careful notes about plumage, size, eating habits, and behavior, and make as detailed a sketch as possible. When an oddball sparrow I simply could not identify showed up at my feeder, I spent hours trying to convince experts I had something rare, but no one could

It looks like a fairytale, but a great blue heron landed at my feeder in winter and gobbled millet with the juncos. Keep a camera ready for your unusual guests!

identify the bird until I showed them a snapshot. Then they informed me my bird was a hybrid between a slate-colored junco and a white-throated sparrow. Keep in mind the possibility of albinism, too, when you consider a bird. One fellow I knew thought he had a brand new blackbird species at his feeder: all black he said, with a pure white head. One look at the bird in real life showed me that it was a cowbird in all ways except for its albinistic white head. Still, it was definitely a bird you don't see every day.

That's the pleasure of rare birds: No matter how you define it, a bird of a different color makes feeder watching more exciting—even after it leaves!

Raspberries and Blackberries

Attract many kinds of birds when berries are ripening

As a HEDGEROW OR SPOT PLANTING in your bird-friendly yard, raspberries and blackberries can't be beat. You can use bramble bushes like these to create an inviting area of cover near feeders, or you can plant them in a sunny corner of your yard, where the arching canes can recline against a fence. When you plant bramble bushes to attract birds, there's no need to worry about trellising or pruning—birds don't care what the plants look like! In fact, an over-grown berry bush is doubly inviting to birds because of the extra protection they find among the dense, prickly branches.

Untidiness pays off with bramble bushes, which birds visit most often when they are grown into a jungle rather than when the bushes are neatly pruned for maximum fruit. The larger size of the unshorn bush and the dense tangle of branches give the birds the protection they desperately need when roosting, nesting, or taking shelter from the storm. I limit pruning to the minimum: I cut out dead canes so that new ones have room to grow.

There are many blackberry and raspberry cultivars to choose from, so you can find plants that will thrive in your yard no matter where you live. In many re-gions, the bushes thrive as part of the wild landscape, especially in old fields that are slowly returning to woods. Be sure to choose a thorny cultivar, not a thornless variety, when planting for the birds, so that your bushes can do triple duty: food source, nesting site, and safe place to hide from predators.

Spotting Birds Among the Berries

Morning is the best time to watch birds feeding at berry bushes. A hedge studded with ripe red rasp-berries or other brambles will attract many species of delightful birds, including some, like the great crested flycatcher and larger vireos, that don't like to visit bird feeders.

I like to settle on a comfy bench or chair about 20 feet from my patch long before the berries ripen, and make it a habit to sit quietly there for a little while as often as possible so that the birds become accus-tomed to my presence. By the time June brings ripe berries, I have a prime seat for viewing the feast. Do pay attention to bird voices in and around the bushes, though. If you hear the sharp "Chip!" note that indicates alarm, the cause for concern may be you. Mature bushes make highly desirable nest sites, and you may be too close to a nest. If you think a bird is telling you to back off, move your seat or yourself back several yards, until life in the bush re-turns to normal.

A Berry Special Feeder Treat

RASPBERRIES AND blackberries cost a mint at the market. You may find them sold for less by local growers, but even so, these small, sweet fruits are too expensive to buy for your birds except as an occasional treat. But birds can help ease the pain you feel when berries you've pur-chased or picked go past their prime before you get to eat them. Toss those faded fruits into a freezer bag, and store them for a time when fresh fruits aren't around, then take pleasure in watching the birds enjoy the berries you missed out on.

It's difficult to tempt fruit-eating birds to a feeder during summer, when raspberries and blackberries ripen in the wild. With woods, fields, and roadsides brimming with natural fruit, birds generally prefer to seek out berries on the bush rather than berries in a tray. The best time to use berries as a feeder treat is from late fall through very early spring, when fresh fruit is just a fond memory to wild birds. Scatter blackberries or raspberries in an open tray feeder that has shel-tering shrubs nearby, and you may lure catbirds, mockingbirds, robins, thrashers, wrens, and even cedar waxwings to feed.

Redbud

Attracts chickadees, hummingbirds, orioles, titmice, vireos, warblers

REDBUD IS THE perfect small tree for a small-scale yard. Redbud delights our hearts with its early bloom, partnering elegant dogwoods and spring flowers with a splash of deep pink color. The trees also delight chickadees, titmice, and other small seed eaters, which seek out the seedpods in winter. The small flowers hum with nectar-seeking insects, which in turn attract hungry orioles, vireos, and warblers. Hummingbirds may also visit for the nectar.

Redbuds belong to the plant family called legumes, which also includes garden peas and beans. Take a close look at redbud blossoms, and you'll see that the shape of the flowers is just like that of the garden pea flowers in your vegetable patch or the sweet peas climbing your picket fence. Another hint of this tree's heritage are the flat pods that decorate the branches after the flowers mature to seed. The small "pea pods" ripen to brown or red and dangle thickly from the branches all winter long.

The leaves have a pretty heart shape and are great for flattening in a heavy book to use in notecards or other crafts. Redbuds are precocious trees that grow fast and bloom early. In my yard, where seedlings sprout from native trees in the surrounding woods, it takes as little as 4 years to reach blooming size. Once you have flowers, you'll have pods. The number of pods varies from year to year; my guess is that cold or rainy weather that inhibits pollinator activity in early spring affects the pod production.

In late winter, when I'm starved for flowers, I clip a few branches of redbud and stick them in a jar of water. When the pink blooms open on the

Pretty redbuds attract seed eaters, insect eaters, and nectar eaters alike.

branches bare of leaves, they have a stylish oriental line that adds elegance even in my cluttered kitchen. I let them linger after the blossoms fade because of the beauty of the brand-new leaves, which unfold into small, shining, tender green hearts.

Redbuds are fine small trees for large or small yards. Native redbuds thrive across most of the United States. Eastern redbud (*Cercis canadensis*) is hardy in Zones 4 to 9. The Texas redbud (*C. canadensis* var. *texensis*) is hardy only to Zone 7, while the Mexican variety (*C. canadensis* var. *mexicanis*) is hardy only to Zone 8. All flourish in full sun to part or light shade. In the West, the native western redbud (*C. occidentalis*), hardy in Zones 9 and 10, and its varieties—*arizonicus*, from Arizona, and *orbiculata*, from Utah—are the trees of choice for a sunny site. White-flowered cultivars and red-foliaged selections are available, too. They vary in mature size, depending on the variety and the characteristics of the individual plant.

Redpolls

MOST OF THE BIRDS AT FEEDERS are finches, thanks to their propensity for eating mostly seeds. Among the most unusual representatives of the family are the redpolls, diminutive birds that wander southward in winter from their nesting homes in the extreme Far North. In some years, "south" may mean only as far as southern Canada, but in other years, the migration may extend into the middle of the United States. During irruption years, when several species of northern birds come for a winter vacation, redpolls may be daily visitors at the feeder for months.

At first glance, both species, the **common redpoll** and the **hoary redpoll,** resemble house finches, with their streaky brown bodies and rosy coloring. Most of the red is concentrated on the breast and on a solid rosy red patch on the top of the head. A black mask around their bills, like a miniature version of the cardinal, accents their face. Living up to its name, the hoary redpoll has a whitish look over its back and belly, as if encrusted with hoarfrost.

Redpolls are a great argument for keeping your binoculars near the window. At a distance, their shape, size, and behavior are so much like goldfinches that even an experienced birder may not notice that this bird is of a different color. When you see groups of small finches with sharply notched tails at your feeders or in your garden in winter, pull out the binoculars. If you're lucky, you may discover a perky, pretty red-capped bird looking back at you. It's a little tricky telling the two redpoll species apart in winter because the rosy flushed breast of the male common redpoll pales after the breeding season ends.

Birds of the Far North, redpolls occasionally come south to delight winter feeder watchers. Seeds of wild plants like milkweed make a fine meal, as do feeder seeds.

REDPOLL FEEDER FOODS

- Birdseed mix
- Grass seeds
- Millet
- Sunflower seeds, black oil or hulled
- Weed seeds, such as common ragweeds, pigweeds, Pennsylvania smart-weed, and common lamb's-quarters

Redpoll Behavior

If you see one redpoll at your feeder, stay at the window for a while—his cronies will soon join him. These finches usually congregate in flocks during the winter, although sighting a single stray bird is possible. They dine like many native sparrows, clinging to weed or flower stems to nibble seeds or picking seeds from the ground. They will also visit higher feeders.

As with most northern finches, a salt block is a prime attraction for redpolls. They also adore fresh water in the wintertime, where they can sip and splash. I have even seen redpolls figure out how to use an icicle shower. When icicles began to melt along the eaves of my roof from the warmth of the sun, the flock of redpolls visiting my feeding station assembled beneath the dripping water, splashing and wriggling as if they were in the most deluxe shower stall.

Roadrunner

As GOOFY IN REAL LIFE as it is on Saturday morning cartoons, the greater roadrunner of the arid Southwest is a most unusual bird. First of all, it's big. It's almost 2 feet long from the tip of its big beak to the end of its perky uptilted tail. Secondly, it's fast. The roadrunner can zip along at 18 miles per hour!

A year-round resident, the roadrunner has adapted well to backyard life. It readily moves between wild deserts and mesquite lands to manicured backyards. It often perches in landscape shrubbery or cactus like an overgrown robin. Its song is a common background soundtrack for the Southwest. Bird experts class the roadrunner with the cuckoo family, a decision that seems very odd when you compare the looks of the long-tailed, graceful cuckoos, which are shaped something like a mockingbird, with the chickenlike roadrunners. It's the toes that give them away: Cuckoo family members have two toes pointing front, two pointing back. You can also hear the family resemblance: Roadrunners sing "Coo, coo, coo, ooh, ooh, ooh" in a voice that sounds like a tired blues singer after a few too many cigarettes.

Roadrunner Behavior

Rattlesnakes are a fact of life for residents of the desert Southwest and West, but there'd be many more of these slithery reptiles if it weren't for roadrunners. Snakes and lizards are mainstays in this desert bird's diet. Ever try to grab a lizard? The roadrunner nabs them routinely, shifting into overdrive and catching the lizards in a burst of speed.

When horse-drawn buggies and wagons dominated the traffic on dusty roads, roadrunners used this to their advantage. They often trotted ahead of the vehicles to snatch up lizards and other morsels that fled from the oncoming traffic. With

Surprisingly big in real life, the roadrunner has long, strong legs built for streaking after lizards and other small prey. Try tempting it closer with fruit.

our faster modern automobiles populating the roads, the birds have given up the habit, although you may still spot one racing beside you along the shoulder.

Roadrunners are a boon to feeding stations because they snack on mice, along with crickets, grasshoppers, scorpions, tarantulas, and other tasty morsels. Unfortunately, they also have a taste for birds' eggs and nestlings, a natural enough habit in the balance of the wild world but not an endearing habit in human eyes. Although roadrunners will consider your entire yard their feeding station, they may sample prickly pear fruits or other juicy fruits from a low feeder or the ground. Individual birds vary in their preferences, with some birds enjoying apples, for instance, while others ignore them. Experiment with your roadrunner's tastes and see what makes it go "Beep-beep."

ROADRUNNER FEEDER FOODS

- Prickly pear (*Opuntia* spp.) fruits
- Other fruits

Robin

THE SIGHT OF ROBINS HOPPING and running about our lawns is so common that most of us take their presence for granted and barely look at them. Yet these common birds are just as interesting as any other species. Watch a robin as it hunts and you'll see a fascinating process, from the first "Did I see something?" suspicion that halts the bird in its tracks, to the zeroing in on the worm's exact location, the swift stab of the bill, and the tug-of-war climax.

Our most common member of the thrush family, the American robin does its best to uphold the musical reputation of its sweet-throated brethren. Their songs are long and beautiful, but when all the robins in the neighborhood are singing their lungs out at once, it's hard to appreciate the beauty of the melody. I make it a point to seek out a single bird each June, just to stand beneath it and focus on its performance.

Most of us think of robins as harbingers of spring, but they are likely to be somewhere nearby at any season of the year. In fall, robins retreat from most of their usual front-lawn haunts and gather in thickets and hedgerows, where they flock together for the winter. When frozen soil and snow make pulling worms impossible, robins fill in their winter menu with berries, seeds, and other edibles.

As harbingers of spring, robins return to our yards just as reliably as the first pussy willows.

ROBIN FEEDER FOODS
■ Apples and cherries, fresh or dried
■ Bayberries (*Myrica pensylvanica*)
■ Berries
■ Bread and other baked goods
■ Bread crumbs
■ Cherries, dried or fresh
■ Corn, cracked
■ Crackers, crumbled
■ Grapes
■ Hawthorn (*Crataegus* spp.) berries
■ Holly (*Ilex* spp.) berries
■ Mealworms
■ Raisins
■ Suet, chopped

Robin Behavior

Everyone knows that robins eat worms, but these common birds also devour plenty of other insects, and they relish fruits and berries. Once they discover a feeding station stocked with their favorite foods, they're likely to visit regularly. Robins also enjoy a good splash in the bath any time of year.

Serve robins in a low tray feeder or directly on the ground. In winter, your handouts can be a literal lifesaver when snow and ice bury natural food. If you live in a cold-winter area, it's a good idea to keep a bag of soft "robin food" on hand in the freezer and extra cracked corn in your seed storage area, in case bad weather brings hungry birds to your yard. When deep snow hits, you may also want to deliver emergency rations along the roadsides, the first place robins go to look for food after a storm.

Although you may see robins year-round, the birds you spot in May may not be the same ones you see in November. Many robins from far northern homelands migrate to spend the winter in the less frigid states, while the summertime inhabitants there head deeper into the South.

R

Rocks

IF YOUR YARD IS FULL of rocks and stones, don't despair, and don't make that call to have them hauled away! Rocks make terrific bird feeders and watering holes and provide natural-looking, decorative touches in your bird garden.

Choosing a Good Rock

For feeder purposes, you'll want a rock with a slightly concave surface, so that it can hold seed, grit, or even water. Low, wide rocks are ideal because their weight is less than that of tall, wide rocks and also because they look more natural in the landscape. If you must use a high rock, bury at least a third of its height below the soil surface, the way it would be settled in nature (unless it had just tumbled down the slope in an avalanche). A single smallish rock—less than 2 or 3 feet across—looks forlorn by itself in a garden.

PROJECT

Learn to Chisel

It's much easier than you think to "improve" the surface of a less than ideal rock. On many kinds of rock, you can carve out a shallow basin in a very short time with simple hand tools and easily acquired skill. All you need is a rock chisel, a mallet, safety glasses, and work gloves—and a big rock to work on. If natural rock is hard to come by, or if you don't trust your leverage skills, you can make a good ground-level feeder from a landscaping stepping stone, sold at garden centers. Usually made of cast concrete, these "rocks" can be hollowed out just like natural stone to make a fine low-level feeder or drinking spot.

MATERIALS AND TOOLS

Large rock

Rock chisel

Mallet

Safety glasses

Work gloves

Step 1. Hold the chisel at a shallow angle and strike it with the mallet, which will gouge chips from the surface of the rock. Depending on the structure of the rock, the blows may loosen small chips or long shards. Sandstone-based rocks are best for this project because they are easiest to carve.

Step 2. Repeat the process until the surface is hollowed out to your satisfaction. A very slight depression is enough to hold small seeds, such as millet, for quail and sparrows.

Step 3. Test your handiwork by pouring a handful of seed onto the rock. If most of the seed stays on top, you're done.

Step 4. You can carve a deeper bowl into your rock for a shallow birdbath.

If a giant rock is out of the question, group three medium-size rocks together to create a "feeder" of good visual weight.

Be sure to use a type of rock that is native to your area. New Mexico lava, for instance, looks very much out of place in a New Hampshire garden, where granite is the norm. Also look for a rock that has a weathered appearance, as though it were sitting in a field or woods for a few hundred years (an instant in rock years). A patina of lichen is a wonderful touch, but be sure to orient it to the same side on all the rocks you install. Freshly quarried rock, such as white limestone, looks too new and raw to suit a garden.

Be Kind to Your Back

BIG ROCKS are better than small ones for birdscaping in your yard, so it's important to think back to your fourth-grade science lesson on leverage. Rocks can be surprisingly heavy for their size, depending on what kind of stone is native to your area. Sandstone is relatively light, but even a breadbox-size chunk of granite can be a backbreaker. When you're attempting to move heavy objects from one place to another, let tools do the heavy work.

If you are of average strength, or a weakling like me, employ a lever instead of straining your back and legs. A crowbar is perfect for prying up a rock and maneuvering it into place, but I usually make do with whatever long, stout stick I have handy, whether it's a length of 2 × 4 or an old hoe handle. Just wiggle the pry bar under the rock, and then place a smaller rock or concrete block in place under the lever to use as a fulcrum. Then push down on the lever, which lifts the rock, and roll it into place.

If your rock is extra large, enlist a helper. Be sure to use a lever that won't snap under the strain of the rock's weight.

Rose Hips

Attract grouse, pheasants, quail, wild turkeys as well as songbirds like bluebirds and mockingbirds

ROSE-HIP TEA IS A POPULAR winter drink, and rose hips are a great winter food for birds and wildlife. Rose hips are the fruits that form after the petals fall from rose blossoms. Multiflora-type roses, with their clusters of many small flowers, produce bunches of little hips; larger blooms mature into bigger fruits, which may be round or elongated. All rose hips are edible, as long as you haven't drenched the bushes in toxic sprays and powders.

Grouse, pheasants, quail, and wild turkeys will pluck rose hips off of rose bushes, as do songbirds such as bluebirds and mockingbirds. Like bramble bushes, roses give your garden the bonus of thick, well-protected cover, where birds can dive during a predator panic attack, seek shelter for the night, or nest safely amid the thorny stems.

Planting Roses for Birds

Roses have a reputation for being finicky, but there are easy-care roses that don't need pampering or spraying to thrive. Your best bet is to choose native roses. Our own American roses are well worth growing for their beauty, fruit, and cover for birds. Meadow rose (*Rosa blanda*), pasture rose (*R. caroliniana*), and dozens of other regional specialties will thrive in gardens as well as in the wild.

Look for native roses in the catalogs of native plant nurseries and "antique" rose specialists. Also ask at your local nursery; they may be willing to order the plants for you. If you spot a promising rose "growing wild," resist an urge to steal it. Ask permission to snip a few 8-inch-long cuttings in spring, and insert them a few inches deep into moist soil to try to root them. Cover with an inverted glass jar to create a mini greenhouse to encourage growth. You can plant containerized rosebushes anytime from spring through summer. Plant bareroot roses in spring, as soon as you bring them home. Native roses flourish without fertilizer, and many are more resistant to blackspot and other disfiguring diseases than nonnative roses.

You may live in an area where the nonnative multiflora rosa (*R. multiflora*) is a widespread weed along roadsides and in fields. You won't want to encourage this plant, but you can collect branches of hips from existing plants. Twist the branches into a wreath or swag for a decorative outdoors accent that also attracts birds. One winter, a mockingbird claimed the rose-hip wreath on my front door as his personal territory and made entering and exiting the house risky business for trespassing humans. After a week or so of that behavior, I snipped off the hips and spread them in tray feeders for the birds (and night-visiting opossums, which also enjoyed the fruits).

Because rose hips are such a popular food with birds, you are likely to find seedlings springing up near the feeder or in your yard, wherever birds make a seed-bearing "deposit." Most of these hardy survivors are likely to be young multiflora rose plants, although they may also be more unusual species. I used to be an antimultiflora snob, but I've changed my position. Now I admire them for their fine bird benefits of shelter, nest sites, and

Rose hips of any shape or color may become bird food. Birds usually wait until wintertime to seek out the tangy fruits. They gulp the small hips whole, and peck the larger ones into beak-size pieces.

food, although I still regret the fact that they have escaped from cultivation into fields and roadsides. But I also recognize that most of the places these roses colonize are those already adulterated by human activity. Still, in order to prevent creating even more problems, I uproot any suspicious bird-planted seedlings I see in the backyard.

S

Safflower

Attracts cardinals

VIVID ORANGE SAFFLOWER (*Carthamus tinctorius*) blossoms are definite attention getters in a garden of birdseed plants. This annual is easy to grow from seed sown directly in sunny soil, and birds will come flocking once its flower heads mature into small, plump white seeds.

At the feeder, cardinals are the main customer for safflower seeds. It may take the red birds a while to discover the seeds, but once they do, they'll be regulars at the feeder. Packaged cardinal seed mix is often nothing more than black sunflower seeds mixed with white safflower—a fine combination tailor-made for cardinal tastes but usually much less expensive to blend yourself from seed bought in bulk.

If your cardinals aren't used to eating safflower, start with just a scant handful of the seeds sprinkled atop a tray of black oil sunflower seeds. Once you can see that the birds have started eating the safflower seeds, you can increase the serving. Safflower seed is a good choice if you prefer not to host jays at your feeder because they're generally not interested in it. With any luck, they'll depart for better vittles at another bird café when you switch to feeding mainly

Golden orange safflower is an asset in the flower garden and at the feeder. The shaggy blossoms yield plump, hard white seeds, which you can also buy.

safflower. Squirrels don't care for safflower seed either and will bypass a feeder filled with it to seek their food elsewhere.

Salt

Attracts house finches plus buntings, doves, purple finches, goldfinches, jays, pigeons, pine siskins, house sparrows, and others

JUST LIKE PEOPLE, birds have different preferences when it comes to adding salt to their diet. Some like to eat it straight, while others can get along fine without even a sprinkling. The easiest way to feed salt is with a long-lasting salt block, available at feed stores for just a few dollars. House finches will be your best customer for salt, but buntings, doves, purple finches, goldfinches, jays, pigeons, pine siskins, house sparrows, and other birds also partake of the mineral.

Rain melts salt, causing it to soak into surrounding soil, endangering plants. To avoid tainting your ground and ending up with a large circle of salted "dead zone," settle your salt block on a sturdy waterproof platform with a lip. An upside-down, concave trash can lid, large plastic plant saucer, concrete birdbath bowl, shallow dishpan, or litter tray will work. For a more attractive presentation, place the salt block on a heavy-duty plastic liner that's held in place with gravel and hidden by a layer of wood chips.

Salt has always been popular with birds and animals. In the eastern half of the country, where an unbroken hardwood forest once stretched, giant shaggy bison and mobs of now-extinct passenger pigeons sought out salt licks and salt springs. Nowadays your neighborhood deer population may cause you to think twice before adding another incentive for them to visit your yard. If deer are a problem, keep the salt block far from any feeders that they can quickly empty. Rabbits, mice, and other animals may also visit a salt block. Nonbird visitors usually visit under the cover of darkness. Shine a strong flashlight on the area or set up a motion-activated light to see who's nibbling on your salt block—or check for teeth marks in daytime.

In days gone by, salt licks were well-trodden gathering places for American bison and immense flocks of passenger pigeons. They're still popular with birds, such as these evening grosbeaks.

Sand

JUST IMAGINE TRYING to survive on a diet of hard, dry corn kernels, acorns, and sunflower seeds—without teeth! That's the dilemma for our bird friends, who can crack open shells with their bills but can't chew the tasty pieces they find inside. They depend on a muscular organ—their gizzard—to grind their food, with the aid of small, abrasive stones, or grit, which the bird must constantly replenish.

Birds find grit in the wild anywhere they can. In regions where slippery roads are a common occurrence in winter, many highway departments spread sand to improve traction. As the snow melts to expose the edges of the road, keep an eye on the birds that gather there. You will frequently see cardinals, doves, and other birds picking up grains of sand from the roadside. The sides of roads that have been sanded for traction in wintertime are popular gathering places.

Coarse sand is an ideal source of grit for birds, which is why you'll want to include it among the offerings in your backyard. Buy the sand at a building supply store, not in the children's play area. Soft, white sandbox sand may be great to play in, but it is too fine for birds. River sand is ideal because of its large-grain size. If you have a gravel or river-rock operation nearby, ask if you can buy a few scoops. In my experience, they'll laugh and say, "Take all you want, it's free!" A bucketful will probably last a year.

Spread sand on the bare ground and let birds help themselves. It's a good idea to keep the supply in the same place year after year, so that your birds get accustomed to a reliable source.

Sand at the feeder is like forks and spoons at a picnic—you're providing utensils so your guests can eat the meal.

S

Sap

Attracts house finches, hummingbirds, orioles, sapsuckers, and woodpeckers

TREE SAP IS NATURE'S VERSION of sugar water, although if you sample it, your human taste buds will discern only a very faint sweetness. The well-named yellow-bellied sapsucker as well as its relatives the red-naped and red-bellied sapsuckers are famed for drilling into trees to create sap runs. The birds return to the sap runs over and over to sip the sweet stuff and pick off the insects drawn to it. In summer, the acorn woodpecker of the West bores into branches of oaks to collect tree sap. House finches, orioles, and other woodpeckers may also visit trees that are oozing sap.

Sapsucker borings are easy to recognize. Look for a closely spaced series of holes in a nice, neat horizontal line. People once believed that such drillings caused serious tree damage, and orchardists killed sapsuckers to defend their trees. The true verdict is still unclear, with some researchers suggesting that the bore holes may not be as harmful as once believed. Diseases and pests that attack trees are also responsible for creating sap flows on the bark of a tree limb or trunk.

As well as enjoying the birds that visit sap, you can also discover many intriguing insects arriving for a sip of sap. In daylight hours, monarchs, red admirals, and anglewing butterflies, to name just a few, come to drink up. I like to take a flashlight out at night to look for large underwing moths (whose top wings look like a fragment of mottled bark, but whose bottom wings are startlingly colored) and big beetles, along with other interesting critters. Occasionally I even come upon a flying squirrel having a bit of dessert after dark.

Hummingbirds get at sap the natural way, hovering before the tree just as they would at a nectar feeder. Birds that never visit a feeder, such as flycatchers and vireos, as well as feeder birds like cardinals and titmice, will come by a sappy tree to pick off butterflies and insects during the day. And owls may come for the flying squirrels at night.

> Sapsuckers and some woodpeckers drill into trees for sap. Once it's flowing, hummingbirds may fly in for a sip.

Scouring Rush

UNCHANGED SINCE PREHISTORIC DAYS, the peculiar, primitive plant known as scouring rush is a species of horsetail (*Equisetum* spp.). As you might suspect from the name, scouring rush makes a great pot scrubber. It also does a superlative job of cutting through the algae in birdbaths, leaving a clean bowl behind after just a few swipes. The odd, jointed stems are so rough with grains of silica that you can feel the grittiness when you stroke the stem with your fingers.

Horsetails thrive in wet soil, but they also tolerate even extremely dry soil. They do so well in containers that they're commonly used in accent planters in commercial and residential landscaping in southern California. These tough perennial plants can put up with just about any conditions. Established plants spread by underground runners to form thick, solid colonies. Although it may take years for a garden planting to reach that stage, be prepared to pull up the extras to control the spread if necessary, or grow the plants in containers to avoid invasive problems.

I like to have horsetails near my water gardens, but the clump I couldn't do without grows at the base of my pedestal-style birdbath. If I had to trek to the house for scrubbing tools every time my birdbath needed a cleaning, I'm afraid to guess what its condition would deteriorate to. But when I can simply stoop, snap off a handful of scouring rush, wad it up, and swish it around the bowl, keeping the birdbath clean becomes more fun than work. The birds appreciate it, too.

Horsetails come in two very different-looking types. Some, such as common horsetail (*E. arvense*), look like little Christmas trees, with branches growing in whorls around the stem; other species have only unbranched, spare, straight green stems about as thick as pencils, marked with contrasting bands of color at the joints. *Equisetum hyemale*, the horsetail I grow, is one of these minimalists. Although horsetails can be aggressive spreaders, I've found this species takes a few years to settle in; if it does spread out of bounds, a quick yank on the unwanted explorers is all it takes to keep it under control.

An architectural ornament in the garden, horsetails also are practical. Their stems are loaded with silica, which makes a handful great for scouring birdbaths.

Seed Hoarding

PUTTING ASIDE SOME SEEDS for a rainy day is such a habit for a few species of birds that they will cache sunflower seed, corn, nuts, and other tidbits even when you offer a fresh supply every day. The nuthatches at your feeder will snatch up a morsel, fly off to a likely hiding spot, and hammer it tightly into place to retrieve later. For every sunflower seed my white-breasted nuthatch splits and eats at the feeder, he stuffs another dozen into cracks in my porch posts and in nearby tree crevices. One fall a red-breasted nuthatch chose a food storage area no other bird had thought of: the crack between the window gasket and door frame of my parked pickup truck. Every time I opened the door, a shower of sunflower seeds fell on my head.

Clark's nutcracker, crows, jays, nuthatches, titmice, and some woodpeckers are all hoarders at heart. Unfortunately, all this careful work often comes to naught when another bird discovers the cache. In winter, when my feeders are hopping, a white-breasted nuthatch often busies itself stuffing bits of my peanut butter and cornmeal dough into the bark of the maple trees. Frequently a brown creeper arrives within minutes to scour the tree and make short work of the unexpected treats. Hoarded nuts and seeds forgotten by jays often sprout into trees to replenish our forests.

The acorn woodpecker of the West turns trees and poles into vertical "Chinese checkers" boards with its hoarding habits. The bird drills shallow holes into trees, then crams an acorn into each hole. Although most storage trees hold dozens of acorns, in 1923 a pine tree was reportedly studded with 50,000 acorns!

> Jays' forgotten hoards of nuts and seeds often sprout into trees to replenish our forests.

Shrikes

LUCKILY FOR ALL of our small songbird friends, shrikes are not common birds. The two American species bear the unsavory nickname of "butcher bird," which speaks for itself. They prey on birds, small animals, and insects, which they impale on stout thorns or barbed wire to eat later.

Both shrikes look much the same: like big-headed, short-necked mockingbirds. Unlike the mockingbird, they sport black wings and tail and a sinister black mask. You may see the **loggerhead shrike** anywhere across the country except for a small strip of the Appalachians and New England, and in most places, at any season of the year. The **northern shrike** nests only in the extreme Far North. Like other birds of this region, it sometimes wanders irregularly southward in winter. Immature birds seem to be particularly prone to wanderlust. Unlike their gray parents, these young birds are dull brown rather than silvery gray.

Shrike Behavior

Take a closer look the next time you spot what appears to be a mockingbird perched on a conspicuous pole, post, or tree top. If it holds its tail nearly horizontally and hunkers its body down, you may be watching a shrike. Like hawks, these energy-efficient hunters spend much of their time perched, waiting for prey to pass. Double-check any "shrike" you see to make sure it's not a mockingbird. The gray-and-white mocker resembles the shrike and may further fool you by chasing other birds (although not for prey).

When a shrike took up residence near my feeding station in Pennsylvania, it chose a wild multiflora rose bush for its habitual perch. The rose thorns provided a convenient place to store

Close to robin-size, the loggerhead shrike is an uncommon predator that impales its feathered prey. Shrikes are classified in their own family.

SHRIKE FEEDER FOODS
■ Bread
■ Eggs, hard-boiled or scrambled
■ Hamburger, raw
■ Meat of any kind, raw
■ Poultry, raw
■ Soup bones with marrow and meat
■ Suet

the accumulating wealth of the shrike's daily kills. The hillside where the bush grew gave the bird a great vantage point to oversee the brush below—and my bird feeders beyond.

Like many other birds of the North, shrikes seem unusually tame and unafraid around humans. None of my usual tactics—mainly running and hollering—had any permanent effect on the shrike. He obediently flew off when I attacked, only to return when I went back inside.

I consoled myself with the thought that the shrike's forays, like those of hawks, were eliminating the weakest birds—those that were most unwary or slowest in reaction time or flight. Still, I found survival-of-the-fittest cold comfort for the loss of my trusting chickadees and gentle juncos.

Shrikes also hang their prey from the crotches of trees as well as stick them on thorns, and like squirrels, they go back to their cache with an unerring memory. Their hunting habits vary, depending on the prey. They may drop from the air or hop about on the ground to drive small birds out of the bushes.

When I encountered a shrike in the date-growing region of California, near Indio, my first reaction was to toss the bird a piece of the honey-sweet fruit that we were eating. It immediately pounced on the date, perhaps attracted by the motion, then took it to a nearby tree to pluck it into pieces and gulp down. At the feeder, shrikes will be very appreciative of a handout of mice, whether you "serve" them scurrying about beneath the feeder or offer contributions from your mouse-traps. For a less squeamish entree, try raw hamburger or other soft food offerings.

Inviting a shrike to dinner won't endear you to the other guests. But providing food for the butcher bird may make it less prone to look for prey. At any rate, keep the "shrike feeder" far, far away from the feeding station, and increase the protective cover you offer your songbirds. They'll need all the help they can get.

The adult northern shrike is paler gray on top than the loggerhead shrike. Immature birds are light brown, with black markings like the adult's.

Pine Siskin

IF YOU LIVE IN THE WEST, pine siskins are most likely frequent guests at your feeder, snacking on niger and sunflower seed like their close relatives, the goldfinches. In the eastern two-thirds of the country, however, siskins are an occasional winter sight and not always a sure thing. Their winter migrations tend to be irregular, sometimes bringing large flocks from the Far North where they nest, and sometimes delivering only a stray bird or two to join the other small birds at your seed feeders.

Both male and female siskins look alike, resembling a streaky brown goldfinch. They have yellow bars on their wings, which expand into noticeable patches of color when the birds fly, and a bit of yellow under their sharply notched tail.

Despite their woodsy-sounding name, pine siskins eat mostly weed seeds, although they do

At first glance, the pine siskin looks like a streaky brown goldfinch. Look closely to see the wingbars that create the flash of yellow when the bird flies.

consume large quantities of pine and alder seeds as well. In the West, the seeds of a nonnative annual flower called filaree (*Erodium* spp.) is the food of choice. Common ragweed is another favorite seed source in all areas where siskins range, a bonus for allergy sufferers.

Siskin Behavior

Siskins nibble daintily at feeders and perform acrobatics to collect seeds as their goldfinch relatives do. Siskins are tamer than goldfinches, and they are fairly easy to coax into eating sunflower seeds right out of your hand. In temperament, they tend to be crabby little guys, often quarreling noisily with their companions at the feeder.

Siskins are very fond of sap and have learned to use nectar feeders. A salt block is a certain enticement to siskins. Like their goldfinch relatives, they enjoy splashing, so a birdbath or other water source is another big draw.

Siskins may show up at your feeders alone or en masse. If only one or a few birds arrive, you may not even notice their presence at first. Their unremarkable streaky brown color blends right in with the female house finches, and in silhouette, their sharply notched tails make them look just like a goldfinch. I find it's a good idea to check the customers, especially at the tube feeders, every morning, scanning with binoculars to get a better view of who's visiting. If you spot a bird that you think may be a pine siskin, keep watching until it flies, when the yellow patches on its wings are more noticeable.

Sleeping

As YOU STRETCH YOUR LEGS in your comfy bed tonight, consider the fact that songbirds sleep standing up. Their extraordinary legs and feet lock into place around a perch, keeping them upright while they snooze. Most birds do snuggle down to sleep, fluffing out breast feathers to cover their legs and tucking their heads under a wing. Listen closely as dusk falls in your yard, and you may hear bird "lullabies": the quiet twitters of sparrows, juncos, and other sleepyheads turning in for the night. Birds usually band together at night, positioning themselves on a comfortable perch in a shared bush or evergreen. Birds favor cedars (*Juniperus* spp.), spruces (*Picea* spp.), and other dense conifers as roosting spots.

In extremely cold weather, cavity-nesting birds such as bluebirds, chickadees, titmice, and wrens seek holes in trees, branches, or wooden fence posts or retreat to bird boxes to help preserve heat. They may crowd together in groups of a dozen or more of the same species. If you spy a bird at your feeder with an oddly curved tail, it may have spent the night in tight quarters. If you're an early bird yourself, you may spot birds leaving a nest-box roosting site. Tap on the box just after daybreak, before birds are flocking to the feeder, and be prepared for a possible rush of wings as occupants leave in a hurry.

I like to sit on my porch near dusk to watch the birds retire for the night into my neighbor's big, dense blue spruce. It's amazing how many birds that tree can hold—60, at the highest count! Native sparrows, house sparrows, juncos, finches, robins, jays, doves, and cardinals all find a place within its sheltering arms.

> Dense conifers, such as cedars or spruces, offer birds a protected place to perch for a good night's sleep.

Snow and Ice Storms

WHEN WINTER STORMS hit your area, it's hard times for birds. Because the ground is covered with snow or ice, birds have to scratch vigorously to reach seeds that may— or may not—be underneath the white stuff. Tree buds, berries, nuts, and even the last withered crab apples may be encased in ice or frozen to impenetrable hardness. Weed stems are bent and bowed under a layer of snow. What's a hungry bird to do?

Why, come to the feeder, of course, where the food is plentiful even when snow keeps falling. Snowflakes and sleet are your signals to bring out the stuff you've been hoarding. Reach for the freezer and pull out the suet balls, the muffins, and the scraps of sandwiches, and offer them with a free hand. Don't hold back on seed or other foods now because your handouts can literally keep birds alive.

Getting caught short when birds are depending on you is a hard way to learn to keep emergency food supplies. If you can't get out, birds will go hungry.

Winter Fuel for Birds

You can't serve hot cocoa to your birds, but you can do the next best thing: Give them high-fat, high-carbohydrate foods that will quickly refuel their calorie-burning bodies and supply the store of energy they need to survive through long, cold nights. Add bacon grease, doughnuts, nuts, and peanut-butter recipes to the menu of standard seeds and suet.

Be an Early Bird

Birds are out early the morning after a storm, and you should be, too. Keeping your guests waiting while you brew coffee and find your galoshes is not just rude right now, it's dangerous to their well-being.

At least make sure the covered feeders are fully stocked before you turn in for the night. Your mission is to keep food available as long as birds need it.

Falling snow or freezing rain and ice can cover feeders fast, so erect lean-tos and other temporary shelters over and around your feeders to divert falling or drifting snow.

Lots of items will do the trick as a temporary lean-to. I keep a few scraps of plywood and a prized section of corrugated metal siding on my porch, ready to grab in case the need arises. I've even pressed empty pizza boxes into service during unexpected snowstorms. Any piece of stiff, flat material will work. Use two or three sturdy sticks or 2 × 4s to prop up the protective shelter. I save the broken handles of garden tools for props, too. Make sure the supports are strong and evenly spaced, so that the weight of snow doesn't cause a collapse of your impromptu shelter.

If you have a multitude of customers, you can serve seed and other foods directly on the ground. Clear the loose snow, scatter the food, and before you get back in the house, the birds will be eating. If snow keeps falling, sweep aside the new snow as often as you have time and patience to do so.

Soda Bottles

BEFORE YOU HAUL those plastic soda pop bottles out to the curb for recycling, set a few aside to transform into bird feeders. Large, 2-liter bottles can be easily adapted into feeders with the aid of commercially made screw-on devices that attach to the former cap end. Smaller 20-ounce plastic soda bottles also make fine additions to your nectar feeder collection. And, as an added bonus, they are also a handy item in your first-aid kit for baby birds: Use them as hot water bottles to keep nestlings cozy until you can deliver the birds to a rehabilitator.

For more free feeding devices, slice the bottom from a large soda bottle, using a sharp-bladed kitchen knife. Nail two or three of these plastic cups to a board. Fill with raisins, chopped apples, ground suet, and other treats.

You can even make a tube feeder from a small bottle. Here's how to do it:

`PROJECT`

Simple Soda Bottle Bird Feeder

Turning a plastic soda bottle into a bird feeder is about as easy as projects get—this is a great activity for kids, or just for your own satisfaction. The paper towels in the bottom of the bottle are meant to prevent a layer of wasted seed that birds can't reach—be sure to use them or some other barrier in your feeder. Don't expect to be overrun with compliments on the beauty and style of your soda bottle bird feeder, but you can congratulate yourself for creating an extremely functional feeder out of an object that, at best, was destined for recycling of some sort. In fact, one of the great things about this homemade feeder is that you can recycle it when its useful life as a feeder has ended.

MATERIALS

20-ounce plastic soda bottle, empty and dry, with cap

Dry paper towels

2 wooden skewers

Wire for hanging

Step 1. Stuff a dry paper towel into the bottom of the bottle, using the handle of a wooden spoon. Repeat if necessary until the bottom ½ inch of the bottle is filled with paper towels.

Step 2. Insert a pointed wooden kitchen skewer for a perch, about ½ inch from the bottom of the bottle, just above the paper towel. Push the skewer in one side, through the bottle, and out the other side.

Step 3. Repeat, inserting a second skewer a couple of inches above and perpendicular to the first one. Trim so that only 2 inches of each perch extends outside the bottle.

Step 4. Insert more paper towels, filling the bottle to a total height of about 1½ inches with paper. This will prevent unreachable seed from being wasted in the bottom of the bottle.

Step 5. Use a utility knife to cut a narrow slit, about ⅛ inch wide, about 1½ inches above each perch.

Step 6. Use a funnel to fill the bottle with niger seed, and replace the cap.

Step 7. Loop a piece of wire around the neck, twist to tighten, and hang the bottle feeder from a handy branch or hook.

Soft Foods

Attract bluebirds, catbirds, mockingbirds, robins, thrashers, thrushes

BREAD, FRUIT, SUET, day-old doughnuts, and leftover pizza and pasta all fit into the category of soft foods. Soft foods include anything a bird can swallow straight down the hatch, without first cracking through a hard shell. Both seed eaters and nonseed eaters enjoy soft foods. Bluebirds, catbirds, robins, thrashers, and thrushes are difficult to attract to feeders that offer only seeds and suet because that menu is foreign to these insect and fruit eaters. Only in times of scarcity will these birds come to rely on the handouts you offer. The rest of the time, they can find their own favored foods easily enough, thank you. All of these species, plus other more common feeder visitors such as mockingbirds and Carolina wrens, are likely to be drawn to a feeding station that offers soft foods, which are similar in beak appeal to the natural foods these birds eat. Like fruits and insects, they are swallowed gulp by gulp, with no pecking necessary except to extricate a bite-size morsel.

Soft foods can be a real lifesaver in the cold months, especially after storms that make natural food hard to come by. I go through dozens of loaves of bread after a snowstorm, when the many robins that winter in my area are desperate for a bite to eat. It's a good idea to stock your freezer with soft foods so you have plenty on hand in case of a weather emergency. I keep a shelf reserved for resealable plastic bags filled with meat scraps, leftover spaghetti, pizza crusts, sandwich scraps, and other goodies. When it's time to feed, I thaw the delicacies in the microwave and spread them in a feeder. The mix may not appear palatable to me, but the birds seem to enjoy picking through the smorgasbord. It's fun to see what they go for first.

In times of need, the very presence of feeding birds of any kind will attract the attention of other species, even if they are not usually inclined to sit shoulder to shoulder with sparrows. I serve soft foods directly on the ground or in open tray feeders, where the birds that aren't accustomed to the feeding station can easily spot them. Avoid going overboard with this approach, though, because starlings are also big fans of soft foods. If starlings become a problem, save these foods for desperate times, unless you don't mind accommodating a horde of starlings in exchange for the occasional sighting of a brown thrasher. Or unless, like me, you also enjoy feeding starlings.

Soft Foods to Avoid

These soft foods do not usually attract desirable birds, but crows and starlings may find them interesting.

- Cheese
- Potatoes, any type (mashed, baked, boiled)
- Salad greens
- Tomatoes
- Vegetables, except corn

Soft Foods to Keep in Stock

OFFER THESE foods in a tray feeder, or place them in a weighted feeder that prevents large birds like crows and starlings from gaining access to the treats.

- Bacon
- Bread
- Cake
- Canned corn
- Cereal
- Cookies
- Dog food
- Doughnuts
- Eggs
- Fruit, dried or fresh
- Lunch meat
- Meat scraps
- Muffins
- Pancakes and waffles
- Pasta, cooked
- Peanut butter
- Pizza
- Raisins
- Sandwich scraps
- Suet
- Toast

Sparrows

FIGURING OUT the grosbeaks, jays, and other large birds at your feeder is the easy part of bird identification. You'll know you've graduated from the novice stage when you start to sort out sparrows. More than 32 different species of native sparrows fill just about every niche in the country, flocking in companionable groups that usually include more than one species.

To preserve the reputation of our native sparrows, it's important to know that house sparrows (or English sparrows) are neither sparrows nor native birds. The sparrows we're discussing in this section are all-American birds that belong to the several genera of the finch family that ornithologists consider sparrows.

All sparrows have small, conical beaks, typical for birds that eat mostly seeds. These little birds devour millions of seeds of weeds-to-be including ragweed (*Ambrosia artemisifolia*), curly dock (*Rumex*

The chipping sparrow is a dapper backyard resident that often nests in a foundation shrub or tree. Listen for its distinctive song, a series of rapid chips.

crispus), and dozens of other plants. They also eat insects, and many of them enjoy fruits and berries.

All sparrows have brown backs, except for a few species that live in sagebrush country in the West. Of these western birds, the **black-chinned sparrow** is deep

---

SPARROW FEEDER FOODS

- Baked goods
- Birdseed mix
- Blackberries (*Rubus* spp.)
- Blueberries (*Vaccinium* spp.)
- Bread crumbs
- Cereal
- Cherries
- Chick scratch

- Corn, cracked or ground
- Crackers, crumbled
- Elderberries (*Sambucus* spp.)
- Evening primrose (*Oenothera* spp.) seeds
- Foxtail grass (*Setaria* spp.) seeds
- Grapes

- Grass seed
- Millet (*Panicum* and other genera)
- Milo (*Sorghum bicolor*)
- Oats (*Avena sativa*)
- Rapeseed (*Brassica napus*)
- Seeds of garden flowers, including cockscomb (*Celosia cristata*), bachelor's

buttons (*Centaurea cyanus*), sweet alyssum (*Lobularia maritima*), and marigolds (*Tagetes* spp.)
- Suet, chopped
- Weed seeds, including pigweed, common ragweed, smartweed, dandelion, and many others

charcoal with brown shoulders, the **sage sparrow** is lovely gray with a white belly, and the **black-throated sparrow** is a soft gray-brown. The **lark bunting** is another sparrow that doesn't dress in brown. This midwestern species is black with snazzy white wing patches. Juncos are sparrows, too; check the Juncos entry on page 182 for more information on them.

A sparrowlike bird of grainfields and farm country, the **dickcissel** bears a silly-sounding name that echoes its call of "Dick, dick, dick, sissel!" The dickcissel looks like a cross between a sparrow and a meadowlark, with a streaky brown back and a bright golden breast boldly marked by a black bib. In summer, it rarely visits feeders, but on its wintering grounds along the Gulf and Atlantic coasts, it may turn up with the sparrows at your feeder.

Sparrows at the Feeder

Although America holds dozens of sparrow species, only a handful regularly partake of the fare at feeding stations. Expect to enjoy regular visits from the **song sparrow** in all seasons and the **white-throated** and **white-crowned sparrows** especially in winter. In the far West, look for the **golden-crowned sparrow** in winter. The golden-crowned closely resembles the smaller white-crowned species, and members of the two species often flock together.

You may also play host to the **chipping sparrow** in spring and summer and the **American tree sparrow** in winter. The **field sparrow** may visit in any season. One of the largest sparrow species, the beautiful rich-colored **fox sparrow** may come to call in various seasons depending on where you live.

Many native sparrows, even widespread species such as the **grasshopper sparrow, lark sparrow, savannah sparrow, and vesper sparrow,** do not usually frequent feeders. These birds stick to their natural haunts in prairies and meadows, fending for themselves without needing extra assistance. Other sparrows of more limited range, including the marsh-loving **LeConte's sparrow, Nelson's sharp-tailed sparrow,** and **seaside sparrow,** also tend to ignore even the most inviting feeder setup in favor of natural food. But don't be surprised to see any

The wide-eyed look of a white eye ring identifies the field sparrow, a bird that frequently forsakes wild places for the abundance at a winter feeding station.

The fox sparrow is one of the easiest to identify and one of the largest. In the West, these feeder birds are dark umber; in the East, they're ruddy chestnut.

sparrow in this book turn up at your spread of tempting seeds, especially in times of severe weather or during migration.

Millet and other small seeds are the primary feeder food of all sparrows. These birds will visit higher feeders, but they are more at home closer to ground level. Supply a low tray feeder for them, or feed directly on the ground. Sparrows often feed under feeders, where they scratch to turn up fresh seeds dropped by other feeder guests.

Identifying Sparrows

No, all sparrows don't look alike—it only seems that way sometimes, which is what leads many bird watchers to lump them together as "LBBs"—little brown birds, or "LBJs"—little brown jobs. These small members of the finch family are a challenge to identify because their differences are subtle, and their behaviors are often similar.

Naming sparrows at the feeder is only a matter of patience because you can compare the visitor to the pictures of the field guide while the bird eats its fill. But when a sparrow is in the yard or in the wild, giving you only a quick, tantalizing glimpse, identification is a different story. Is it a swamp sparrow or a tree sparrow scolding you from the hedge? By the time you pull out your field guide—usually after the bird has flown—you may forget many of the fine points, if you noticed them in the first place.

Sparrows' distinguishing differences are noticeable if you have an eye for details. Look for the dark "stickpin" on a song sparrow's streaky breast.

When I spot an unfamiliar sparrow, I first make a quick sketch of its head, noting stripes, if any, and colors. Sometimes that's as far as I get before the sparrow skedaddles. If I have the luxury of a longer look, I run down a quick checklist of other features that could help me identify the bird, such as wing bars or a dark "stickpin" mark on the breast. Look specifically at head markings and tail shape when

8 Steps to Sparrow I.D.

NOTICING THESE features will help you figure out who's who.

- Streaked or unstreaked breast?
- Dark central spot on breast?
- Color of head cap?
- Eye stripe?
- Color of throat?
- Wing bars?
- Length of tail?
- Shape of tail notch?

Head cap
Eye stripe
Wing bars
Throat color
Tail length
Breast streaks
Central breast spot
Tail notch

you're trying to sort out sparrows; these characteristics are often enough to make a final classification.

I also note the habitat in which I saw the sparrow. This is a big help in nesting season, but less so during migration and in winter, when sparrows range far afield of their usual haunts. I make quick notes of any behavior I notice, too, which help me remember the bird the next time. If the sparrow is feeding, I jot down what and how: "scratching for seeds beneath dock," for instance, or "perched on goldenrod stem, fluffy stuff flying." You don't have to be scientific with these field notes; just record information that you will understand when you read it later.

A winter feeder visitor, the tree sparrow sports an interesting two-toned bill. Disregard the name—this bird usually hops about in fields, gardens, and brush.

Sparrow Behavior

Native sparrows are the perfect teachers for a course in weed appreciation. If you keep a less-than-perfect lawn, you get extra points with these spritely brown birds. In winter, song sparrows keep me company as I hoe off clumps of chickweed and toss the clumps out of the patch for them to enjoy the seeds at leisure. In late spring, when my lawn is dotted with puffs of dandelions gone to seed, migrating white-crowned and white-throated sparrows squabble over the parachute seeds. In fall, when the crabgrass that kept the yard green in summer has stretched out into seedheads, the same species come to visit again on their trip southward, drawn to the banquet of weed seeds that my slightly shaggy yard offers them.

In addition to eating weed seeds, sparrows also scour asters (*Aster* spp. and other genera), goldenrod (*Solidago* spp.), and garden flowers such as tickseed sunflower (*Bidens aristosa*), cosmos (*Cosmos* spp.),

---

Weed Eaters Deluxe

SPARROWS DEVOUR zillions of weed seeds every year. The list of their favored edibles sounds like a gardener's worst nightmare. Here are some of the plants you'll see less of, thanks to sparrows:

- Pigweeds (*Amaranthus* spp.)
- Common ragweed (*Ambrosia artemisifolia*)
- Common lamb's-quarters (*Chenopodium album*)
- Tarweed (*Cuphea petiolata*)
- Crabgrasses (*Digiaria* spp.)
- Filarees (*Erodium* spp.)
- Yellow wood sorrel (*Oxalis stricta*)
- Pennsylvania smartweed (*Polygonum pensylvanicum*)
- Knotweeds (*Polygonum* spp.)
- Common purslane (*Portulaca oleracea*)
- Sheep sorrel (*Rumex acetosella*)
- Docks (*Rumex* spp.)
- Foxtail grasses (*Setaria* spp.)
- Nightshades (*Solanum* spp.)
- Common chickweed (*Stellaria media*)

and marigolds (*Tagetes* spp.). Visiting sparrows are the main reason I let my garden plants stand through winter. The stems provide a sheltered place where these small birds, very conscious of their low rung on the food ladder, can forage for seeds without fear of hawks or other predators.

Watch as sparrows move across a stretch of open space, and you will see how they have perfected flight patterns to avoid being picked off by predators. Some skulk from one clump of low vegetation to another, while others make a mad dash, zigzagging evasively across the dangerous open ground.

Sparrows usually behave well at the feeding station, even when they visit in flocks. They peck busily at the seeds with quick motions, always ready to take flight in an instant. Many sparrows scratch as they feed. Some use a one-legged technique, while others hop front, then back, to turn over the debris.

If you live in an area of winter snows, you may see a song sparrow working industriously beneath your

The white-crowned sparrow looks highly alert, thanks to the eye-catching bright white stripes atop its head. Juvenile birds wear duller colors.

feeder after a fresh snowfall. I have seen song and fox sparrows feeding in 6-inch-deep pits shortly after daybreak, when hunger urged them to try to reach the seed buried beneath the deep white blanket.

Sparrows appreciate fresh water, and several species, including the chipping sparrow, are fans of

A Weed to Plant

HOLDING THE number-one place in the stomachs of many sparrow species are smartweeds (*Polygonum* spp.), a genus that includes many common and widespread plants. You probably have smartweeds (or the similar knotweeds) growing in your yard right now, or in nearby wild places. All have spikes of close-packed tiny flowers, usually pink but also white, depending on the species.

Once you pay attention to smartweeds, you'll notice that many species have definite garden potential. Taller, shade-loving species are appealing with ferns and hostas; low growers are best en masse. Experiment with those that grow well in your own area; you will encounter some smartweeds with fine garden potential. Many bloom for weeks, providing an understated ruff of color with perennials or other plants.

I encourage a ground-hugging variety (*Polygonum persicaria*) that has vibrant, deep pink flowers to cover the spaces among my native ornamental grasses. This smart-weed is a very late bloomer that comes into its own when the purple top grass (*Tridens flavus*) is standing tall and somber in bloom, and the panic grass (*Panicum virgatum*) is mellowing into tawny fall color, making a beautiful combination of color and texture. The finishing touch is another sparrow-beloved weed, purple love grass (*Eragrostis spectabilis*), which produces soft, low clouds of pale pinkish purple seedheads. After I enjoy the show of grasses and smartweed, my many winter-resident sparrows work at the seeds for months.

salt. In spring, some sparrows, such as the golden-crowned, like to nip off the petals and buds of garden flowers. Tender green sprouts of weeds and veggies tempt others—I've learned to cover my peas until after the white-crowned sparrows have left in spring. Small fruits are also a staple in their diets.

There are so many sparrows in America and they eat so many insects that the USDA issued a publication 80 years ago (before pesticides were commonly used) ranking sparrows by their useful-ness to farmers. Their yen for beetles, cutworms, grasshoppers, weevils, and other garden menaces make sparrows a presence to be encouraged in your backyard.

The white-throated sparrow has a beautiful but melancholy song. You may hear it at the feeder as spring nears. It prefers dense plantings and shrubs.

Spring Feeding

TRAFFIC REMAINS HIGH at backyard feeders in early spring. Mating season hasn't begun or is just starting for most species. Migration is getting under way, bringing temporary bird visitors as well as the resident birds of summer into your area. Snow-storms and other severe weather can still sweep through, causing a rush on the feeding station. Keep your supplies well stocked just in case. I usually add an extra jar of peanut butter and a few more suet blocks to the larder, just in case. Should cold weather hit hard, these will help the birds through the tough time. Purple martins and bluebirds are particularly susceptible to cold weather, which keeps insects out of sight. During a cold snap, invest a few dollars in meal-worms and offer them with a free hand at an open tray feeder for these birds—it can mean the difference between life and death. Spring also brings humming-birds to nearly every part of the country, so make sure your nectar feeders are ready and waiting.

What to Watch For

Although you won't notice much of a change in the number of birds at your feeders early in the season, you will see a change in behavior. Instead of congre-gating in congenial groups, many species are now be-ginning courtship maneuvers and forming pair bonds. Sparring over females is common, and territorial jousting can occur between males of the same species.

Feeder birds sound different in spring, too. Their hormone levels are changing, triggering them to begin singing their love songs. Blackbirds, bluebirds, chickadees, meadowlarks, nuthatches, song spar-rows, starlings, and titmice are among the first to start singing. Watch them to see whether they're trying to impress a mate or stake out a territory.

Arriving spring migrants are cause for big excite-ment at the feeders because now is the time when some of the most colorful, most unusual birds may show up. Insects are still scarce, and the need to refuel quickly is paramount, which means that tanagers may choose an hour of feasting at your feeder over an afternoon of foraging for themselves.

If your feeders offer generous helpings of favored foods, you may find an ever-increasing number of birds as migrants come into the area and stop for a few days. Goldfinches, particularly, can build into enormous flocks at a well-stocked feeder. In spring, my usual number of 6 goldfinches swells to 200. They fill the trees over the feeders and make the air come alive with their musical twitterings. Even my dozen feeders aren't enough to accommodate them, so for a couple of weeks, I resort to pouring black sunflower seed directly on the ground. When the sunny horde descends on the seeds, it looks as though a big patch of dandelions has come into bloom overnight.

Watch for the birds that passed through on their way south to stop again on their way north. Often, I'm convinced, it's the self-same bird. I remember a fox sparrow that lingered for 3 or 4 days on both legs of its migratory voyage. I had moved my feeding station between fall and spring, but this sparrow returned to where the feeder used to be.

Migration is usually gradual. Not every bird species has a departure ticket for the same day. I like to keep a head count once a week to stay on top of the changes; otherwise, one day I look out the window and notice that there's not a single junco in sight. As winter residents leave for more northerly

Rose-breasted grosbeaks may stop at your feeder on their spring trip northward. The feeder scene changes as winter residents move on and summer birds return.

breeding grounds, you won't need to fill your feeders as often.

As spring progresses and the birds move to nesting territories, their visits to your feeder will likely become fewer and farther between. By late spring, nesting season is in full swing, migration is over, and feeder traffic usually drops off dramatically. Don't worry, though: Some of the faithfuls will stay regular customers right through summer.

10 To-Dos for Spring Feeding

1. Increase the amount of millet in your feeders to satisfy the many small seed eaters that may be stopping in, such as indigo buntings, finches, siskins, and native sparrows.

2. Add another tube feeder if needed to accommodate the burgeoning numbers of goldfinches.

3. Pull out the special treats to keep birds loyal to your feeder: nuts, peanuts, fruits, peanut-butter delicacies.

4. Put out hummingbird feeders.

5. Serve mealworms, a real treat for migrating tanagers, thrushes, and other insect eaters.

6. Offer crushed eggshells to replenish minerals.

7. Keep a ready supply of fresh water available to the birds.

8. Watch for plumage changes in male goldfinches, as they switch from winter olive drab to dandelion yellow spring dress.

9. Learn bird songs as you begin to hear them from courting couples.

10. Note the arrival dates of spring migrants this year on a calendar page for the same day the coming year; it's fun to know when to expect them next year.

Sprinklers, Drippers, and Misters

ANY DEVICE THAT makes water audible is a prized addition to a bird-attracting yard. Recirculating pumps fill the bill, as do fountains in garden pools. Keep in mind that you don't need to create a torrent to attract birds. Their hearing is acute, and they can pick up just a ripple or a drip. In the days before water meters and water-table awareness, I often let my garden hose run on the ground. (I still do sometimes when I forget to turn it off after watering.) That very low-tech approach attracted a multitude of birds to the yard, including thrushes and towhees from the nearby woods.

A lawn sprinkler delights birds as well as kids. Keep watch to see who's frolicking in the water. Hummingbirds, like this Anna's, are fond of a bath on the wing.

Sprinklers

A good old lawn sprinkler makes a low-tech, low-cost approach to creating water music. Robins and flickers are particularly fond of this bath; they will linger beneath the spray for a long time, fluttering their wings as they luxuriate in the gentle water. Birds prefer a sprinkler that waters the same area for a long time rather than an oscillating sprinkler that swings from one place to another.

If hummingbirds visit your yard, the spray of a sprinkler may serve as a hummingbird shower—an event that is a delight to watch. Instead of alighting like other birds, hummers swing back and forth through the spray, then retire to a nearby perch to freshen their feathers. These endearing little birds may even bathe in the spray from a handheld hose nozzle.

Drippers

On a smaller, more sensible scale, a gentle drip-drip-drip is also highly effective. You can create your own dripper, albeit a funny-looking one, by suspending a leaky bucket over the birdbath. Poke a nail into the bucket from the inside to make a single hole in the center. Fill with water and let 'er drip. If you want a splashier sound, poke two or three holes, but be aware you'll have to refill the bucket more often.

Commercial dripper devices are widely available for attachment to your garden hose. They are a simple piece of copper or other tubing, bent into a curve at the top like the handle of a cane, with a connection for attachment at the other end. These accessories are perfect for a ground-level birdbath or garden pool.

Misters

Misting devices, which break up spray into superfine droplets, are a real treat for birds. They exult in the fine spray regularly once they discover it. A mist head that attaches to your hose is a real bargain at about $20. The attachment may tempt bright-colored orioles and tanagers, as well as robins, sparrows, and a host of other songbirds to the delights of the bath. Hummingbirds will also soon be regulars. You can attach the mist head to a branch, post, or other support. Point the spray toward a place where birds can alight to enjoy it. Hummingbirds, of course, need no perch for the pleasure of their bath; an upward-pointing mister is ideal for a hummingbirds-only bathing area.

Hoses

No matter how good I try to be, invariably at least once a season I forget to turn off the garden hose. The running water is a big attraction for robins, towhees, and other birds, which sip and splash until I remember my lapse and the water dries up.

A pair of inexpensive misters offers water for songbirds, hummingbirds, and butterflies. In summer, birds may find water more tempting than food.

Y-connector

Squirrels

NOBODY IS NEUTRAL ABOUT SQUIRRELS. When it comes to these bushy-tailed rapscallions, we either laugh at their comedy routines and put up with their raids on the birdseed, or we declare a vendetta and do everything we can to bar the door.

Unfortunately, squirrels are darn smart. They can figure out how to raid almost any feeder, including those sold as squirrel-proof. Combine that native intelligence with an agile body and dexterous front paws, plus the leaping ability of Superman, and it's no wonder that the Great Squirrel Wars have been going on almost as long as folks have been scattering bread crumbs.

Tales from the Front

Everyone who keeps a feeding station has their own tales of battle, and some of them are downright incredible. Even I have a hard time believing some of the squirrel antics I've witnessed, and I was there!

One early winter morning after a fresh snow, I watched two squirrels cooperate to drag away an entire plastic bag of corn on the cob—10 pounds'

Cunning squirrels will put their wits to work to outsmart your antisquirrel tactics. A tube feeder with metal guards will at least slow their seed consumption.

worth. Each squirrel had a corner of the bag in its teeth, and they dragged it between them as if pulling a sled over snow. How they split up the spoils, I don't know, but I did find the empty sack in the woods, far behind the house and up a steep hill.

I have watched squirrels vacuum up a tray feeder of sunflower seeds in less than half an hour—and as far as I could tell, there were only four of them working at it. I have watched squirrels leap outward a distance of 12 feet (I measured), attempting to reach a peanut feeder. They completed the jump by wriggling violently in midair to throw their bodies upward at the end of the arc. I have seen squirrels launch an aerial attack on a feeder, misjudge a landing, fall from a branch 20 feet off the ground, and scamper off, none the worse for wear.

My favorite squirrel feat stars one determined creature who inched his way *upside down* along 30 feet of skinny-wire wash line to reach a feeder hanging in the center of it. Naturally I had no camera to record that acrobatic stunt and no binoculars handy to see how he managed to grip the wire while supporting his body weight beneath it. Sometimes it still seems unbelievable.

Such tales fill the annals of bird feeding, which is one reason why many of us choose to live with squirrels rather than without them. They're too much fun to watch to give it up over the cost of a few extra bags of birdseed.

Like other species, the fox squirrel may spend an hour or more dining. Birds shy away from a squirrel-occupied feeder; offer them alternative feeding sites.

Nasty Habits

Squirrels do have a dark side. Those strong rodent teeth just love to chew through plastic tube feeders to get at the seeds inside. Along with chewing feeders to smithereens, they may also enlarge the entrance holes of birdhouses to turn them into cozy squirrel shelters for the long winter nights. (A metal entrance guard will keep them out.)

Squirrels can consume enormous amounts of birdseed and other feeder treats. Although they are often willing to eat peaceably beside birds, the presence of the animal in the feeder is enough to keep away most of the regulars. Once a squirrel arrives, it's often there for the long haul. It sits quietly in the feeder, snacking through seeds for an hour or more

Chip off the Block

FOR AN easy way to feed squirrels, chipmunks, and other close-to-the-ground animals, try a block of birdseed. These all-in-one feasts come in a hefty size that holds several pounds of seed and nuts in a large, tightly compressed block. It's fun to watch the animals nibble at their favorite morsels in the block, and it slows consumption and saves bird feeders from squirrel visits. Cardinals, jays, and other birds may also visit the feeder-in-a-block when squirrels are taking a temporary break.

Friend of the Forest

THE ACTIVITIES of squirrels play a huge role in the health of our forests. These animals believe in saving for a rainy day, so to speak, so they bury their nuts and seeds in the soil to retrieve later, when stores are running low. Often they overlook a hickory nut, an acorn, or other seed, which sprouts the next season into a seedling tree. Along with jays, which also bury food, squirrels are the chief natural reforesters of our native woodlands.

If you host squirrels in your yard, you will often discover many squirrel-planted trees springing up after winter cold subsides. I let these seedlings grow if they fit well in my landscaping scheme. They mature faster than transplanted nursery-grown trees, with oaks reaching 4 feet tall in just 3 years or so and nut trees growing even faster. Although it will take years for the young trees to bear a crop, the trees provide valuable cover for birds and often host a bounty of insects for bird food. Native tree species, including sweetgum (*Liquidambar styraciflua*), walnuts (*Juglans* spp.), and wild cherries (*Prunus* spp.) even when young, also provide vital home sites for the caterpillars of giant moths, such as the gorgeous luna and the huge cecropia.

before it's had enough and moves on—only to make way for the next squirrel in line.

Squirrels live in cavities or in leafy nests. But once in a while, an intrepid individual may take up residence in your house or use your attic as personal storage space for its winter cache of nuts and seeds. One autumn, I thought for sure I had ghosts in my attic—and they apparently had a bowling league going in full swing. My ghosts turned out to be squirrels rolling black walnuts across the attic floor. Of course, the furry fellows couldn't stay; the bowling was bad enough, but squirrels also may gnaw on the insulation of electric wires, a little habit that can start a house fire. I evicted mine with the aid of a live trap baited with peanut butter and then took measures to screen or otherwise seal up any openings that might grant them readmission to my attic.

Far worse than their gluttony at the feeder is their appetite for birds. Tree-dwelling squirrels are notorious for the havoc they wreak on nesting birds, devouring eggs and nestlings at will, and parent birds when they can grab them. One study estimated that a single red squirrel may eat 200 birds a year. Before you start casting an evil glare toward your local squirrels, remember that these creatures are part of nature's checks and balances. They're just doing what comes naturally.

It is we humans, with our destruction and alteration of wild habitat, that have pushed songbirds to the danger point. With fewer numbers of birds around, the destruction wrought by squirrels takes on a more ominous weight. We can't eliminate all the dangers birds face. But we can do our part to provide nesting habitat on

SQUIRREL FEEDER FOODS

- Acorns
- Amelanchier (*Amelanchier* spp.) berries
- Apples
- Blackberries, raspberries, and other small fruits
- Bread and other baked goods
- Buckeyes (*Aesculus* spp.)
- Cereal
- Chestnuts (*Castanea* spp.)
- Corn, any kind
- Crackers
- Dried peas and beans
- Eggs, hard-boiled or scrambled
- Holly (*Ilex* spp.) berries
- Leftovers
- Leftover "trail mix" snacks
- Meat scraps
- Nuts, any kind
- Peanut butter
- Peanuts
- Pine nuts (*Pinus cembroides*)
- Suet
- Sunflower seeds

our property and keep birds thriving with nutritious foods.

Squirrels themselves face fatal encounters with other menaces of civilization: cars and cats. Hawks and owls also help keep them in check, as does hunting in wild places. In backyards, there's not much you can do to get rid of squirrels. Live trapping works, but moving the squirrel to an unfamiliar territory only passes along the predator and confuses the squirrel that you dump in an unfamiliar area. We can only hope that squirrels and birds manage to regain a balance that keeps both kinds of animals thriving for generations to come.

If You Can't Beat 'Em . . .

I gave up on trying to keep squirrels away from my feeders a long time ago. Once I learned that all I had to do was give them their own setup stocked with corn and the occasional sunflower seed handout, I called a truce. Where else can you get so much entertainment for such a small investment?

Of course, now and then a greedier—or smarter—individual comes along, who refuses to stay where he belongs and moves into the bird feeders instead. I usually put up with the thievery for a while, then make a concerted effort to shoo Mr. Squirrel away from the no-trespassing area. If my madwoman dashes, accompanied by clapping hands and loud shouts, don't do the trick, I move the bird feeders within the fence that holds my dogs. Squirrels don't dare tread there.

To reach your bird feeders, squirrels will undertake feats that a ringmaster might describe as "death-defying." Grab a window seat and enjoy the show!

See Ya, Squirrels

A dog is your best weapon against squirrels, unless the bushy-tails learn that Rover can't reach them. If that happens, they seem to take pleasure in taunting the poor pet as he lunges below them, barking frantically. But the presence of a dog will definitely make squirrels think twice about treating your yard as their own private nature preserve.

Many manufacturers sell squirrel-proof feeders. Some designs attempt to exclude the animals by

---

Don't Kill Them with Kindness

IN MY small town, where almost every block holds at least one squirrel corn feeder, the squirrels often battle the bulge. They put on weight quickly once we stock our feeders in the fall, at first looking lovely and sleek as they fill out from their usual skinny selves. But soon their overindulgence shows.

The extra weight eventually hinders their movements, and they aren't nearly as nimble as they were when lean and rangy.

This is bad news for the squirrels, and in winter the population drops dramatically once hawks and cats discover the easy pickings. Many of the unathletic individuals also fall victim to cars, whose drivers expect them to scamper out of the way with the

same speed they exhibited in their summer prime.

If the squirrels were wild woods dwellers instead of tame town squirrels, they would probably burn the extra calories in their daily forays around the forest. But here, it seems, their only activity is getting from nest to feeder and back again. Perhaps what we need now is a low-fat corn cultivar, just for feeding sedentary city squirrels.

dropping a lid when a heavy visitor lands on the feeder. My squirrels outwitted one model of this type by reaching from above for the seeds. I have switched to all-metal tube feeders, after one too many plastic models yielded to squirrel teeth. Tube feeders with metal guards at the seed slots may also deter them from gnawing their way in.

Conical or dome-shaped baffles also slow squirrels down. At first, your squirrels will look as if they're at an amusement park, as they slip and slide over the baffle, trying to reach the feeder it protects. I use baffles to discourage squirrels from most of my hanging and post-mounted feeders. While it may not stop them completely, it makes them work for their food and they return more readily to the squirrel-feeding area, leaving the birds alone.

The newest development in the antisquirrel battle is seed treated with hot-pepper extract. The great news is that it works. The bad news is that it costs more than untreated seed, although prices will probably drop as more suppliers get into the game. I've experimented recently with a homemade version of the commercial products (see "Chemical Warfare" on this page), and it also seems to be effective.

Meet the Squirrels

Growing up in eastern Pennsylvania, I thought the gray squirrels in our woods and backyards were the only squirrels that existed. Then I discovered that the **gray squirrel** is just one of the arboreal, or tree-dwelling species. The feisty **red squirrel** of the Northeast and Great Lakes areas is another arboreal species, as are the **Fremont's squirrel** of the Rockies and the wonderfully named **Douglas' chickaree**, a rusty red fellow of Pacific conifer forests. Even the gray squirrel has western relatives: the **western gray squirrel,** which has a broader tail than the eastern species, and the perky long-eared **Abert's squirrel** and its subspecies, the **Kaibab squirrel.** Some color variations keep gray squirrels interesting. In isolated regions, the squirrels may be so dark we call them black squirrels, or they may veer to the other extreme and become albino white squirrels.

Moving down from the trees, you'll find animals that spend much of their time at ground level,

Chemical Warfare

THE SUBSTANCE in hot peppers that makes your skin burn, your mouth breathe fire, and your eyes water furiously should you get it near them is capsaicin. Hot peppers vary in their levels of this naturally occurring compound, with the degree of heat being measured in Scoville Heat Units (SHUs). A fairly mild jalapeño pepper checks in at about 5,000 SHUs; a hotter-than-heck habanero leaps off the chart at 500,000 SHUs!

Since I had a bumper crop of hot-hot habaneros last year, I decided to experiment with treated feeder foods. I didn't bother with birdseed, which I don't mind sharing with the squirrels. But I did want to protect my stockpile of nutmeats and whole peanuts, which birds treasure, because I feed them in small amounts that squirrels quickly wipe out.

My experiment was very simple. Wearing rubber gloves to protect my hands, I tossed about a dozen ripe peppers into a gallon of water and let it sit for two days. Then I poured some of the firewater into a recycled pump-spray bottle. Out of curiosity, I made the mistake of dipping my finger in and taking a lick, just to see how hot it was. Whoo-ee!

Now that I knew I had bottled fire, I spread 5 pounds of walnut meats on a window screen and spritzed them with the pepper solution. I was very careful not to touch my hands to my eyes or risk any other exposure to my skin because these babies burn. The nuts dried quickly in the sun. I turned them with a spatula and sprayed the other side. When the nuts were thoroughly dry, I scooped them into plastic resealable bags for storage (still wearing gloves). The bags make it easy to pour out the nuts without touching them.

At feeding time, the nuts entice the squirrels but the confused critters soon retreat, rubbing their faces and shaking their heads. The birds don't seem to notice any difference.

The red squirrel is a smaller species with a bad temper. Fights erupt frequently among red squirrels; gray squirrels that trespass are swiftly driven away.

A cob of dry corn on a spike pleases this gray squirrel and keeps it out of the bird feeder. Woodpeckers and jays may share the corn when the squirrel is away.

although they also climb trees. In western campgrounds, I met the friendly **rock squirrels**, which are chubbier and slower moving than tree squirrels. **Ground squirrels** are similar to chipmunks, and some have similarly striped backs. Here in southern Indiana, the most abundant squirrel is the **fox squirrel**, a beauty with a tawny golden belly and tail. Nonarboreal squirrels seem to be tamer than those that roam the treetops, or maybe they simply spend less time in the frenetic activity of scurrying and leaping. **Flying squirrels** (see that entry on page 128) are the nocturnal replacement for the daytime tribe.

All squirrels are nut and seed eaters. Their diet varies, depending on what's available where they live. Those that reside in conifer forests fill their bellies with the seeds of cones from pines, Douglas fir, hemlocks, and other evergreens. In deciduous woodlands or mixed forests, acorns, beechnuts, hickories, and other meaty nuts are also mainstays on the menu. Farm

fields and game plots provide some squirrels with a big part of their food, including corn and wheat.

Squirrels also eat fruit, particularly wild species like blackberry, mulberry (*Morus* spp.), wild grapes, and amelanchiers (*Amelanchier* spp.), and the berries of dogwood (*Cornus* spp.), black gum (*Nyssa sylvatica*), and other trees and shrubs.

At the feeder, squirrels will devour just about anything you serve them, though they will dine on their natural foods first. Put out corn and peanuts, and you'll have squirrel friends forever.

Squirrel Behavior

Squirrels are easy to observe. They are large, active creatures, and they quickly become semi-tame around the feeder. Enjoy their antics as they attempt to reach off-limit feeders or snack at the squirrel station. Because squirrels often sport *(continued on page 274)*

A Box for Munchies

This hinged box lets you serve squirrels their favorite treats in a hopper protected from the elements. When the squirrel wants a snack, it uses its hands or head to lift the lid and take a sample. Stock the munch box with whole peanuts, acorns, nuts in the shell, or other treats.

MATERIALS

1 × 6 lumber, cut to the dimensions shown

Plexiglas, cut to the dimensions shown

Nails

2 hinges

Step 1. Cut ⅛-inch grooves 1 inch from the short end of the sides to serve as channels for the Plexiglas.

Step 2. With the grooves vertical at what will be the front of the box and facing inward, nail the floor to the sides.

Step 3. Nail the back to the sides and floor. Nail the second back to the first one.

Step 4. Attach the lid at the rear by the hinges.

Step 5. Slide the Plexiglas into the grooves in the sides.

Step 6. Nail the finished box to a tree or post.

Step 7. Fill with peanuts and other squirrel treats.

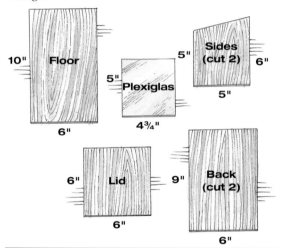

Squirrel-Friendly Mix

Serve up this crunchy mix in a squirrel-operated munch box or in an open tray feeder and it might keep the squirrels so busy that they leave your bird feeders to the birds! Of course, when squirrels aren't around, birds will drop in to nibble on the sunflower seeds and shelled nuts.

INGREDIENTS

4 parts whole-kernel dried corn

2 parts peanuts in the shell

2 parts striped or black sunflower seeds

2 parts walnuts, in shell

1 part shelled peanuts

1 part small dry beans, such as navy beans

1 part walnut, almond, or pecan pieces

Measure ingredients into metal pretzel can or large metal popcorn tin. Stir to combine. Replace lid tightly after filling your squirrel-friendly feeders.

distinguishing characteristics—a ratty tail, a fat belly, a white forehead star—you may soon be able to identify some of the troupe. Recognizing individuals will give you a more personal connection to the varmints.

I like to keep sketches of squirrel "tail language." Squirrels use these fluffy appendages to signal all kinds of communications, from danger to aggression to playfulness. Squirrels are great game players, often indulging in an apparent game of tag with as much abandon as a bunch of 7-year-old kids. They chase each other up and down trees, across the ground, and in and out of rock and brush piles.

Plenty of trash talk accompanies such games. Listen for "chirrs," rattles, and barking cries.

During courtship and mating season, usually in fall to late winter, squirrel games take on a new seriousness. The promiscuous males attempt to run down any female they see, and battles between suitors are intense.

The list of favored feeder offerings is a long one for squirrels; most will try anything you serve. Inexpensive whole corn is a staple, as are sunflower seeds. They are fond of fresh water, too. A low-level pool or dish is easiest for them to reach, but they will also visit a pedestal birdbath.

Starling

STARLINGS ARE CERTAINLY A NUISANCE. They're noisy, they gobble up feeder food like gluttons, they travel in crowds, their bathroom habits are none too delicate, and they aren't even pretty. Worse yet, they outcompete cavity-nesting flickers and other native birds for prime real estate in dead trees and bird boxes.

That's the bad news.

The good news is that starlings are extremely useful at controlling another imported pest, the Japanese beetle, which makes lacework out of your grapevines and devours your rosebuds before they open. They eat both adults and larvae, stabbing into the soil with their dagger beaks to extract the plump grubs. The starling's destruction of weevils, cutworms, and other beetles and their larvae also helps polish the starling reputation.

Starlings are clever and interesting, once you begin observing them with a more tolerant eye. And, though they do engage in shrieking contests, they also have a pretty, gurgling love song. Although often dismissed as plain or even ugly, starlings have an understated beauty, with their plumage decorated with a delicate pattern of creamy white "stars" in winter and an iridescent sheen in spring. Starlings can help predict when spring is coming or winter nears, as their beak changes color with the seasons.

Imported from overseas 100 years ago, starlings are here to stay. Although messy and loud, they're not all bad, as they consume their fair share of insect pests.

Welcome to America

Starlings are not American natives, and they are not "blackbirds." They belong to the myna or starling family and originally hail from Eurasia, where they have been just as pestiferous and just as useful as they are in America. In the late 1800s, starlings saved the day when they descended in enormous numbers to contain a potentially disastrous outbreak of the spruce moth in Bavaria. A couple of decades later, they descended like "black clouds" on Swiss vineyards, stripping the vines bare of fruit.

Eugene Scheifflin performed the first successful introduction of starlings from 1890 to 1891 in Central Park, New York. Like the alien house sparrow, starlings quickly found their niche in this country, settling into cities and countryside, usually living close to humans.

Bluebirds, flickers, great crested flycatchers, purple martins, house wrens, and other woodpeckers have all suffered loss of nest sites thanks to starlings. The house-hunting starling stands by while the other birds do the work of carving out a home, then make a determined move to oust the original dwellers. Thanks to birdhouses with custom-size holes that exclude the larger starlings, we can help provide suitable homes for nearly all of the starling-displaced birds. Flickers, larger woodpeckers, and the great crested flycatcher, however, must still battle the interlopers. Because of their size, these bigger birds are often successful in ejecting the starling squatters. However, it's often an ongoing battle, with another starling ready to slide in when the nest defender discourages the first.

In winter, the starling shows why it bears that name. Each feather is tipped with a tiny chevron of pale yellow, which gives the body a star-spangled look.

Starling Behavior

These rowdy, ungainly looking birds lack the svelteness and delicacy of many songbirds, and even a few starlings make quite an impact on your food supply as they scarf down seeds and monopolize suet feeders and soft foods. Basically, the birds are gluttons. (See the Nuisance Birds entry on page 217 for tips on discouraging them from interfering with your feeding station.)

Starlings usually forage on the ground for their natural food, but I serve them in higher tray feeders so the leftovers don't attract vermin. At night, they gather in huge communal roosting

STARLING FEEDER FOODS			
■ Apple peelings	■ Cereal	■ Holly (*Ilex* spp.) berries	■ Milo (*Sorghum bicolor*)
■ Birdseed mix	■ Corn, cracked	■ Leftovers	■ Pasta, cooked
■ Bones, to clean off bits of meat or marrow	■ Crackers	■ Meat scraps	■ Raisins
	■ Dog food	■ Millets (*Panicum* spp. and other genera)	■ Suet
■ Bread and other baked goods	■ Fruit		■ Wheats (*Triticum* spp.)

S

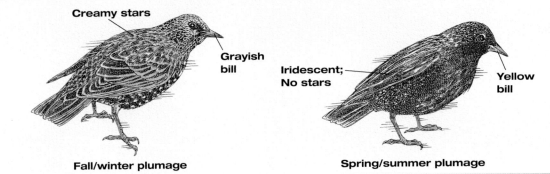

Changing with the Seasons

WATCH THE plumage and bill color of your starlings change with the seasons. In fall, the birds lose their glossy green and purple irides- cence and acquire the speckled look that gives them their name. Their bill becomes grayish in color. As spring approaches, the pale tips of the feathers gradually wear away, and the bird soon shines in iridescent black breeding plumage, accented by a bill that has changed to bright yellow. Imma- ture starlings have fooled many a bird watcher because their soft brown-gray color, with paler belly, bears little resemblance to their parents' plumage.

Creamy stars

Grayish bill

Fall/winter plumage

Iridescent; No stars

Yellow bill

Spring/summer plumage

groups to seek shelters on buildings, in conifers, or other protected sites.

Listen for the warbling courtship songs of star- lings, which usually start up in late winter. Some birds may also mimic barking dogs, crows, and other birds as well as inanimate objects like a squeaking door.

To their credit, starlings also protect themselves and other birds from foraging raptors. Should a hawk appear at your feeding station, starlings will rush to the attack. They form a tight group around the flying bird, mobbing it with a mass escort that is apparently so annoying that the hawk soon flies elsewhere.

Storing Seed

PUT SOME THOUGHT INTO WHERE you will store your seed supplies because you'll be visiting them frequently—probably every morning during the busy fall and winter feeding seasons. When choosing a storage location, look for a site that meets these criteria:

- **Close to feeders and close to house.** Every step counts when it's cold or raining.
- **Easy to clean.** Spills are a frequent occurrence; keep a dustpan and broom handy.
- **Out of reach of deer, raccoons, and squirrels.** You don't want your seed devoured before you get it to the feeders.

- **Away from human food.** Keep possible grain pests, such as meal moths, from infiltrating your pantry.
- **As cool as possible.** Oils in seed can turn rancid in hot weather; metal containers heat up fast if placed in direct sun.
- **Dry.** Moldy seed is a waste of money.

An unheated garage is an ideal spot for seed storage. It's under cover, convenient to feeders and your house, and protected from larger animals.

Storage Containers

A metal can with a tight-fitting lid is the best con- tainer for storing birdseed, corn, and other dry feeder items. The metal provides an impenetrable barrier to the hungry teeth of mice and other rodents, and the lid keeps out insects and animals bent on pilfering from your supply.

If you keep only small amounts of seed on hand, a pretzel or popcorn tin will work well. For storing seed in bulk, a metal trash can is ideal. I usually keep my big bags of seed in the larger can, and I use the smaller can for keeping 1 or 2 days' supply of birdseed at the ready. My birdseed "pantry" actually holds a few smaller cans, in which I keep my own custom seed mixes for restocking various feeders. One holds a mix of black oil sunflower and safflower—my "cardinal blend"; another holds millet, grass seed, canary seed, and niger—my "finch magnet" mix. A third can stores peanuts in the shell, plus whole kernel corn, nuts in their shells collected from the wild, and acorns—that's the "squirrel treat" can. A fourth can keeps auxiliary bird supplies at the ready: a giant jar of peanut butter, a sack of cornmeal, bags of raisins and stale bread, and, in winter, a few extra suet balls ready to hang. I also keep a large plastic mixing bowl and a supply of disposable wooden paint stirrers in the can for stirring up concoctions with these ingredients, a job that's swift and less messy outdoors than at the kitchen table.

Protect your precious seed supplies from insects, mice, other unmentionable rodents, and moisture by storing them in a metal container with a tight-fitting lid.

I label the cans with waterproof black marker on a strip of masking tape across the lid, so that I don't waste time fumbling to see what's what at morning refill time. Just to make sure I don't confuse my seed mixes, I also stick a label across the can itself in case I mix up the lids.

Strawberries

Attract catbirds, mockingbirds, robins, thrashers

IT'S HARD TO KEEP BIRDS AWAY from strawberries in the garden. Those juicy red fruits peeking from beneath the leaves are just too tempting. So use that appeal to lure fruit-eating birds such as catbirds, mockingbirds, robins, and thrashers by planting strawberries (*Fragaria* spp.) wherever you can squeeze them in: Use them as an edging along a driveway or walkway, as groundcover around a birdbath, or as a border at the front of your flowerbeds or birdseed gardens.

Birds aren't particular about what variety of strawberry you plant. Their sharp beaks can easily nip a slice out of even the biggest strawberry, while small wild (*F. vesca*) or alpine strawberries (*F. montana fraga*) go down the hatch whole. Select a variety that thrives in your area and is disease-resistant. Or locate native wild strawberries at a specialty nursery. Order your strawberry plants early from a catalog for the best selection of your favorite varieties. Plant the bareroot plants as soon as they arrive in spring, following the directions included in the package. Or buy plants in early spring at local nurseries; they are usually sold in bareroot bundles. Plant so that the growing tip of the plant, from which the leaves will emerge, is above ground. After the ground freezes in the fall, cover your strawberry bed with several inches of hay or straw mulch for winter protection. Remove the mulch in the spring before the plants begin to grow. Strawberry plants send out runners from the parent plant in subsequent seasons. Expand your planting by slicing off the plantlets at the ends of the runners and transplanting them.

You can save strawberries for later bird feeding by drying them. (If you don't grow your own, buy berries in bulk at the height of the season when prices are low.) Slice the berries and dry them on cookie sheets in the sun, turning the slices occasionally. Cover the drying fruits with a layer of cheesecloth or a piece of window screen to keep the birds from enjoying their treat early. Store dried berries in a jar or in resealable bags in a cool, dry place. In fall and winter, when your feeders are hopping with hungry birds, you can add the dried berries to birdseed mixes or other recipes for a real treat for fruit-loving birds.

Birds like strawberries as much as we do—maybe more. Squeeze in a few plants wherever you can find room—along a sidewalk, as a groundcover, or in a container on the patio.

RECIPE

Quick and Easy Strawberry Pancakes for Birds

Blackbirds, bluebirds, doves, grackles, jays, mockingbirds, robins, starlings, and others may arrive for this special breakfast treat.

INGREDIENTS

*1 cup dried strawberries, chopped into small pieces**

Pancake mix to make 10–12 pancakes, prepared as directed on package

Stir dried strawberry pieces into pancake batter. Pour into hot, lightly oiled skillet until bottom of pan is almost completely covered. Cook over medium heat until bubbles appear. Flip pancakes; cook other side until lightly browned. Remove to plate; cool. Repeat until all batter is used.

Using a sharp knife, slice across each pancake at about 1-inch intervals. Rotate plate one-half turn and repeat, so that you end up with small, 1-inch-wide sections of cooked pancake. Serve pancake sections and any crumbs in an open tray feeder or directly on the ground.

* Fresh or thawed frozen strawberries will also work just fine in this recipe. They're a lot juicier than dried berries, which means you'll need to reduce the amount of water you add to the batter by one-third or so. An interesting side effect: Strawberry juice makes pink pancakes!

Suet and Fat

Attract many kinds of birds

ADDING A SUET FEEDER to your bird-supply station is one of the best investments you will make. The ready-made wire baskets sold in bird-supply stores, discount chains, and hardware stores cost only $5 or so, and the suet to fill them adds only another dollar to the cost. A constant stream of chickadees, jays, nuthatches, titmice, and woodpeckers jockeying for a bite of their favorite food will reward you. You may also get unexpected visitors, including bluebirds, catbirds, kinglets, mockingbirds, and yellow-rumped warblers. Resurrect Grandma's meat grinder to turn chunks of suet or beef fat into the hamburger-like "worms" that these birds adore, maybe because they look like the grubs and caterpillars on their natural menu. Cardinals, juncos, native sparrows, and other birds will eagerly consume any bits that fall to the ground. To make it easier for low-level eaters, I drill a 2-inch-diameter, ½-inch-deep cavity just above ground level in my wood feeder posts to accommodate a few dabs of the prized fat.

Birds favor all types of fat including greasy drippings in your roasting pan, trimmings from the supermarket, and prepackaged blocks of suet that slide neatly into a feeder. You may even spy woodpeckers and other birds working away at the carcasses of deer and other roadkill, although that option is one you won't want to include at the feeder.

Preventing Pests

The major drawback to suet is that it is also one of the favorite foods of starlings, crows, raccoons, and cats. If you prefer not to feed every suet

"Suet" is used to include other animal fat, which birds like just as well. Beef fat trimmings cost less than pure kidney-fat suet and are available at any meat counter.

eater in the neighborhood, the solution is simple, though a little more costly. Pest-proof feeders that allow access only to desirable birds are widely available through catalogs such as those listed in "Resources" on page 348 or on the shelves at bird-supply stores.

Because I like to feed any hungry bird or animal that comes along, I supply suet and fat in abundance. Wire feeders are at many locations in my yard, and in winter my shrubs and trees take on a festive air, thanks to my collection of homemade red mesh-covered suet balls hanging from their branches. A few hanging, horizontal sections of log, drilled with holes underneath to stuff suet into round out my suet stations. These log feeders are easily accessible to acrobatic woodpeckers, nuthatches, and brown creepers, but not to starlings, which leave them alone in favor of suet offerings that are easier for them to reach.

Bark Slab Sandwich Feeder

Recently, an interesting new pest-proof feeder has come on the market. Although it is synthetic, it looks very much like two slabs of natural bark with a narrow slit between, which you can fill with fat, peanut butter, or other treats. Woodpeckers, with their long bills and longer tongues, have no trouble clinging to the feeder and reaching into the crevice for the fat.

You can duplicate this feeder easily by visiting a sawmill and buying a couple of slices of bark backed by a thin layer of wood. Screw the slabs together at top and bottom corners and add a wire handle for hanging. To prevent the suet from falling out at the bottom, stuff the bottom of the crack with a wood shim.

MATERIALS

2 trimmed bark slabs, about 6 × 12 inches

4 long bolts and nuts to fit them

Plastic tubing to fit over bolts

Wood shim

Wire for hanging

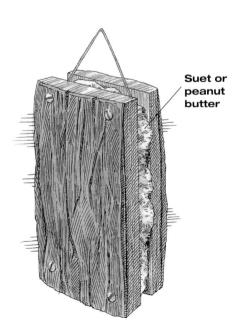

Suet or peanut butter

Step 1. Drill a hole in each corner of both bark slabs.

Step 2. Insert bolts through holes in one slab; slip a ½-inch piece of plastic tubing over each to hold space between the slabs.

Step 3. Run the bolts through the holes in the other slab and secure with nuts.

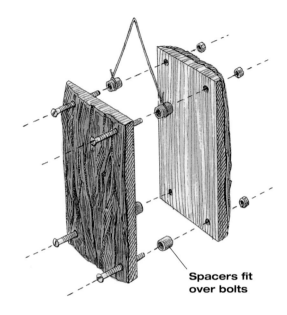

Spacers fit over bolts

Step 4. Wrap wire around the two bolts/spacers on one end to create a hanger.

Step 5. Push the shim into the opposite end between the slabs to keep the suet from falling out the bottom.

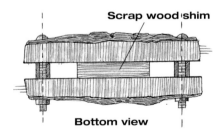

Scrap wood shim

Bottom view

Step 6. Stuff the spaces between the slabs on the sides with suet or peanut butter.

Step 7. Hang the finished feeder.

How to Buy Suet

Prepackaged slabs, wrapped in plastic and purified so they stay fresh for a long time are the most convenient form of suet. At about a dollar or two apiece, they are a great buy, lasting for several weeks in the feeder, depending on the traffic.

Because I feed lots of fat to my birds, I buy beef trimmings from the supermarket, too, stockpiling them in the freezer so that I always have a good supply on hand. Ask at your local meat counter for beef trimmings, and you may get the precious fat for free or quite cheaply. Some butchers will grind the fat for you if you ask, which makes it easier to include in recipes or offer to birds that have a hard time clinging to wire feeders, such as bluebirds and native sparrows.

You may also be able to buy pure suet, which is the layer of fat that covers an animal's kidneys, from the butcher. Since this is more expensive than just plain old fat, I usually don't bother with it, although birds welcome it.

You can also pour bacon grease, beef drippings, or other melted fat into washed cat food or tuna cans for quick fat feeding. I save my cooking fats in a large coffee can in the refrigerator so that I can prepare feeders when I have a convenient amount of grease. It stays soft enough to scoop out with a spoon.

How to Feed Suet and Fat

There's no need to melt the suet or fat before offering it to birds. If you're working with true suet or beef trimmings, just slice off chunks or strips with a

> Use a meat grinder to turn suet chunks or beef fat into "worms" that birds gobble up just like live worms.

stout chef's knife and fill your containers. I save the plastic mesh bags from onions for instant suet feeders: Just fill the empty mesh bag with fat, tie the top closed, and hang from a branch, hook, or nail.

Most suet feeders hang near our eye level, but many ground-feeding birds also like some fat in their diets. To accommodate these guests, I feed ground or chopped suet in a tray feeder near ground level.

Small, shallow cans left over from cat food or tuna are time-honored bases for suet feeders. Punch a hole in the can with a nail and attach a wire for hanging, then fill with melted suet, let it solidify, and hang.

To keep my throngs of wintertime starlings occupied, I also feed the largest chunks of fat I can find. I put these hunks of fat in a feeder away from the main feeder area, but in a place where I can watch the action. It's fun to watch them peck and pull at the offering. When hunger and the presence of other birds drive crows to investigate my feeders, they also like the big chunks of fat at the starling area.

Added Ingredients

Some of the products marketed for birds have more appeal to those that feed them than to the birds themselves. You'll find suet blocks with fruit, suet with nuts, and suet with seed offered for sale. Sounds

---

Greasy Bird Stuff

FEED SOFTER fats, such as meat drippings and bacon grease that you have accumulated, by spreading the stuff onto a rough piece of bark. Don't try this trick on porch posts or living trees: The grease creates an unsightly stain. A local sawmill can supply a thin piece of wood with bark still on, or you can use a rough-cut wood shingle called a shake. Even a rough-cut piece of 2 × 6 board will do the trick. If the surface of the wood is too slick for the fat to adhere to, collect fallen pieces of bark from your trees and staple them into place for a more textured surface. You can also spread soft suet into a corner of a wooden tray feeder, if you don't mind grease stains. Smear some fat low on the wood post near ground level for juncos and sparrows. If you'd prefer something other than this sort of "smear" campaign, use the grease to moisten leftover cereal, crushed crackers, or small bits of bread. See the Cereal entry on page 58 for tips on which types of cereal work well for this feeding method. Offer the resulting food mix in a tray feeder.

tempting, especially when it's marked with a label like "Suet for Bluebirds" or "Suet for Orioles." Feel free to experiment with such specialties, but be aware that suet alone is enough of a draw to attract all kinds of birds without other enticements. Once a bluebird discovers your suet feeder, it will return again and again whether or not peanuts or other tidbits enhance the fat. The presence of the additives won't make birds come to the feeder any sooner than they would otherwise.

Steer clear of suet that includes birdseed mix, such as millet and other small seeds. The main customers for fat do not eat these seeds, and the ground-feeding birds that do eat the seeds don't visit suet cages. Also, birds can get their feathers greasy if they try to reach in for the seeds, which may affect the vital insulation properties of their plumage.

I prefer to save my special treats for use in recipes with ground or chopped suet, not melted fat. In an impromptu test I tried, I filled a wire suet feeder in a new location with a block of suet sold specifically to entice bluebirds. Then I filled a new tray feeder next to it with a fast mix of chopped suet, raisins, and chopped peanuts that I squeezed with my hands into a loose loaf. The bluebirds ignored the "bluebird block" and flocked to my homemade mixture along with a catbird, robins, and Carolina wrens. After 2 weeks of regular forays, the bluebirds still hadn't tried the suet cage, perhaps because of the frequent visits of chickadees, nuthatches, titmice, and woodpeckers, who apparently didn't know they were feasting on fat for bluebirds.

Benefits of Feeding Fat

The reason suet is so popular as a bird food is that it is pure fat, and that means lots of calories to fuel the high-speed metabolism of your feathered guests. Suet and fat are ideal foods for winter feeding when high-calorie foods are vital to keep birds cozy through the long, cold nights. The smaller the bird, the faster its body burns calories. The time a bird spends at a suet feeder provides an excellent ratio of energy expended to calories consumed. Compared to the expense in energy of foraging in

A mesh bag filled with fat chunks makes a fine feeder as far as these pygmy nuthatches are concerned. If raccoons are a problem, serve fat in pest-resistant metal cages.

the wild and flitting from tree to tree or from field to hedgerow, sitting at a suet feeder is as close to being a couch potato as it gets in the bird world.

Summer Suet Feeding

The peak of customers occurs in winter, but suet and fat are popular all year. In spring and autumn, they attract migrants such as flickers and yellow-bellied sapsuckers as well as resident birds. In summer, parent birds often select these soft foods for their nestlings and fledglings. Keep a suet feeder up in summer, and you're apt to receive a visit by a family of fuzzy-headed chickadees, nuthatches, or titmice. If you see a bird take a beakful of fat and fly away instead of swallowing it on the spot, watch to see where it goes. You may discover a nest, or even better, a lineup of adorable juveniles on a nearby branch.

Suet and fat can melt quickly in the heat of summer. This is the time when feeding purified blocks makes sense. Commercial suet blocks are very slow to melt or turn rancid in warm weather. If you're feeding your own collection of fats, keep the offerings small, so that the stuff stays palatable. Move feeders to the shade or keep them out of direct sun to slow the melting. For a more solid, slower-melting product, heat fat and suet over low heat on the stove, discard the bottom layer of particles in the pan, and use only the top layer to fill feeders.

Beef trimmings can look pretty disgusting after they sit for a while in warm weather: They turn gray or black and may shrivel. Despite the unappealing appearance, birds will continue to visit as long as they can uncover a bit of fresh white fat. When the offering is no more than an empty shell, pitch it and replace with fresh fat.

Better'n Bug Eggs

This combination provides plenty of protein and fat. It also offers a dollop of carbohydrates. If you can get ant eggs or mealworms, add them to the mix. All suet-eating birds will gobble it up. Serve in a tray feeder for best visibility.

INGREDIENTS

5 cups unseasoned bread crumbs

5 cups hulled sunflower seed pieces

1½ cups fine-chopped or ground suet

1½ cups hamburger (high fat, not lean, is best!)

1½ cups raisins, dried berries, dried cherries, dried figs, or dried apples, chopped (a mix is fine)

Mix with hands (wear rubber kitchen gloves if desired) until all ingredients are well combined. Spread a small amount in tray feeder. Call birds for dinner.

Suet Feeders

SUET IS A REASONABLE FACSIMILE of natural insect food, which is why it's such a favorite of chickadees, nuthatches, titmice, woodpeckers, wrens, and other bug-eating birds. When you add suet feeders to your yard, you'll soon notice that these wire cages and mesh-covered bags are almost constantly in demand.

It's interesting to note the various suet-eating styles of different birds: While high-energy chickadees and other small birds tend to dart in, snatch a beakful, and dart out, woodpeckers are much more slow and deliberate in their undertaking. A single red-bellied woodpecker, for instance, may spend more than an hour quietly pecking away at the soft white fat.

Suet Strategies

Simple wire cages are an excellent way to serve suet. You can either slide in a preformed commercial

Wire cages for suet blocks are so convenient: Slip a block in the feeder and suet's on! Feeders with drilled holes take longer to refill but birds like them, too.

block, or stuff the cage yourself with chunks of fat from the butcher. The sturdy grid of wire protects the suet from being carried off whole by other feeder visitors, especially nocturnal prowlers like cats and coons. Suet cages are so inexpensive to buy (about $5) that you will save little money by attempting to duplicate them yourself. If, however, you come across an old-fashioned coated-wire soap dish at a yard sale, snap it up: Its design is very similar, and when nailed to a board or post, it will do a fine job of holding fat.

Some feeder designs incorporate a suet feeder at the side of the seed tray or hopper. I steer clear of combination feeders so that the suet eaters can have their favorite food all to themselves, without the interruptions of arriving and departing seed eaters.

If the traffic is heavy at your suet feeder, you may want to add more than one outpost for the food, or invest in a large-capacity suet feeder, which holds two or three preformed blocks, rather than just one.

Mesh Suet Feeders

Because suet is so popular, I save my mesh onion and potato bags year-round so that I can hang lots of minisuet feeders during the months of peak demand. You can stuff these strong plastic mesh bags with as much or as little suet or beef fat scraps as you like.

When I have some time to spare, I fill the bags with fat and fasten them tightly with a long twist-tie. I store the bags in my freezer, where they look like an arsenal of red snowballs, and pull them out whenever I want to give the birds a treat. Sometimes I hook these bags onto a nail or other hanger, and sometimes I hang them from a length of string attached to the branches of shrubs or trees.

I save one 5-pound mesh potato sack to make a giant-size suet bag to keep the starlings happy. It lasts for weeks. Given their own easy-access supply, the big birds stay away from other suet feeders where they have a harder time keeping their balance while eating. I hang the bag from a length of strong fishing line to prevent raccoons from demolishing it wholesale.

Suet Cups and Cans

I also serve suet and other fats in a collection of cat food and tuna cans. Once they're washed and their labels are removed, they make surprisingly attractive containers for the soft stuff. I nail the filled cans to a vertical board or wood post, pounding in a large nail partway so it can double as a perch. When the cans are empty, it takes just a minute to pull out the nail with a claw hammer, replace the empty can with a full one, and reset the nail.

Containers from yogurt, cottage cheese, sour cream, and other products also can be easily recycled into fat feeders. Melt suet or collect bacon grease or other meat drippings, cool, and pour into the containers. It will solidify into a delectable bird treat. Because these fats are softer than suet, they are best served in cold weather to prevent them from oozing out of containers mounted with the open side down to discourage starlings. Or you can mount the containers with open end up. I keep a board handy with nails driven through it as spikes, on which I can impale the fat-filled cups. This "feeder" doubles for fruit when my collection of meat grease is low.

One of my favorite impromptu suet containers is a jar lid. These shallow containers are perfect for two reasons: (1) You can fill them quickly with just a few tablespoons of melted fat, and (2) birds empty them quickly, so they're ideal for summer feeding when the fat disappears before it begins to drip. I raid my local recycling center for lids as well as saving my own from jars of coffee, peanut butter, and other staples. To turn a lid collection into a suet feeder, just nail the lids to a board in whatever configuration you like. Metal lids are getting harder to find, but plastic is just as utilitarian. I made a simple, 5-minute horizontal deck-rail suet feeder from a scrap of 2 × 4 and three snazzy red plastic lids nailed in a row. A heat-proof glass measuring cup makes it easy to pour the warm but not hot melted fat into the lids when it's time to refill.

Jar lids, tuna or cat food cans, yogurt cups, and other containers work well for serving up suet and bacon fat.

Anti-Starling Suet Feeder

Starlings are notorious suet lovers. If they begin hogging your feeders so that woodpeckers can't enjoy their favorite food, treat your less aggressive birds to a feeder designed to keep starlings at bay. The trick is simple: Instead of suet being held within easy reach for a perched bird, the fat is hidden on the underside of the feeder. Only birds with acrobatic skills need apply—and that means no starlings!

MATERIALS

Wire suet cage feeder

½-inch plywood

2-inch-wide furring strips

Staple gun and staples

Screw eye

Chain

Step 1. Measure a standard wire suet cage feeder. Make a sketch, marking the dimensions of the four sides and the bottom.

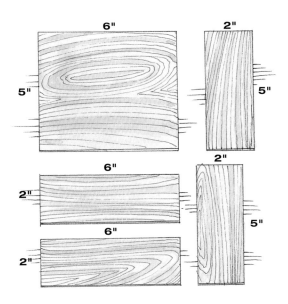

Step 2. Cut a piece of ½-inch plywood to the length and width of the suet cage bottom.

Step 3. Cut strips of 2-inch-wide wood furring strips to the length of the four sides.

Step 4. Staple the furring strips at the corners into an open box shape.

Step 5. Staple the plywood bottom to the firring strip frame.

Step 6. Insert the wire cage into the wooden box, making sure that the side that opens faces outward from the box.

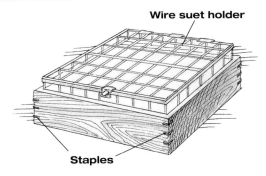

Wire suet holder

Staples

Step 7. Staple the cage to the walls of the frame. Staple the cage to the plywood bottom.

Step 8. Screw in a screw eye for hanging to the center of the plywood back. Attach the chain to the hook.

Step 9. Open the cage and insert the suet.

Step 10. Hang from the chain.

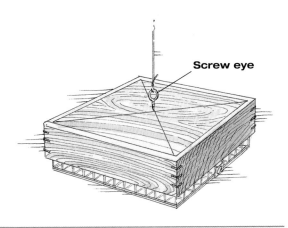

Screw eye

Sumac

Attracts more than 20 kinds of birds, from bluebirds to wrens to game birds

SUMACS (*RHUS* SPP.) GET SHORT SHRIFT in most home landscapes, probably because they're such common wild plants across the country that they become part of the background scenery, hardly drawing a second glance. Only in autumn, when sumac leaves become burnished crimson or orange, and in winter, when their branches stand bare and stark with a candelabra of deep red fruits, can sumacs be considered eye-catching. This doesn't mean these shrubs and small trees are unappealing plants. On the contrary, their compound, sometimes glossy leaves and graceful form make them good additions to a casual or natural garden.

In spring and summer, birds search sumac foliage for insects, just as they do any other plant. The panicles of whitish green, pink, or yellow flowers attract many small insects, a veritable feast for vireos, warblers, and other bug snatchers. But it's in winter that sumac becomes a standout with birds. Those spires of fuzzy fruits provide long-term food in the leanest months of the year. Sumacs flourish from Zone 2 through 10, depending on the species, and in an assortment of conditions. Most grow best in full sun to light shade and are very drought-tolerant.

A male purple finch echoes the color of sumac berries. Sumacs attract all kinds of takers in winter, when other foods are scarce or snow-covered.

Sumac Appreciators

Name a bird that dwells in your region in winter, and it's a sure bet that it samples sumac fruits at some time from late fall to very early spring. Only sparrows seem to disdain sumac for reasons they haven't yet told me. Although sumac isn't a preferred food, like acorns or nuts, it is very much appreciated by birds as a food of last resort. More than 50 species of birds, plus an assortment of rabbits and chipmunks, flock to sumac.

Some of my best winter bird watching has been done from the bench that overlooked a sumac thicket I planted. I'll never forget one cold, brilliantly clear winter day, when a flock of 26 eastern bluebirds settled onto the bushes to feed. It was a beautifully color-coordinated scene, with the birds' breasts echoing the red of the berries, their backs mirroring the sky, and their white bellies as soft as the snow underfoot.

When snowstorms move in with a vengeance, sumac is a natural for birds. The berries rarely go ignored in bad weather because their shape and position shrugs off most of the snow, so that birds can reach life-giving food. After one overnight snowstorm, which left the feeders piled high with the white stuff, I stepped outside to find golden evening grosbeaks sharing sumac with robins and a brown thrasher who was probably wondering why he hadn't flown south, while beneath the bushes, a busy flock of juncos picked up leftovers as they dropped.

When I go afield in winter looking for birds, I never pass a copse of sumac without waiting awhile to see what turns up.

Summer Feeding

THE SUMMER SCENE at the feeding station is sparse compared to the overflow crowds of fall and winter. With insects abundant and wild fruits ripening, birds don't need to depend on your generosity to satisfy their needs. Many species are nesting, too, which means they'll be spending most of their days in a frantic search for insects rather than leisurely kibitzing among themselves at your backyard feeders.

Still, you'll find that some loyal customers remain regulars at your feeders throughout the dog days. Cardinals, chickadees, finches, grackles, jays, and other birds will drop in to grab a snack daily. And, for better or worse, house sparrows and starlings will never desert you!

The summer feeding season is the time to enjoy the fruits of your landscaping labors. Now the payoff of all that planting is at hand, as birds flock to your yard to find food in your shrubs, trees, and garden beds. They'll be looking for fruit and berries, but they'll also be patrolling for creeping, crawling food like caterpillars and beetles. This is a great time to watch birds acting naturally in your yard, as they gather food for nestlings and a bit later bring the young'uns to your sanctuary.

Many feeder keepers take a break from stocking seed in summer. With gardening in full swing, many of us are no longer lingering over coffee with the

Add a plastic bottle full of sugar water to a screw-on feeder, and you're ready for hummers. Instead of cleaning the bottle, simply rinse, recycle, and replace it with another one.

chickadees but are instead strolling the yard before work or other daily routines to see what's sprouting or blooming. Birds won't suffer if you stop feeding them in summer as they would in winter, but I still like to keep a few feeders stocked with fresh seed, for

10 To-Dos for Summer Feeding

1. Cut back on your servings so that seed doesn't go to waste in feeders or attract undesirables.

2. Monitor seed supplies for webbing, larvae, or other signs of insect infestation.

3. Clean up hulls beneath feeders and replace mulch.

4. Move suet feeders to the shade to slow melting.

5. Replace beef-fat trimmings with processed suet blocks, which resist melting.

6. Add an oriole nectar feeder for sweet-toothed songbirds.

7. Give nectar feeders a weekly cleaning, especially around feeding holes, and refill anti-ant moats or renew petroleum-jelly ant barriers as needed.

8. In early summer, plant a hedge or windbreak of sunflowers or corn; birds will devour the seeds for weeks.

9. Freeze blueberries and other small fruits for winter feeding when the birds will really appreciate a sweet treat.

10. Keep birdbaths scrubbed free of algae. Install a misting sprinkler for irresistible bird bathing.

my own enjoyment as much as theirs. A tube feeder of niger and one or two hopper or tray feeders accommodate the summer seed-eating guests, while a suet feeder or two and the popular nectar feeders satisfy the other birds. I don't bother with fruit feeders in summer, since my offerings can't compete with natural fruit and berries, but I do keep up the regular handout of mealworms for the bluebirds and wrens.

The slowdown at the feeders may or may not dovetail with your seed supply. If you have only a few pounds of seed at the end of the spring season, that's great—you can replenish it by buying small amounts as you need it over the summer. I usually end up with most of a big sack or two of sunflower or other seeds. In my steamy southern Indiana summer, insects quickly infest the seed in storage, making it much less appealing to birds. Cracked corn not only suffers infestation by meal moth larvae and other pests, it also turns rancid in heat. To prevent waste, when feeder traffic slows to a handful of birds, I dump out most of the seed directly on the ground, where it attracts hordes of house sparrows and grackles, which quickly polish off most of it. Suet acquires an unappealing black mold in summer and melts in the sun. Move your suet feeder to a shady spot; your loyal woodpecker customers will soon find it.

Summer is the ideal time to thoroughly clean and repair feeders and to rake hulls and freshen mulch beneath feeders. Remove and store any unused feeders for tidiness' sake.

If you've been hankering for a garden pool, this is the season to install one. Summer heat and drought will bring glorious orioles, tanagers, and other bright-colored beauties to water. And the sound of water in your yard will make your place a favorite hangout for doves, finches, robins, sparrows, and other backyard regulars. Be sure to include a place where you can put your feet up and watch the birds near the water!

Sunflowers

Attract cardinals, chickadees, finches, grosbeaks, jays, nuthatches, titmice, woodpeckers

SUNFLOWER SEEDS ARE SO IRRESISTIBLE to birds that you could make them the only foods you ever offer at your bird feeders and *still* please the crowd. Both gray-striped and black oil sunflower seeds are high-fat, high-protein, and apparently delectable foods that give birds maximum food value for minimum effort. Grow sunflowers in your garden, and you'll have birds snitching the seeds before you even realize they're ripe. Serve sunflower seeds in a feeder, and you'll have all the customers you can handle as soon as the word gets around.

Sunflower Eaters

Who eats sunflower seeds? Cardinals, chickadees, finches, grosbeaks, jays, nuthatches, titmice, woodpeckers, and other birds with stout beaks will crack the hulls of sunflowers seeds to reach the

The birds that eat sunflowers at a feeder will also pick them from the plant. Here a tufted titmouse extracts a seed. Act fast if you plan to harvest some yourself.

meat inside. Blackbirds, juncos, sparrows, and towhees don't have large enough beaks to crack sunflower shells, but they'll search through the feeder or on the ground below to garner bits left behind by larger-billed birds. Tanagers and buntings may also show up to dine occasionally on sunflower seeds.

Squirrels, chipmunks, and ground squirrels also can't resist a banquet of sunflower seeds. These eating machines can empty a feeder faster than a horde of evening grosbeaks—and those big yellow-and-black birds go through the seeds so fast it makes a crackling noise that sounds like the feeder is on fire! Rodents will also use your sunflower feeders to stock their larders for a later snack. They can stash their cheek pouches full and transport sunflower seeds back to their cozy dens.

To deter squirrels and other gluttons, you'll need armored feeders that keep them from reaching the seeds. No feeder is entirely squirrel-proof because these intelligent and determined animals can figure out how to outwit just about any trick, from counterbalanced perches to slippery baffles. (For more on discouraging squirrels, see the Squirrels entry on page 267.)

This male goldfinch will happily pick out seeds from sunflowers with small, large, or gigantic blossoms, so grow the varieties with the flowers you like best.

Annual Sunflowers

Sunflowers are happy-face flowers. We've rediscovered the joys of growing these all-American flowers, and plant breeders have responded by releasing a flurry of new varieties to cash in on the craze. You can still find the classic tall, single-headed sunflower on seed racks and in catalogs, but you'll also see a fantastic range of new sunflowers, all selected from the parent species, *Helianthus annuus*, the common sunflower.

Growing Annual Sunflowers

A FENCE or wall is the perfect backdrop for a planting of tall annual sunflowers. It will shelter them from summer wind storms that could topple unprotected plants. Branching sunflowers, which bear a multitude of small flowers, are less prone to toppling than the big monsters that may suddenly keel over from top-heavy seedheads.

Tall sunflowers make a great hedge for attracting birds and creating privacy, at least for the summer. Use them to enclose a sitting area or patio or to create visual boundary lines in your yard. Shorter varieties are easy to work into flowerbeds. All sunflowers add appeal to a vegetable garden, but be sure to plant them where they won't block the sun from lower-growing plants.

Plant these agreeable annuals in full sun and in average to lean soil to encourage flowering rather than leafy growth. Learn to recognize sunflower seedlings—once your yard is busy with birds, you'll find volunteer seedlings popping up here and there, wherever a bird dropped a seed. These work-free seedlings will grow into a fine feast for birds.

You can grow sunflowers in dramatic autumnal shades of rust and copper; in pint-size versions with full-size blooms on knee-high plants; with fluffy, double flowers that look more like a cactus-flowered zinnia than a sunflower; and in varieties that are pollen-free, so that cut flowers don't dust your end table with a golden shower. You can even grow ancient varieties that were bred by native Americans, with seeds of burnished chestnut, deep charcoal-blue, or creamy white.

As far as birds are concerned, tasty seeds are the main reason for growing sunflowers. So choose the varieties that appeal to your personal taste, as long as they bear a bountiful crop. How can you tell? The birds will let you know. If cardinals, chickadees, goldfinches, titmice, or other sunflower eaters aren't perched on the seedheads after the petals wither, you've planted a dud.

Plants that sprout from dropped birdseed also produce excellent seeds for birds, but the plants won't look like their parents. Instead, they'll have stout, single stems, and the flower heads may be much less flashy-looking. These volunteer plants are the same type of sunflower (*Helianthus annuus*)

that decorates roadsides from Missouri to the Rockies each summer in a wide swath of shining yellow. If you're experimenting with new varieties, do your birds a favor and find a spot where you can plant some plain old birdseed sunflowers for insurance, just in case your prettified plants don't produce good seeds.

Perennial Sunflowers

North America, the home of sunflowers, boasts dozens of species of native perennial sunflowers. The flower heads are much smaller than those of the annual sunflower, but they're still crammed with small, bird-attracting seeds. All have sunny yellow daisy flowers on plants of varying height, form, and foliage. Maximilian sunflower (*H. maximilianii*), for instance, is a regal plant, stretching 8 feet or taller, with flowers borne thickly along the top 2 feet of each stem. Soft sunflower (*H. mollis*), on the other hand, tends to flop or recline against neighboring plants. Its velvet-soft gray foliage and clusters of furred buds are as pretty as its buttery yellow flowers, which usually appear about 2 feet from ground level.

Growing Perennial Sunflowers

PERENNIAL SUNFLOWERS are used to fighting for space among the tall grasses and stout flowers of the American prairie, so they can be pushy. Most species spread like lightning from underground roots. Be forewarned: It can be very frustrating to try to pull out all those roots if you decide you don't want a sunflower plantation in one particular location. Jerusalem artichoke (*H. tuberosus*) is the worst offender because its brittle roots snap easily when you attempt to dig or pull them up, and each piece of

left-behind root sprouts a vigorous new plant.

Plant perennial sunflowers in average soil in a sunny to partly shady location, depending on the species. They laugh at drought, bloom their heads off in high heat and humidity, and come through bitter cold without a qualm.

Combine perennial sunflowers with equally tough plants, such as prairie grasses (*Andropogon gerardii, Panicum virgatum, Sorghastrum nutans,* and others), goldenrods (*Solidago* spp.), and ironweeds (*Vernonia* spp.), and you'll have an instant, self-maintaining garden that's super appealing to many birds.

Luckily, climate and growing conditions are often effective at limiting a sunflower's spread. But before you invite perennial sunflowers into your treasured beds and borders, give them a trial run in an isolated part of your yard. Because they're so determined, perennial sunflowers are ideal plants to use in a naturalized area or meadow or prairie planting.

Most perennial sunflower species bloom late in the season and continue blooming even after light frost. Birds are fond of their small seeds and begin eating them as soon as the first flower head matures.

T

Thrashers

THRASHERS ARE large, slim birds with long bills and tail feathers. In some species, such as the **California thrasher** and its western cohorts, the **curve-billed, LeConte's,** and **crissal thrashers,** the beak is extravagantly long, with a decided down curve. The birds are easy to recognize as thrashers but difficult to tell apart because most are equally plain with soft gray-brown feathers. The **brown thrasher, long-billed thrasher,** and **sage thrasher** are much more distinctive, thanks to their streaked white breasts. The brown thrasher is the only representative east of the Rockies. The other species roam in the Southwest, with the California thrasher making its home in far western California.

A thrasher's businesslike bill comes in handy as it feeds on the ground beneath bushes and trees. The habit of threshing or thrashing through litter in brushy thickets to dislodge insects earned the bird its common name.

Thrashers fill their bellies with insects, fruits, and occasionally seeds in the wild. The most common thrashers at the feeder are the brown thrasher and the California thrasher, although the crissal and others may occasionally stop in for a bite. Fruit and soft foods are the big temptations for thrashers. Occasionally, a bird will linger north of its usual winter

Big and beautiful in its cinnamon garb, the brown thrasher may come to a feeder for suet, a food attractive to insect eaters. Thrashers also like fruit.

range, and those hardy souls often become feeder regulars until insects are once again plentiful.

Use a low tray feeder to lure thrashers to the feast. Once they are accustomed to visiting your feeding station, they may join other birds at higher feeders. Thrashers often visit birdbaths and other water features, especially in the dry West and Southwest.

Thrasher Behavior

Members of the mockingbird family, thrashers are talented singers with sweet, melodious songs. They engage in extended songfests, usually from

THRASHER FEEDER FOODS			
■ Amelanchier (*Amelanchier* spp.) fruits	■ Cactus fruits	■ Holly (*Ilex* spp.) berries	■ Suet, chopped or ground
■ Apples, halved or chopped	■ Cooked pasta	■ Leftovers	■ Sunflower seeds, hulled
■ Bread and other baked goods	■ Cracked corn	■ Meat scraps	
	■ Grapes and other small fruits	■ Nuts	

a perch atop a shrub or tree. The brown thrasher and California thrasher carry on the family tradition of mimicry, inserting imitations of hawks, other birds, and inanimate objects into their extended songs.

In the feeder area or in your yard, you will notice that thrashers tend to go on foot or use short flights to make their way from one patch of cover to the next. They are agile runners, too. The California thrasher is the speedster of the group pointing its tail up when it darts across open spaces. Thrashers fly low, a behavior that causes many collisions with cars when the birds are moving from bushes on one side of the road to the other.

Western thrashers, including the sage and the curve-billed, may seem almost tame once they begin visiting your yard. But all thrashers are fierce defenders of the nest, particularly when it comes to snakes. That long, sharp bill is a good deterrent to most slithering predators, but the thrasher adds to the attack with flashing wings and fanned tail.

The California thrasher's beak looks lethal, but the bird uses it mainly to scythe through leaves in search of insects or to pluck fruits from spiny cactuses.

Thrushes

IT'S A RED-LETTER DAY when a thrush shows up at the feeder. These quiet, docile birds usually forage for themselves in the woodsy areas where they make their homes. But one of the members of the family may visit your feeder during fall and spring migration or at other times if your property is near thrush habitat.

Thrushes are famed for their singing, not their looks, but the western **varied thrush** is a beauty as well as a vocalist. Dressed in glowing orange and deep blue, this bird's haunting melody of drawn-out single notes is common in the mossy woods of the Northwest. More typical of the thrush clan are several species with brown backs and dark-spotted white bellies. The **wood thrush,** once a common nesting bird of eastern woods and suburbs, and the **veery,** a wider-spread species with a few spots on its white underside, are endangered by the parasitic

The hermit thrush's habit of raising and lowering its tail makes it easy to distinguish from its similar relatives. Listen for its clear, bell-like tones at dusk and dawn.

THRUSH FEEDER FOODS

- Amelanchier (*Amelanchier* spp.) fruits
- Bayberries (*Myrica pensylvanica*)
- Birdseed mix
- Blackberries (*Rubus* spp.)
- Blueberries (*Vaccinium* spp.)
- California peppertree (*Schinus molle*) berries
- Cherries, fresh or dried
- Common greenbrier (*Smilax rotundifolia*) berries
- Dogwood (*Cornus* spp.) berries
- Elderberries (*Sambucus* spp.)
- Figs (*Ficus carica*)
- Grapes
- Mealworms
- Millet
- Mulberries (*Morus* spp.)
- Peanut butter
- Raisins
- Rose hips, small
- Spicebush (*Lindera benzoin*) berries
- Strawberries (*Fragaria* spp.)
- Suet, chopped
- Sumac (*Rhus* spp.) berries
- Virginia creeper (*Parthenocissus quinquefolia*) berries

cowbird. Other thrushes, including the **hermit thrush, Swainson's thrush,** and **gray-cheeked thrush,** may also be in jeopardy, although they seem to be less affected by the cowbird.

Loss of habitat and the carving up of woodlands in both their summer breeding territories in North America and their wintering grounds southward are also causing a decline in thrushes. Unlike chickadees and many other birds, these quiet songbirds do not adapt easily to life in suburbia. While we can't put an end to development, we can fill our yards with thrush-friendly berry bushes and supply suitable feeder foods, such as millet and mealworms, to nourish them, especially during their long migration flights.

Thrush Behavior

All thrushes have glorious voices, including the most common species, the American robin (see the Robin entry on page 245). Some sing complex, fluting melodies, while others offer quiet, pretty whistled phrases. If you are lucky enough to live near nesting habitat, take the time to enjoy their concerts at dusk and dawn.

With so many singers in springtime, it can be tricky to sort out individual voices, much less identify them. Start learning thrush songs by listening to the most familiar thrush of all, the American robin. Notice the way the phrases slide into one another—that's a hallmark of this group of superb singers. Other species have a breathy quality to their voices, as if playing a woodwind instrument rather than whistling. I've found bird recordings to be a great help in figuring out thrushes singing around me. I play the recording in the house in April, when thrushes are due to make their appearance, to get a basic familiarity with their varied songs. Then, on a spring morning or evening, I pop the cassette into a portable player, pause it at the thrush section, and step outside. When a bird starts up, I play the tape, and use the process of elimination to identify the real singers I hear.

Birds of the forest floor, thrushes prefer to eat at ground level or in very low feeders. Fruit and berries, plus a few other soft foods, are the big draw for all thrushes. These birds prefer to forage for the berries themselves, although they will take them from feeding areas, too. Common pokeweed (*Phytolacca americana*) is a magnet for thrushes, thanks to its bounty of black-purple berries that ripen during fall migration. If you allow this common weed into your garden, you may wake up one morning to find dozens of thrushes have descended on it, dropping in for breakfast after a long night of flying through the dark. The varied thrush also welcomes millet and other small seeds.

Water is another must for thrushes, which welcome naturalistic pools and low-level baths. An inexpensive dripping device—basically a bent tube above a birdbath—is a great way to grab the attention of migrating thrushes. Mount the skinny drip tube above a shallow clay saucer near ground level to increase the allure of your birdbath..

Titmice

In habits and actions, titmice resemble their relatives, the chickadees. They forage through trees, searching out insects, nuts, and other delicacies every season of the year. These small gray birds are instantly lovable, thanks to their perky posture and active behavior. Their bright black eyes shine with alertness. Unlike chickadees, they have jaunty crests capping their heads.

The most familiar of the titmice is the **tufted titmouse**, a gray-backed bird of eastern North America with pale belly and a pink flush along its side. The very similar **plain titmouse** takes over in the West, overlapping in range with the fancy **bridled titmouse** of the Southwest, a species with striking black head stripes decorating its face. In parts of Texas, the **black-crested titmouse,** a subspecies of the tufted titmouse, is common.

Titmice are common feeder birds in all seasons, although fall and winter are prime times because insect food is less abundant. One of the delights of having titmice as regulars at the feeder is that they are apt to bring their young ones to visit when they leave the nest. Keep your suet up in summer, and you

Active and friendly, the tufted titmouse and others of its clan don't migrate. The ones you see at the suet in winter are the same birds you saw nesting in summer.

may get to see a lineup of adorable youngsters begging a bite of suet from their parents.

Titmouse Behavior

At the feeding station, these well-mannered birds rarely squabble with other birds. They make frequent visits for their favorite sunflower seeds and nuts, which they hold in their feet and hammer with their small, strong bills.

TITMOUSE FEEDER FOODS			
■ Acorns (*Quercus* spp.)	■ Bread and other baked goods	■ Doughnuts	■ Peanuts
■ Apples	■ Cereal	■ Hamburger, raw	■ Pine (*Pinus cembroides*) nuts
■ Bayberries (*Myrica pensylvanica*)	■ Cherries, fresh or dried	■ Meat scraps	■ Suet
■ Beech (*Fagus* spp.) nuts	■ Corn, any kind	■ Nuts	■ Sunflower seeds, any kind
	■ Crackers	■ Peanut butter	

In winter, titmice join mixed flocks of chickadees, kinglets, and yellow-rumped warblers to range through yards and wild areas. Watch as they scour your trees for insects and their eggs and larvae or peck at cocoons to extract the plump tidbit inside.

Almost as tame as chickadees, titmice are good birds on which to practice your hand-feeding skills. They will quickly accept an offering, particularly if you tempt them with nuts. Like nuthatches and chickadees, titmice often carry seeds and nuts away from the feeder to hammer them open elsewhere. Usually the bird alights on a nearby branch, grasps the food in its feet, and pecks away at it without dropping even a nibble of the prize.

Titmice are talkative. They socialize with thin, high-pitched notes that sound very much like chickadees, and some species even emit an occasional "Chick-a-dee-dee-dee," although in a screechier tone than the namesake's call. Also listen for their harsh, scolding calls and for their sweet whistles any time of year, but especially when courtship begins in late winter. The clear, whistled "Peter, Peter" call of a titmouse is surprisingly loud for such a small bird.

PROJECT

Feeder of Titmouse Favorites

Treat titmice to a special feeder loaded with their favorite foods, and these cheery little birds will provide you with hours of entertainment. This simple setup holds a buffet of suet, apples, doughnuts, and shelled peanuts. Chickadees and woodpeckers will visit, too.

MATERIALS

Several long nails

Board, approximately 18 inches square

Empty cat food or tuna can

¼-inch or smaller wire mesh

2 screw eyes

Wire

Step 1. Drive 4 long nails through the back of the board so they protrude on the front of the feeder. One is for impaling apple halves, with a second nail below that to serve as a perch; the third nail is hold a doughnut, and the fourth will provide a perch beneath the can of suet.

Step 2. Nail through the bottom of the cat food can to attach it to the front of the feeder.

Step 3. Use the mesh to create a wire "pocket" on the bottom half of the board. Staple it in place.

Step 4. Attach the screw eyes to the top edge of the board.

Step 5. Add favorite foods: Press suet into the cat food can, hang a stale doughnut on one nail, and impale an apple half on the other one. Fill the mesh pouch with whole shelled peanuts.

Step 6. Run wire through the screw eyes and hang the feeder from a branch.

Wire mesh "pocket"

Towhees

TOWHEES ARE FOUL-WEATHER feeder friends, usually making their first appearance only when snow or food shortages cause them to seek out other sources for sustenance. Once they discover your feeder, though, they are likely to become everyday visitors no matter what the weather.

You'll notice the male **rufous-sided towhee** first because the plumage of these birds is so eye-catching, with a velvety black back and reddish sides contrasting with the pure white belly. Bright red eyes accent the plumage like ruby stickpins. (The white-eyed race of the Southeast lives up to its name for eye color.) Females are just as pretty, though not as snazzy, wearing warm brown on top instead of black. The **western rufous-sided towhee**, a race of the species, adds further ornament with white spots and stripes on its black wings. In the Southwest and along the Pacific Coast, the well-named **brown towhee** and the similar **Abert's towhee** are common in brush and shrubbery. Another western species, the **green-tailed towhee**, looks like an overgrown sparrow with its olive back, gray sides, white throat patch, and chestnut cap.

A rufous-sided towhee scratching for insects in dead leaves makes so much noise, you'll expect a larger animal. The bird will announce himself: "Toe-WHEET!"

Towhee Behavior

Like their sparrow relatives, these long-tailed members of the finch family kick and scratch in the leaf litter for seeds and insects. A single bird can make a remarkably big fuss as it tosses aside dry leaves.

The unusual name of the bird comes from the call of the rufous-sided species, which clearly announces itself with a loud, whistled "Toe-WHEET." Towhees can fool you with their variety of calls, trills, and chips, plus their whistled songs. Identifying the birds can also be tricky when you spot a juvenile or female without a male. Your first guess is likely to be "sparrow." Check the elongated tail, though, and try to match it with sparrows in your field guide.

Like sparrows, towhees rarely sit still. They hop rapidly from one sheltering shrub to another, moving from branch to branch. As they leave or arrive at your feeding station, watch for the flashing white spots in the outer feathers of the rufous-sided towhees.

Towhee tails come in handy during courtship, when the male goes all out to impress the female. Spreading those long, pretty tail feathers works well.

TOWHEE FEEDER FOODS			
■ Acorns (*Quercus* spp.)	■ Blackberries (*Rubus* spp.)	■ Corn, cracked	■ Oats (*Avena sativa*)
■ Barleys (*Hordeum* spp.)	■ Blueberries (*Vaccinium* spp.)	■ Flax (*Linum usitatissimum*)	■ Strawberries (*Fragaria* spp.)
■ Bayberries (*Myrica pensylvanica*)	■ Bread and other baked goods	■ Grass seed	■ Suet, chopped
■ Birdseed mix	■ Bread crumbs	■ Millet (*Panicum* and other genera)	■ Wheats (*Triticum* spp.)

Tray Feeders

A SIMPLE, SHALLOW tray is the kind of banquet table birds like best. The seed is in plain view, so it attracts visitors quickly to a new feeding station. The feeder accommodates many birds at a time, thanks to its ledges and the wide-open tray. There's plenty of room for all birds, even when aggressive types visit, because of the large feeding area. And the birds can fly in and out freely, plus have a clear view in all directions.

An open tray feeder has great bird appeal. It offers plenty of seating—see the blue jay sharing space with two red-bellied woodpeckers!—and allows an unobstructed view for you.

Nearly all birds will accept a tray feeder, which is also known as a platform feeder. Chickadees, finches, grosbeaks, jays, and titmice will be your best customers right from the start, followed soon after by buntings, cardinals, nuthatches, redpolls, siskins, sparrows, and all other seed-eating birds. Even quail will vault to a tray filled with tempting seed. If you offer such taste treats as dried cherries, grapes, raisins, and chopped suet, your tray feeder may also lure catbirds, mockingbirds, thrashers, and the much-sought-after bluebirds. Woodpeckers, too, will be regulars—from the diminutive downy to the bigger-than-life pileated.

The long list of customers is one of the best reasons to install a platform feeder. The other big incentive is that this type of feeder also gives you the best view of the birds. With no tubes or hoppers to hide birds on the opposite side, you can see at a glance all your satisfied customers and enjoy watching their interactions.

Bad Weather, Hungry Squirrels

Tray feeders offer many benefits to birds, but there are a couple of negative considerations to keep in mind before you install one. In inclement weather, the seed in a tray feeder may get soaked by rain, covered by snow, or blown out by strong gusts of wind.

Despite this drawback, the tray feeder is an excellent model to anchor your feeding station—unless you are overrun with squirrels or deer.

Squirrels, raccoons, deer, and other animal guests see tray feeders as a 24-hour smorgasbord. With abundant food free for the taking, they will stuff their stomachs, fill their cheek pouches, and come back for more. If you don't mind the neighborhood bushytails putting on winter weight thanks to your offerings, leave the food open to all takers. But if squirrels and their ilk are zipping through the birdseed, you may want to install an antipest grid over the feeder to deny them access (see the Feeder Covers entry on page 99 for details).

Tray Feeder Construction

Most tray feeders are made from wood or plastic, although a clay saucer or even a plastic cafeteria tray can adequately serve the same purpose. As with any other bird feeder that will get heavy use, inspect before you buy to look for signs of solid construction.

Before buying a wood feeder, check to make sure it has screws or nails at the joints, not staples, and solid wood lumber instead of plywood or pressed fiberboard. A plastic feeder should be made of material that includes an ultraviolet inhibitor so that it doesn't degrade quickly in sunlight. Also check for a heavy, solid feel; a flimsy feeder won't last for long.

All tray feeders should have drainage so that rainwater doesn't puddle in the seed. Many wood feeders have a stiff screened bottom that helps the seed drain quickly and increases air circulation to help stave off mold. Other wood models, and most plastic feeders, have drain holes drilled in the bottom to accomplish the same objectives.

It's an Investment

The price of a well-constructed bird feeder may seem outrageously high—about $20 and up for an open tray, $40 for one with a roof. But good construction and solid lumber is worth the money because the feeder will last for years. It's better to invest in a higher quality feeder, even though it carries a steeper price tag, than to replace cheap feeders every couple of years.

If the price deters you, consider building your own tray feeder. It's an easy project, even if you've never wielded a hammer before. Ask a lumberyard or home supply store to cut the wood and the bottom screen to your specifications so that all you have to do at home is assemble the feeder. Having these cuts made by the pros will cost you just pocket change—usually 50 cents or less per cut. Since there are only five pieces of wood in the feeder, this labor-saving trick will set you back less than the price of a fast-food lunch. And you won't have to invest in power tools to build a one-time project.

Room—with a view—makes tray feeders ideal for offering a variety of foods to many kinds of birds.

An open, unroofed feeder is easiest to make. If you don't fill it to the brim with seed when rain is in the forecast, an unroofed feeder will serve your birds well without breaking your birdseed budget on moldy seed. If your carpentry skills are beyond beginner status, you can find many plans for roofed tray feeders at your library, or you can design your own.

Treats for a Tray Feeder

Fill your tray feeder with bird staples, such as black oil sunflower seed or millet, or a combination of seeds. This menu will satisfy both large and small seed eaters. Foods scavenged from your kitchen cabinets—crushed crackers, cereal, bits of bread, and other tidbits that don't fit well into hoppers or tubes—work well in a tray feeder, too. You can also use a tray feeder to serve low-cost foods, such as cracked corn or chick scratch, for a crowd.

The tray feeder is also the ideal place to offer new foods. The intended recipients will be able to spot the new foods immediately, while they are filling their bills with more familiar items. When I scatter a handful of pecan nutmeats in the feeder, savvy chickadees and titmice dive on these treats, while finches and juncos around them continue to peck at their usual millet. I've used my tray feeders to introduce mealworms for bluebirds, safflower seeds for cardinals, and chopped suet for juncos and Carolina wrens.

High or Low?

You can mount tray feeders at about waist-height, the traditional level, or you can place them closer to ground level, where birds that normally stay low, such as doves and towhees, are more comfortable patronizing the feeder.

If you have only one tray feeder, mounted at the higher level, you'll find that you soon end up with a two-tier system after all. As sparrows and other birds hunt and peck for seeds in the tray, they will invariably scratch seeds over the edge onto the ground. That's where you'll see juncos, quail, native sparrows, and other ground-feeding birds eagerly picking up the overflow.

Treasures from Trash

MANY OF YOUR HOUSEHOLD CAST-OFFS hold potential for the feeding station—and we're not talking about food scraps. Jar lids, chipped or cracked cups and plates, wire clothes hangers, and other goodies can be reclaimed to help tempt birds to your yard with food offerings. The recycling bin holds other possibilities: Plastic soda bottles, yogurt cups, cottage cheese containers, and the like are golden garbage.

Your trash is not the same as mine, so what you'll find to reuse may be different. But a few general considerations apply, when you're sizing up an object for bird use. Before you give it the old heave-ho, ask yourself:

- Is the object waterproof?

- Can it hold seed?

- Can it hold suet?

- Can it be smeared with peanut butter?

- Can it hold water?

Generally, trash treasures fall into three categories: those that serve as containers; those that can be spread with peanut butter (and rolled in seed); and those that can function as hangers or other supports. Use your imagination to transform your everyday throwaways into useful objects.

A pair of scissors, a wire cutter, and pliers are usually all you need to complete any trash-transformation project. A handful of screw-in hooks or eyehooks for hanging, a spool of wire, and perhaps a piece of scrap wood to serve as a backing will round out your workshop for these projects.

Ask your kids for bright ideas about trash, too. One snowy winter day, when school was closed, my son and I made tube feeders out of cardboard paper towel tubes and paper plates. They weren't built to last, but they did feed some extra birds that day, and we both felt proud that the birds accepted our efforts. Since the process is easy, with no need for exactitude, and results are quick, with birds flocking to the new feeders fast, these projects are ideal for kids. Most

Recycle unwanted items into feeders, scoops, and other useful goods. A strong scissors or utility knife, a spool of wire, and some ingenuity are all you need.

projects are as simple as nailing an old plastic dinner plate to a post for a fruit feeder. Check the Suet and Fat entry on page 279 for ideas on using cans and plastic containers for holding the prized soft food.

I have a strong streak of scavenger in me, so I also keep an eye on the piles along the street on trash day. At the recycling center, I sometimes cart home more than I came in with. Once you start considering objects creatively, you'll find lots of potential in throwaways. I've reclaimed sections of lattice, clay drainpipe, and other utilitarian trash that is easy to recycle into posts and pedestals to hold feeders or birdbaths or to use as additions to the feeding station area. Trim the edges of a broken piece of lattice, for example, add a new frame of 1 × 4s for a finished look, mount it against a wall or privacy fence, and you have a great holder for half a dozen feeders. In my experience, local recycling centers and the individuals who generate curbside trash don't mind if you lighten their load, as long as you ask permission and don't leave a mess after sorting through the leavings.

Muffin-Tin Suet Sampler

Baking pans often remain durable and "perfectly good" long past their usefulness in the kitchen. Try your own recipes for special suet treats and serve them up in a dented or rusted muffin tin that was destined for the trash.

MATERIALS

Suet, melted or ground

Chopped orange pulp, chopped peanuts, or chopped raisins

Old muffin tin

Wooden kitchen skewers

Sturdy nail for hanging

Step 1. Combine suet with chopped orange pulp, chopped peanuts, chopped raisins, or other bird treats.

Step 2. Fill cups of muffin tin to the brim.

Step 3. After the suet hardens, insert a 3-inch piece of wooden skewer near the bottom of each cup to serve as a perch.

Step 4. Hang on nail from post or tree.

PROJECT

Apple-Core Mini-Wreath

You like the apple, but birds love the core. The remnants left over from making an apple pie include enough cores to make a treat for the birds.

MATERIALS

Floral wire

Apple cores

Step 1. Wrap two or three turns of floral wire around the first core.

Step 2. Repeat with the rest of the cores. Leave about ½ inch of space between cores to form a wreath; allow about 6 inches of wire between cores if you'd prefer to hang them garland-style along a fence.

Step 3. Bend the string of cores into a circle and wire the last core to the first one. Hang where birds can enjoy the seeds and bits of apple.

Step 4. If you've made a garland of cores, drape it horizontally along a fence or staple it vertically on a wooden post.

Chipped-Cup Mini-Feeders

Even badly chipped teacups can seem too pretty to simply toss out. Save those chipped beauties, and use them as a decorative set of feeders for holding special bird treats to add a touch of whimsy to your feeding station.

MATERIALS

Scrap lumber or plywood

Cup hooks

2 screw eyes

2 sturdy nails

Chipped teacups with handles intact

Walnuts, peanuts, hazelnuts, chopped almonds, or other nuts

Step 1. Cut a piece of scrap lumber to the size you desire—can vary to accommodate the number of teacups you have, the size of the space where you want to mount the feeder, or the size of the scrap wood you have on hand.

Step 2. Mark positions for the cup hooks, leaving 4 to 6 inches between them and space for cups to hang below them if your layout includes more than one row of cups. Screw in the cup hooks.

Step 3. Attach two screw eyes to top edge of board for hanging. Hang board from nails.

Step 4. Hang cups on cup hooks and fill with special treats for chickadees, titmice, and other small birds. Walnut meats, peanuts, hazelnuts, and chopped almond pieces all are appreciated.

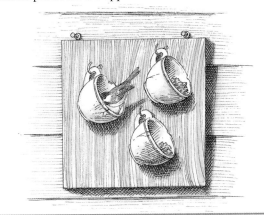

Squirrel IQ Test

Here's another use for the ever-versatile plastic soda bottle: Use it to test the intelligence of the squirrels in your yard! Warning: Genius squirrels may tire of being tested and chew through the bottle to reach its contents.

MATERIALS

Empty 20-ounce plastic soda bottle

Wire

Peanuts in shells

Step 1. Fill bottle with peanuts in the shells.

Step 2. Securely wire the uncapped bottle upside down to a post or railing.

Step 3. Watch squirrels reach inside to get the peanuts in position for removal.

Skillet Splasher

Is your nonstick skillet too scratched for further use as cookware? Give it new life as a birdbath with a sturdy "bowl" that is just the right depth and can stand up to freezing with no ill effects.

MATERIALS

Scratched nonstick skillet

Bricks, cinder blocks, or other items for base

Step 1. Remove the handle from the skillet to disguise the origins of your new birdbath.

Step 2. If pan is still slippery, scratch the bottom with a fork or sharp knife to give birds better footing.

Step 3. Set the pan on a double-layer stack of bricks (or on cinder blocks or other supports). Use whatever number of bricks looks best for the size of the pan.

Step 4. Fill with water to a depth of about 1½ inches.

Holiday Treats

Pizza boxes and other pieces of corrugated cardboard are sturdy enough to convert to other uses. Turn them into cheery holiday ornaments that your birds will appreciate, too.

MATERIALS

Pizza boxes or other corrugated cardboard

Wire or twine for hanging

Peanut butter

Bird seed or chopped nuts

Wire coat hanger (optional)

Step 1. Cut shapes, about 6 inches long, from the cardboard.

Step 2. Poke a hole through the top of each, string wire or twine through the hole, and tie in a loop.

Step 3. Coat one side of the shape lightly with peanut butter.

Step 4. Press into bird seed or chopped nuts in a rimmed cookie sheet.

Step 5. Hold by loop hanger and coat other side with peanut butter.

Step 6. Press into seed, being careful not to dislodge seeds on top.

Step 7. Hang ornaments individually on branches of trees or shrubs, or hang a few of them from a coat hanger and bend the top crook of the hanger into a loop that you can hook over a nail or branch.

Tree Seeds and Buds

Attract many kinds of birds at various times of the year

YOU CAN SEE why trees that bear large, meaty seeds, like acorns and nuts, and those with fleshy or juicy fruits, like crab apples, attract birds. Dining on these seeds and fruits fills a bird's belly fast. But smaller tree seeds and even tender buds are also relished by some birds, particularly crossbills, finches, game birds, and grosbeaks.

One winter day I was strolling around my yard when I noticed a flurry of tuliptree seeds drifting to the ground around me. This was odd because there was no wind to stir the tree, and at first I thought perhaps it was just the time for the conelike seedheads to shatter. Then I looked up into the top of the 100-foot tree and discovered a flock of about a dozen evening grosbeaks, quietly and industriously working at the cones to pull free individual seeds.

The strong, conical bills of grosbeaks are as efficient as a pair of pruners at nipping off buds of maples, ashes, and other trees, and even conifers aren't safe from their nibbling. I was pleased to host pine grosbeaks one year until I noticed that they were devouring the tender growing tips of my young pear tree.

Although dedicated scientists have done painstaking inventories of birds' stomach contents for decades, it can still be a surprise to see what your birds are dining on. When an irruption year brought common redpolls to my yard in Pennsylvania, I discovered that the birds enjoyed the plump buds of my lilac bushes as much as they liked the sunflower seeds at the feeder.

Look to the Trees

It's easy to forget about looking up as you wander your backyard, but if you do, you'll discover that birds are often above you. If they're not actively flitting after insects or combing the bark and branches, they may well be dining on the seeds still held on the tree or nipping off fat buds. Look down to find

The tender buds or tasty seeds of trees are favored foods of many birds, especially finches. Fluffy down from cottonwoods is often used as nest material.

evidence of birds at trees, too: Nipped branch tips on the willows at the garden pool may be the clue to grouse or turkeys. Doves, juncos, towhees, and other ground-feeding birds often pay close attention to the ground beneath trees, where seeds may have dropped from the branches above.

Keep a Record

I keep an informal diary to help me remember when to look for certain birds in my trees: In early spring, for example, I check my elms for pine siskins; in winter, I look for them in tulip trees. The data I collect from my own sightings of birds dining in my neighborhood trees also helps me select bird-attracting plants to add to the garden.

Tree Seeds and Buds for Birds

KEEP AN eye on the trees in your backyard and in your neighborhood, and you may spot birds munching on their seeds or buds. Double-check with your binoculars when you see a bird apparently feeding in a tree—it's fascinating to watch how various birds approach the task of freeing the seeds or reaching for buds. You may see other birds besides those listed here at trees; the wild foods that birds eat is an area that needs more study, and your own anecdotal notes are important. (Trees that bear acorns, nuts, cones, and fruits or berries are not included here.)

TREE SEEDS

Tree	Seed Eaters
Acacias (*Acacia* spp.)	Doves, quail
Maples and boxelders (*Acer* spp.)	Chickadees, prairie chickens, finches, grosbeaks, grouse, nuthatches, quail, wild turkeys
Alders (*Alnus* spp.)	Goldfinches, grouse, pine siskins, redpolls, woodcocks
Birches (*Betula* spp.)	Chickadees, crossbills, purple finches, common redpolls, pine siskins, fox sparrows, tree sparrows
Hornbeam (*Carpinus caroliniana*)	Bobwhites, grouse, pheasants, myrtle warblers
Catalpas (*Catalpa* spp.)	Cardinals, finches, grosbeaks
Ashes (*Fraxinus* spp.)	Cardinals, finches, grosbeaks, quail, wild turkeys
Sweetgum (*Liquidambar styraciflua*)	Bobwhites, chickadees, purple finches, goldfinches, white-throated sparrows, towhees, Carolina wrens
Tuliptree (*Liriodendron tulipifera*)	Redwing blackbirds, cardinals, chickadees, purple finches, goldfinches, evening grosbeaks
Magnolias (*Magnolia* spp.)	Towhees, red-eyed vireos, woodpeckers
Ironwood, hophornbeam (*Ostrya virginiana*)	Purple finches, rose-breasted grosbeaks, downy woodpeckers
Sycamores (*Platanus* spp.)	Finches
Aspens, poplars, cottonwoods (*Populus* spp.)	Crossbills, finches, quail
Mesquites (*Prosopis* spp.)	Doves, quail, ravens
Black locust (*Robinia pseudoacacia*)	Quail
Elms (*Ulmus* spp.)	Chickadees, purple finches, goldfinches, rose-breasted grosbeaks, grouse, pheasants, wild turkeys

Tree Seeds and Buds for Birds—*Continued*

TREE BUDS

Tree	Bud Eaters
Conifers (many species of *Abies, Picea,* and *Pinus*)	Crossbills, finches, grosbeaks
Maples (*Acer* spp.)	Cassin's finches, purple finches, goldfinches, grosbeaks
Birches (*Betula* spp.)	Prairie chickens, grouse
American hornbeam (*Carpinus caroliniana*)	Bobwhites, grouse, pheasants
Ashes (*Fraxinus* spp.)	Finches, grosbeaks
Aspens and poplars (*Populus* spp.)	Prairie chickens, purple finches, grouse, quail, Abert towhees
Cottonwoods (*Populus* spp.)	Pyrrhuloxia
Willows (*Salix* spp.)	Grosbeaks, grouse, redpolls
Elms (*Ulmus* spp.)	Cardinals, finches, grosbeaks, pine siskins

Trellises and Arbors

WHETHER YOU HAVE a large garden or a small one, adding height with trellises and arbors will make it look more interesting. These structures also supply more growing room because plants tend to go up, not out. Around the feeder area, trellises and arbors supply shade, serve as windbreaks, and block the force of winter rains and snow so that feeder birds can eat in a sheltered nook. The vines on these vertical supports give birds quick shelter, too, should danger threaten.

Another advantage to using trellises around your feeders is that they provide a visual barrier to territorial birds. Should an aggressive mockingbird decide to lay claim to its favorite feeder, you can install another feeder on the far side of the trellis or arbor barrier where other birds can eat in peace.

The more plants in your yard for food and shelter, the better for birds. Multiply your plantings by growing upward. Here American bittersweet climbs a trellis.

Best Plants for Bird Trellises

CHOOSE PLANTS to cover arbors and trellises using the same criteria as you would for other plantings in your bird-friendly yard. Select those that do double duty, offering a food source as well as shelter.

Native vines are an excellent choice for bird arbors because they have evolved along with the birds that use them. Their fruits ripen when birds need them most, and the tasty treats they provide stay edible into winter. Here are my four top picks for fast-growing, fruitful native vines:

American bittersweet (*Celastrus scandens*): A tough, twining vine hardy to Zone 2. The bright orange-and-red fruits are eaten by bluebirds, grouse, pheasants, quail, robins, and wild turkeys. Plant both a male and a female vine to assure fruiting.

Virginia creeper (*Parthenocissus quinquefolia*): A relative of Boston ivy, Virginia creeper is hardy to Zone 3 and has five-part leaves that glow translucent crimson in fall. Its clusters of deep blue berries on bright red stems are eagerly sought by many birds, including bluebirds, chickadees, flickers, great-crested flycatchers, nuthatches, robins, sapsuckers and other woodpeckers, sparrows, thrushes, thrashers, titmice, and vireos.

Greenbriers (*Smilax* spp.): An interesting and unusual choice. Native mostly to the eastern two-thirds of the country, these glossy-leaved, woody vines bear fleshy fruits that are favored by cardinals, catbirds, flickers, grouse, mockingbirds, pheasants, robins, sparrows, thrushes, wild turkeys, waxwings, pileated woodpeckers, and, in Florida, fish crows. Both thorny and smooth species are available for Zones 4 through 10. Some species are evergreen.

Wild grapes (*Vitis* spp.): Native to almost all parts of the country, except for the northern mountains. Wild grapes are vigorous, fast growers, and their usually tiny fruits are devoured with relish even when old and dried in winter. If you can't find a native wild grape, any cultivated variety will also attract birds. Grape lovers include bluebirds, cardinals, catbirds, purple finches, grackles, grosbeaks, jays, juncos, kingbirds, orioles, robins, sparrows, thrushes, woodpeckers—you get the idea. There are few birds that won't be tempted by grapes. All game birds, including doves, pheasants, quail, and turkeys also eat them readily.

Tube Feeders

ONE OF THE MORE RECENT INNOVATIONS in bird feeder technology, tube feeders were an instant hit when introduced a few decades ago and have remained popular ever since.

Why such universal acceptance? First, tube feeders are ideal for the frugal. They save you money because they conserve seed. Because birds pull out just a seed or two at a time, little is wasted to spills or messy eaters.

Tube feeders are easy to use, too. Slide up the lid, pour in the seed, and the feeder is stocked for as long as a few weeks, depending on the size of your feeder and the traffic it gets. With limited seating area, the seed lasts a long time.

Tube feeders are also the only practical way to offer niger seed, an extremely small and lightweight seed that gets lost in most seed mixes and is easily blown out of other feeders. Goldfinches, house finches, purple finches, redpolls, and pine siskins are regular customers at feeders filled with niger seed.

Another factor in the popularity of tube feeders may be that they are used only by small birds, including finches, redpolls, and pine siskins. Starlings and other larger perching birds can't get a grip on the short perches, and they're at least a slight deterrent to seed-seeking squirrels.

Seeds for Tube Feeders

The first tube feeders were fit for only niger seed, but today's models have adapted the design to accommodate larger seeds, such as seed mixes, sunflower seed, and even nuts.

Choose your tube feeders according to the kind of seed you want to serve in them. Of course, you can always include a variety of tube feeders at your feeding station! Multitube models can serve a mixed banquet all at once, with one tube holding niger, another millet or mixed seed, and a third sunflower seed.

Holding capacity isn't as important to keep in mind when you choose a commercial tube feeder because the seed is doled out slowly to a limited number of consumers. Still, bigger is better if you want to save yourself frequent refilling trips or if you plan to be away during the peak bird-feeding season from fall to early spring.

Tube Feeder Construction

Tube feeders are usually made with a plastic tube and metal lid, bottom stopper, and metal perches, although the materials may vary depending on the quality of the feeder. Feeders with metal guards around the seed openings help prevent the holes from becoming enlarged through use over time. Metal parts also add weight to the feeder, which helps keep it stable in winds that can rock and tilt the feeder and cause seed to spill.

Niger seed is one of the costlier bird foods, and I'm a real penny pincher, so I'm always on the lookout for ways to avoid waste. I've discovered that the longer the chain or hook attached to my tube feeder, the greater the arc the feeder will sway in when the wind blows—and that means a greater possibility of spilled seed. Instead of dangling my tube feeder on a chain, I prefer to hook the metal feeder handle directly to a stationary support, such as a bracket arm attached to a porch post, so that there is as little free play as possible. You can also mount some models atop a wood or metal post. If

A tube feeder with ports below the perches helps slow niger consumption by less-agile house finches. Goldfinches don't seem to mind dining upside down.

Goldfinches, pine siskins, and house finches feed in harmony at a tube feeder. Metal reinforcements prevent squirrels from enlarging the feeding holes.

you see your post-mounted feeder swaying, either you have giant moles at work or you'd better grab the earthquake preparedness kit.

Outwitting the Squirrels

If the squirrels in your neighborhood are particularly determined (or if my squirrels have been e-mailing them about tricks of the trade), they may try to gnaw their way into a tube feeder. A feeder that contains niger is of little interest to squirrels, but one that's chock-full of nuts, corn, peanuts, or other favored foods will certainly get their attention. Thin plastic walls are not much of a barrier to the incisors of a hungry squirrel, which can mean a new feeder for you and a full belly for your furry friend. If you suspect that squirrel attacks may be likely, try an all-metal tube feeder or add a baffle above the feeder to deter them—at least for a while.

Make a Wire Tube Feeder

You can make your own tube feeder from a cylinder of wire hardware cloth, sized to serve larger seeds such as sunflowers, peanuts, and corn. With this type of feeder, you don't need to include perches because chickadees, nuthatches, titmice, woodpeckers, and other birds can cling to the wire itself. I like to supply a perch near the bottom of the feeder, though, so that less athletic birds, such as cardinals, can get a bite to eat, too.

MATERIALS

½-inch mesh hardware cloth

2 jar lids of the same size

Wooden dowel

Wire for hanging

Duct tape

Step 1. Measure and cut a piece of ½-inch-grid hardware cloth to 14 inches high and 8 inches wide. Cut one end of the 14-inch side through the grids, so that loose ends are left on the cross wires.

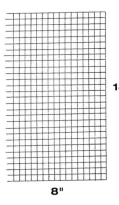

14"

8"

Step 2. Roll the wire so that the ends overlap to form a tube just slightly smaller in diameter than your jar lids. Bend the loose ends of the cross wires around the grids of the mesh where they meet. A needlenose pliers makes short work of this job. Wear gloves so you don't get poked by sharp wire ends.

Step 3. Insert a wooden dowel through the feeder, about 2 inches from the bottom of the feeder. Trim to 3-inch-long perches on either side of the wire feeder.

Step 4. Insert a strong wire through the sides of the feeder near the top; this serves as a handle for hanging.

Step 5. Cap the bottom of the feeder with a jar lid or other close-fitting cover. Tape to the wire with duct tape to hold it in place.

Step 6. Use another lid to serve as the feeder cap; this one need not be as close-fitting as the bottom cap. Fill the feeder with seed, close the feeder cap, and hang.

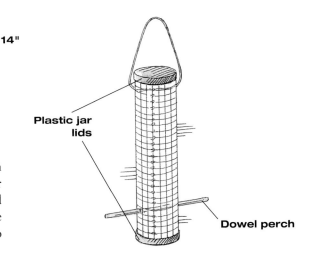

Plastic jar lids

Dowel perch

V

Vegetable Gardens and Birds

Attract many kinds of birds at various times of the year

ALTHOUGH BIRDS can be friends or foes in your vegetable garden, most of the time they're your good friends. When you notice a bird bustling through your garden, don't assume it's there to grab a strawberry or a kernel of corn—it's probably searching beneath the leaves for insects to feed to its hungry babies.

When veggie gardens are reaching their peak in early to midsummer, bird life is at its busiest, with many a shrub and tree holding a nest of baby birds. This is perfect timing for us gardeners because parent birds with a nest near the garden will quickly adopt our patch as part of their regular food-finding beat.

Nestlings need soft foods such as fat caterpillars, beetles, ants, and aphids. Every 10 minutes or so, there's another baby bird in the brood waiting to be fed, so parent birds are almost constantly on food patrol. Catbirds, song sparrows, and wrens are just three of the many species that frequent vegetable gardens in search of insects, and practically any bird in your neighborhood may turn up in your garden. I've even seen purple martins, which spend nearly all their time nabbing insects from the air, plucking squash bugs from my pumpkin vines without ever alighting.

Bring On the Birds

Because birds do such a good job of controlling pests in vegetable gardens, you'll want to do everything you can to encourage them to visit yours. The vegetation alone will attract birds because they know there are bound to be bugs there. Even though you may do a fine job of hand-picking beetles and other

Provide housing for birds, and they'll gladly patrol your garden for pests. Some birds may also nibble tender sprouts; be ready to discourage them if necessary.

pests, you're bound to overlook some creepy-crawlies, and those are the ones birds will zero in on.

Put shrubs on the side. A vegetable garden is typically set in an isolated sunny spot, surrounded by lawn grass. To make your veggie garden more bird-friendly, try planting a corridor of shrubs (raspberries and blackberries, perhaps) nearby, so that birds can move to and from the garden in safety.

Set up a nearby feeder. A feeder near the garden is a good idea, too, especially in fall and winter. That's when birds will move from the feeder to the garden itself to pick over the soil for any weed seeds or slumbering insects. Ground-feeding birds are what you want to attract to this area, so make the feeder a low-level tray and fill it with millet, flax, and other seeds favored by doves, juncos, native sparrows, and towhees.

Plant a nest box in your garden. House wrens, which are remarkably unafraid of humans, may quickly adopt a nesting box mounted on a post right in your garden—which gives them easy access to creeping, crawling food. The wrens that lived in the birdhouse in my garden were particularly adept at keeping the cabbage loopers from devouring my broccoli and cabbage.

Install the birdhouse in an area of the garden that has at least 4 feet of private space around it, so you won't disturb the birds at their nest. This is a great place to sprinkle a "surprise garden" packet of mixed annuals that won't require much tending from you. Wrens are vocal birds and quick to voice their displeasure, so if you find your wrens scolding you with "Chirrs" and rattling sounds, back off quickly. If your garden is small, place the nest box nearby instead of in the middle of it to make the real estate more appealing to potential tenants.

Add water. A nearby birdbath will also draw helpful birds to your garden. The old-fashioned pedestal-type bath makes an appealing centerpiece, and nearby garden plants will appreciate the extra water you splash on them when refilling the bath.

Keep an eye out for interesting and unusual visitors in your garden. If you live near woods, you may spot fox sparrows, thrushes, or towhees ferreting out insect food on the ground beneath your plants. Even grosbeaks, orioles, and bright-colored tanagers may visit a vegetable garden to glean what they can. In times of drought, when insects are especially drawn to your succulent, well-watered veggies, birds will soon follow because the pickings are much better there than on the parched vegetation in the wild.

Keep Out! This Means You!

Occasionally, birds will enjoy raiding your garden for seeds or plants; for example, birds may forget their good manners if you're growing sweet corn. Newly planted seeds and some sprouts, such as those of peas and lettuce, may also bring in birds to feast on your prized plantings. If you plant strawberries in your vegetable patch, you may come out to pick your morning bowl of berries and find the berries marred by beak marks or, worse, completely consumed by your bird buddies.

The best way to protect your garden from losses is to use barriers to deter marauders. Netting, floating row covers, and wire cages (for berry bushes) will absolutely keep birds from getting even a nibble. Less drastic measures, such as making a scarecrow, hanging cat's head cutouts, or distributing rubber snakes among your crops may discourage birds for a while, but when the devices prove harmless, the birds will move in again. Flashy strips of silver Mylar or Grandma's trick of hanging aluminum pie pans to dangle in the sun may also prove effective, at least for a while.

Appreciating House Sparrows

THE VEGETABLE garden is one place where I appreciate hosting house sparrows. When the lean-to shed near my vegetable garden had a thriving colony of these community nesters, I was sure they were planning some kind of raid on the patch, though I couldn't imagine what. I just couldn't imagine that house sparrows would be beneficial birds, but that's exactly what they proved themselves to be. When cucumber beetles reached dangerous numbers, they spent a couple of days snapping up every beetle they could find. Same thing when Colorado potato beetles moved in.

In Boston, Massachusetts, I saw more evidence of helpful house sparrows in a thriving urban garden. Every square inch of the backyard was crammed with crops, from oregano to heirloom tomatoes to grapes and figs. The gardeners kept a small patio bare of everything except a couple of chairs and a scattering of bread crumbs. "Why the bread?" I asked. "Sit down and see," they invited. As I watched, house sparrows approached from neighboring rooftops, drawn to the bread. After the birds squabbled over the last crumbs, they moved into the garden and gobbled up invisible insects like a flock of animated vacuum cleaners. Then they were off, back to another busy day among the Boston rooftops.

Viburnums

Attract cardinals, catbirds, robins, sparrows, thrashers, waxwings

BERRIES ARE THE BIGGEST bird draw that a viburnum offers—but they're not the only bird-friendly feature of these plants. The berries come in red, blue, and orange, and robins, thrashers, waxwings, and other berry-eating birds love them. Viburnums are a diverse group of shrubs and small trees—there are more than 150 different kinds. They bear plentiful blooms and some have fall foliage that's as brilliant as a sugar maple.

Viburnum foliage is dense, making the shrubs a protected location where birds can search for insects or hide nests. Cardinals, catbirds, and sparrows all like to nest in viburnums. These shrubs are fast-growing, too, so they're a fine choice for a hedge or shrub grouping to provide the cover that makes your yard more appealing to birds in general. A mixed group of viburnums staggers the berry-ripening schedule, so birds don't clean off all the bushes in one fell swoop.

Plant breeders have developed dozens of garden-worthy viburnum cultivars, but in some cases, changes due to breeding have caused the berries to lose their appeal to birds. If you want surefire berries for birds, stick to the native species that grow in your region. Don't discount the cultivars altogether, though. Even if birds don't eat the berries, the clusters of small flowers will attract a myriad of nectar-seeking insects. Those insects will draw insect-eating birds such as vireos and warblers to the shrubs.

Six Bird-Friendly Native Viburnums

IT'S UNFORTUNATE, but true, that native viburnums are not as widely available in nurseries and garden centers as introduced species. And the introduced species very often are not attractive to our native birds. To get you started on your search for homegrown viburnums that birds will come flocking to, here are six fine viburnums to seek out:

Mapleleaf viburnum (*V. acerifolium*): An ideal cover or hedge plant, this 4- to 6-foot-tall, multi-stemmed shrub often spreads by suckers to form a small colony. Pretty maplelike leaves are beautiful in fall, when they turn crimson and purple. Many small clusters of white, mildly fragrant flowers ripen into red fruits that gradually turn black. Hardy to Zone 3.

Arrowwood (*V. dentatum*): One of two viburnums commonly called arrowwood (the other is *V. rafinesquianum*), this large, fast-growing shrub reaches its mature height of 8 to 15 feet in as little as 3 years. Its new branches are remarkably straight and were long ago used as arrow shafts. Like most viburnums, its shape is undistinguished—this one has an upright form widening at the top. Fuzzy, white, slightly fragrant flowers bloom in spring, followed by deep blue berry clusters held above reddish foliage in fall. Hardy to Zone 2.

Nannyberry (*V. lentago*): Tall shrub or small tree grows to 25 feet tall and has creamy, fragrant flowers followed by clusters of red fruits that turn black when fully ripe. Beautiful red fall color. Hardy to Zone 2.

Black haw (*V. prunifolium*): Branching, tall shrub or small tree grows to 25 feet tall, with rounded oval leaves that flash red and yellow in fall. Deep blue, nearly black fruits in autumn. Hardy to Zone 3.

Southern blackhaw (*V. rufidulum*): A tall species that may eventually grow into a small tree to 30 feet tall. Lovely shiny, rounded leaves and checkered bark on older trees. Large clusters of sweet-scented white flowers, followed by clusters of dark blue fruits. Fall color varies; may show red and yellow. Hardy to Zone 5.

American cranberrybush (*V. trilobum*): An eye-catcher in fall, when heavy crops of red fruit glow on this upright, 9-foot-tall shrub. White spring flowers may have some fragrance; fall color can be striking or muted, in shades of yellow to red. Hardy to Zone 2.

Viburnums differ greatly in hardiness, although most can adapt to a range of soil, moisture, and light conditions. Some species, such as the blue-black fruited American natives nanny-berry viburnum (*Viburnum lentago*) and *V. rafinesquianum* flourish as far north as Zone 2; others, including many of the Chinese species and cultivars, are far more tender, surviving only to Zone 9. In general, most species are hardy to at least Zone 6. Check the catalogs and nurseries of native plants specialists to find viburnums that are adapted to the climate, conditions, and bird life of your area. (See "Resources" on page 348 for mail-order possibilities.)

Viburnums' flowers attract birds indirectly by attracting insects. The twiggy branches also make good cover for birds like this white-crowned sparrow.

Vines

Attract many kinds of birds at various times of the year

FOOD AND COVER ARE THE NAME of the game when it comes to attracting birds, and flowering vines can provide both. Planting annual and perennial vines is also a great way to add an interesting new feature to your garden or yard. You can plant a vine in a flowerbed to add a tall accent or to create the impression of a "wall" between one area of your yard and another. A trellised vine can also serve as a windbreak or as shade to protect your feeding area from the glare of summer sun and the brunt of blustery winter winds.

Annual Vines

Annual vines grow as fast as Jack's beanstalk, always a plus if you like almost-instant gratification from a garden. Here are some ideas for adding bird-attracting annual vines to your yard. It's best to start from seeds sown in place because many annual vines grow a deep taproot that doesn't transplant well. For faster germination, soak the seeds overnight in a saucer of water to soften their seed coat and keep the planting area moist until they sprout. A sunny spot of average, well-drained soil is all you need for success with annual vines. Avoid fertilizing, which encourages leafy growth and can delay flowering.

- Easy-to-grow climbing beans are a terrific vine for birds. Plenty of insects like to feed on their foliage, and the birds will feast on those juicy morsels and feed them to their nestlings, too. The flowers of scarlet runner bean (*Phaseolus coccineus*) will bring hordes of hummingbirds to your yard.

- Purple-flowered hyacinth bean (*Lablab purpurea*) is great for covering a wall of your house or a masonry retaining wall; its dense, high-climbing vines are so sturdy that birds may be tempted to nest there as well as seek shelter in them.

- The flowers of morning glories (*Ipomoea* spp.) and cardinal creeper (*I. × multifida*) attract hummingbirds, and Carolina wrens and other small birds may nest among the thicket of stems. Use these vines to cover chain-link fences or other spots that could use some camouflaging greenery. In just a few weeks, you'll transform ho-hum features into corners of bird-attracting beauty.

- Climbing roses, while not truly vines, provide similar benefits for birds: a safe place to perch, plus insects on flowers and foliage, and tasty roseships in the fall and winter. Climbing 'New Dawn' is one of the best because of its disease resistance and long, arching stems.

- Birdhouse gourds, pumpkins, and squash cover fences and trellises with superfast greenery, and they offer a bonus at harvest time. You can make gourds into seed scoops, feeders, or birdhouses, while pumpkins and squash yield seeds for winter bird feeding.

If your yard is short on shrubs and other permanent cover, install trellises of annual vines near your feeding station so that birds can make a quick getaway when danger threatens. Bathing birds will also appreciate a simple lattice trellis of annual vines near the birdbath, where they can find secure perching places among the vines to preen their feathers after bathing. Hummingbirds and mockingbirds like to perch on trellises, regardless of what vine is growing there because they can get the high vantage point that these feisty, territorial birds desire.

Perennial Vines

Annual vines die away each fall, but when you plant perennial vines, they grow bigger and better every year, as well as heavier. Weight is something to keep in mind when you're deciding what vines to grow and what kind of support structure to use.

> A trellised vine creates a beautiful backdrop for a birdbath and gives wet birds a safe place to dry off and preen.

Dress up a fence with handsome Virginia creeper. In fall, the dark blue berries with their pretty red stems attract wonderful surprises like this hermit thrush.

Plant them in spring, starting with potted plants to get a head start. Although it is possible to grow perennial vines from seed, results are two to three years swifter and much easier if you begin with potted plants. Choose your perennial vines according to the conditions of your yard: Some thrive in shade, while others flourish in full sun. All will grow well in average, well-drained soil. Most of the plant's energy will go into producing roots the first year, so don't be disappointed to see little new growth aboveground. By the second growing season, your perennial vine should be settled in and ready to push out new growth in earnest. A wisteria vine or trumpetvine (*Campsis radicans*) may look puny when you put it in the ground, but in a few years, it may be threatening to swamp your yard like some tropical nightmare. Of course, most birds would like nothing better!

Most perennial vines are vigorous growers, but they are easy to keep in bounds with a haircut every now and then. Pruning perennial vines is easiest in winter, after the vine has dropped its leaves and you can easily see the branch structure. But you can keep established plants in bounds by snipping them back with pruners at any time of year if they stray from their supporting trellis. Don't be shy about cutting back a perennial vine; these hardy specimens will quickly recover from even a drastic pruning session. Usually, nipping back side branches is all the pruning you'll need to do. But you can even cut a mature vine to the ground and expect vigorous regrowth.

Exploring perennial vines pays off for both gardeners and birds. As with an annual vine, a trellised perennial vine adds height to your garden. The dense growth makes it a good choice for creating a shady nook to shelter a garden bench or to protect a bird feeder. The tangled stems deter predators, making it a sought-after site for nesting and roosting birds. Catbirds, for instance, often seek a vine to hold their cupped nest.

Vining Vegetables

Because it's cover and insects that attract birds to vines (plus any edible fruit), some of the plants you relegate to the vegetable garden are worth considering in other areas. My favorite veggie vine is the birdhouse gourd, not because of the gourds it yields for musical shakers or bird dwellings, but because it has delicate white flowers, as beautiful as any

> Even dead or dormant vines benefit birds: They provide shelter, roosting spots, and nesting material.

poppy, that open in the evening. Vining squash, melons, and pumpkins also make a good, quick fence cover—and you can serve the seeds to birds and squirrels later. You can even grow cherry tomatoes as a vine—just keep tying the stems to a fence or trellis as they grow. The plump tomato hornworms that occasionally plague the plants are a fine snack for catbirds, wrens, and other garden friends.

One year, a particularly energetic gourd vine I grew outstretched its trellis, crawled across the roof of the house, and clambered high into the branches of a maple overhead. Amazed at its prowess, I let it ramble. In fall, when all that was left was a tangle of bare stems, the vine became an access route to my feeders. Chickadees, jays, and downy woodpeckers, among others, used the ladder of dead, twisted stems to move from the sheltering treetop to the deck feeder.

Off-Season Vine Care

Birds still find vines useful even after the stems are dead or the leaves have dropped because they pro-

---

Vines to Try

PLAYING WITH perennial vines holds interesting possibilities for the bird-friendly yard. Try these ideas when you're deciding what to plant.

■ Native perennial vines are often overlooked, but there are many good choices among them. Passionflowers (*Passiflora* spp.), for instance, support butterflies as well as birds. Natives are easier to care for and weather extremes of climate better than

most imported plants. Another big advantage to choosing regionally native vines—or native shrubs, trees, and perennials—is that you'll avoid introducing or contributing to ecological disasters. Japanese honeysuckle (*Lonicera japonica*), anyone? Or maybe a nice little sprout of kudzu (*Pueraria lobata*)? Birds find both these introduced species very useful, but these rogues have become a bane to gardeners and wildflower enthusiasts.

■ Think like a bird when choosing vines for your yard, and you'll find many good selections that will suit your own taste, too. The perennial morning glory known as blue dawn flower (*Ipomoea indica*), a tender perennial hardy only to Zone 9, is perfect for covering an arbor and attracting birds to its sheltering tangle of stems. Its ethereal blue flowers will lift any gardener's heart. Grapevines (*Vitis* spp.) and some clematis species (*Clematis* spp.) are also ideal bird plants.

vide shelter and places to perch. A chain-link fence covered in morning glories, for instance, has value even in winter, when the vines have dried to tan, twisting stems. Sparrows and other birds often use the remains of annual vines as a place to gather on fall and winter days, and the branches of honeysuckle or other perennial vines may host a congregation of birds and even shelter them at night. Another advantage to letting annual vines stand is that they will drop their seeds, giving you a fresh crop of volunteers next season without spending a penny! Of course, if you prefer a tidier look to your yard, you can cut back your annual vines at the end of the growing season and replant them next year.

For the most benefit to birds, let perennial vines stand all winter as a roosting haven and windbreak. Prune them back into shape if desired in very early spring. Nearly all perennial vines bloom on "new wood," that is, stems that sprout from older branches in spring, so you won't have to worry about snipping off next season's flowers when you prune. Consider how severely grapevines in vineyards are routinely pruned—allowing only a few short branches on the main stem of the vine—and you'll see that vines are forgiving plants. Even if you should sacrifice flowers, the vines will still attract birds with their abundant insect-hiding foliage and sheltering stems.

Reduce maintenance chores for trellises and arbors by using supports made of wood that can weather naturally or weather-resistant metal or PVC. Plastic trellises and arbors continue to improve from the early days when they looked flimsy and fake. Many of today's plastic structures are almost indistinguishable from classic painted wood, and they come in plain or fancy styles and price ranges. Avoid painted supports for perennial vines because you'll discover it's tricky work to touch up the paint when there's a vine wrapped around the posts. Check your trellises and arbors in early spring to make sure they are still firmly seated in the ground; repair any weak parts if necessary by replacing or bracing damaged sections.

Walnuts

Attract chickadees, jays, nuthatches, titmice, woodpeckers

WANT TO HAND-TAME A CHICKADEE? Invest in a pound of walnuts. Before you reach the bottom of the bag, you'll have a little bird nibbling nuts right out of the palm of your hand.

Walnuts are a welcome treat for many birds, including jays, nuthatches, titmice, and woodpeckers as well as chickadees. Of course, your bushy-tailed "friends" also adore them, and that means you'll want to dole them out a bit at a time to prevent squirrels or chipmunks from skedaddling with bulging cheeks, leaving a suspiciously empty feeder in their wake.

Serving Up Walnuts

Birds will quickly snatch up big walnut pieces, but they will fly away from the feeder to a tree limb or other protected spot where they can eat the meat bit by bit. If you want the birds to linger, use a rolling pin to break the nuts into smaller chunks before you put them in your feeders. If you'd rather sharpen your skills at bird watching away from the feeder, put out larger pieces and follow the birds with your eyes or binoculars as they fly off to a tree, and then watch them break the nut down to size.

Shelled nuts are best at the feeder, but birds also appreciate broken pieces of walnuts still in the shell.

It's fun to watch how skillfully they extricate the nutmeats from the shell, especially black walnuts (*Juglans nigra*), which don't yield their tasty morsels easily. If you've ever tried to clean a bucket of black walnuts, you'll appreciate the finesse and sometimes frustration with which birds attack the nut.

Birds like both English (*J. regia*) and black walnuts. If you're lucky enough to have your own tree, collect some nuts (quickly, before the squirrels do!), and store them away for winter bird feeding. Black walnut is a native American tree, and the nuts are often available free for the asking along country roadsides (do be sure to ask permission). Whack the nuts with a hammer to break them for the bird feeder. Wear rubber gloves if you're handling black walnuts; the husks and shells will stain unprotected fingers deep brown. If you've managed to collect a large amount of black walnuts, you can crack them quickly by driving over them. Don't try this if an unblemished driveway is important to you—the nuts will stain concrete, gravel, and any other material.

Shelled walnuts are widely available, but you'll generally find the best prices at supermarket bulk-food bins or through co-ops or health-food stores. During prime baking season from Thanksgiving to

Strategy for Survival

WALNUTS AND other members of the *Juglans* genus have evolved a highly effective way of making sure their species survives: Their roots exude a toxin called juglone that stunts or kills many other plants that dare to trespass near the tree. Although walnuts, especially the black walnut, are notorious for this "allelopathic" defense system, other plants use the same trick, with chemical toxins that differ according to the plant. Sunflowers, for instance, will inhibit the growth of many other plant neighbors; even the seed hulls can have a negative effect on other plants.

In most cases, the reaction is mild enough to go unnoticed by us gardeners. But black walnut is a real thug when it comes to claiming its space. The chemical lingers in the soil for years after a tree has been cut down. Even its leaves and nuts are toxic to other plants to a lesser degree, which is a good reason to be tidy and clean up the shells after the birds are done with them. Wood chips from a black walnut tree can also have a negative effect on other plants.

Before planting a black walnut, think about where its roots will reach. Keep the tree well away from prized flowerbeds and other ornamentals, and forget about planting your nut grove near the veggie garden: Tomatoes are highly sensitive to the black walnut's warfare.

Christmas, stores often sell walnuts at discounted prices. Store extras in your refrigerator to prevent the oil from turning rancid at room temperature.

Nocturnal Nut Nibblers

A nighttime offering of walnuts, spread in the feeder after dark, especially in fall and winter, may bring you the enchanting surprise of a flying squirrel in your feeder. These gentle, dark-eyed creatures are unusually fearless around humans, and if you approach quietly, they will let you watch close up while they eat. They're particularly fond of walnuts.

Start a Shady Grove

If you have been offering whole walnuts in your feeders or if you have walnut trees in the neighborhood, you may already have a start of a backyard walnut grove, thanks to the efforts of your friends,

the squirrels. Both English and black walnuts will sprout from whole nuts, a neat trick to try yourself, especially if you let the kids help: Just poke a few whole walnuts, still intact in their shells, 3 inches deep into the soil, spacing them several feet apart. To keep squirrels from digging up your nuts, lay a piece of wire mesh hardware cloth over the site.

You can also buy walnut trees from catalogs and garden centers. English walnuts grow into large, graceful shade trees with wide-spreading branches, while black walnuts are more upright in shape. Birds also favor the related Japanese walnut, or heartnut (*Juglans ailanthifolia*). Several cultivars are available that yield nuts with thinner shells or larger meats than the usual unimproved variety. Choose a cultivar that is hardy in your climate (English walnuts thrive through Zone 5; black walnuts into Zone 4), and plant it in a sunny spot where it will have room to spread its limbs.

PROJECT

Bird Treat Balls

Birds—and other feeder visitors—adore these tasty balls shaped from walnut pieces and chopped peanuts. To make the treat extra special for mockingbirds, cedar waxwings, and Carolina wrens, mix in dried cherries along with the nuts. Unflavored gelatin holds the treats together, and a sprig of holly berries adds a festive touch. Treats such as this one are best offered only in cold weather, when you can rely on the gelatin to hold the goodies together.

MATERIALS

Packet unflavored gelatin

1 quart walnut pieces

1 quart chopped peanuts

1 to 2 cups dried cherries (optional)

Wire for hanging

Sprig of holly berries (optional)

Step 1. Mix the packet of unflavored gelatin according to the label. In another bowl, combine walnut pieces, chopped peanuts, and dried cherries (if desired).

Step 2. Spread the nut mixture onto a cookie sheet.

Step 3. Fill a squirt bottle with the liquid gelatin, and spritz the nut mix liberally. Stir the mixture with your hands, and mold into 3-inch-diameter balls.

Step 4. Push a length of wire through each ball, bending at the bottom to prevent slippage and making a loop at the top for hanging. Top the ball with a sprig of holly berries.

Step 5. Place the balls in the freezer to solidify them; store in cool conditions until use.

Yellow-Rumped Warbler

WARBLERS ARE TINY BIRDS, chickadee-size but slimmer, that live almost entirely on a diet of insects. Dozens of species roam the country from spring through early fall, but most of us rarely see them because the birds pursue their daily bugs far above our heads, in the treetops. Learning the warblers is a challenge because the little birds are perpetual-motion machines, flitting from one branch to another before you can get your binoculars glued on them. This would be okay if each species was a bird of a different color: a red one, a blue one, a yellow one. But the rest of the bad news is that many warblers look alike, being yellowish green with only tiny details—an eye ring here, a wing band there—to tell them apart. Worse yet, in fall, the males lose their distinguishing bright colors and become the notorious "confusing fall warblers."

Sorting out warblers is an intriguing challenge, but you won't have to worry about it at the feeder. Of the 40 or so wood warblers, only 3 or 4 species eat anything other than insects, which means you can eliminate most of them right off the bat. To make matters even simpler, only one species is more than a rare visitor to feeders: the yellow-rumped warbler.

The myrtle and the Audubon's races of the yellow-rumped warbler are almost identical, but the myrtle has a white throat and the Audubon's throat is yellow. Named for its fondness for wax myrtle and the related bayberries (*Myrica* spp.), the myrtle warbler ranges across the country but is most abundant near the coasts. The Audubon's breeds across the West, retreating westward and southward in winter. Poison ivy berries are another favorite of these birds. Whenever I

Once known as the myrtle warbler, the yellow-rumped warbler frequents the coasts in winter, where it feasts on myrtle berries. Suet may attract it to the feeder.

spot one of these plants with ripe fruit, I pause for a few minutes, keeping my ears alert for the distinctive call note, a low-pitched "Chuck."

Warbler Behavior

Look for the flash of white in the tail and wings and the eye-catching yellow rump, easily visible as the well-named bird flits among branches or hovers briefly to probe a likely spot or snatch a berry. In winter, when bands of chickadees, creepers, and kinglets roam the woodlands and backyards, a myrtle warbler or two may accompany them.

I never see yellow-rumped warblers at the feeders until fall, no doubt because insect food is so abundant in other seasons. At the feeder, insect eaters love suet, and yellow-rumped warblers are no exception. I spread chopped bits of suet in an open tray to tempt them and Carolina wrens, although they will also peck the fat from a suet holder.

WARBLER FEEDER FOODS

- American persimmon (*Diospyros virginiana*) fruits
- Bayberries (*Myrica* spp.)
- Figs
- Red cedar (*Juniperus virginiana*) berries
- Suet
- Sumac (*Rhus* spp.) berries

Water Features

You may have noticed that the species that come to dine at your feeders are just a fraction of the birds that live in or pass through your area. Many birds ignore feeding stations, preferring to forage for natural food on their own. So while you can realistically hope for every woodpecker under the sun to visit your feeder, waiting for wood warblers to drop in from the sky is unrealistic. Like other nonfeeder birds, warblers feed almost entirely on insects, and no matter what delicacies you offer, you can't compete with the largesse of Mother Nature. Flycatchers, tanagers, and vireos will largely be no-shows, too.

The sound of trickling, dripping, or gently flowing water is music to birds' ears. Song sparrows and many other bird bathers will regularly visit shallow, moving water.

The best way to entice these hard-to-get birds to your yard is with water. All birds need H_2O for drinking, and nearly all birds enjoy a splashing bath in fresh water. Birds are quick to visit natural ponds, streams, and other areas, as well as backyard water features, but they are also adept at making do with even a temporary source of water. After a rain, or when snow melts, they will flock to a shallow puddle. Even a melting icicle may slake their thirst. Watch your garden after a rain, and you may be lucky enough to spot a chickadee, hummingbird, or other small feathered creature sipping or even splashing in the thin layer of water held by a cupped leaf. Dew supplies many birds with necessary liquid, too.

Guaranteed to Please

Water is so irresistible that the sound of it dripping or burbling or splashing is a guaranteed draw, no matter where you live. Not only will it bring regular customers to the bath day after day, but it will also tempt migrants in spring and fall and unusual backyard visitors any time of year.

One summer, during a drought, visiting birds overwhelmed a small bubbling "spring" I created at ground level. Bobwhites jockeyed for space with mourning doves, wood thrushes shyly waited until the bluebirds finished drinking, and goldfinches were a noisy, constant presence. Cedar waxwings perched on nearby shrubs, awaiting the unspoken agreement of the flock to descend en masse. At daybreak, it wasn't unusual to see a plain-red summer tanager sipping beside a red-and-black scarlet tanager—both species among the earliest visitors. Phoebes and flycatchers visited late in the afternoon, and in the heat of the day, bank swallows and barn swallows traveled from their colony a quarter-mile away to quench their thirst.

My traditional pedestal-type birdbath was not nearly so successful as the water feature that attracted birds with the quiet murmur of running water. The birdbath still attracted plenty of catbirds, doves, finches, and robins, but the naturalistic water feature got the lion's share.

Keep It Shallow

It feels great to us to sink into hot water up to the chin, but birds don't feel safe in anything but shallow water. Knee-deep is perfect; belly-deep is scary. If a bird loses its footing in deep water, it can quickly become helpless and thus vulnerable to attack or to drowning. No wonder shallow water with secure footing is so important!

Here's yet another place to take a lesson from the way birds behave in the wild. Keep your eyes open for bathing birds, and you'll soon see that shallow places attract them. Lakes hold no appeal, except around the very edges, and then usually for drinking, not bathing. Isolated puddles are the top temptation for birds—an idea you can mimic in your own yard very successfully. Like people who have a fear of the vastness of the ocean, birds seem to feel safer when their bathing spot is finite. At creeks, you will see them splashing in the small stretches of quiet, shallow water sheltered by surrounding rocks—not in the wide open areas.

Bath Mat for Birds

Think rough when designing a water feature or selecting a birdbath. A nonslippery surface gives birds a feeling of security just as a rubber bath mat provides that for you in your bathtub.

The most beautiful birdbath in the world will stand unused if the surface beneath the water or on the rim is slick metal or glazed pottery. If birds can't get a grip when they land on the edge, they are unlikely to risk stepping down into the bath. I learned this lesson the hard way after buying a beautiful birdbath glazed cobalt blue—my favorite color. It made a pretty yard ornament, but birds wouldn't stop to sip until I covered the blue interior with a layer of rough sandstone that let them feel safe.

Concrete, sandstone and other rough-surfaced rock, and synthetic materials topped with a grainy surface are ideal for birdbaths. Vinyl pond liners,

Songbirds like this blue grosbeak prefer the safety of shallow water and a nonslip surface for bathing. Create water features that slope gradually at edges.

smooth metal or ceramic saucers, and slippery plastic containers are trouble, from a bird's perspective. Although they may visit a water feature with these surfaces, it will only be when they can't find water elsewhere.

Keep It Low

You won't find natural water at waist height unless it's dropping over a cliff. Water pools near the ground, and that's the first place birds look for it.

Anything you can do to recreate natural circumstances will increase the numbers and kinds of birds that visit your water features. Setting up a bath at ground level is an easy first step. See the Birdbaths entry on page 19 for more details on creating a simple low-level bathing area.

Best Water Features for Birds

Once you're ready to graduate from a simple pedestal or hanging birdbath, your next thought is likely to be of a garden pool. Now that even discount stores are stocking preformed garden pools, the hobby of water gardening is available to anyone who can invest a weekend's work and around $100. That's all it takes to add the pleasure of a permanent water feature to your yard. A single free-form or more formal pool, a suitable pump, a few hours of digging, and the basics are in place.

Before you leap for the shovel, though, consider the benefits of a garden pool to birds. Remember what's important to them—shallow water and a good drip—and you'll see that a garden pool is actually not very effective as a bathing place for your feathered visitors. The water is too deep. Worse yet, instead of a gently sloping approach, it drops almost instantly from the rim to a depth that birds will avoid.

You can alter a garden pool to serve birds better, but it's probably easier to turn your sights to a different kind of water feature. Create a bath just for birds that imitates the shallow, protected wild places they seek.

Design Considerations

Seeing things from a bird's point of view is vital when you're choosing a water feature to add to your yard, but don't forget to factor in your own sense of style, too. Birds won't notice if you arrange the rocks around the water casually or symmetrically in a formal style—but *you* will. A rippling "stream" or naturalistic waterfall is perfect for an informal garden or country look. But if your tastes run to straight-edged beds and a more controlled appearance, an informal water feature would stick out like

A water-lily pond is too deep for bird bathing. But it will attract nonfeeder birds like this prothonotary warbler that come to dine on insects found around the water.

Old Faithful. In a more formal garden, a rectangular pool with a gentle bubbler would be more at home.

When you shop for ready-made water features, you'll find products that run the gamut from unabashed tackiness to elegant simplicity, and every stop in between. Before the plastic revolution, which has put good taste (and bad taste) in the hands of the masses, choices were much more limited. "The shell

Improving a Pool for the Birds

INCREASE THE accessibility of your garden pool by making these improvements to a standard pre-formed installation. All will provide bird visitors with a secure place to perch while drinking or access to shallow water for bathing.

- Lay rocks into one end of the pool, so that their surfaces are just below water level, with part of the rock above the water. This will give birds a place to stand for drinking and perhaps a place to splash.

- Leave spaces between some of the rocks around the rim of the pool to provide a sheltered nook where birds can get a drink or wet a feather.

- Place potted aquatic plants close to the edge of the pool, in the water, so that the surface of their containers extends to or very near the rim of the pool.

Birds may use the pots' edges as perches.

- Pile a wide plastic container, such as a dishpan or kitty-litter tray, with rough stones or gravel, mounding it higher in the center. Settle the container onto bricks or an overturned pot beneath the water, so that the heaped stones in the center of the container are above water level, while those at the edges are just under water.

of the giant clam (*Tridacna gigas*) makes a most attractive birdbath," suggests one older book on my shelf, noting that garden-supply shops can supply specimens. The run on giant clams may have contributed to today's scarcity. They are now an endangered species, and apparently those old birdbaths didn't last because I can't remember ever seeing one of these natural wonders outside a museum.

Buy It or Build It

Thanks to the buying power of backyard bird watchers, all sorts of great water features are on the market, with more added every year. Some are for connoisseurs, such as estate-quality cast iron constructions that cost about the same as college tuition. Others are designed for everyone, with lightweight plastics that will give several years of good use.

If you like working with your hands, you may prefer the creativity of making your own water features instead of the convenience of buying ready-made ones. Working with concrete or PVC liner material to make a permanent puddle is as messy as making mud pies, and just as much fun. Once you give it a try, you may decide to graduate to making a recycling stream or even a waterfall—both entirely possible projects for even a rank novice. I can testify to this: I started with common sense and a memory of favorite wild places. Armed with several feet of ½-inch tubing and a small recirculating pump, I lugged four big, flat rocks into place and made a very satisfying waterfall that spilled into a sunken plastic tub.

Whichever route you choose, keep the "Big Three" criteria in mind:

- Shallow water for safety
- Rough surface for sure footing
- The tempting sound of running water to lure birds from a distance

Adding a naturalistic water feature to your yard will bring wonderful surprises. Even the ungainly-looking beak of the red crossbill can sip from shallow water.

Commercial Products

Manufacturers have made it easy for us bird lovers. Just make a trip to the garden center, home-supply store, or discount center, and you can carry home a self-contained kit that includes everything you need to attract birds with water. Best of all, it takes no installation—just choose a spot, fill the container with water, and plug in the pump.

Availability of the products may vary with regional markets and suppliers. Keep the "Big Three" desired features in mind when you go shopping, and you'll have no trouble satisfying your sense of aesthetics and making the birds happy, too.

One of the most appealing commercial products I've seen had two tiers of basins, a large bottom one and a smaller top one, made of molded plastic that looked just like stone. A small pump kept water spilling over the top ledge into the lower basin. The surface felt like sandstone, rough and grainy the way birds like it. At a little over $100, the water feature was an investment that would pay off fast with increased bird traffic. I saw it in a country greenhouse,

(continued on page 324)

Simple Pool for Bird Bathing

Working with concrete was the only choice for making birdbaths just a few decades ago. Today heavy-duty plastic liners make it much easier for the average klutz to create a water feature. The liner material prevents water from seeping into the soil. All you need to do is scoop out a depression, lay the liner in place, decorate the edges, and fill with water. You can cut the liner material with a utility knife to tailor it to the size of your excavation.

MATERIALS

Pond liner

Mix of medium and large rocks for rim

Sand

Gravel

Landscaping materials: shrubs, grasses, perennials, and/or groundcovers

Small recirculating pump

Step 1. Dig a shallow, sloping hole, about 3 feet across, 6 inches deep in the center. The hole can be circular, oval, free-form, or even rectangular if yours is a formal garden. Slope the sides gradually from the edges.

Step 2. Lay a piece of pond liner in the hole. The size of your pond liner will need to be the length and width plus the depth. The liner for this pool should be about 4 feet × 4 feet. Trim off excess material around the edges, allowing a 6-inch overlap onto surrounding soil.

Step 3. Anchor the liner with rocks around the edges.

Step 4. Cover the liner with 2 inches of coarse sand or river rock or other smooth stones or gravel. If you use rough gravel, cover the liner with a layer of sand first to prevent cuts from the sharp edges on the gravel.

Step 5. Landscape around the pool.

Step 6. Install a small recirculating pump to attract birds. Fill with water, plug in the pump, and watch for your first customers.

A typical garden pool drops off sharply at the edges. Re-dig this one so that the sides make a very slight transition in steepness, and you won't have to fiddle with laying in rocks or bricks so that birds can walk into the water.

where an open door allowed some of the accumulated heat to escape. The greenhouse was alive with hummingbirds and butterflies, and several of them were drinking at the trickling fountain.

Concrete is still a good option for making water features. It's inexpensive and fun to do with kids. And it gives you the pride of saying "I did it myself," even if the result is less slick than a purchased model. A sack of quick-setting concrete makes the job fast and simple. I mix it in an old metal wheelbarrow, using a garden hoe for stirring and a wide mason's trowel for spreading it. Plan your water feature, collect any materials, and do the digging before you mix the concrete—it hardens remarkably fast.

Unless you're an expert, stick with a simple design. I made a serviceable pool for my birds by digging a sloping, shallow hole and spreading a 2- to 3-inch layer of concrete in the depression. I don't like the stark look of whitish concrete, so I used a commercial dye to tint the mix to a deep charcoal gray. Before the concrete hardened, I stuck a few rocks into place in the pool and at the edges to give it a natural look and to provide perching opportunities. Two coats of waterproofing compound after the concrete dried gave me added insurance against leaks. I was a little worried about the pool being damaged in my Zone 6 winters, but it lasted for almost a decade before finally cracking—and then I simply patched the crack.

PROJECT

Almost-Natural Waterfall

If you have a slightly sloping area in your yard, you can build a natural-looking waterfall in just a couple of weekends. Enlist a helper to lessen the load and make it easier to lay out the liner. Sketch your design on paper and collect your materials before you dig the first scoop of soil, so you can easily follow the steps. Collect some long, flat rocks if you want a curtain effect for the waterfall, or, if you prefer a wild tumble, use irregular rocks to make the spillway. It's fun to play with water and easier than it looks to do this project. If needed, break it up into steps that you can accomplish gradually.

MATERIALS

Sandbags, as needed

Sand

Pool liner

A mix of rocks for the rim and waterfall

Solvent

Small recirculating pump

Flexible tubing

Landscaping materials: shrubs, grasses, perennials, and/or groundcovers

Step 1. Excavate a channel and pool. Keep the channel shallow, about 8 inches deep, and use the removed soil to create a berm along each side to contain the water. Gradually slope the pool to as deep as you wish in the center.

Step 2. Pile removed soil as a foundation for the head of the waterfall. Add sandbags for extra fill.

Step 3. Level the pool hole, and pour in a layer of sand. Moisten it and smooth it, so that it follows the contours of the pool.

Step 4. Measure and cut the liner for the pool, allowing extra for overhang at the edges. To figure the liner size, measure the width of the pool, add the depth of the two sides, and add another 12 inches for overhang. Do the same calculations for the length of the pool.

Step 5. Lay the liner over the hole (easier with a helper). Smooth out wrinkles as much as possible.

Step 6. Lay rocks around edges to hold the liner in place. Trim off excess liner.

Step 7. Measure and cut liner for waterfall/stream channel, allowing 1 foot overlap onto pool liner. Use solvent (available at home-supply stores and garden centers) to weld the overlap to the pool liner.

Works of Art

Don't we all want a stream in our yards? How about a waterfall? Thanks to the wonders of flexible pond liners, we can have it all. The technique is simple. Basically, you dig a sloping channel, line it with sand, lay in PVC liner, edge with rocks, and install pump and tubing that continuously returns water to the headwaters of your creek.

These ambitious water features may take a couple of weekends to get just right, but they will give you years of pleasure. Running water is just as delightful to our eyes, ears, and psyches as it is appealing to birds. The stream or waterfall you install will be a major attraction in your yard for as long as you live there. It will become such a part of your place that you may find yourself forgetting that once you had nothing but lawn.

Use some thought when deciding where to place your stream. The first criterion is to locate it in a place where you can watch the activity from a favorite window inside the house, or from a garden bench or other sitting area outside. Make sure it won't be an obstacle to foot traffic—wading across stepping stones is a charming thought, but a lot less fun if you have to do it every time you pick up the mail. You will also need to select a sloping area to build the watercourse—water flows downhill. It's the job of the pump to return it to its starting point. Also be sure you have

Step 8. Set large rocks in place along the channel and at the waterfall to anchor the liner. Experiment with the placement until you find it pleasing, lifting and lowering rocks carefully so as not to rip the liner.

Step 9. Install a recirculating pump in the pool and run flexible tubing back to the waterfall, disguising it among the rocks.

Step 10. Slowly fill the pool, until you are satisfied with the volume of water flowing through the stream.

Step 11. Add additional rocks in the streambed and at the waterfall to create bathing and drinking pools for birds. Mark off a few shallow areas of the pool by placing rocks between them and the deeper water, so birds can feel safe in shallow water.

Step 12. Landscape the area with shrubs for preening after bathing and perennials and ornamental grasses to give it a natural appeal.

Once your garden pond and waterfall are installed, plant around it to create a more natural setting. Branching and fruit-bearing shrubs near the water will provide damp birds with safe places to sit and preen.

a convenient outdoor electrical outlet to power the pump.

You can use preformed garden pool sections to create the stream and waterfall, or use an earthen bed topped with sand and a pond liner. Good-sized rocks are another necessity. They disguise the edges in a natural way and help anchor the construction. If you don't have a handy supply of fieldstone around your property, you can find dealers in stone and rock who will deliver the material or let you pick it up yourself. Be sure to select rock that fits your area, so that it doesn't look incongruous in your landscape.

Faux rocks are another possibility. They've come a long way from the first "that's a fake" effect. Now plastic boulders and stones look so natural that you can't tell even by touching. Their slight weight is a welcome improvement over real stone, which always seems heavier than it looks.

See Your Stonemason

Stone fountains and other stone water features usually carry exorbitantly high prices because of the limited market, the shipping weight of the material, and the amount of design and labor that goes into them. If you yearn for one of these beautiful objects and won't settle for plastic, you can cut costs—often dramatically—by finding a stonecutter to do the work for you.

Thankfully, cutting stone is an art that's still alive, and you can find its practitioners in your Yellow Pages. Your nearest supplier of cemetery headstones may also have the equipment and skills necessary to transform a block of sandstone, granite, or limestone into a work of art. As with any custom job, be sure you and the craftsperson agree on what work is being done, what the schedule is, and how much it will cost.

Put your birdbaths and other water features where you can see them so that you don't miss the fun. Here a chipping sparrow indulges in a morning splash.

Think from a bird's point of view as you arrange rocks to make your water features. This white-throated sparrow and other birds seek out shallow places with easy access.

W

Weather Predictors

Is a big snow coming? Just take a look at the feeders. If they are jam-packed with birds, and if the birds linger until past their usual last-call time, you can bet bad weather is on the way. Birds are sensitive to atmospheric pressure, and the lows that precede a storm are a signal to stock up while the getting is good.

Here in the tornado belt of the Midwest, I take my severe-weather cues from the birds as well as the Weather Channel. If the birds fall silent during daylight hours, I know something big is coming, and I head for cover. Long before the meteorologists issue the all-clear, the birds let me know that the danger is past. That first chirping robin or trilling song sparrow sounds glorious after a bad storm.

Yellow-billed and black-billed cuckoos, which rarely visit feeders, are known as "rain crows" in some areas because of their habit of calling before a thunderstorm. On heavy summer afternoons, when humidity is thick, their mournful "Coo-coo-coo" is a common sound in the woods and hedgerows they frequent.

Birds have a knack for knowing a winter storm is approaching. You can count on a mob before a blizzard as birds keep the feeders hopping.

Weeds

Attract many kinds of birds at various times of the year

Stop mowing your grass, put away the dandelion digger, and by the end of summer you'll have every bird for blocks hanging out in your yard. Of course, you might also encounter the zoning officer at your door reminding you of the need to conform to neighborhood standards. The fact is, birds love weeds, but you (and your neighbors) might not.

To birds, weeds mean just one thing: food, and lots of it. Find a stand of giant ragweed in winter, and you're sure to find a horde of cardinals, finches, and native sparrows, which come to feast on the abundant seeds until the spiky seedheads are picked clean. Same thing with lamb's-quarters: A thicket of the 4-foot-tall plants will attract scores of buntings, chickadees, finches, siskins, sparrows,

and others. Even a single plant doesn't escape notice. I've watched white-crowned sparrows desert the easy pickings at my feeder in favor of a single stem of lamb's-quarters growing nearby, which they fought over as if it were candy. Lamb's-quarter seeds must definitely be delicious to attract as many birds as they do, but to my uneducated palate, the tiny seeds don't taste like much. I'd take sunflower seeds any day.

The Best Weed for Birds

The number-one weed for birds is the pretty annual grass known as foxtail, or bristlegrass. You've probably seen the fuzzy spikes of this common weed along roadsides and fields nearby or even sprouting in your own flowerbeds. The bristly seedheads may be arching or they may stand erect, depending on species, but birds gobble them no matter what position they're in. Practically every seed-eating bird in America seeks out foxtail grass, a close cousin of the millet so popular at the feeder. Doves, ducks, grouse, quail, and other game birds are huge fans. Among the songbird clan, everyone from cardinals and grosbeaks to sparrows and thrashers—at least 46 species—relish the small, crunchy seeds. This is one of the most abundant American weeds and one of the easiest to collect for later offerings at the feeder. In fall, I pick a lavish bouquet of tan, ripe foxtail grass seedheads for the fat brown crock on my kitchen table. When I get tired of my dried arrangement indoors, I just tie the stems together and hang it below the feeder.

Weedy Gardens Are Great for Birds

If you can tolerate a few weeds in your yard—or better yet, if you have a discreet corner that you can let "go wild" with weeds—you'll increase your bird life by a bushel. Plus you'll get to observe the interesting ways birds devour different seeds. You may see an indigo bunting neatly pulling one tuft after another from a dandelion puff or perhaps a tree sparrow hopping off the ground to pull down a seedhead of curly dock so it can stand on the stem while it eats. Acrobatic goldfinches and siskins are amusing to watch as they go after every remaining seed in a stem of wild mustard that bends beneath their weight.

If you can't bear the thought of encouraging "plain old weeds," at least consider some of the weeds that have been civilized for garden use: The ornamental amaranths are almost as seedy as their pigweed cousins. And chicory bears garden-worthy blue flowers; just plant it behind something low and bushy to hide its ratty foliage.

Weeds are so attractive to birds that (shhh! don't tell) I sometimes resort to subterfuge and hide a weed plantation behind a fool-the-neighbors strip of annual flowers. Tall, branching sunflowers on the out-

Pretty flowers help people accept weeds like chicory; goldfinches and others like their seeds. A diverse, weedy corner will welcome many hungry birds.

side, lamb's-quarters, pigweed, and whatever else wants to come up on the inside—it's a fine arrangement that doesn't distress the neighbors, and it gives me months of good bird watching on the "weedy" side of the garden.

I also let the occasional weed grow in my more traditional flower gardens, and I haven't had a sudden bumper crop of weeds after tolerating their presence. I credit the birds with that—they clean up the seeds so thoroughly that few get added to the reservoir of weed seeds already in the soil.

The moral of this story? If you want more birds to visit your yard and to linger longer, invite a few weeds to stay. You may find yourself beginning to look on common weeds with a brand new perspective. From there, it's just a small step to actually cultivating these scorned plants.

Four Seasons of Weeds for Birds

FAMILIAR WEEDS that we remove from our gardens and yards are great sources of food for many birds. Weeds generally mature fast, and they often set staggered crops of seeds. These adaptable habits mean that there are ripe weed seeds available for birds year-round. Accept a bit of untidiness during the growing season and leave some weeds standing for the fall and winter because they will draw extra birds to your backyard.

Weed	Description	Comments
Pigweeds (*Amaranthus* spp.)	30-plus species of coarse, annual weeds with fuzzy stalks of tiny flowers and seeds	Eagerly eaten by all small seed-eating birds, including buntings, doves, finches, goldfinches, juncos, horned larks, pheasant, quail, redpolls, native sparrows, and towhees. Large-beaked rose-breasted grosbeaks also devour the seeds.
Ragweeds (*Ambrosia* spp.)	Annual and exceedingly common weeds whose spikes of tiny, nondescript flowers produce masses of airborne irritating pollen, the bane of the allergy-prone	Seeds relished by song sparrows, swamp sparrows, white-throated sparrows, and other native sparrows; also blackbirds, bobolinks, buntings, crossbills, grosbeaks, juncos, horned larks, meadowlarks, redpolls, robins, siskins, towhees, and even cedar waxwings. The seeds of giant ragweed (*A. trifida*) are hard for small-beaked birds to crack but are a top favorite of cardinals.
Star-thistles (napa star-thistle, *Centaurea melitensis*; yellow star-thistle, *C. solstitialis*)	Common annual prickly plants of western grainfields, especially in California; flowers mature to bristly clusters of seeds	Seeds sought by mourning dove, house finch, goldfinches, Oregon junco, California quail, pine siskin, golden-crowned and other western native sparrows, titmice, and towhees
Lamb's-quarters (*Chenopodium album*)	Annual weed growing to 4 feet tall; multiple branches from single stem; arrow-shaped leaves and packed clusters of small, greenish flowers	Oily seeds eagerly sought by doves, grouse, quail, and other game birds as well as buntings, finches, goldfinches, juncos, horned larks, pyrrhuloxia, redpolls, and native sparrows
Chicory (*Cichorium intybus*)	Tall perennial weed with dandelion-like rosette of toothed leaves in winter, followed by a tall branching stem of light blue flowers in spring and summer	Buntings, finches, juncos, siskins, and native sparrows eat the seeds.
Filarees (*Erodium* spp.)	Also known as stork's bill, these annual weeds are especially common in the West. Have fernlike leaves and dainty pink-purple flowers that mature into long, pointy seeds.	Highly popular with almost all small seed-eating birds, including blackbirds, buntings, doves, finches, goldfinches, juncos, horned larks, meadowlarks, quail, siskins, native sparrows, varied thrush, towhees, wrens, and waxwings
Smartweeds (*Polygonum* spp.)	Ultracommon annual weeds, sprawling in habit, low to tall in height, with tight-packed spikes of tiny, usually pink or white flowers	Highly popular with doves, grouse, quail, and other game birds and almost all seed-eating songbirds such as blackbirds, buntings, finches, goldfinches, juncos, horned larks, redpolls, and nearly all native sparrows
Chickweed (*Stellaria media*)	Winter annual weed that sprouts in fall on bare ground; grows in a low, sprawling clump of tiny green leaves and even smaller white flowers that bloom in winter to early spring	White-crowned, white-throated, and other native sparrows relish the multitude of tiny seeds, which ripen during spring sparrow migration. Also sought by buntings, doves, finches, goldfinches, juncos, horned larks, quail, pine siskins, and towhees
Dandelion (*Taraxacum officinale*)	Familiar perennial weed with rosette of long, toothed leaves and familiar yellow flowers	Indigo buntings, goldfinches, pine siskins, and native sparrows adore the seeds. Look for groups of these birds and an occasional rose-breasted grosbeak at dandelion patches during spring migration. Yellow-headed blackbirds, Brewer's blackbirds, and towhees also enjoy the seeds; game birds eat both seeds and leaves.

SEASONS WHEN SEEDS ARE PLENTIFUL ☐ SPRING ☐ SUMMER ☐ FALL ☐ WINTER

Wheat

Attracts blackbirds, doves, grouse, pheasants, quail, house sparrows, some native sparrows, starlings

"Eat Your Wheaties" is a slogan that most birds pay no attention to, except in times when wheat is about all there is for breakfast, lunch, or dinner. Even so, wheat seed is a common ingredient in birdseed mixes probably because it's less costly than other types of seeds and because its relatively large size takes up lots of space in that 25-pound sack.

Blackbirds, doves, grouse, pheasants, quail, house sparrows, some native sparrows, and starlings do eat wheat, but in my experience, they prefer to pick it from standing stalks of the grain. At the feeder, birds ignore wheat seeds and eventually kick them to the ground where mice, ants, and other not-so-picky eaters are quick to carry them off. So if you want to offer wheat to feeder birds, start with a small amount. If your regular customers start to eat it, you can make it a low-cost part of the menu.

Birds usually scorn wheat in the feeder unless it's the last resort. But when the grain matures, birds seek it out on the stem or forage for dropped kernels.

Wheat in the Garden

Wheat is a pretty addition to a birdseed garden. The long bristles (called "awns") on the seed kernels catch the light and lend a delicate, silky look to plantings. Some varieties are particularly ornamental, such as the extravagantly long-awned types and black wheat, which has a dramatic dark-shadowed look.

All wheat is simple to grow. Scratch up a planting bed, scatter the seed kernels, cover them lightly, keep watered, and in a few days you'll have a thick crop sprouting and growing fast. By mid- to late summer, your grain crop will be ripening to gold.

Since few of us keep a tractor in the driveway, planting wheat at home is usually on a small scale. This fast-growing grass is an excellent cover crop in the garden, but birds won't benefit because it's turned under to enrich the soil long before seedheads ripen.

One spring, I tilled a strip of land along my yard, planning to put in a mixed hedge fronted by bright flowers for butterflies. I got the shrubs into the ground, but then I got sidetracked. By the time I got back to it, weed seedlings were sprouting a mile a minute. With no time to get fancy, I dumped a sack of wheat along the 2-foot-wide strip and wished it well. Lo and behold, the wheat grew so fast and thick that it crowded out most of the burgeoning weeds.

As seedheads ripened, the birds arrived. Every house sparrow and mourning dove in town found their way to the wheat. Red-winged blackbirds flew in, and even a few meadowlarks made the trek, plus blue jays, juncos, song sparrows, and even a white-breasted nuthatch. More than 20 species of birds visited from late summer through spring, when the wheat eaters were still picking seeds from the ground.

Wildlife at the Feeder

KEEPING TRACK OF THE ANIMALS that visit your feeder is almost as much fun as watching birds. Unfortunately, many visitors will come to call during the hours of darkness, when you are apt to miss their visits. You may want to install a motion-sensitive light to alert you to the arrival of guests and to make viewing easier.

Because larger animals such as deer and raccoons can damage smaller feeders and nearby plantings, it's a good idea to establish a separate feeding station for such guests. Supply low and high tray feeders without roofs so that you can watch the action. Corn is an excellent all-purpose choice for wildlife that visits the feeding area, and it's inexpensive enough to offer generously.

Fruit is also a favorite. Because animals can devour fruit in a jiffy, scout out apple, pear, or other fruit trees in your neighborhood, and ask for permission to collect those that fall to the ground when the crop ripens. Homeowners and businesses are often happy to have you collect the fruit, which they wouldn't use anyway. You can also find low-cost or free fruit in quantity at nearby orchards; ask for windfalls or blemished fruit. Your animal guests won't mind a few bruises or wormholes.

A salt block is another temptation for wildlife. Porcupines, deer, mice, and other critters, as well as birds, will enjoy it. Water features, especially garden pools and ponds, are also popular with animal visitors.

If you live in an area with snow, use your detective skills to see who's been visiting your feeding station. Tracks will be clear, from the diminutive paw prints of mice to the distinctive cloven hooves of deer. Investigating prints in snow or mud is a great activity to do with kids; an inexpensive field guide will tell you who's who. It's fun to make a scrapbook of footprint drawings, matched to photos or sketches of the animals that made them and the date they visited your feeder.

A separate feeding station for nonbird wildlife may show neighbors you've never seen and keep them out of your bird feeders. If you live near wild places, you may attract chipmunks, raccoons, squirrels, quail and other game birds, deer, rabbits, opossums, and maybe even a fox. Birds will visit it, too.

Windows and Birds

Collisions with windows are one of the chief causes of bird fatalities. The bird never sees the glass—only the deceptive scene of backyard and blue sky reflected in it. An inexpensive sheet or roll of plastic fruit-tree bird netting, sold for protecting fruit crops from the depredations of birds, is the best preventive for window accidents. Cut it to size with a pair of scissors and staple it to your window frame for the best defense. The fine grid of the mesh breaks up those dangerous reflections in glass that bring many a bird to its doom.

Stick-on silhouettes of owls and hawks are sold to keep birds from windows, but in my experience, these just don't work. You can also fiddle with strips of mylar, outside window shades, or other devices. But fruit-tree netting is a highly effective, unobtrusive solution. The netting is usually black, and when stretched tightly, it is barely visible to human eyes inside or outside the house.

Aggressive, territorial male birds (cardinals and robins seem to be the worst offenders) may attack their own reflection in a window, car mirror, or other shiny surface in the belief that they are fighting a competing male. If a male bird starts sparring with your windowpane, relieve him of his defensive duties by attaching a piece of netting over the frustrating glass.

Large expanses of glass, like patio doors, are highly dangerous to birds. Hang barely visible netting to break up reflections on windows that birds crash into.

If you haven't had any bird accidents yet at your windows, count yourself lucky—or unaware. Keep your birds safe by taking preventive measures before you hear the first thump.

Winter Feeding

The main reason that feeder traffic takes a dramatic jump in winter is that natural food is much scarcer then. The few foods that do remain are hard to find, and birds can save considerable precious energy by zeroing in on your feeder instead of hunting for their own breakfast, lunch, and dinner. In cold-winter areas, insects are just a summer memory, except for the stray cocoon or overwintering egg—no more easy pickings of caterpillars and beetles and their myriad kin. Fruits and seeds are mostly all eaten, too, by the time winter rolls around.

This is good news for us bird watchers, who can enjoy feeling really needed as the birds dine on our handouts. It's also a good reason to stock your yard with plants that hold their food into the winter months. Birds appreciate variety in their diet. Natural foods may also draw in birds, such as cedar waxwings and thrushes, that normally don't visit feeders.

What to Watch For

Not only is the demand higher for bird-feeder foods in winter, but the sheer number of birds that visit your

Winter Food Plants

STOCKING YOUR yard with plants that hold their seeds, berries, or cones into the winter months is a great way to draw foraging thrushes, cedar waxwings, and other birds that may be reluctant to visit a feeding station. Natural foods also provide a welcome change of pace for your feeder regulars. All conifers (pines, spruces, hemlocks, firs, and others) are a good source of winter food, but consider rounding out the menu with a few other possibilities, such as the following:

Long-Lasting Seedheads

Amaranths (*Amaranthus* spp.): Annual weeds or decorative garden plants, this genus holds seed-packed fuzzy spikes relished throughout the cold months by buntings, doves, finches, goldfinches, juncos, horned larks, pheasants, quail, redpolls, native sparrows, and towhees.

Ragweeds (*Ambrosia* spp.): Common annual weeds, ranging from knee-high to head height, depending on species, produce abundant small, oily seeds sought by cardinals, doves, finches, pine siskin, native sparrows, waxwings, and many other birds.

Big bluestem (*Andropogon gerardii*): Very tall native perennial prairie grass, to 6 feet, with interesting "turkey foot"–shaped seedheads that eventually keel over in late winter, providing food for juncos, native sparrows, towhees, and other ground-feeding birds.

Broomsedge (*A. virginicus*): Perennial grass almost identical to little bluestem (*Schizachyrium scoparium*), with more of a "whisk-broom" look near the tops of the stems; acquires rich orangeish color in fall and winter. Small seeds sought by rosy finches, juncos, native sparrows, and game birds.

Little bluestem (*Schizachyrium scoparium*): Clump-forming native perennial prairie grass that grows to 3 feet tall and turns beautiful warm orange in fall and winter. Fuzzy seed clusters along stems furnish food for finches, game birds, juncos, and native sparrows as well as small mammals.

Winter Berries or Fruit

Manzanitas (*Arctostaphlyos* spp.): Striking smooth, red bark characterizes many of the shrubby species of this western and southwestern genus, which also includes ground-hugging bearberry (*A. uva-ursi*). Red or brown berries are prime food for grouse, grosbeaks, jays, mockingbird, and fox sparrow as well as for small mammals—skunks particularly like them!

Hackberries (*Celtis laevigata, C. occidentalis,* and other spp.): Lovely shade trees with interesting warty gray bark and a multitude of small fruits that ripen in late fall to early winter. Source of food for catbirds, flickers, jays, mockingbirds, orioles, robins, sapsuckers, starlings, thrashers, thrushes, titmice, woodpeckers, and wrens, which devour the bounty while still on the tree. Towhees, fox sparrows, and other native sparrows join in the feast when the fruit drops.

Persimmons (*Diospyros virginiana, D. texana*): Native trees with alligator-hide–checkered bark, large, simple leaves, and astringent orange to orange-red fleshy fruit that softens and sweetens when ripe. Beloved by bluebirds, catbirds, mockingbirds, robins, sapsuckers, starlings, wild turkeys, yellow-rumped warblers, and waxwings. Also a favorite of the raccoon and its close relative, the unusual ring-tailed cat of Texas, the Southwest, and West.

Cedars (*Juniperus* spp.): Deep green or gray-green conifers with often prickly foliage and lovely blue berries, much sought by bluebirds, catbirds, crossbills, doves, finches, flickers, grosbeaks, jays, mockingbirds, robins, sapsuckers, thrashers, thrushes, yellow-rumped warbler, and waxwings as well as game birds.

Sumacs (*Rhus* spp.): Native shrubs or small trees with foliage that turns brilliant red to orange in fall and dense, pointed clusters of red (white in some species) fuzzy berries held upright. A food of last resort, the berries are eaten in winter by crows, ruffed grouse, pigeons, quail, wild turkeys, and many songbirds, including bluebirds, cardinals, catbirds, purple finches, flickers, jays, magpies, mockingbirds, starlings, thrushes, woodpeckers, and wrens.

Greenbriers (*Smilax* spp.): Evergreen or deciduous native climbers, some thorny-stemmed, absent in parts of the West and abundant in the Southeast. Berries may be yellow, black, blue, or green and are devoured eagerly by many birds: Bluebirds, catbirds, fish crows, flickers, mockingbirds, robins, fox sparrows, white-throated sparrows, thrushes, cedar waxwings and pileated woodpeckers are among the prime customers.

yard increases because of flocking patterns. Blackbirds and house finches may arrive in large flocks, and cardinals, finches, grosbeaks, sparrows, and other birds now pal around in groups instead of living the solitary life.

The cast of characters at your feeder remains fairly stable in winter, except that the numbers will swell temporarily when bad weather moves in. Occasional rare birds, either unusual for your region or unusual for your feeder, also appear at feeders in the winter, driven by hunger. For example, from spring through fall, I never see a crow anywhere near my small town yard. But I can count on several big black birds stalking the feeding area during the winter season, particularly when snow (even a light dusting) covers the ground. Often they join the starlings at the dog-food pan or turkey carcass.

If you live in the Deep South or southern California, the scene at your winter feeders may be quite different than the view in cold, snowy areas. Rufous and black-chinned hummingbirds are in winter residence along the Gulf coast, busily visiting nectar feeders. Red-breasted nuthatches, a southern rarity in spring and summer except during migration, now settle in across the southern half of the country for a sunny winter vacation, as do chipping sparrows and fox sparrows. In the West, the beautiful varied thrush moves in, giving winter feeder keepers all the way to Baja some color to enjoy. Western and mountain

This is the scene that warms a feeder host's heart: birds filling their bellies at the feeding station when natural food is scarce.

bluebirds move into the southern regions of the West. In the Deep South and along the southern Atlantic coast, house wrens may visit for mealworms; catbirds, robins, and brown thrashers may turn up at the chopped suet or fruit feeder; and Bullock's and Baltimore orioles may grace the nectar feeder. As the days gradually start to lengthen at the end of winter, you'll notice that the birds at your feeders are beginning

10 To-Dos for Winter Feeding

1. Stock up! Lay in a week's supply of your most popular seeds in reserve.

2. Be sure you have plenty of suet on hand; extra fat in the freezer is easy to pull out when needed.

3. Keep feeders free of ice and snow. Erect lean-tos or add roofs so that at least some feeders are covered.

4. If you're blessed with deep snow or frequent treacherous ice, temporarily move a few feeders very close to the house, so that you can refill them easily without risking your neck.

5. Try hand taming: It's easy in cold weather, when birds are motivated to take the food.

6. Keep a calendar of daily visitors, or a weekly census. It's fun to know exactly whom you're feeding.

7. Save leftover soft foods, such as bread and pancakes, for catbirds, robins, wrens, and other soft-food eaters. If you run out of kitchen leftovers, serve these birds moistened dog food.

8. Watch for hawks patrolling from above or perched to wait for your feeder birds.

9. Recycle your Christmas tree into a windbreak alongside a low-level tray feeder.

10. Make homemade treats for the bird, such as the ever-popular peanut-butter–smeared pinecones. Kids love to help, and it gives them an early sense of connection to the birds outside their window.

to behave differently. Male cardinals, juncos, native sparrows, and other males of the same species that formerly ate companionably side by side now become short-tempered, turning to each other with flashing wings and threatening opened beaks. It's only natural—longer daylight hours kick the reproductive hormones into gear, and battles over elbow room and mates become a more frequent occurrence. Doves, owls, and woodpeckers are among the earliest to actually start a family, often in late winter.

Plan Ahead

The most important rule of winter feeding is: Be prepared. Storms can move in quickly, making that little jaunt to the birdseed store a nightmare or just plain impossible. Besides, your own family's needs will no doubt take precedence over feeder birds. That's why you'll want to keep an extra sack or two of birdseed on hand for emergencies. I keep at least a week's worth in reserve during winter, which for my feeders means a 50-pound bag of sunflower seed, a 50-pound sack of cracked corn, and 20 pounds of millet, plus about 10 ears of whole corn for my squirrels.

You'll appreciate your freezer and pantry in the winter months, too, if you have stockpiled them with bird treats such as the following:

■ Chopped suet and raw hamburger are prized foods at the winter feeder, as are meat scraps and leftovers.

■ Nuts of any kind offer excellent nourishment and are so popular that they may be the cause of bird disputes.

■ Grain-based foods from the kitchen, such as cereal recipes, bread crumbs, and baked goods, are a hit with many kinds of birds.

■ Frozen or dried fruits and berries come in handy for bluebirds, catbirds, robins, thrashers, wrens, and other birds that usually eschew seeds.

■ An extra jar of peanut butter, economy-size, is a treasure in winter, when severe weather is likely to bring any bluebirds in the area to your feeders.

■ Mealworms are snatched up fast at the winter feeder.

Feeder birds don't mind sharing space at the table when a snowstorm sends everyone fluttering to find food. Here a Carolina wren dines with a cardinal.

If you've included a salt block at your feeding area, you'll see it's as popular in winter as at other times of the year. Winter brings winter finches sweeping down irregularly from the North, and salt is a big hit with these unusual birds. Keep an eye open for crossbills, redpolls, and siskins at your salt block along with the usual doves and house finches. Focus your binoculars on the odd scissors bill of crossbills at the salt lick, and you will see that they make this food live up to its name: they actually lick up the salt with their tongues.

Birds still search for water in winter, too. Since most natural sources of water are frozen, a birdbath or other water feature free of ice will make your yard a magnet for birds. They splash about in fresh water even when the temperature is frigid, as long as they find a sunny perch afterward where they can dry their feathers. You can set out a shallow basin of warm water daily or invest in an electric heater for the birdbath that will keep at least part of the water ice-free. The Birdbaths entry on page 19 has more helpful hints for ensuring a steady supply of precious water.

Woodpeckers

If my only feeder visitor was a woodpecker, I could be quite content (at least for a while!). Even when they're motionless, these highly specialized birds are wonderful to watch. They are beautiful birds with complex feather patterns, variations of head markings between species and sexes, and an intriguing structure and use of the tail. In action the birds are fascinating as they use their heavy beaks to pry, chisel, chop, whack, and delicately probe. They also have fascinating feet that help them cling to tree trunks.

Eighteen different American woodpeckers (not counting the flickers, which you can learn about in their own entry on page 121) ensure that no matter where you feed birds, a woodpecker will accept your hospitality. Supply suet, supplemented with seeds and other treats, and you'll have feeder friends for life. Year after year, woodpeckers return to feeding stations where they have learned to find food.

Most Common Feeder Visitors

Several woodpeckers are frequent feeders across the country. These common species are among the most adaptable of the family, often leaving their traditional forest homelands for new dwelling places in suburbia and towns. Not only will they visit your feeders regularly, they are also likely to quickly adopt a nest box or a dead branch in your yard for raising their family.

The downy woodpecker is a regular at feeders across most of the country. A nonmigrating species, the downy will visit daily in all seasons.

Every feeder host has a soft spot for the little **downy woodpecker,** the smallest of the tribe, and a reliable year-round guest at the suet and seed tray. This black-and-white bird occurs across nearly the entire country, except for a few areas of the Southwest. Its larger look-alike cousin, the **hairy woodpecker,** is less common but just as widespread. If a

WOODPECKER FEEDER FOODS			
■ Acorns (*Quercus* spp.)	■ Elderberries (*Sambucus* spp.)	■ Holly (*Ilex* spp.) berries	■ Pecans (*Carya illinoiensis*)
■ Almonds	■ Figs	■ Mealworms	■ Pine (*Pinus cembroides*) nuts
■ Amelanchier (*Amelanchier* spp.) berries	■ Grapes	■ Meat scraps	■ Suet
■ Cherries, fresh or dried	■ Hazelnuts (*Corylus* spp.)	■ Mulberries (*Morus* spp.)	■ Sunflower seeds
■ Corn, on cob, whole, or cracked	■ Hickory (*Carya ovata*) nuts	■ Nectar	■ Walnuts (*Juglans* spp.)
■ Dogwood (*Cornus* spp.) berries		■ Peanut butter	

bird shows up at the feeder looking like a downy on steroids, it's probably a hairy. The hairy's body is bigger and its beak is heavier than the petite downy's.

In the eastern half of the country, another likely feeder guest is the **red-bellied woodpecker,** a bird that's big enough to give even a jay a hard time. The first thing you'll notice about this deceptively named woodpecker isn't its belly—it's the head splashed with vivid red from bill to nape (crown to nape in the female). One of the "ladderbacked" group of woodpeckers, this bird has finely barred black and white feathers on its back that look like rungs on a ladder. Bird watchers in bygone years called it the "zebra bird." If you can get a glimpse of the bird's belly, you may see the flush of reddish feathers that gives it its common name. But since woodpeckers typically cling against a support to eat, the red patch is hard to spot. Like other ladderbacks, this nonmigratory bird doesn't budge when the seasons change; the red-belly eating suet in December is the same bird you see in July.

The **yellow-bellied sapsucker** is a common bird, but not so commonly seen. While most woodpeckers are noisy and outgoing, this species is an introvert. It's so shy that it will hitch its body around to the other side of the tree if it notices you watching it. One sapsucker I spotted was shy but not too savvy. Like a 2-year-old playing peekaboo, the bird hid only its head under a branch, as if positive I could no longer see it. Western sapsuckers include the **red-breasted sapsucker** and **Williamson's sapsucker.** Sapsuckers have other behaviors peculiar to their kind—they don't drum on resonant dead branches or other percussion "instruments" like other woodpeckers, and they drill for sap. Their work produces rows of small holes, spaced closely together, in the bark of trees. The birds sip the sap as it flows from

The red-bellied woodpecker gets my vote for most poorly named bird. I'd call it red-naped—that red on the back of its neck is the first thing you see.

the tree. A wonderful array of butterflies, hummingbirds, gorgeous underwing moths, large beetles, and other interesting visitors also enjoy the sap.

Locally Common Woodpeckers

The presence of some woodpeckers is a matter of luck. These "locally common" birds are thick in some areas and rare just a short distance away. Why this occurs is a mystery as suitable habitat doesn't seem to matter. If you're lucky, the **red-headed woodpecker** may visit you. Shining black on the back, with a snow white breast, this bird wears a hood of rich crimson that covers its head and neck. Large white wing patches meld with its white rump when the bird flies, creating a tricolor picture of red, black, and pure white. It ranges across the eastern two-thirds of the country, but this bird is a now-you-see-it, now-you-don't species. If you have a red-headed woodpecker at your feeder, count yourself a privileged person.

Lewis's woodpecker, named for one-half of the intrepid exploring team of Lewis and Clark, is another of those tantalizing "locally common" species. It's a possibility across most of the West. This bird looks like a smudged facsimile of the red-headed species, with greenish black back, red face, pink belly, and mottled grayish breast. Sticking to a narrower western range is another teaser, the locally common and vividly distinct **white-headed woodpecker.** This striking bird is solid black except for a bright white head and throat, a white wing patch, and a dash of red at the nape.

Even more limited in range is the **black-backed woodpecker,** which ranges through some Northwest and Far North conifer forests. It peels slabs and flakes of bark from dead trees to get at insects. Along with a black back, this bird has a bright yellow crown, like the **three-toed woodpecker,** another locally common western and northern bird. You may have a hard time counting his toes, but the three-toed woodpecker has a bright yellow crown that's visible from quite a distance.

A Woodpecker for Every Tree

With so many kinds of woodpeckers guarding our forests and shade trees from insects, you're sure to have some interesting individuals in or near your backyard. One you won't miss, should it deign to visit, is the giant-size pileated woodpecker. Almost as big as a crow, this super bird sticks mainly to fallen logs and stumps, although, it may also visit feeders for suet, seeds, peanut butter, and other offerings.

Western feeding stations may host the **acorn woodpecker,** which has a quizzical look, thanks to its white head markings, and a nifty habit of stashing acorns in any handy hiding place. Often it bores its own larder, hollowing out a honeycomb of holes in a dead snag, perfectly sized to hold a single acorn apiece. In saguaro country of the Southwest, the harsh cries of the **gila woodpecker** ring out. If you live in the Southeast, keep your eyes peeled for the rare **red-cockaded woodpecker** and maybe the last surviving **ivory-billed woodpecker,** a species that may already be extinct. Both these species have suffered from loss of their natural piney woods habitat.

Woodpeckers at the Feeder

Several species of woodpeckers are common, everyday feeder visitors. But even those that stick

Count yourself lucky if you host a red-headed woodpecker at your feeders. Although they're not all that rare, these birds keep to extremely local ranges.

mostly to wild places may come to sample your goodies. As with all insect-eating birds, suet is a big attraction, whether it's served in a solid block or chopped in a tray. Many woodpeckers welcome sunflower seeds, corn, and nuts, too.

Any kind of suet feeder will serve woodpeckers, unless it's routinely overrun with starlings. They prefer higher feeders for other offerings.

A recent development in feeder preferences is spreading fast as an apparently learned behavior. Nectar feeders are irresistible to many woodpeckers. Once a woodpecker homes in on one, the bird may sit for hours sipping the sweet stuff and fending off any hummingbirds that venture near. It's quite a sight to see a large, heavy-bodied, red-bellied woodpecker or other species clinging to the feeder—the whole contraption tilts madly when the bird lands on it, scrambling for a foothold. In addition to your hummingbird feeders, provide a large-capacity feeder with sturdy perches to accommodate any woodpeckers that drop in. Those sold for orioles are serviceable, but it may not be long before we see woodpecker nectar feeders on the market.

PROJECT

Woodpecker Feeder Tree

This special "tree" of woodpecker treats gives these striking-looking birds a place of their own where they can enjoy their favorite foods and you can enjoy watching their fascinating behavior. If you have a wooden fence post already standing on your property, it's easy to modify it to make this feeder and you can leave it right where it is.

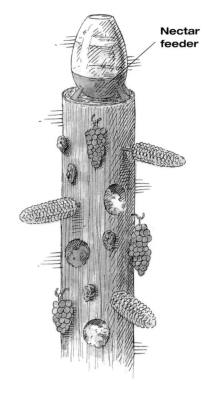

Nectar feeder

MATERIALS

Wood 4 × 4 fence post or length of log

Several large nails

Cup hooks

Smaller nails

Nectar feeder

Suet and/or peanut butter

Whole ears of dried corn

Bunches of grapes

Figs

Step 1. Drill 1½-inch-deep, 2-inch-diameter holes in a fence post to hold suet or peanut butter.

Step 2. Use large nails to nail a few ears of corn to the sides of the post.

Step 3. Screw in cup hooks between holes and ears of corn for holding bunches of grapes.

Step 4. Use smaller nails to fasten some figs to the post.

Step 5. Nail, wire, or otherwise fasten the nectar feeder to the top of the post.

Step 6. Mount or hang the feeder vertically (if not a standing fence post).

Step 7. Fill the nectar feeder and suet/peanut butter holes. Replenish corn, grapes, and figs, as needed, and as these treats are available.

Woodpecker Behavior

Woodpeckers are single-minded at the feeder: They arrive, quickly locate a favored food, then usually sit tight until they have eaten their fill. Watch for their viciously threatening head gestures, especially among the larger species, should another bird dare to come near while the woodpecker is eating. Woodpeckers will even take on a much larger squirrel, should it dare to come near the cob of corn or other delicacy that the bird is dining at. If the animal doesn't get the hint, the woodpecker may rout the squirrel with a swoop straight at it. Starlings are another story. Perhaps it's because starlings usually travel in a gang, or maybe they're just more persistent, but the woodpeckers I've watched, so fierce with squirrels, turn to sissies around starlings.

At any season but especially during breeding time, you will hear a whole litany of weird rattles, "Chirrs," squawks, and other vocalizing from the woodpeckers in the area. Their voices carry quite a distance—I can tell when my neighbor two blocks away is hosting a red-headed woodpecker by listening to its "Yowps" as it arrives. Woodpeckers are great percussionists, too, pounding in staccato rhythms on a favored hollow tree or other noisemaker. When I lived in a tin-roofed Pennsylvania farmhouse, an ear-splitting drum roll was my reveille at the crack of dawn every morning for weeks—a red-bellied wood-pecker found the corner of the roof above my bed-room exactly to its liking. Just about the time I was ready to take drastic measures, the bird switched to an empty metal barrel by the barn.

Be sure to pull out your binoculars when a wood-pecker arrives at the feeder. First look at the way the tail feathers prop up that big body perfectly. They're stiff, strong, and sharply pointed (as well as intricately patterned or polka-dotted in many species). Then check out the bird's feet. Unless you're looking at a three-toed woodpecker, you'll see the short legs and long toes that make it possible for the birds to cling close to tree trunks. Notice, too, how the bird holds two toes facing forward, two toes pointing back, in-stead of the three-and-one arrangement typical of songbirds. This helps the bird maintain a firm grip.

Chisel Beaks and Spear Tongues

I'd often watched woodpeckers rip through dead wood to snack on grubs, but it wasn't until I dumped a handful of whole black walnuts into a feeder that I found out just how powerful the muscles are that drive that chisel beak. Black walnuts are notoriously hard to crack—I resort to a hammer instead of a nut-cracker—but the red-bellied woodpecker at my feeder calmly assessed the nut, drew back his head, and with two solid whacks had the thing split open. That dead-eye aim and strength are just part of the amazing de-sign of woodpeckers. Some behind-the-scenes details can give you a new appreciation for these birds.

Ever blow a coiled-paper New Year's Eve party whistle? That's a reasonable facsimile of the way a woodpecker tongue works. Until the bird is ready to snatch its prey, the extraordinarily long tongue lies coiled around a special pair of bones in the skull.

You can't have too many acorns, says the acorn woodpecker, a bird of extreme single-mindedness. It stows its hoard in holes drilled just for that purpose.

Then it zips forward when the bird zaps an ant or delves for a deep grub.

Even with the aid of binoculars, you probably won't be able to see the other niceties that make woodpeckers so successful at their jobs. But if you watch closely when a woodpecker eats, you will see the effects of these adaptations. All species, except for sapsuckers, have a sharp spear-tipped tongue and backward-pointing barbs that make sure the grub or other morsel stays impaled despite its squirmings. Sticky saliva coats the tongue, too, snagging ants and other insects like a piece of sticky tape sucks up lint. Sapsuckers have unique tongues, too, with small hairs at the tip that work like the bristles of a paint brush to soak up sap.

Wreaths and Swags

A WREATH ON YOUR FRONT GATE says welcome to family and friends, and if you make it from the right materials, birds will also drop by to get a close-up view of your decorating skills. In late summer to fall, when the yard is brimming with ripening berries and seeds, I collect anything that looks as if it has bird potential. I watch for vines of wild grapes and bittersweet, for privet berries on the hedge, for sunflowers going to seed in the garden, and even for likely candidates among the weeds. A smattering of fuzzy foxtail grass and a sprawl of the common pink-flowered smartweed appear as weeds in the garden, but when I work the seedheads into a lush arrangement for the front-door lamppost, the "weed bouquet" gives my house a country touch and supplies the birds with weeks of good eating.

You'll need a surprisingly large amount of plant material to make a wreath or other decoration. I stockpile my treasures in shallow cardboard boxes (recycled pizza boxes work great) in a dry, sheltered area until I have a big stash. Then, on a bright fall day when it's a pleasure to work outdoors, I sort and separate the plants at the picnic table.

(continued on page 343)

Eat-It-Up Winter Wreath

Sticky gelatin holds seeds to a cardboard base for a wreath that birds can peck away at for weeks. Save this project for winter: Unless temperatures are below or close to freezing, the gelatin may slide off the base. This is a good, messy project that kids will enjoy. If your winter temps hover in the fifties or below, you can substitute peanut butter for the gelatin to make a reasonable facsimile. Cover your kitchen table with a plastic tablecloth and dig in!

MATERIALS

Piece of corrugated cardboard

Packet clear gelatin

2 quarts mixed seeds and nuts

Length of wire

Bow or cluster of California pepperberries (optional)

Step 1. Cut a circle of corrugated cardboard to a diameter of 10 inches.

Step 2. Mix packet of clear gelatin, according to the package directions.

Step 3. Pour 2 quarts of seeds and nuts into the gelatin.

Step 4. Stir to coat the seed mixture. If the mixture is too loose and doesn't hold together when you squeeze a handful, add more seed.

Step 5. Mold by hand onto the cardboard form.

Step 6. Attach loop of wire for hanging. Attach a bow or cluster of California pepperberries for decoration, if desired.

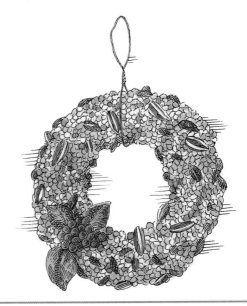

A Fruitful Della Robbia Wreath

Fruit-loving birds will enjoy this colorful circle of fruit. Depending on the time of year when you hang it, you may see catbirds, house finches, purple finches, flickers, grosbeaks, magpies, orioles, robins, tanagers, thrushes, waxwings, and woodpeckers flying in for a treat. You can vary the fruit on the wreath according to what you have available.

MATERIALS

Greenery (fir, pine, boxwood, bayberry)

Heavy-duty wire wreath form

Floral picks or wire

A variety of fruit, including orange halves, figs, persimmons, small apples, crab apples, pepperberries, grapes

Step 1. Wire greenery to the form.

Step 2. Use floral picks or wire to secure large fruits to the form.

Step 3. Fill in between the large fruits with figs, crab apples, persmimmons, and grapes or other small fruits.

Swag for Cedar Waxwings

Berry-laden juniper branches are a magnet for handsome cedar waxwings. Use a decorative swag of evergreen boughs and juniper branches to bring these attractive birds to your yard for a visit.

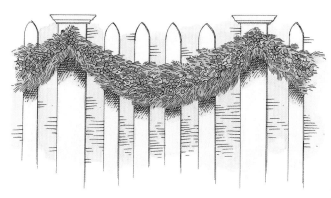

MATERIALS

Length of wire

Evergreen boughs (fir, pine, boxwood, bayberry)

Rope, cut to desired swag length

Juniper branches with berries, 4 to 6 inches long

Holly berries or California pepperberries (optional)

Step 1. Wire overlapping bunches of greenery to rope.

Step 2. Wire on juniper branches amid greenery.

Step 3. Accent with holly berries or pepperberries and hang.

PROJECT

Garland of Grains

Recycle the seedheads of grasses and grains from craft shops or your own yard to make a swag brimming with nutritious seeds. As cardinals, finches, and other birds work at the seedheads, their spills will be quickly cleaned up by juncos, towhees, doves, and other ground-feeding birds not acrobatic enough to cling to the garland. I like to make this swag when I put up my fall decorations—it adds a homemade harvest touch to my fence. Use whatever grass and grain seedheads you can find— they're natural foods that birds eagerly eat.

MATERIALS

Lightweight floral wire

*Any grasses or sedges with seeds still in seedheads (examine to be sure), such as little bluestem (*Schizachyrium scoparium*), big bluestem (*Andropogon gerardii*), Indian grass (*Sorghastrum nutans*), crabgrass, yellow nut sedge, fescue (*Festuca spp.*), bluegrass (*Poa pratensis*), purpletop (*Tridens flavus*), northern sea oats (*Chasmanthium latifolium*), foxtails*

Any grains with seeds, such as milo (sorghum), oats, wheat, rye, barley

Heavyweight wire

Wire cutters

Step 1. Use lightweight floral wire to tie grasses into bunches. Keep seedheads in a bouquet, and snip off extra lengths of stems so that they are even and about 6 inches long.

Step 2. Using heavier wire, wrap bunches into a continuous garland, overlapping as for a wreath. Wire seedheads of the second bunch over the stems of the first, so that the heads of both bunches are snugly side by side. Continue in this fashion. The length of heavier wire holding the bunches together will form the support for the swag.

Step 3. Hang and wait for birds to discover your tasty decoration.

A Simple Spray

Got 5 minutes? That's all it takes to make a lush, beautiful, and bird-attracting "weed bouquet." Just gather a thick double handful of plant material together and wrap the stems tightly with floral wire to make a bouquet. Top with a bunch of corn cobs wired together or a few sunflower seedheads, and your country feast is ready to hang

You can use any combination of handy plant material. I aim for a variety of textures, including twining vines, stiff seedpods, and soft grass seedheads. It's fun to see who arrives to dine on what.

Among the most popular-with-birds combinations I've tried are:

- Bright orange bittersweet, tiny black-purple wild grapes, and clouds of tickle grass (*Panicum* spp.), all common weeds in my area—robins loved it until a mockingbird claimed it.

- Deep brown rose mallow seedpods (*Hibiscus* spp.), masses of foxtail grass seedheads, and catalpa tree (*Catalpa* spp.) beans attracted evening grosbeaks and purple finches.

- Sprays of pale tan ash-tree seedpods (*Fraxinus* spp.), spiky tuliptree cones (*Liriodendron tulipifera*), and zinnia seedheads were a favorite of goldfinches and siskins.

- Oak tree branches with acorns attached, sunflower seedheads, and miniature corn ears—chickadees, jays, titmice, and woodpeckers adored it.

A Circle of Seeds

Fashioning a wreath is a bigger project than making a spray, but it's such fun that you won't want to stop at just one. I purchase a wire form for only a dollar or two to use as the base for my bird wreaths. I can reuse the forms over and over. You can also use straw or grapevine circlets as the base. A roll of floral wire, wire cutters, and a pair of pruners are my only other aids. You can also use long twist-ties to fasten plants to the wreath. A large wreath makes a fine focal point on the front door or gate, but birds enjoy small, quick-to-make, 4- to 6-inch wreaths just as much.

To make your wreath, take a handful of plant material, clip the stems to about 5 inches, and wire securely to the form. Take another bunch of material, snip off extra stem length, and overlap the seed heads onto the stems of the first bunch, so that the "seedy" parts of your material fit snugly together. Wire in place. Repeat until you fill the entire wreath. To hide the bare stems of the last bunch, poke some plants, a sunflower seed

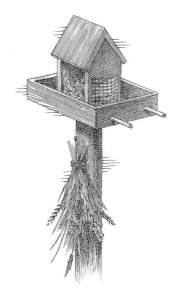

Fasten bird food wherever there's space, keeping in mind the way birds eat. Dining from overhanging seedheads is a natural for the birds that will enjoy this.

head, or a few ears of miniature corn through the stems and wire them into place on the back of the wreath.

Fruit is a great addition to a bird wreath. I keep small apples fresh for months in the fruit bin of my refrigerator to use for wreath making. You can also use orange slices and grapes wired into place. Dried fruit is easy to add to wreaths, too.

Beautiful and Useful

FOLLOW THESE tips to create a pretty country-style wreath with plenty of bird appeal.

- Select a variety of colors and textures when choosing your materials, so that your bird-food wreath looks good to your eyes, too.

- Hang the wreath where birds can visit freely, without being disturbed by activity within the house.

- Debris beneath the wreath is a sign that it's a success! Hulls and bits of broken plants will naturally accumulate there as may bird droppings. A fence or feeder post may be a better location than your front door.

- Fasten materials securely, so that birds can perch on plants and tug at seeds without fear of falling.

- Hang the wreath as solidly as possible so that it doesn't swing under the weight of birds. Unexpected movement when they alight may cause them to avoid it.

- Don't forget ground-feeding birds! Supply wreaths or hang a spray of seedheads at low levels, too.

Drape a Swag

A swag is an elongated spray, or a wreath without the circular backbone of a rigid form. A spool of versatile floral wire does the trick here, too, holding the overlapping bundles of plant material into one continuous rope. In fact, if you are making a thick swag or using heavy plants such as evergreens, a real rope can come in handy. I use a piece of wire-reinforced plastic clothesline as the supporting player for my swag, wiring the branches all along its strong, flexible length.

I save my swag making for Christmastime, when I drape ropes of greenery and berries across the fence and around the entrance, but you can also use fall-themed plants to create a harvest-home decorative swag. As with other crafty decorations, think like a bird when you choose plants to put together. Items that are popular with birds in the garden or at your feeder are fine candidates for a swag.

At my house many birds enjoy a swag of hemlock branches with the cones attached and dotted with sprigs of bright holly berries. Bluebirds, chickadees, visiting crossbills, nuthatches, berry-eating robins, and the troublesome "It's mine, all mine" mockingbirds visit repeatedly. One year, I delighted my squirrels and cardinals by wiring ears of yellow field corn together end to end. The simple golden chain looked lovely draped across a latticework trellis—at least at first! When the corn swag began to look moth-eaten as kernels disappeared, I wrapped it around a tall feeder post for further squirrel and bird forays.

Sometimes it's easy to forget that the reason you're making these decorations is to feed the birds. Don't expect your bird food wreaths and swags to stay in their original state for long. Celebrate the lively birds they bring to the garden, and accepting the eventual fate of your creations will be easier.

Wrens

WHEN AUTUMN feeder traffic swings into gear, the juncos and white-throated sparrows crowd the trays and goldfinches swing on the tube feeders. I get so caught up in the excitement that I forget all about one of my favorite feeder birds: the **Carolina wren.** I'll be filling the feeders on a crisp October morning when I hear an almost mechanical chirring sound that halts me in my tracks for the split second it takes me to place it. Then a jaunty, toasty brown bird swings into view, and I remember the pleasure of wrens at the feeder. Carolina wrens have expanded their range northward, so that now anyone with a feeder in the eastern half of the country might spot them summer or winter. If you live in the Southwest, watch for the thrush-size **cactus wren,** a giant among this family. It's a frequent visitor to feeders.

Most familiar among backyard bird watchers with its almost nationwide range, the small brown

A white eye stripe and warm buffy breast identify a Carolina wren, as does its repertoire of loud, clear whistled phrases and odd whirrs and chirrs.

house wren is much less common at feeders. This insect-loving bird retreats to the deep southern edge of the country and southward once cold weather arrives. **Bewick's wren,** common in the West and ranging into the Southeast and Midwest, is as unafraid of humans as the house wren and often takes up residence around houses and farms. Other wrens, including the tiny **winter wren** of the far West and East, the wetland-loving **marsh wren,** and the rock-dwelling **canyon wren** and **rock wren** of the West, are usually not feeder regulars. But as with any bird, individuals may show up when natural food is scarce or if your yard is part of their territory.

Win a house wren's heart with mealworms, suet, and peanut butter. This tiny but talented singer practically spills over with burbling song in spring and summer.

WREN FEEDER FOODS
■ Apple, halved or chopped
■ Bread and other baked goods
■ Bread crumbs
■ Elderberries (*Sambucus* spp.)
■ Leftovers
■ Mealworms
■ Meat scraps
■ Peanut butter
■ Suet

Wren Behavior

You'll hear wrens long before you see them because these little birds can't seem to help sounding off. They have beautiful singing voices that ring out with liquid notes, performing long, complicated songs in some species or short carols in others. A grab bag of scolding rattles, harsh chirrs, and general jabbering comes along with the virtuoso performances. If you hear a repeated unmusical birdcall from your yard, it's probably a wren.

Wrens eat mostly insects, so they are great little pals to have in the garden. At the feeder, they like suet, bread crumbs, and other soft foods. Active and acrobatic, they can easily reach any type of feeder. Wrens are feisty toward other birds at the feeder but never are pests because they usually show up singly or in pairs.

Most wrens nest in cavities, which may explain why the birds have a propensity for exploring nooks and crannies. Or they may just be curious. Leave a garage door open, even a crack, and you may find a Carolina wren exploring when you return. Several types of wrens nest and roost in sheds, garages, and other outbuildings or in dense vines against a porch.

Zinnias

Attract buntings, cardinals, doves, goldfinches, hummingbirds, native sparrows, titmice, towhees

ZINNIAS (*ZINNIA* SPP.) are one of the easiest annual flowers to grow—and that's good news for bird lovers. Zinnias have bright, daisylike flowers that attract a bounty of butterflies when they're in full bloom, but that's only the beginning. Red- and orange-flowered zinnias also lure hummingbirds to their nectar. And when the flower heads begin to go to seed, goldfinches are first on the scene. If you leave your zinnia patch standing through fall and into winter, you'll spot buntings, doves, native sparrows, and towhees, busily scratching for seeds around the plants.

Colorful and foolproof, zinnias will attract butterflies and hummingbirds all summer long. Let the plants stand in fall and winter to feed songbirds.

Zinnias take only 10 to 12 weeks to burst into bloom, counting from the time you plant the seeds. They flourish in full sun, in rich or lean soil, and in clay or sandy places. Traditional cactus-flowered or double-flowered zinnias (*Z. elegans*) are excellent for songbirds, hummingbirds, and butterflies; for smaller seed-eating species, the lower-growing zinnia cultivars 'Bonita Red' and 'Bonita Yellow' or old-fashioned Persian carpet (*Z. haageana*) are tops.

Zinnias are prone to powdery mildew, which causes a whitish dusting on their foliage. The effect is cosmetic: It's not fatal to the plants, and flowers are usually unaffected. Because mildew is most noticeable when the plant is a tall one, I add mid-height and dwarf zinnia cultivars in front of my giants to hide their foliage, just in case it becomes disfigured. Or you can stick to planting mildew-resistant cultivars.

If you plant a large sweep of zinnias, you can easily snip off seedheads and offer them in feeders later in the season, or work them into a wreath for birds. Try cutting the ripe seedheads with long stems attached, tie them together with twine, and attach them to a lamppost, fence post, or door—they'll attract cardinals, titmice, and other birds. Save some of the seeds for planting next year. If you save seed of named cultivars, you may find the next generation doesn't look very much like its parents. If your garden color scheme is important, sow the saved seeds in an out-of-the-way spot, where a sudden unexpected jolt of fuchsia or scarlet won't disrupt your soft pastels. I like the surprises of color and flower form I get from saved seed, but if reliable results are what you want, stick to packaged seeds.

Zinnias are great flowers for first-time gardeners: They sprout in just a few days, the seedlings are big and hearty, and they grow fast and bloom quickly. If you want to give a child a love of gardening, pass along a packet of zinnia seeds. They're as close to foolproof as gardening gets.

Resources

Bird-Feeding Supplies

The ever-growing popularity of bird feeding means that sources of feeders, food, and other bird-related items abound. Your best source of supplies may be your local garden center or wild-bird specialty shop, but you'll also find bird feeders and birdhouses at most discount stores and hardware stores. Feed mills are a great source of low-cost birdseed and grains if you buy in large quantity. Fast-dissolving superfine sugar, which melts instantly even in cold water and is great for making nectar, is available at some supermarkets or from restaurant- and bar-supply shops.

Many cottage-industry bird box and feeder makers have entered the market. Check the back pages of any bird or wildlife magazine (see "Recommended Reading" on page 352 for listings) for advertisements and places to send for catalogs. You may also want to shop for supplies from the mail-order firms listed here.

The Audubon Workshop
5100 Schenley Place
Lawrenceburg, IN 47025
Phone: (812) 537-3583

Down to Earth
4 Highland Circle
Lucas, TX 75002
Phone: (800) 865-1996
Fax: (972) 442-2816
E-mail: sales@downtoearth.com
Web site: www.downtoearth.com
Makes simple cypress-wood houses and wonderful see-through bird feeders and birdhouses that you can attach to windows.

Droll Yankees, Inc.
27 Mill Road
Foster, RI 02825
Phone: (800) 352-9164
Fax: (401) 647-7620
E-mail: custserv@drollyankees.com
Web site: www.drollyankees.com

Duncraft, Inc.
102 Fisherville Road
Concord, NH 03303-2086
Phone: (800) 593-5656
Fax: (603) 226-3735
E-mail: info@duncraft.com
Web site: www.duncraft.com

Plow & Hearth
P.O. Box 5000
Madison, VA 22727-1500
Phone: (800) 627-1712
Fax: (800) 843-2509
Web site: www.plowhearth.com

Wellscroft Farm Fence Systems
167 Sunset Hill-Chesham
Harrisville, NH 03450
Phone: (603) 827-3464
Fax: (603) 827-3666

Wild Bird Centers of America, Inc.
Phone: (800) 945-3247 (to locate a store near you)
Web site: www.wildbirdcenter.com

Wild Birds Unlimited
Phone: (800) 326-4928 (to locate a store near you)
Fax: (317) 571-7110
Web site: www.wbu.com

Wild Wings Organic Wild Bird Foods
220 Congress Park Drive #232
Delray Beach, FL 33445
Phone: (800) 346-0269
Fax: (800) 279-5984
Web site: www.wildwings organic.com
Certified organic bird foods

Organizations and Programs

American Bird Conservancy
P.O. Box 249
The Plains, VA 20198-0249
E-mail: abc@abcbirds.org
Web site: www.abcbirds.org

A nonprofit organization that builds coalitions of conservation groups, scientists, and the public in order to identify and protect important sites for bird conservation. Annual membership fee includes ABC's quarterly magazine about bird conservation and a newsletter on policy issues affecting birds.

**Backyard Wildlife
  Habitat Program**
National Wildlife Federation
11100 Wildlife Center Drive
Reston, VA 20190-5361
Phone: (800) 822-9919
Web site: www.nwf.org

Free information on developing a bird-friendly backyard; provide a certificate if you follow through.

National Audubon Society
700 Broadway
New York, NY 10003
Phone: (212) 979-3000
Fax: (212) 979-3188
Web site: www.audubon.org

Founded in 1905, this is one of the biggest nonprofit conservation organizations and is active worldwide in all kinds of conservation issues as well as birds. Join a local branch to meet other birders, participate in bird counts, and enjoy other bird-related activities.

National Bird-Feeding Society
P.O. Box 23
Northbrook, IL 60065-0023
Phone: (847) 272-0135
Fax: (773) 404-0923
Web site: www.birdfeeding.org

Organization devoted to bird feeding. Annual fee includes bimonthly newsletter and other information on bird feeding.

**North American Bird Banding
Program**
Learn how to create your own banding research program or volunteer with other banders.

For U.S. residents, contact:

Bird Banding Laboratory
U.S. Geological Survey—
  Biological Resources Division
Patuxent Wildlife Research Center
12100 Beech Forest Road, Suite
  4037
Laurel, MD 20708-4037
Phone: (301) 497-5790
Fax: (301) 497-5784
E-mail: BBL@mail.fws.gov
Web site: www.mbr-
  pwrc.usgs.gov/bbl/bbl.htm

For Canadian residents, contact:

Bird Banding Office
National Wildlife Research Centre
Canadian Wildlife Service
Hull, Quebec, Canada K1A 0H3
Phone: (819) 994-6176
Fax: (819) 953-6612

**North American Rare Bird Alert
(NARBA)**
P.O. Box 6599
Colorado Springs, CO 80934
Phone: (719) 578-9703
Web site: www.americanbirding.org
  (go to the Rare Bird Alert link)

Project FeederWatch
Winter counts of feeder birds are conducted by "regular people" all across North America. The data collected contribute to scientific understanding of changes in bird populations and distribution. Annual fee covers project newsletter and participation.

For U.S. residents, contact:

Project Feeder Watch
Cornell Laboratory of
  Ornithology
159 Sapsucker Woods Road
Ithaca, NY 14850-1923
Phone: (800) 843-BIRD
E-mail: feederwatch@cornell.edu
Web site: birds.cornell.edu/pfw

For Canadian residents, contact:

Project Feeder Watch
Bird Studies Canada
P.O. Box 160
Port Rowan, Ontario N0E 1M0
Phone: (888) 448-BIRD;
  (519) 586-3531
Fax: (519) 586-3532
E-mail: pfw@bsc-eoc.org

Songbird Foundation
5215 Ballard Avenue NW
Seattle, WA 98107
Phone: (206) 374-3674
Fax: (206) 374-3675
E-mail: info@songbird.org
Web site: www.songbird.org

Nonprofit group working to raise awareness about the negative impact of sun-grown coffee production on songbird habitat. Funds projects that promote shade-grown/organic coffee growing.

Sources of Seeds and Plants

When you shop for plants, visit local nurseries that grow their own plants or buy from mail-order firms. Plants from discount stores often haven't been cared for properly and may not establish themselves as well in your garden. Some mail-order companies charge a small fee for their catalogs; you'll often get a credit on your first order.

The following is just a small selection of mail-order nurseries. Ask gardening friends what companies they recommend, too.

Native Plants

Boothe Hill Wildflowers
921 Boothe Hill
Chapel Hill, NC 27514
Phone: (919) 967-4091
Specializes in seeds and plants of native and naturalized wildflowers for the Southeast and throughout the United States

Busse Gardens
17160 245th Avenue
Big Lake, MN 55309
Phone: (800) 544-3192
Fax: (763) 263-1473
Web site: www.bussegardens.com
Reliable and beautiful perennial plants that can take cold but also thrive in milder gardens

Edible Landscaping
P.O. Box 77
Afton, VA 22920-0077
Phone: (434) 361-9134
Fax: (434) 361-1916
Web site: www.eat-it.com
Plants for you and the birds (and other wildlife); lots of fruit-bearing trees and shrubs

Finch Blueberry Nursery
P.O. Box 699
Bailey, NC 27807
Phone: (252) 235-4664
Web site: www.danfinch.com
Wide selection of blueberries for your bird garden

Forestfarm
990 Tetherow Road
Williams, OR 97544-9599
Phone: (541) 846-7269
Fax: (541) 846-6963
Web site: www.forestfarm.com
More than 2,000 plants, including wildflowers, perennials, and an outstanding variety of trees and shrubs

Kurt Bluemel, Inc.
2740 Greene Lane
Baldwin, MD 21013-9523
Phone: (800) 498-1560
Fax: (410) 557-9785
Web site: www.kurtbluemel.com
Specializes in ornamental grasses

Louisiana Nursery
5853 Highway 182
Opelousas, LA 70570
Phone: (337) 948-3696
Fax: (337) 942-6404
Web site: www.durionursery.com
Vines for hummingbirds; many trees, shrubs, and perennials

**Meadowbrook Nursery–
We-Du Natives**
2055 Polly Spout Road
Marion, NC 28752
Phone: (828) 738-8300
Fax: (828) 287-9348
Web site: www.we-du.com
Impressive selection of wildflowers and perennials, including lots of woodland plants

Niche Gardens
1111 Dawson Road
Chapel Hill, NC 27516
Phone: (919) 967-0078
Fax: (919) 967-4026
Web site: www.nichegdn.com
Generous-size plants of grasses, nursery-propagated wildflowers, perennials, and herbs

Plant Delights Nusery
9241 Sauls Road
Raleigh, NC 27603
Phone: (919) 772-4794
Fax: (919) 662-0370
Web site: www.plantdelights.com
A broad and eclectic selection of new and unusual perennials, along with many old favorites; many natives

Prairie Moon Nursery
Route 3, Box 163
Winona, MN 55987-9515
Phone: (507) 452-1362
Fax: (507) 454-5238
Web site: www.prairiemoon
 nursery.com
An outstanding variety of native prairie grasses and wildflowers; also lots of seeds

Prairie Nursery, Inc.
P.O. Box 306
Westfield, WI 53964
Phone: (800) 476-9453
Fax: (608) 296-2741
Web site: www.prairienursery.com
An excellent source of native wildflowers and grasses, many of them ideal for bird gardens

Raintree Nursery
391 Butts Road
Morton, WA 98356
Phone: (360) 496-6400
Fax: (888) 770-8358
Web site: www.raintreenursery.com
A wide selection of fruit trees and shrubs

Shooting Star Nursery
444 Bates Road
Frankfort, KY 40601
Phone: (502) 223-1679
Fax: (502) 227-5700
Web site:
www.shootingstarnursery.com
Diverse assortment of plants and seeds native to the forests, prairies, and wetlands of Kentucky and other eastern states

Sunlight Gardens, Inc.
174 Golden Lane
Andersonville, TN 37705
Phone: (800) 272-7396
Fax: (865) 494-7086
Web site:
www.sunlightgardens.com
Terrific selection of wildflowers, all nursery propagated, of southeastern and northeastern North America

Tripple Brook Farm
37 Middle Road
Southampton, MA 01073
Phone: (413) 527-4626
Fax: (413) 527-9853
Web site:
www.tripplebrookfarm.com
Lively catalog of wildflowers and other northeastern native plants, plus fruits and shrubs

Wildlife Nurseries
P.O. Box 2724
Oshkosh, WI 54903-2724
Phone: (920) 231-3780
Fax: (920) 231-3554
Excellent, informative listing of plants and seeds of native grasses, annuals, and perennials that attract birds and other wildlife; also water garden plants and supplies

Woodlanders, Inc.
1128 Colleton Avenue
Aiken, SC 29801
Phone/fax: (803) 648-7522
Web site: www.woodlanders.net
A fantastic collection of native trees, shrubs, ferns, vines, and perennials, plus other good garden plants. It's a list only, no pictures or descriptions, so if you're a newcomer to plants, pull out a plant encyclopedia to consult as you go.

Native Roses

Forestfarm
990 Tetherow Road
Williams, OR 97544-9599
Phone: (541) 846-7269
Fax: (541) 846-6963
Web site: www.forestfarm.com

Hortico, Inc.
723 Robson Road, R.R. #1
Waterdown, Ontario, Canada
    L0R 2H1
Phone: (905) 689-6984;
    (905) 689-3002
Fax: (905) 689-6566
Web site: www.hortico.com

The Roseraie at Granite Ridge
3202 Friendship Road
P.O. Box R
Waldoboro, ME 04572-0919
Phone: (207) 832-6330
Fax: (800) 933-4508
Web site: www.roseraie.com

Water Garden Plants and Supplies

Lilypons Water Gardens
6800 Lilypons Road
P.O. Box 10
Buckeystown, MD 21717-0010
Phone: (800) 999-5459
Fax: (800) 879-5459
Web site: www.lilypons.com

Van Ness Water Gardens
2460 North Euclid Avenue
Upland, CA 91784-1199
Phone: (800) 205-2425
Fax: (909) 949-7217
Web site: www.vnwg.com

Recommended Reading

Books

Adams, George. *Birdscaping Your Garden*. Emmaus, PA: Rodale, 1998.

Barnes, Thomas G. *Gardening for the Birds*. Lexington, KY: University Press of Kentucky, 1999.

Burton, Robert. *National Audubon Society's North American Birdfeeder Handbook*. Rev. ed. New York: DK Publishing, 1995.

Ellis, Barbara. *Attracting Birds & Butterflies: How to Plan and Plant a Backyard Habitat. Taylor's Weekend Gardening Guides*. New York: Houghton Mifflin, 1997.

Harrison, George H. *Garden Birds of America: A Gallery of Garden Birds & How to Attract Them*. Minocqua, WI: Willow Creek Press, 1996.

Kress, Stephen W. *National Audubon Society: The Bird Garden*. New York: DK Publishing, 1995.

National Audubon Society. *The Audubon Society Handbook for Birders*. New York: Charles Scribner's Sons, 1981.

Proctor, Noble. *Garden Birds: How to Attract Birds to Your Garden*. Emmaus, PA: Rodale, 1996.

Ricciuti, Edward R. *Backyards Are for the Birds: Creating a Bird-Friendly Environment Outside Your Window*. New York: Avon Books, 1998.

Roth, Sally. *Attracting Birds to Your Backyard: 536 Ways to Turn Your Yard and Garden into a Haven for Your Favorite Birds*. Emmaus, PA: Rodale, 1998.

Roth, Sally. *Natural Landscaping*. Emmaus, PA: Rodale, 1997.

Sunset Staff. *An Illustrated Guide to Attracting Birds*. Menlo Park, CA: Sunset Publishing Corporation, 1990.

Terres, John K. *Songbirds in Your Garden*. Chapel Hill, NC: Algonquin Books of Chapel Hill, 1994.

Terres, John K. *The Audubon Society's Encyclopedia of North American Birds*. New York: Random House Value Publishing, 1995.

Thompson III, Bill. *Bird Watching for Dummies*. Foster City, CA: IDG Books Worldwide, Inc., 1997.

Tufts, Craig, and Peter Loewer. *The National Wildlife Federation's Guide to Gardening for Wildlife*. Emmaus, PA.: Rodale, 1995.

For a unique series of books about American birds, chock-full of anecdotes and lively, informative reading, check at your local library or secondhand book store for the *Life Histories of North American Birds* series by Arthur Cleveland Bent, first published in the early decades of the twentieth century, and reprinted in paperback by Dover Press. A few titles in the series are:

Life Histories of North American Marsh Birds (1927)

Life Histories of North American Gallinaceous Birds (1980)

Life Histories of North American Flycatchers, Larks, Swallows, and Their Allies (1989)

Life Histories of North American Woodpeckers (1992)

Magazines

Audubon
700 Broadway
New York, NY 10003
Phone: (800) 274-4201
Web site: magazine.audubon.org

Birder's World
21027 Crossroads Circle
P.O. Box 1612
Waukesha, WI 53187-1612
Phone: (800) 533-6644
Web site: www2.birdersworld.com

Birds and Blooms
5400 South 60th Street
Greendale, WI 53129
Phone: (800) 344-6913

Bird Watcher's Digest
P.O. Box 110
Marietta, OH 45750
Phone: (800) 879-2473
Web site:
    www.birdwatchersdigest.com

Living Bird
c/o Cornell Laboratory of
    Ornithology
159 Sapsucker Woods Road
Ithaca, NY 14850-1923
Phone: (800) 843-BIRD
Web site: www.birds.cornell.edu

Organic Gardening
Rodale
33 East Minor Street
Emmaus, PA 18098
Phone: (800) 666-2206
    (subscriptions)
Web site:
    www.organicgardening.com

Wild Bird
P.O. Box 52898
Boulder, CO 80322-2898
Phone: (800) 365-4421

Bird Field Guides and Recordings

The beauty of a field guide lies in its portable nature: These compact books fit easily into a daypack or glove compartment, so you can always have one handy when there's a bird you want to identify. They're also nice to keep near your favorite feeder-watching window, so you can look up any unusual guests. Their small size doesn't mean that field guides lack information—on the contrary, they're packed with useful identification tips and may also tell you what foods each bird eats and a little about its nesting habits. Here are a few good ones.

A Guide to Field Identification: Birds of North America by Chandler S. Robbins, Bertel Bruun, and Herbert S. Zim (New York: Golden Press, 1983) Birds are illustrated in lifelike poses and on a plant where you're likely to see them. Range maps are inserted at each bird's entry, so you don't have to flip to a separate section in the back of the book as you do with Peterson's. The book includes all birds of North America, which will give you a wider perspective.

The Peterson Field Guide series (Boston: Houghton Mifflin Co., 1998) is also excellent, but they're regional guides and birds are drawn in flatter, less lifelike poses than in the Golden field guide, without any hint of habitat in most pictures. Peterson uses arrows to point out field marks to look for, for definitive identification. Also look for the audio series *Birding by Ear*, which includes *Birding by Ear: Eastern/Central*, edited by Richard K. Walton (Houghton Mifflin Audio, 1999); it includes three CDs or audiotapes.

The Audubon Society Field Guide series (New York: Alfred A. Knopf, 1987), another regional set of guides, uses photos instead of illustrations, which are not as accurate for identifying field marks. The guides also include a lot of interesting information about each bird.

Stokes Field Guide to Birds: Eastern Region and *Stokes Field Guide to Birds: Western Region* (Boston: Little, Brown and Co., 1996) are two photographic field guides that also offer information on feeding and nesting habits and other behavior. There is also a *Stokes Field Guide to Bird Songs: Eastern Region* (or western region) that is by Lang Elliot (Time Warner Audio Books, 1997) and includes three CDs or audiotapes and a booklet.

Photo Credits

Index

Note: Page references in **boldface** indicate illustrations. Page references in *italics* indicate photographs.

USDA Plant Hardiness Zone Map

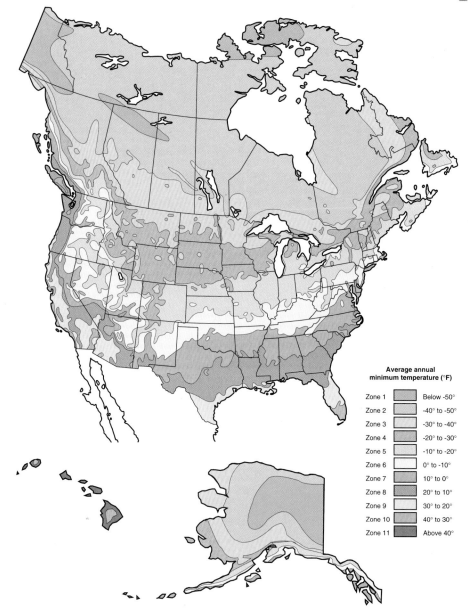

Average annual minimum temperature (°F)

Zone 1	Below -50°
Zone 2	-40° to -50°
Zone 3	-30° to -40°
Zone 4	-20° to -30°
Zone 5	-10° to -20°
Zone 6	0° to -10°
Zone 7	10° to 0°
Zone 8	20° to 10°
Zone 9	30° to 20°
Zone 10	40° to 30°
Zone 11	Above 40°

This map was revised in 1990 and is recognized as the best indicator of minimum temperatures available. Look at the map to find your area, then match its pattern to the key above. When you've found your color, the key will tell you what hardiness zone you live in. Remember that the map is a general guide; your particular conditions may vary.